THE TRUE FACE *of* Sir Isaac Brock

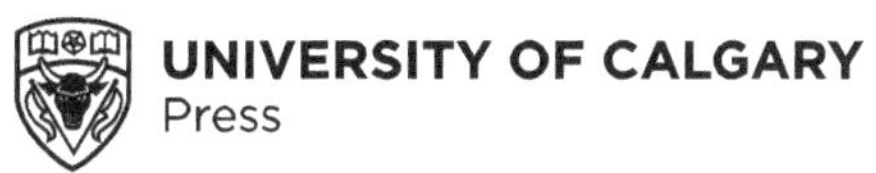

THE TRUE FACE *of* Sir Isaac Brock

Guy ST-DENIS

University of Calgary Press
2500 University Drive NW
Calgary, Alberta
Canada T2N 1N4
press.ucalgary.ca

Library and Archives Canada Cataloguing in Publication

St-Denis, Guy, 1960-, author
The true face of Sir Isaac Brock / Guy St-Denis.

Includes bibliographical references and index.
Issued in print and electronic formats.
ISBN 978-1-77385-020-7 (softcover).—ISBN 978-1-77385-021-4 (open access PDF).—
ISBN 978-1-77385-022-1 (PDF).—ISBN 978-1-77385-023-8 (EPUB).—
ISBN 978-1-77385-024-5 (Kindle)

1. Brock, Isaac, Sir, 1769-1812. 2. Generals—Canada—Biography. 3. Lieutenant governors—Canada—Biography. 4. Canada—History—1791-1841. 5. Canada—History—War of 1812. I. Title.

FC443.B76S83 2018 971.03'2092 C2018-904211-7
C2018-904212-5

The University of Calgary Press acknowledges the support of the Government of Alberta through the Alberta Media Fund for our publications. We acknowledge the financial support of the Government of Canada. We acknowledge the financial support of the Canada Council for the Arts for our publishing program.

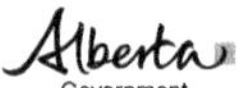

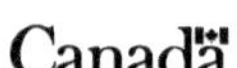

Canada Council for the Arts
Conseil des Arts du Canada

Cover image Lieutenant George Dunn misidentified as Major General Sir Isaac Brock by J. Hudson, 1816.
© Royal Ontario Museum.
Copyediting by Kathryn Simpson
Cover design, page design, and typesetting by Melina Cusano

For

Gillian Lenfestey
La Dame du Fief le Comte

Contents

Preface

Oddly enough, this book began without my knowing it. A more curious distinction would be difficult to imagine, this I grant. Whereas most historians have some notion of the books they intend to write, I did not (at least, not in this particular instance). The research used here was actually intended for a biography, not an art history. The origins of this latter, inadvertent endeavour can be traced to May of 2001, when the acclaimed British historian John Sugden alerted me to the fact that Major General Sir Isaac Brock was in need of a new biography—by which he meant that I was the right person for the job. It was quite the compliment, but no amount of flattery could persuade me to launch headlong into such an audacious undertaking. Still, Brock was one of my childhood heroes and so the idea did hold a certain appeal. But then I began to fear that I might be out of my depth. While I knew that Brock was the British commander who died defending what is now Ontario during the War of 1812, the rest of his life was a mystery to me. I felt a sudden urge to familiarize myself with the great man, and the authoritative *Dictionary of Canadian Biography* provided a useful overview.[1]

In 1785, when Brock was just fifteen years old, he entered the British army with the purchase of an ensign's commission in the 8th (or King's) Regiment. Five years later, he used the same method to become a lieutenant. When the opportunity to raise an independent company presented itself, Brock was rewarded with a captain's rank on half-pay (or semi-retirement). It was also in 1790 that he returned to full service by exchanging into the 49th Regiment, which he joined the following year in Barbados. After a near-fatal illness in 1793, Brock resumed his military career by recruiting in England. In 1795, he purchased a majority and two years later a lieutenant colonelcy was attained through similar means. His first taste of battle was in 1799, during the Anglo-Russian expedition to the Netherlands. He next came under fire in 1801, when his regiment participated in the naval operation against Copenhagen. But with the Treaty of Amiens early in 1802, Brock's exploits were abruptly put on hold. It was during this lull in hostilities between Great Britain and the French Republic that the 49th Regiment was ordered to garrison duty in British North America. Despite the seclusion of his postings, first to Lower and then to Upper Canada (Quebec and Ontario), Brock's rise up the chain of command continued unabated.

In 1808, three years after a promotion to full colonel, he was appointed a brigadier general on the staff of Sir James H. Craig at Quebec City.[2] Towards the end of 1811, during a return to the command of Upper Canada, and having been promoted major general, Brock was designated to administer the government of that province in the absence of the lieutenant governor. He was still acting in this capacity when news of the American declaration of war reached him in June of 1812. Less than two months later, he forced the surrender of Detroit. That calculated risk worked in his favour, but a similar gamble the following October backfired with deadly consequences. Brock was killed by a gunshot wound to the chest while leading a charge against American invaders at the village of Queenston, twelve kilometres down river from Niagara Falls.

Because Brock did not achieve great fame until near the end of his life, and since those last few months had already been thoroughly scrutinized by earlier historians, I wondered if yet another biography could be anything more than a repetitious waste of time. Had I not come so highly recommended, I might have abandoned the idea altogether. But with John Sugden's encouragement, I decided to take up the challenge. Although I was still occupied with the writing of *Tecumseh's Bones*, I began looking into Brock's life whenever time permitted—and I soon found my niche. By seeking out previously unexplored archival holdings, I would amass the fresh insights necessary for a new biography.

As my Brock research progressed, it occurred to me that I should also begin gathering illustrations for the upcoming publication. While I was interested in any and all portraits of Brock, one dating to near the time of his heroic death was also the most desirable. And I had good reason to believe there was such a portrait, given all the internet images labelled as such. Most of these claims were clearly false, but I was still cautiously optimistic that an authentic portrait of Brock as a senior officer could be found among all the digital misinformation. My approach to this problem was a very simple one. I simply kept an eye open, and whenever a picture of Brock's portrait came my way, it was copied and filed for future reference. This slap-dash routine seemed to work extremely well, and I congratulated myself for having things well in hand. However, it soon became evident that my system was becoming clogged with paper. Eventually, I had to resign myself to the necessity of a major sorting out. I dreaded the task, but the exercise did allow me to weed out a good number of files on various paintings, drawings, and even a few sculptures—all of which were obviously artists' impressions and therefore beyond the scope of my project.

Having thus narrowed down the number of potential Brock portraits, my focus shifted to testing the authenticity of those that remained. A literature search consumed a great deal of time, and produced little to show for it. But delving into primary sources was well worth the effort—even if it seemed to take forever to accomplish the task. After consulting diverse and far-flung manuscript collections for the better part of a decade, I was finally able to reveal the true face of Sir Isaac Brock. In doing so, I developed a better understanding of the circumstances in which it and the other portraits were commissioned and carried out. And while I worried about not having enough material for so much as an appendix to Brock's biography, the envisioned appendix gradually began to look more like an article, then two articles, and finally the manuscript for a book—this book.

Notes on Abbreviations and References

Published sources are cited fully in the first instance of each chapter, with a shortened format thereafter. Manuscripts receive a consistently expansive treatment; however, multiple references to the repositories preserving them are abbreviated as follows:

AO	Archives of Ontario
BU	Brock University
CWM	Canadian War Museum
ECG	Ecclesiastical Court of Guernsey
FARL	Frick Art Reference Library
LAC	Library and Archives Canada
MMCH	McCord Museum of Canadian History
NARA	National Archives and Records Administration
RAM	RiverBrink Art Museum
NAUK	National Archives of the United Kingdom
TRL	Toronto Reference Library
TU	Trent University
UCCA	United Church of Canada Archives
UM	University of Michigan

Minor spelling mistakes in quoted passages have been corrected.

Plates

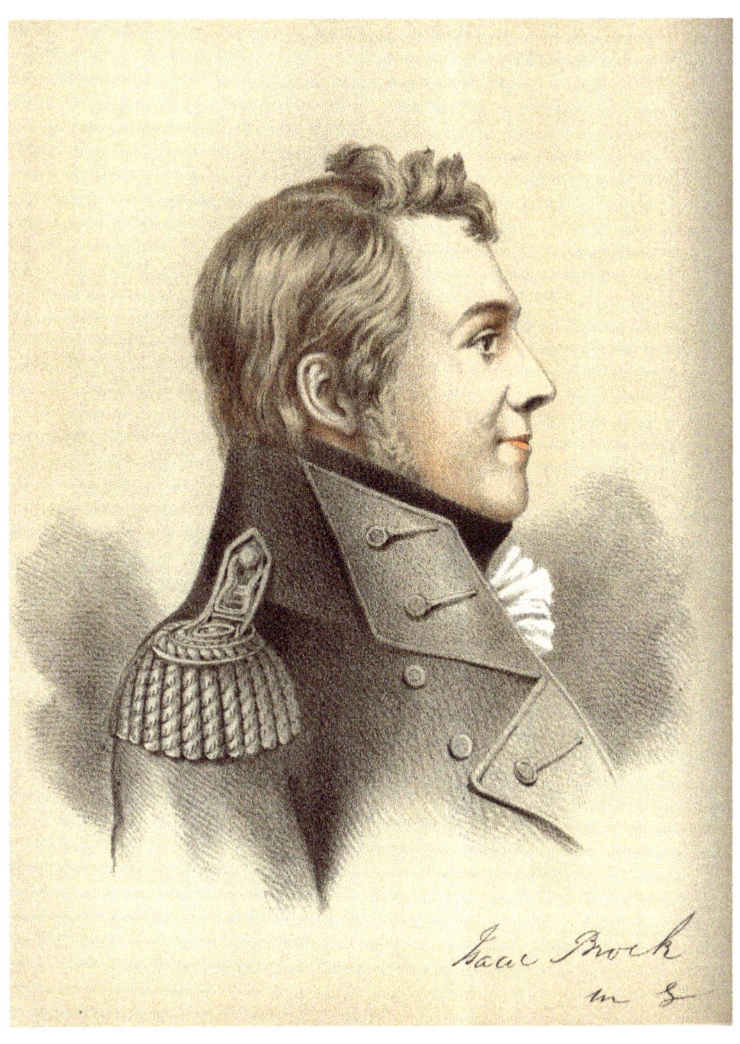

PLATE 1. Rolph, Smith and Company (after Gerrit Schipper, 1809/1810), *Isaac Brock M[ajor] G[eneral]*, 1880, chromolithograph, 23.9 x 17.9 cm, *Canadian Portrait Gallery*.

In 1880, John Charles Dent began publishing *The Canadian Portrait Gallery*, a four-volume set showcasing biographies of individuals who made significant contributions to Canada. Included in the first volume was Major General Sir Isaac Brock, whose profile portrait by Gerrit Schipper (pl. 3) inspired this chromolithographic variant. Despite the addition of a bushy sideburn, Brock has a distinctly dandified look about him. As for the uniform, which is actually that of a brigadier general and staff officer, it should be red with dark blue facings. Moreover, the epaulettes and buttons ought to be gold.

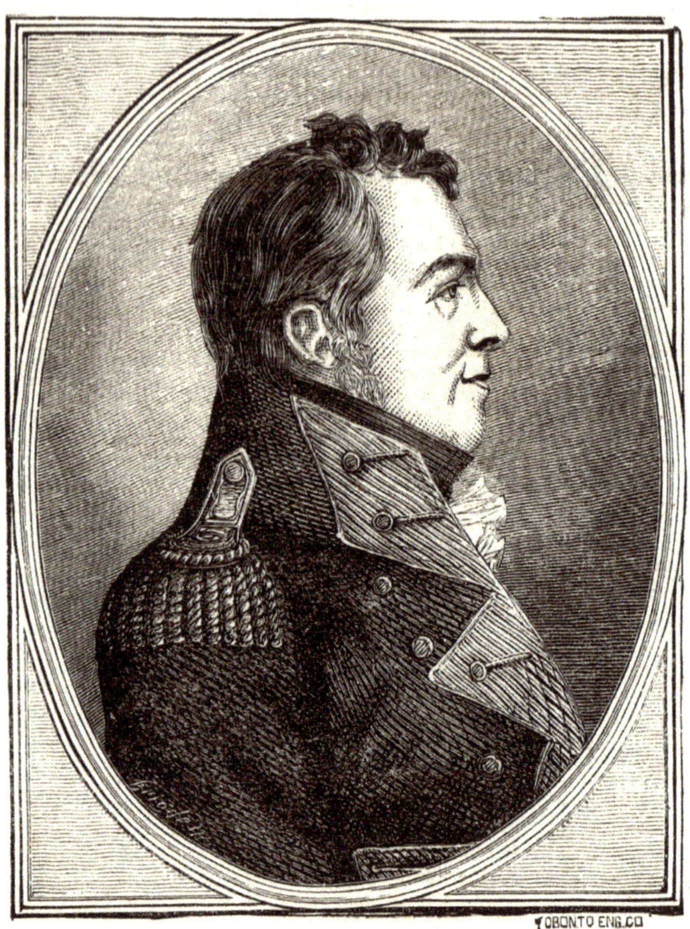

SIR ISAAC BROCK.

Plate 2. Frederick Brigden, Toronto Engraving Company (after Gerrit Schipper, 1809/1810), *Sir Isaac Brock*, 1877, wood-engraving, 11.2 x 8.7 cm, *Globe*.

Also commissioned by John Charles Dent, this wood-engraving appeared in an 1877 edition of the Toronto *Globe*. Like the later chromolithograph (pl. 1), it was based on a photograph of Gerrit Schipper's profile portrait of Brigadier General Isaac Brock (pl. 3). Both of Dent's illustrations helped to convince Ontario's lieutenant governor, John Beverley Robinson, that a portrait of Brock had been preserved by his relatives in Guernsey. While the engraving pictured here is relatively faithful, the sideburn is an unfortunate elaboration. It may have been inspired by the mutton chops enhancing Brock's statue, which was hoisted to the top of his monument in October of 1855. An extra button was also added to the oversized collar patch, and this error—along with the sideburn—was repeated in the chromolithograph mentioned above.

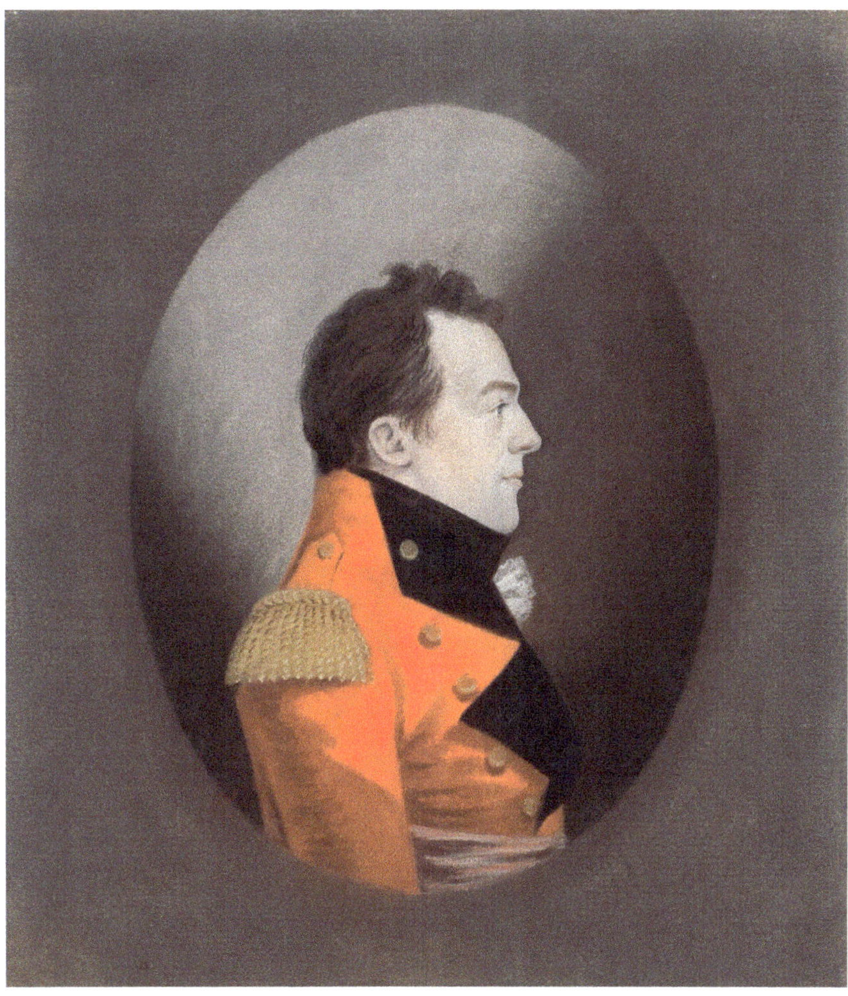

Plate 3. Gerrit Schipper, *Brigadier General Isaac Brock*, 1809/1810 (restored by Jane McAusland, 2010), pastel painting with chalk and graphite on paper, 20.3 x 23.4 cm, Guernsey Museums and Galleries, States of Guernsey (accession GMAG 2009.52).

At Quebec City, sometime between late May of 1809 and early July of 1810, Brigadier General Isaac Brock sat for the Dutch itinerant artist Gerrit Schipper. The resulting profile portrait, done mainly in pastels with some chalk and graphite, is the only authentic likeness of Brock known to exist from near the end of his life. Brock was portrayed in his colonel's uniform, which he continued to wear while he awaited the delivery of his new outfit. However, the coatee had been altered to represent Brock's appointment to brigadier general and staff officer. This process involved replacing the full green facings of the 49th Regiment with new ones of dark blue, as well as collar patches of the same colour and appropriate epaulettes. The buttons, normally set in pairs for a brigadier general, were left in their original settings and spaced evenly—as specified for the regiment.

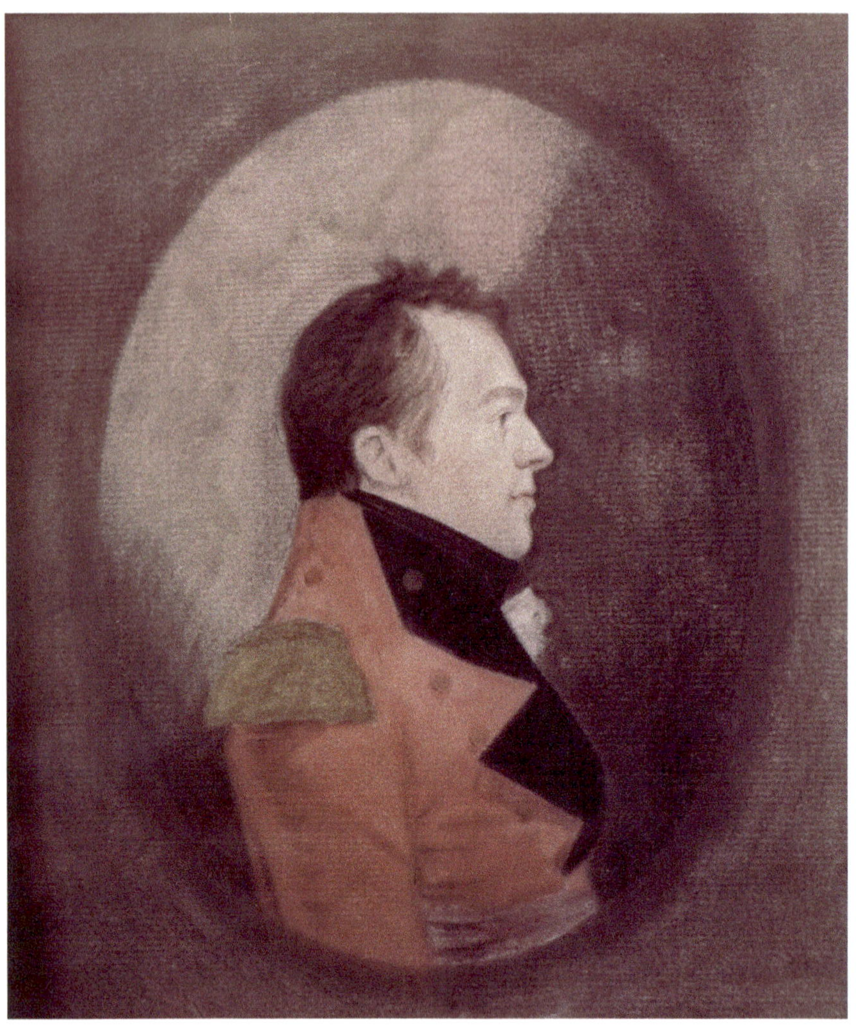

Plate 4. Brian J. Green (after unknown copyist, date unknown; after Gerrit Schipper (1809/1810), *Brigadier General Isaac Brock*, circa 1980 (restored by Alan Noon, 2009), photograph in film format, 12.8 x 11.3 cm, Military History Research Centre, Canadian War Museum.

This copy of Gerrit Schipper's profile portrait of Brigadier General Isaac Brock (pl. 3) appears to have been commissioned by Brock's brother, John Savery Brock, and was often mistaken for the original. A telltale feature of the copy is the area of staining in the upper left background, which also appears in the duplicate made by Alyn Williams for Miss Agnes FitzGibbon in 1897 (pl. 19). © Brian J. Green.

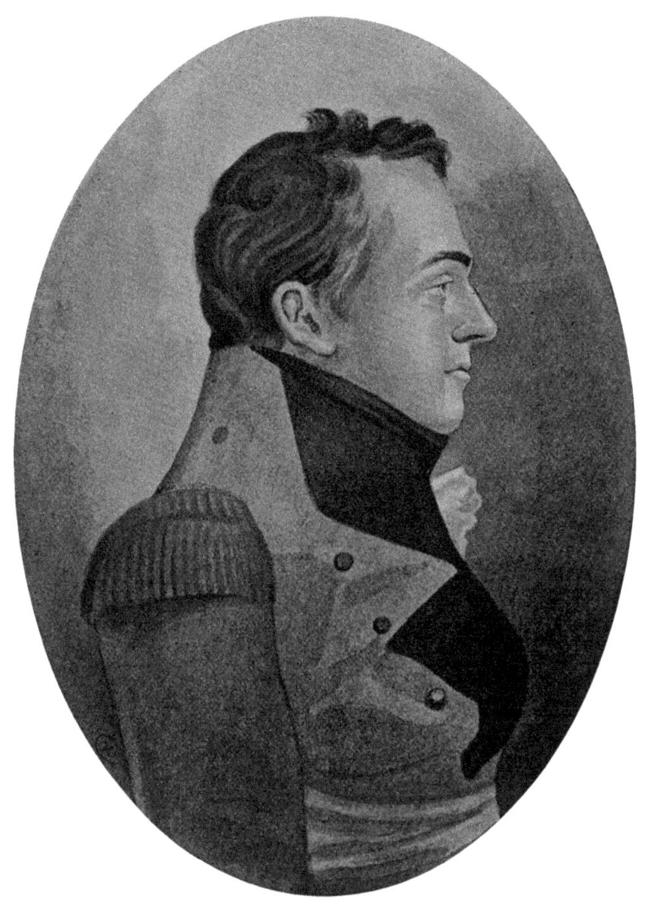

Plate 5. Bailliage Printing Works (after Alice Kerr-Nelson, 1882; after Gerrit Schipper, 1809/1810), *Major-General Sir Isaac Brock, K.B.*, 1892, halftone print of sepia watercolour painting, 28 x 21 cm, Priaulx Library.

In 1882, Miss Alice Kerr-Nelson was commissioned to paint a watercolour copy in sepia tones of Gerrit Schipper's profile portrait of Brigadier General Isaac Brock (pl. 3). Her client was Colonel Charles W. Robinson, who wanted the reproduction for the Royal Hospital at Chelsea. Unfortunately, the sepia copy is now lost; however, a reproduction dating from 1892 still exists in the form of a halftone print (pictured here). While this image gives the impression of a very fatigued-looking Brock, Colonel Robinson claimed to have been pleased with the results.

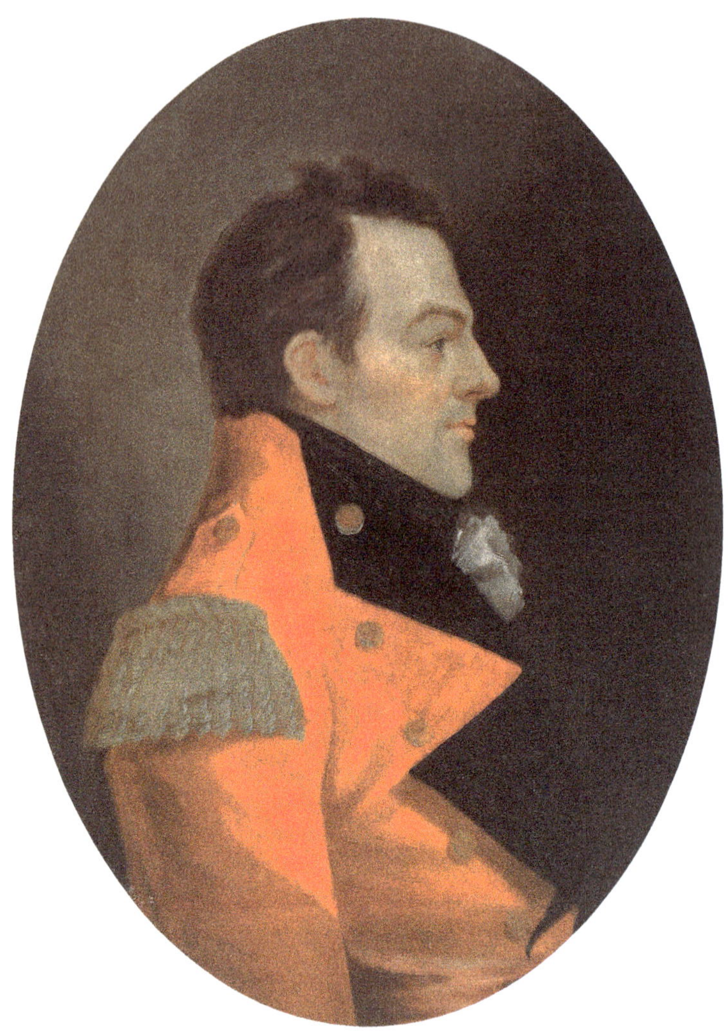

Plate 6. Alice Kerr-Nelson (after Gerrit Schipper, 1809/1810), *General Brock*, 1881, oil painting on cardboard, 55.9 x 40.6 cm, Archives and Special Collections, James A. Gibson Library, Brock University (catalogue BC-028-6-6).

Painted in oils by Miss Alice Kerr-Nelson, this copy of Gerrit Schipper's profile portrait of Brigadier General Isaac Brock (pl. 3) was commissioned by Colonel Charles W. Robinson in 1881. He did so on behalf of his brother, the lieutenant governor of Ontario. Although the painting was not found suitable for Government House in Toronto, it remained in the Robinson family for many years. A recent inspection revealed that the artist had to adjust the epaulette, as it was originally painted too high on the shoulder.

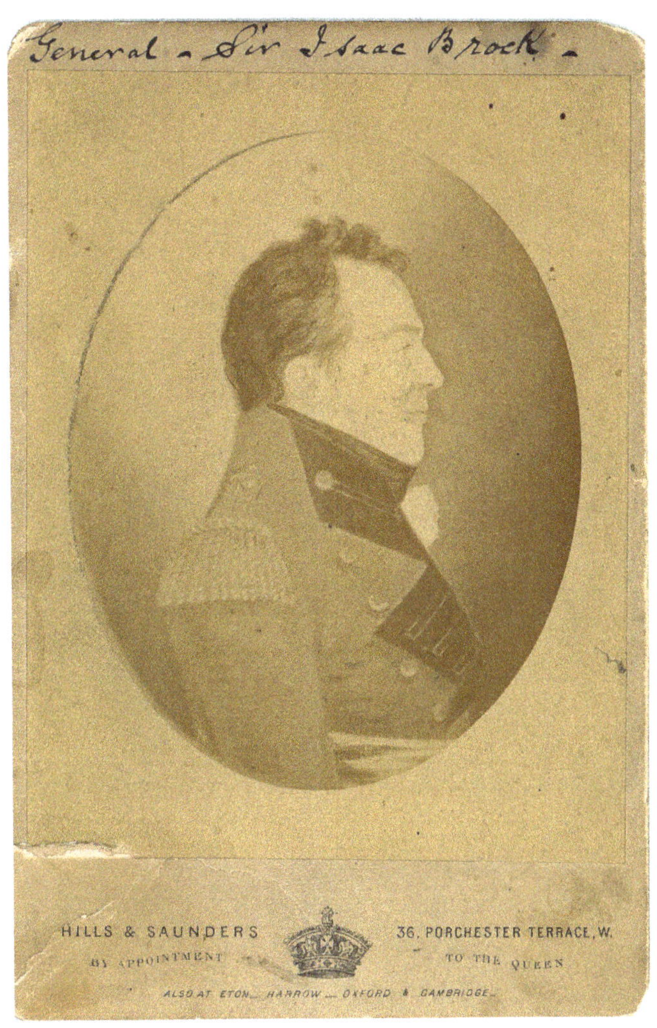

Plate 7. Hills and Saunders (after Gerrit Schipper, 1809/1810), *General Sir Isaac Brock*, 1881, photograph in cabinet card format, 16.5 x 10.8 cm, Trent University Archives.

Gerrit Schipper's profile portrait of Brigadier General Isaac Brock (pl. 3) was photographed by Hills and Saunders of London. This is one of six identical cabinet pictures made for Colonel Charles W. Robinson in late 1881, and may be the very one used by George Berthon to paint Brock's portrait (pl. 9).

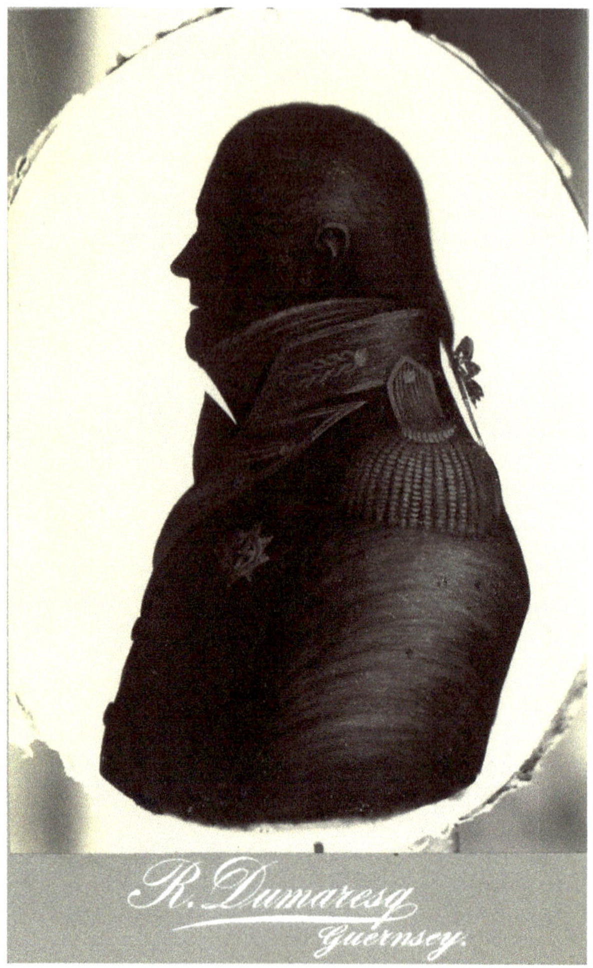

Plate 8. Robert Dumaresq (after John Field (?), circa 1812), bronze profile/silhouette of an *Unknown Officer*, possibly Francis Rawdon-Hastings, Lord Moira (misidentified as "Major General Sir Isaac Brock"), 1897, photograph in cabinet card format, 14.3 x 10.2 cm, Notman Photographic Archives, McCord Museum of Canadian History (catalogue MP-0000.2251.1).

The bronze profile, or bronzed silhouette, was long thought to portray Major General Sir Isaac Brock. But Miss Agnes FitzGibbon had her doubts, as did Ludwig Kosche. The most telling drawback is the Garter Star prominently displayed on the sitter's chest, which represents an honour never bestowed upon Brock. Had he agreed to sit for a bronzed silhouette of himself, it would have looked more like the modern recreation commissioned for this book (pl. 34). Clearly, the sitter was someone other than Brock—possibly Francis Rawdon-Hastings, Earl of Moira and Marquess of Hastings.

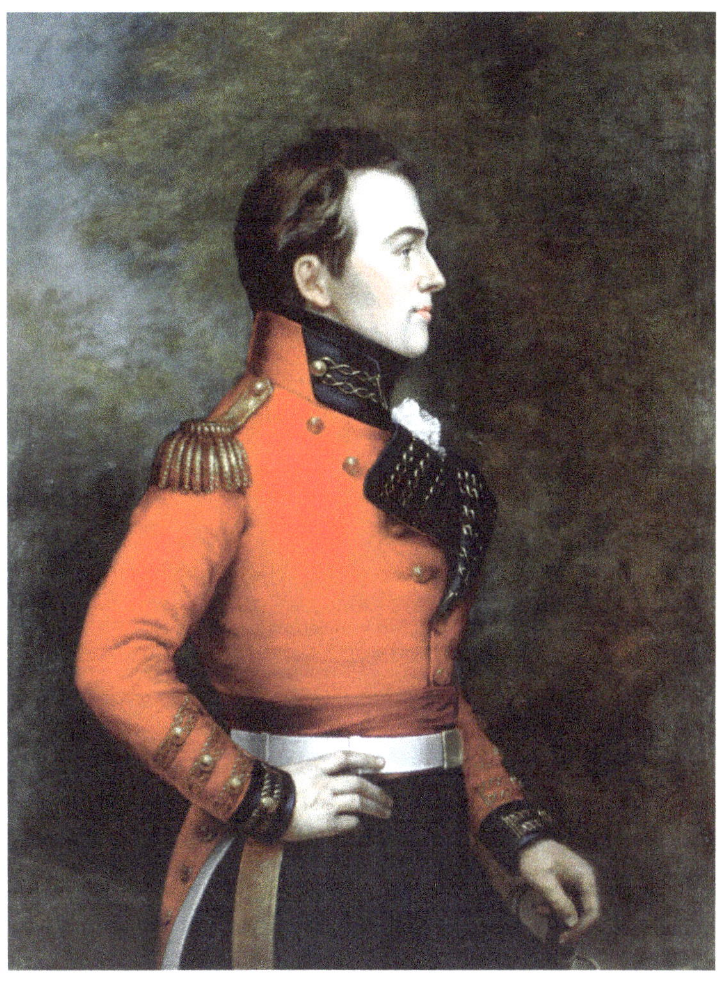

PLATE 9. George Berthon (after Gerrit Schipper, 1809/1810), *Major-General Sir Isaac Brock, KB*, 1882, oil painting on canvas, 111.8 x 83.8 cm, Government of Ontario Art Collection, Archives of Ontario (accession 694,158).

George Berthon's painting of Major General Sir Isaac Brock, one in a series of viceregal portraits, was commissioned by Lieutenant Governor John Beverley Robinson for Government House in Toronto. Berthon's refined style suggests that he worked directly from one of the Hills and Saunders photographs (pl. 7), as opposed to Miss Alice Kerr-Nelson's copy in oils (pl. 6). Berthon took the liberty of portraying Brock in the dress, or formal, uniform of a major general. This painting, previously thought to have been completed in 1883, probably dates from 1882.

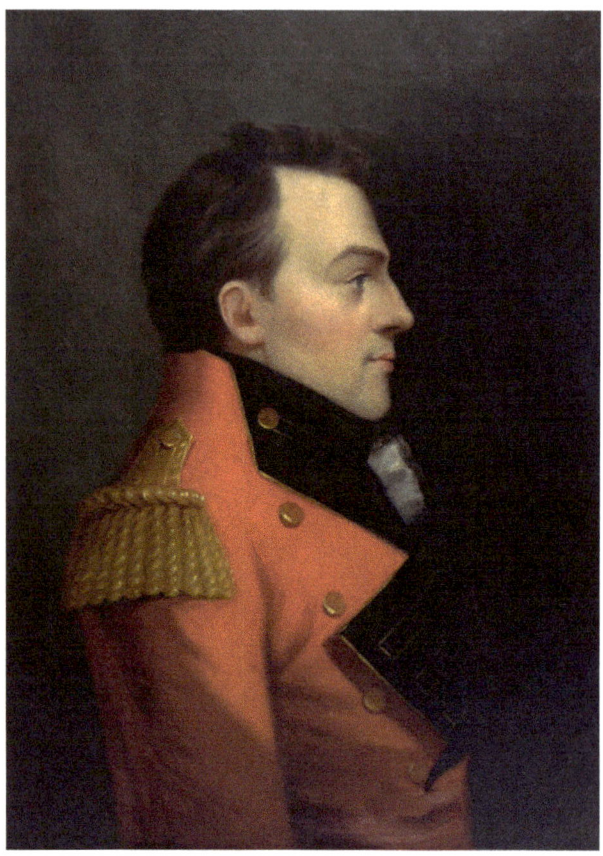

Plate 10. John W.L. Forster (after Gerrit Schipper, 1809/1810), *Portrait of Maj. General Sir Isaac Brock KB*, 1894, oil painting on canvas, 83.5 x 68 cm, Niagara Falls History Museum (accession 995.D.067.005).

In 1894, John Wycliffe Lowes Forster was commissioned by John A. Macdonell to paint this portrait of Major General Sir Isaac Brock. Forster used material supplied to him by Ontario's former lieutenant governor, the Honourable John Beverley Robinson, including Miss Alice Kerr-Nelson's copy of the original profile portrait of Brock (pl. 6). Her work no doubt influenced this painting, which is arguably the best of several Forster produced in honour of Brock. Despite the portrait's label, which identifies Brock as a major general, he is portrayed in the uniform of a brigadier general and staff officer.

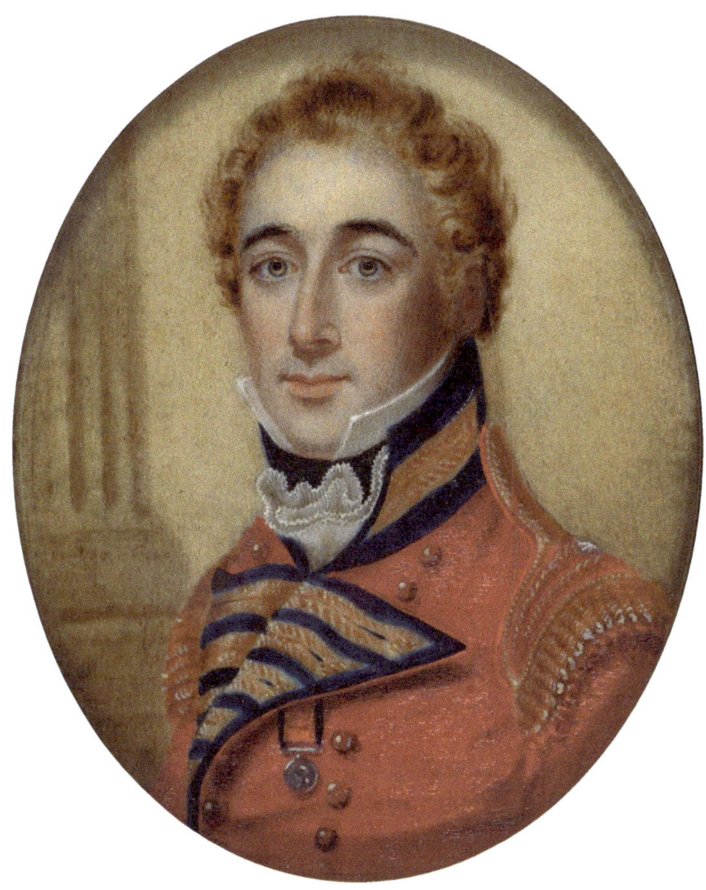

Plate 11. J. (James?) Hudson, *Lieutenant George Dunn* (misidentified as "General Sir Isaac Brock"), 1816, watercolour painting on ivory, 8 x 6.3 cm, Canadian Collection, Department of World Cultures, Royal Ontario Museum (accession 996.58.3.1).

This miniature was discovered in 1896 by Miss Sara Mickle, who was assured by the collateral descendants of Captain James Brock that it portrayed Major General Sir Isaac Brock as a young officer. They were wrong, however, and in 1985 Ludwig Kosche revealed that the sitter is actually Lieutenant George Dunn of the 23rd Regiment (the Royal Welch Fusiliers). At the time the miniature was painted, which was determined to be 1816, Lieutenant Dunn was a youthful veteran of the Battle of Waterloo. © Royal Ontario Museum.

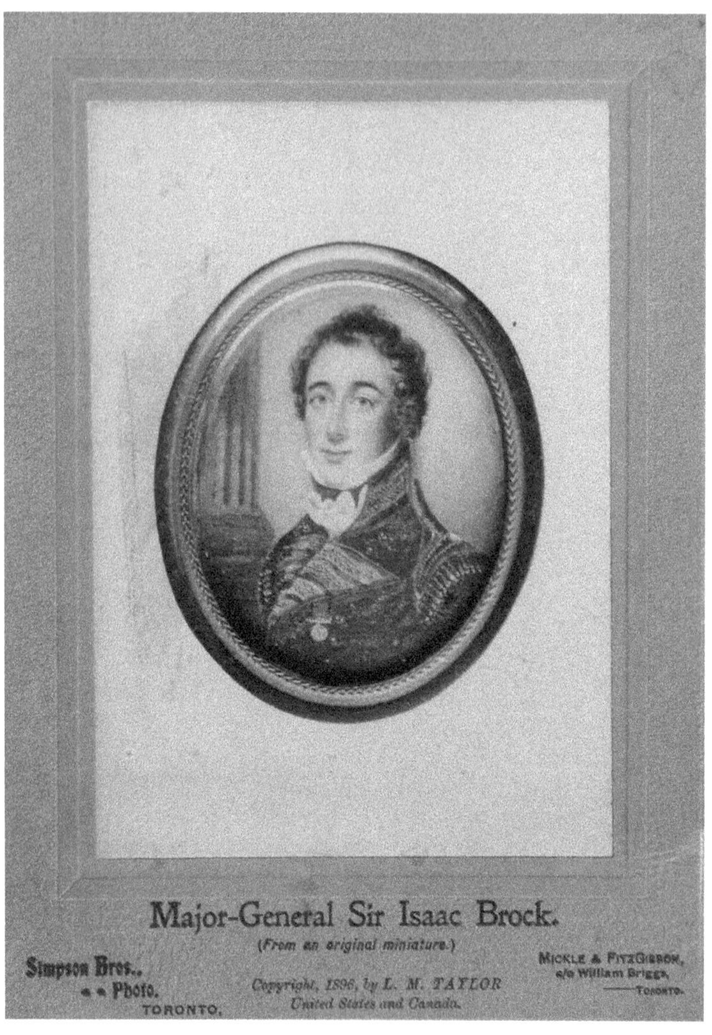

Plate 12. Simpson Brothers (after J. Hudson, 1816), *Lieutenant George Dunn* (misidentified as "Major-General Sir Isaac Brock"), 1896, photograph in cabinet card format, 19.2 x 14.1 cm, Archives of Ontario.

Soon after its discovery, Miss Mickle had the Dunn miniature (pl. 11) photographed by Simpson Brothers of Toronto. Photographic copies were necessary for reproduction in *The Cabot Calendar* (pl. 14), and also for Canadian copyright registration. Since the miniature was still owned by Mrs. Heber (Lucy Short) Taylor, the copyright notice appeared in her name.

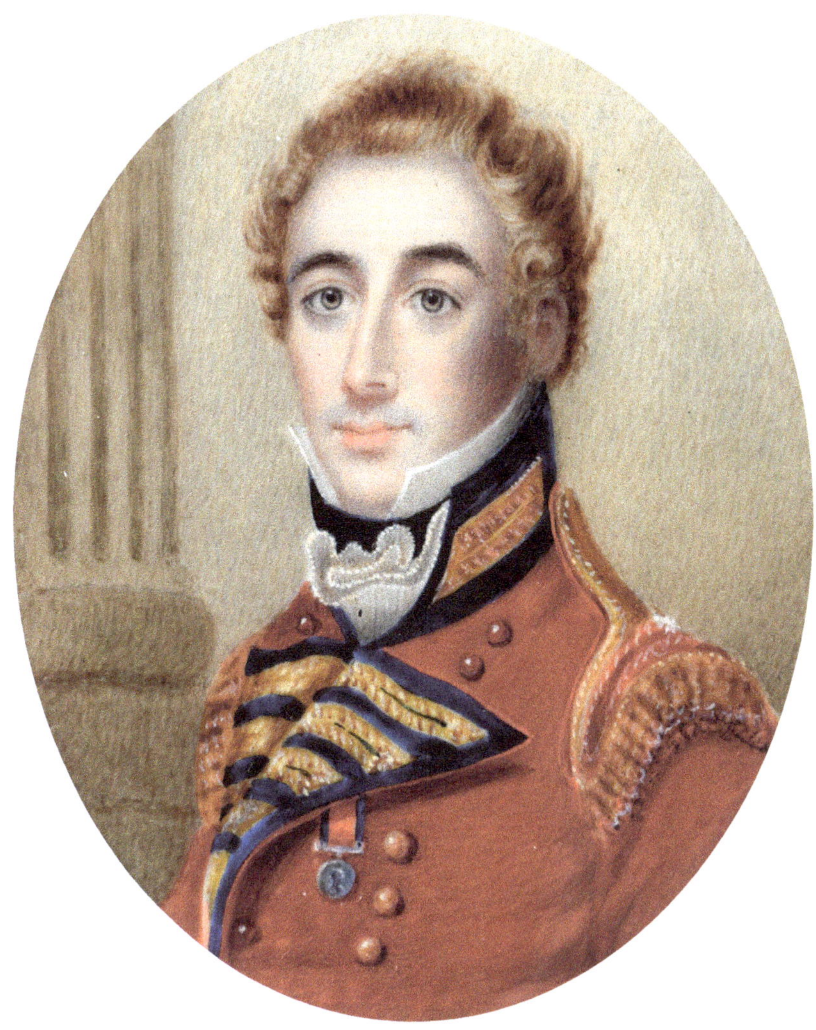

Plate 13. Gerald S. Hayward (after J. Hudson, 1816), *Lieutenant George Dunn* (misidentified as "General Brock"), 1896, oil painting on ivory, 9 x 7 cm, Canadian Collection, Department of World Cultures, Royal Ontario Museum (accession 921.42.2).

In 1896, not long after Miss Sara Mickle had the Dunn miniature (pl. 11) restored by Gerald S. Hayward, she commissioned him to paint this copy of it. Hayward was the first artist to do so, in the mistaken belief that he was portraying Major General Sir Isaac Brock as a junior officer.

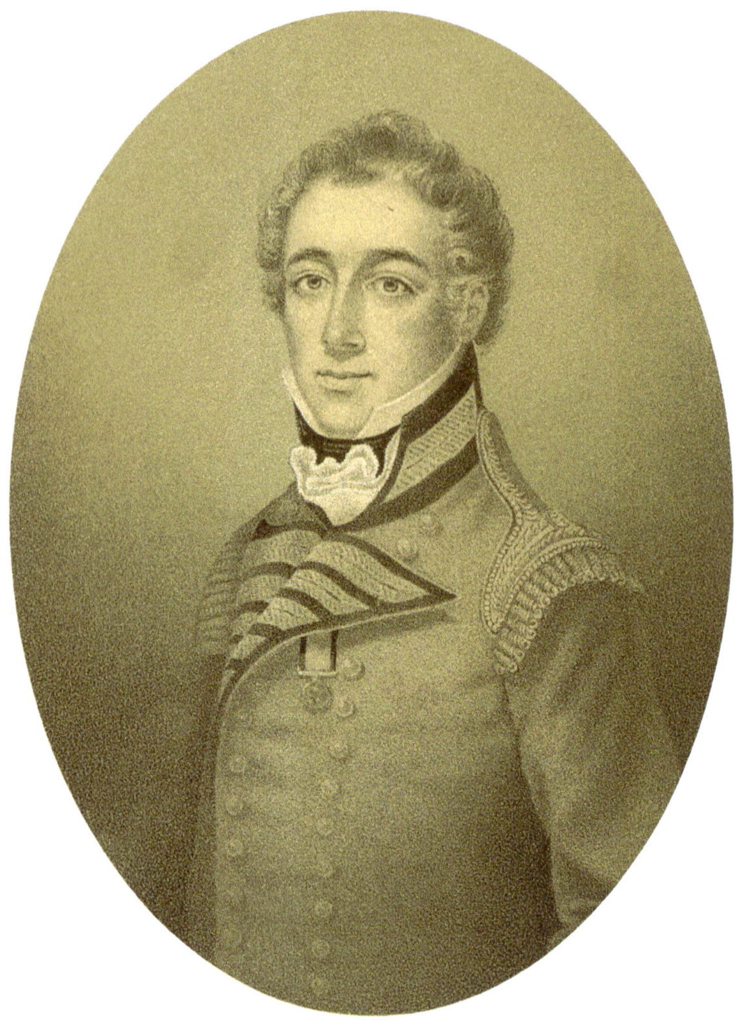

Plate 14. Thomas W. Elliott (?)/Toronto Lithographing Company (after J. Hudson, 1816), *Lieutenant George Dunn* (misidentified as "Isaac Brock"), 1896, lithograph, 24.7 x 17.7 cm, *Cabot Calendar.*

This misidentified portrait of "Isaac Brock" appeared in *The Cabot Calendar*, a commemorative souvenir published in 1897. The calendar was Miss Sara Mickle's idea and in seeking an image of Major General Sir Isaac Brock better adapted to lithographic reproduction, she discovered the original miniature from which this portrait is taken (pl. 11). However, as Ludwig Kosche subsequently determined, the sitter is actually Lieutenant George Dunn of the 23rd Regiment.

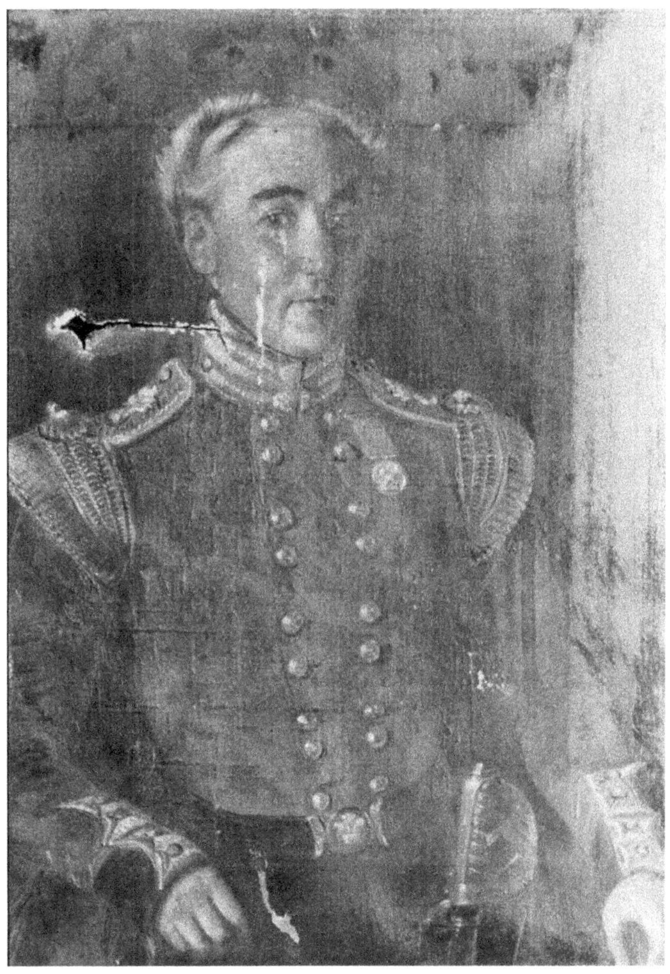

Plate 15. Association of Canadian Archivists (after unknown artist, circa 1840), *Lieutenant George Dunn*, 1985, halftone illustration of oil painting on canvas, dimensions unknown, *Archivaria*.

Although badly damaged, this circa 1840 painting of a middle-aged Lieutenant George Dunn bears a striking resemblance to his younger self, as evidenced by a careful comparison with the miniature painted in 1816 (pl. 11). The most recognizable characteristics are his high and pronounced eyebrows, which in later years gave him a "wild Harum Scarum" look.

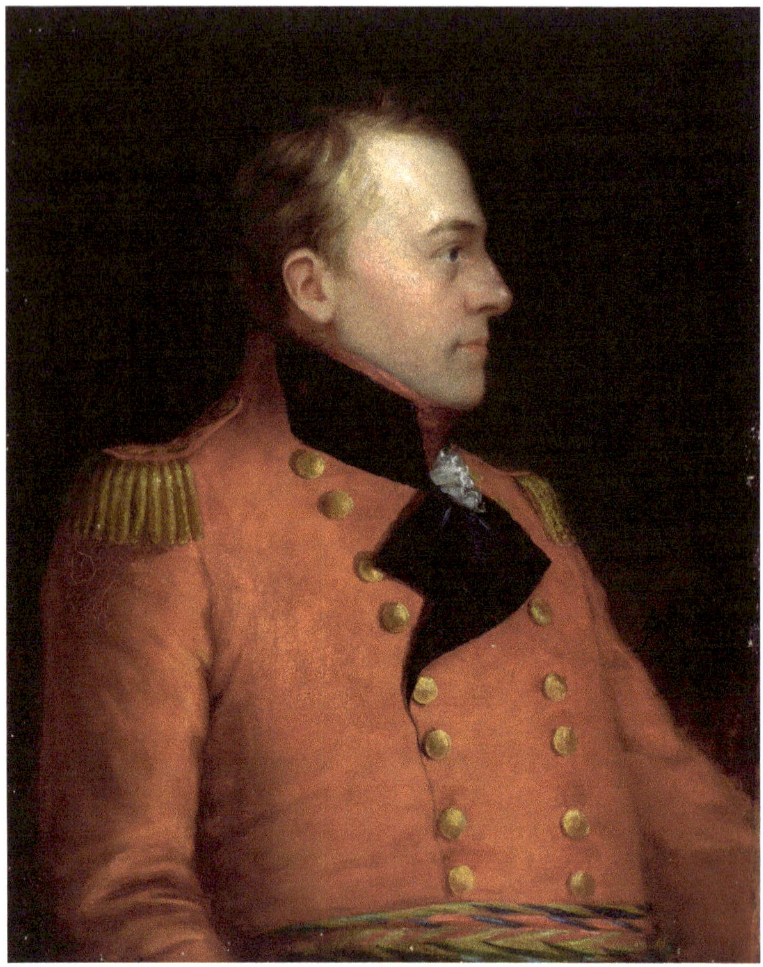

PLATE 16. John W.L. Forster (after unknown copyist, date unknown; after Gerrit Schipper, 1809/1810), *Study of Sir Isaac Brock*, 1897, oil painting on canvas, 76.2 x 60.9 cm, Portrait Gallery of Canada, Library and Archives Canada (accession 1991-30-1).

In 1897, John Wycliffe Lowes Forster visited Guernsey where he painted this study for a portrait of Major General Sir Isaac Brock. The face differs markedly from the portrait Forster undertook for John A. Macdonell (pl. 10). This variance was due, in part, to the copy of Gerrit Schipper's profile portrait of Brigadier General Isaac Brock (pl. 4), which Forster used as a reference after having misjudged it to be the original. Forster's treatment of the uniform is quite accurate, however, as he was given access to the same brigadier general's coatee in which Brock was killed. Unfortunately, the ceinture fléchée (a sash with an arrow design) and the red stock (a neckband of stiff fabric) compromise Forster's careful approach to historical representation, as they are both non-regulation. The sash should have been crimson, and the stock black.

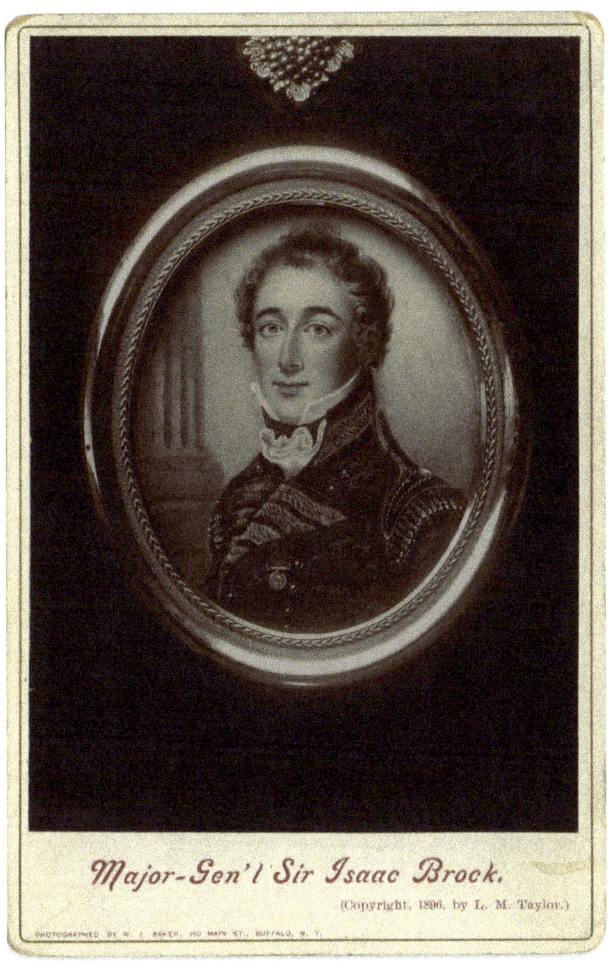

Plate 17. William J. Baker (after J. Hudson, 1816), *Lieutenant George Dunn* (misidentified as "Major-Gen'l Sir Isaac Brock"), 1896, photograph in cabinet card format, 16.5 x 10.7 cm, Military History Research Centre, Canadian War Museum.

Taken by William J. Baker of Buffalo, New York, this photograph of the miniature discovered by Miss Sara Mickle (pl. 11) was necessary for American copyright registration. It was also the photograph Miss Agnes FitzGibbon showed to the art experts in London. The sitter, however, is actually Lieutenant George Dunn and not Major General Sir Isaac Brock as a junior officer.

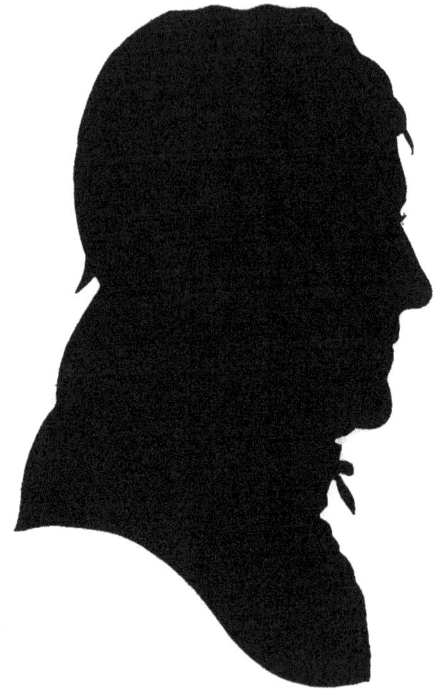

Plate 18. Champlain Society (after unknown silhouettist, date unknown), *Genl. Brock* (otherwise known as the Jarvis silhouette), 1920, halftone illustration of silhouette, 16.5 x 24 cm, *Select British Documents of the Canadian War of 1812.*

The Jarvis silhouette, so-called because it originated with the family of Aemilius Jarvis, was long held to be the profile of "Genl. Brock." Relying on provenance that seemed indisputable, Miss Sara Mickle thought the facial outline would serve to authenticate the miniature she discovered (pl. 11). But the Jarvis silhouette was doubted, and it remains a questionable item to this day.

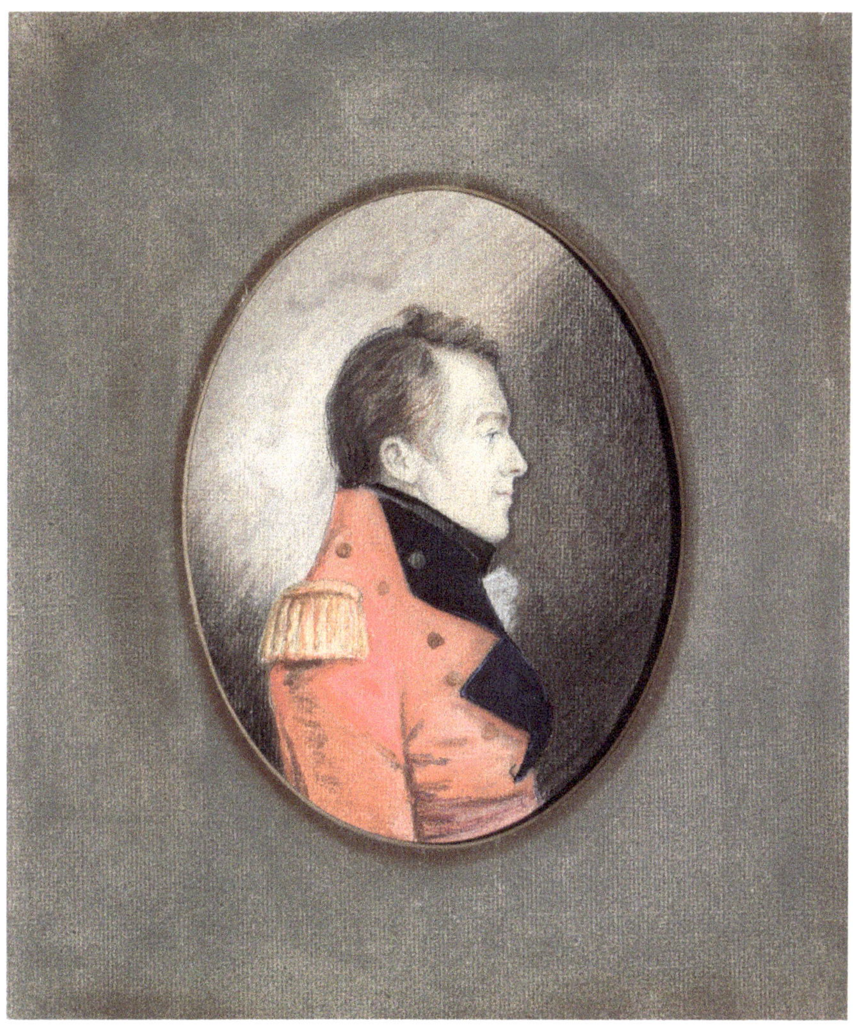

Plate 19. Alyn Williams (after unknown copyist, date unknown; after Gerrit Schipper, 1809/1810), *General Sir Isaac Brock*, 1897, pastel painting with gouache and graphite on paper, 17.8 x 14 cm, Canadian Collection, Department of World Cultures, Royal Ontario Museum (accession 921.42.3).

This miniature was painted by Alyn Williams, one of the art experts Miss Agnes FitzGibbon consulted in London during the summer of 1897. After pronouncing the profile portrait of Brock then owned by John Savery Carey (pl. 4) to be the original, Williams advised a copy and Miss FitzGibbon agreed to the commission. Unfortunately, the portrait Williams copied was itself a copy.

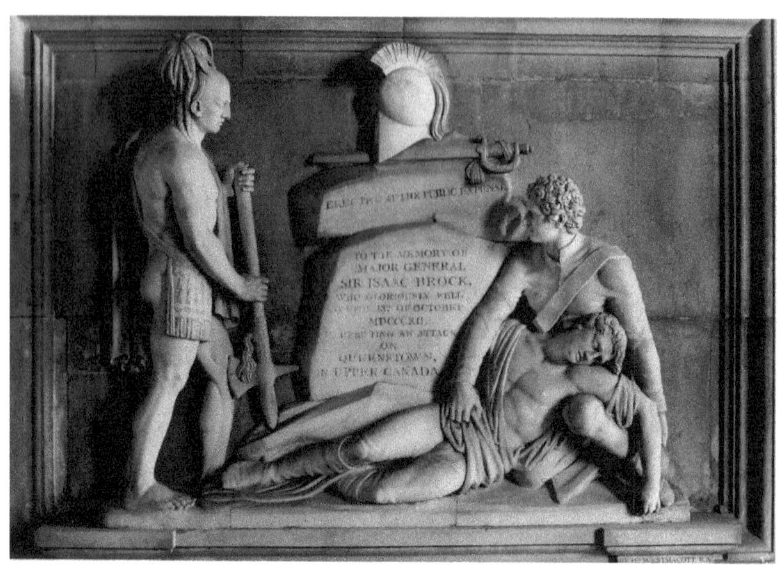

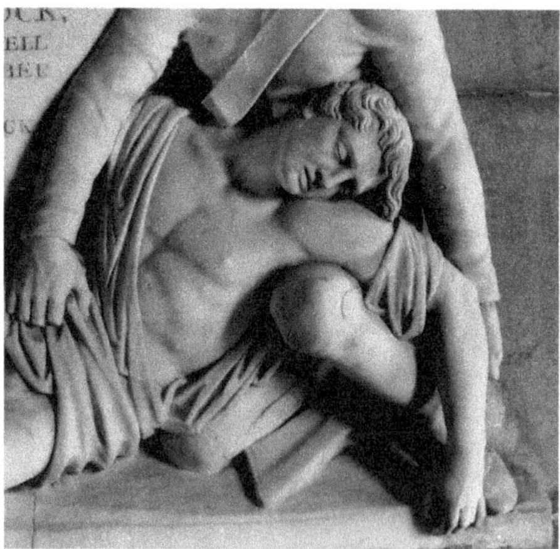

PLATE 20. Richard Westmacott, *Memorial to Major General Sir Isaac Brock*, circa 1815, marble high relief tableau, approximately 161 x 256 cm, St. Paul's Cathedral/The Courtauld Institute of Art. A. Detail of above.

In 1814, Richard Westmacott was commissioned to sculpt this neoclassical memorial to Major General Sir Isaac Brock. After its completion, the tableau was placed in the south transept of St. Paul's Cathedral. The detail illustrates Westmacott's stylized approach in representing Brock's face. © The Courtauld Institute of Art.

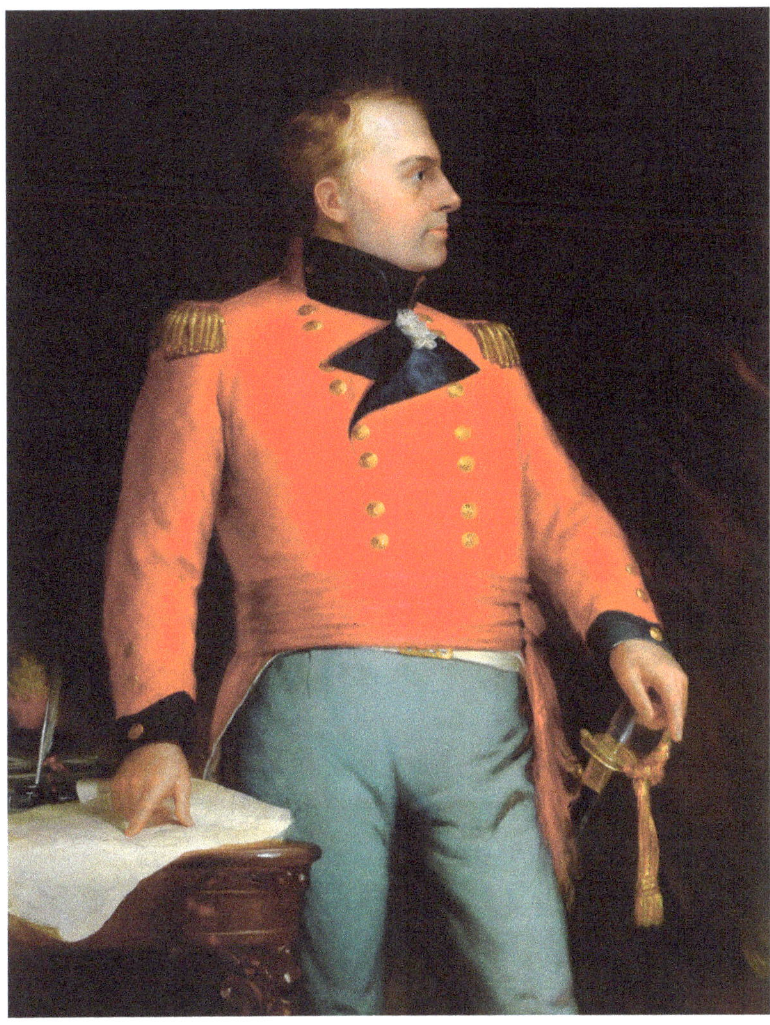

Plate 21. John W.L. Forster (after unknown copyist, date unknown; after Gerrit Schipper, 1809/1810), *Major General Sir Isaac Brock, K.B.*, 1897, oil painting on canvas, 178 x 127 cm, Royal Court, States of Guernsey (accession GUESP:RCT. 22).

Before he left Guernsey in the late summer of 1897, John Wycliffe Lowes Forster painted a larger version of his study for a portrait of Major General Sir Isaac Brock (pl. 16). Its purchase was subject to the approval of the States (or parliament), and after a sometimes-heated debate—during which both the quality of the painting and the artist's talents were scrutinized—the question was put to a vote. Much to Forster's satisfaction, there was a majority in favour of the proposition. The portrait now hangs in the Royal Court.

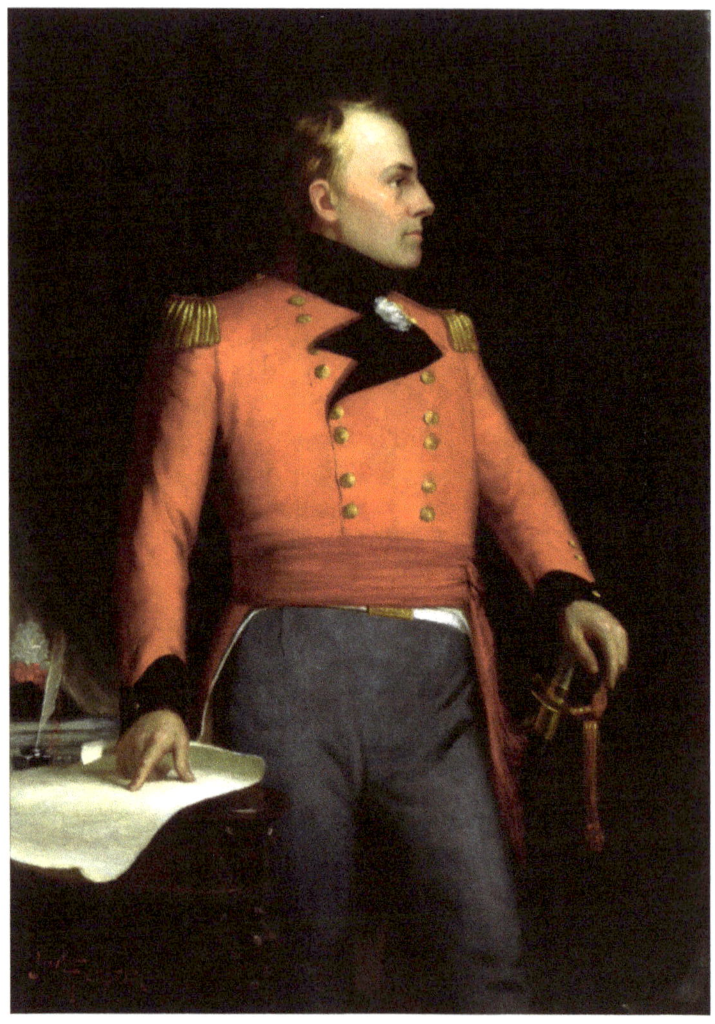

Plate 22. John W.L. Forster (after unknown copyist, date unknown; after Gerrit Schipper, 1809/1810), *Major-General Sir Isaac Brock, KB*, 1900, oil painting on canvas, 150.5 x 109.2 cm, Government of Ontario Art Collection, Archives of Ontario (accession 692,993).

This portrait of Major General Sir Isaac Brock, which has long graced the foyer of the Ontario Legislature, was painted by John Wycliffe Lowes Forster in 1900. It was sold to the Ontario Minister of Education in that same year. © Government of Ontario Art Collection, Archives of Ontario.

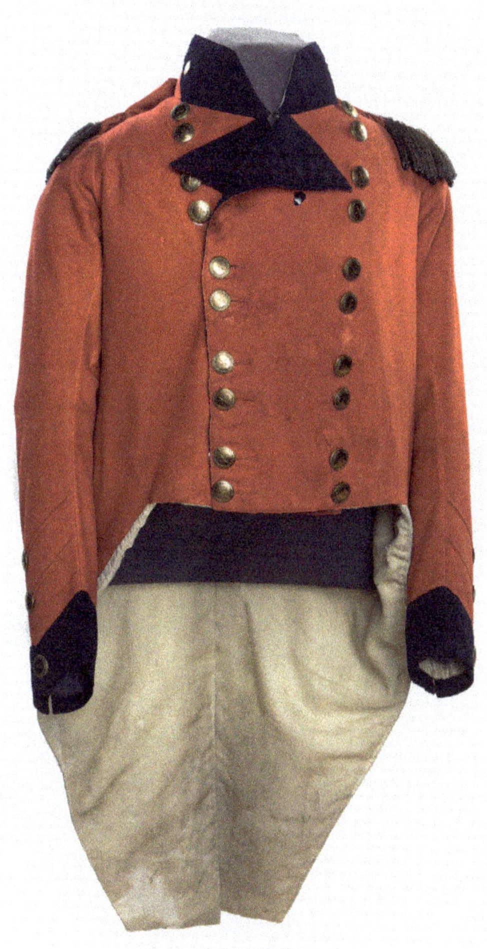

Plate 23. Undress (plain) *Coatee of Brigadier General Isaac Brock* (tailor unknown), circa 1809, wool (superfine), h. 111 cm, Canadian War Museum (artifact CWM 19670070-009).

The coatee which Major General Sir Isaac Brock wore at the time of his death is actually part of his brigadier general's outfit. Unlike the modified colonel's uniform featured in the profile portrait by Gerrit Schipper (pl. 3), this coatee shows the correct arrangement of buttons for a brigadier general (in pairs down the chest). © Canadian War Museum.

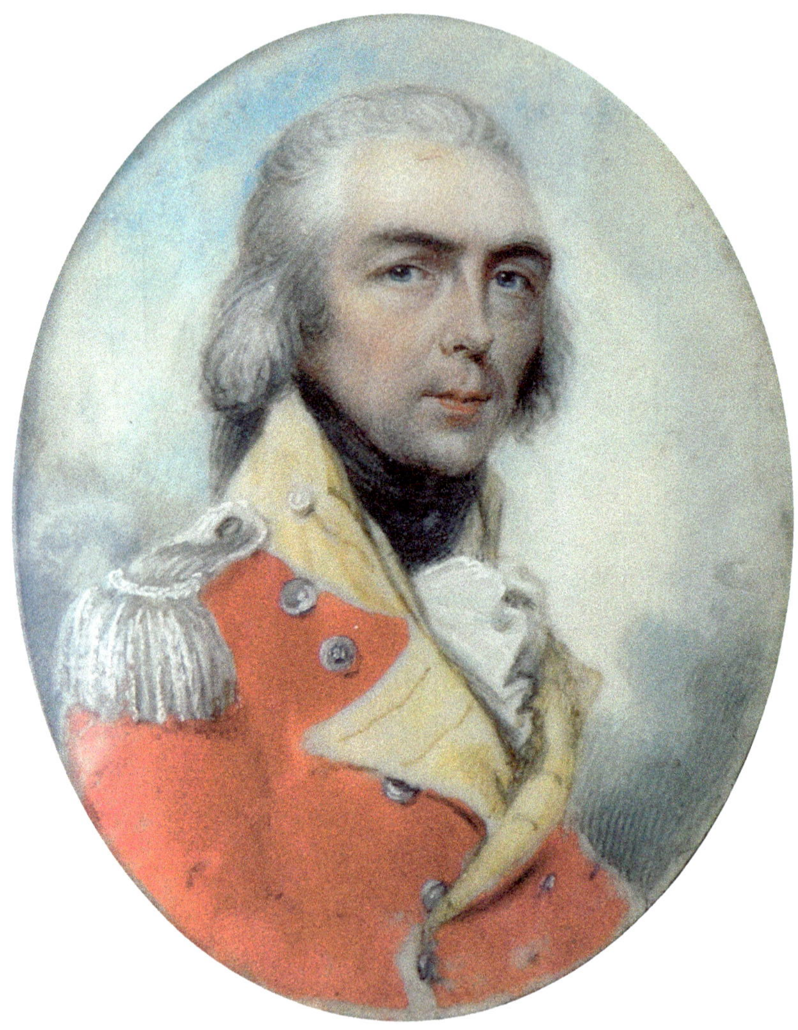

Plate 24. Artist unknown, *Captain John Brock, 81st Regiment* (misidentified as "Major Gen. Sir Isaac Brock"), circa 1795, watercolour painting on ivory, 8.3 x 7 cm, Archives and Special Collections, James A. Gibson Library, Brock University (catalogue BC-024-6-1-1).

Despite an elaborate label on the reverse side of this miniature, which identifies the sitter as "Major Gen. Sir Isaac Brock," the officer is actually his older brother, Captain John Brock of the 81st Regiment, circa 1795. This mistake was rectified by Ludwig Kosche, who discovered the regimental number displayed in one of the uniform's buttons.

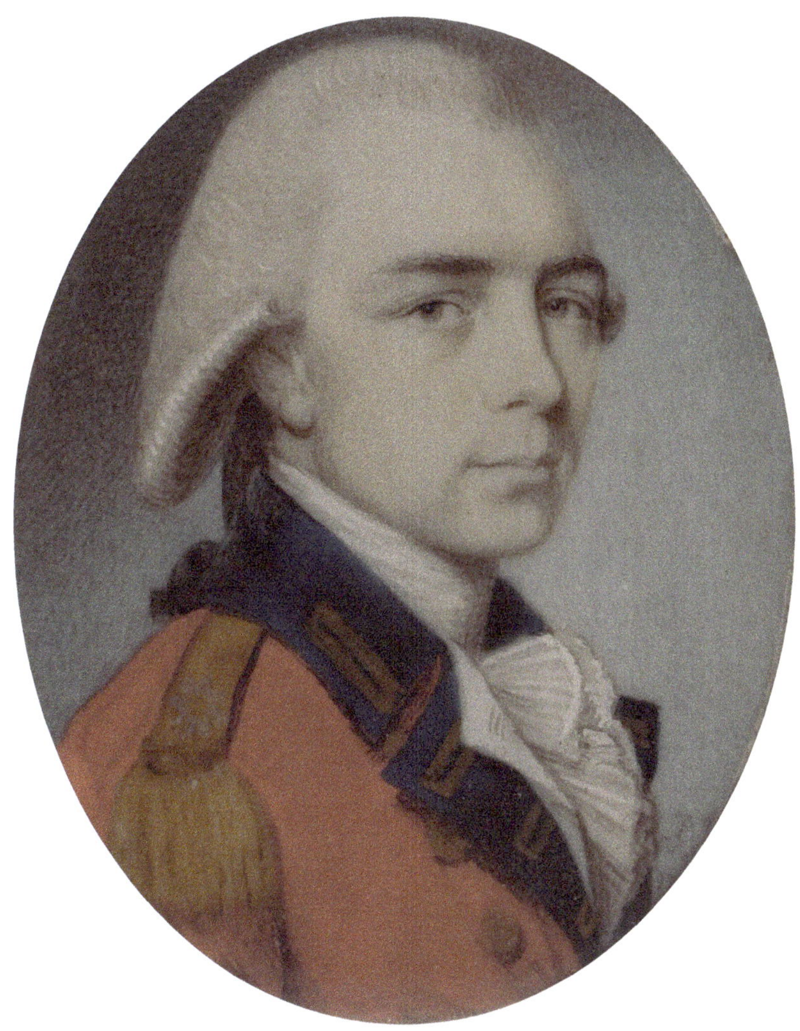

Plate 25. Philip Jean, *Lieutenant John Brock, 8th (or King's) Regiment*, circa 1784–85, watercolour painting on ivory, 4.8 x 3.7 cm, Guernsey Museums and Galleries, States of Guernsey (accession GMAG 2009.54).

When John Brock sat for this miniature, which was sometime in 1784 or 1785, he was still a lieutenant in the 8th (or King's) Regiment. The artist was Philip Jean. © Guernsey Museums and Galleries, States of Guernsey.

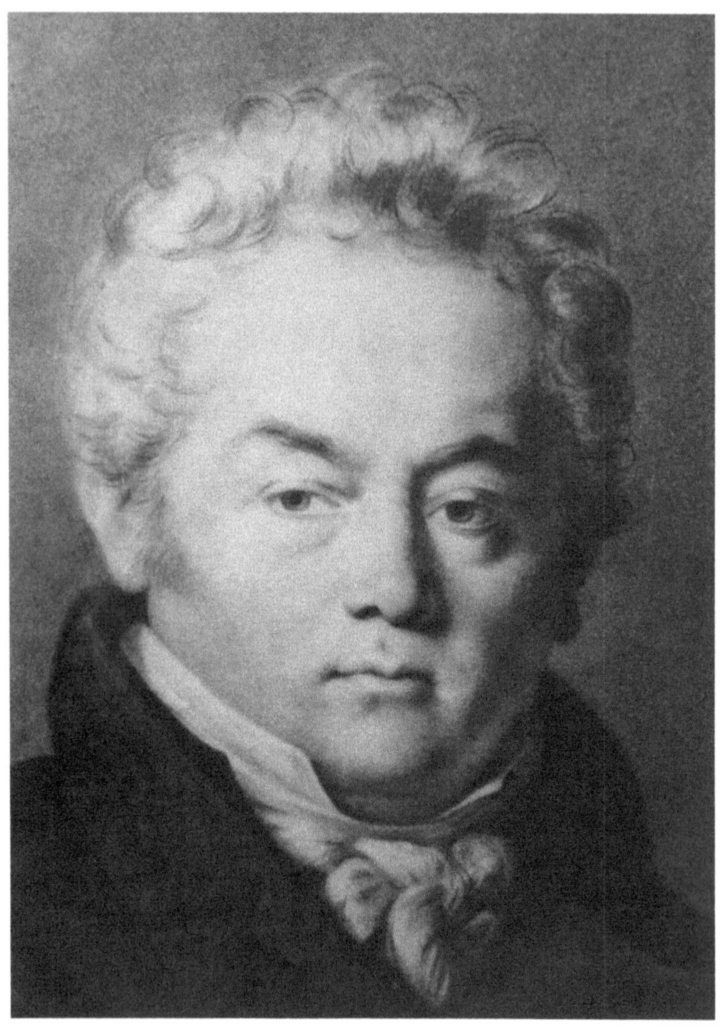

Plate 26. Association of Canadian Archivists (after unknown artist, circa 1820), detail from a *Portrait of John Savery Brock*, 1985, halftone illustration of graphite drawing on paper (detail), dimensions unknown, *Archivaria*.

This detail is taken from a pencil sketch of John Savery Brock, which came to the attention of Ludwig Kosche in 1982—at the same time that he was trying to identify a miniature owned by Brock University (pl. 24). Believing that the miniature portrayed John Brock, the older brother of Isaac Brock, Kosche expected that the sitters in both the miniature and the pencil sketch would resemble one another. However, upon seeing the sketch for the first time, Kosche began to realize that there must have been two Brock brothers named John.

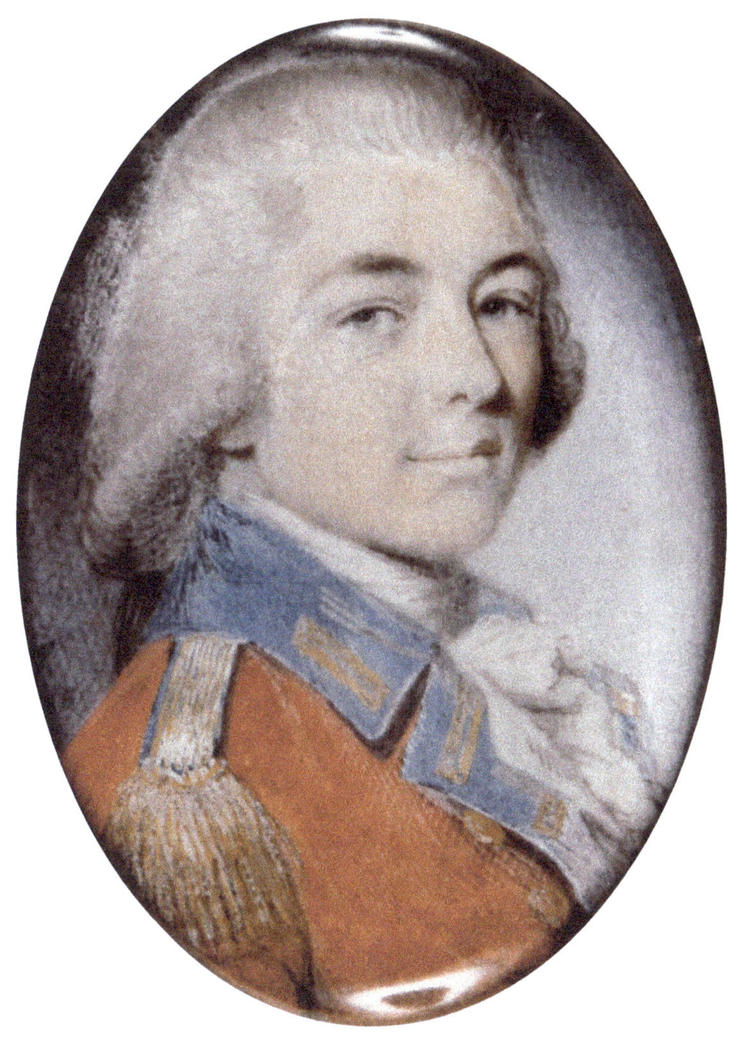

Plate 27. Philip Jean, *Ensign Isaac Brock, 8th (or King's) Regiment*, 1785, watercolour painting on ivory, 4.5 x 3.3 cm, Guernsey Museums and Galleries, States of Guernsey (accession GMAG 2009.53).

The work of Philip Jean, this miniature of a youthful Isaac Brock was painted in 1785—not long after he became an ensign in the 8th (or King's) Regiment. © Guernsey Museums and Galleries, States of Guernsey.

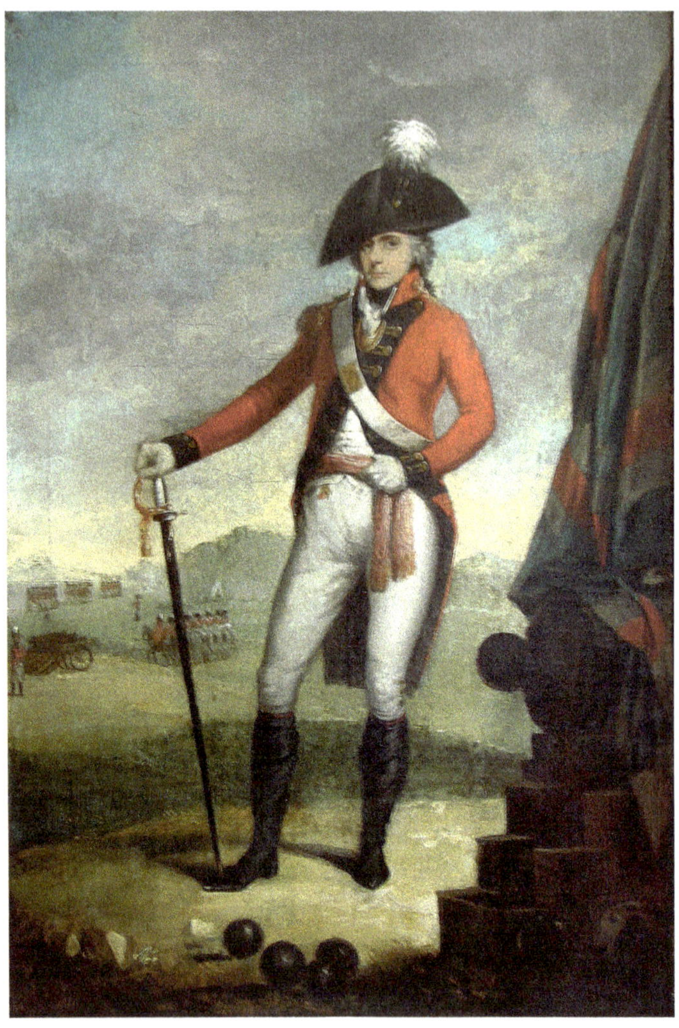

Plate 28. Artist unknown, *Unknown Officer* (misidentified as "Sir Isaac Brock as Captain"), circa 1801–03, oil painting on canvas, 50.8 x 35.4 cm, Honourable P. Michael Pitfield.

Once thought to portray Captain Isaac Brock of the 49th Regiment, this painting was later refuted mainly because of an incorrect uniform. As well, it was determined that the flag dates to circa 1801–03, by which time Brock held the rank of lieutenant colonel. Therefore, the officer depicted cannot be Isaac Brock as a captain. In accepting this conclusion, Ludwig Kosche began to think that the officer might have been Brock's older brother, John Brock. However, this identification is also now questioned.

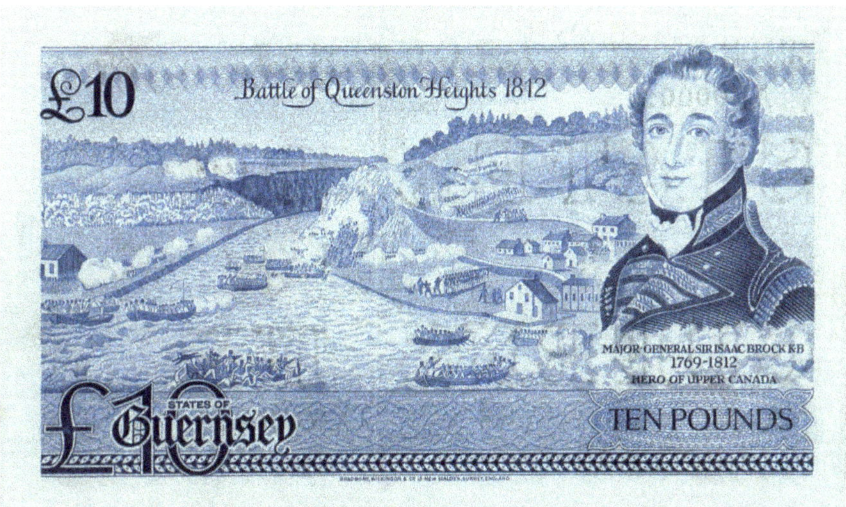

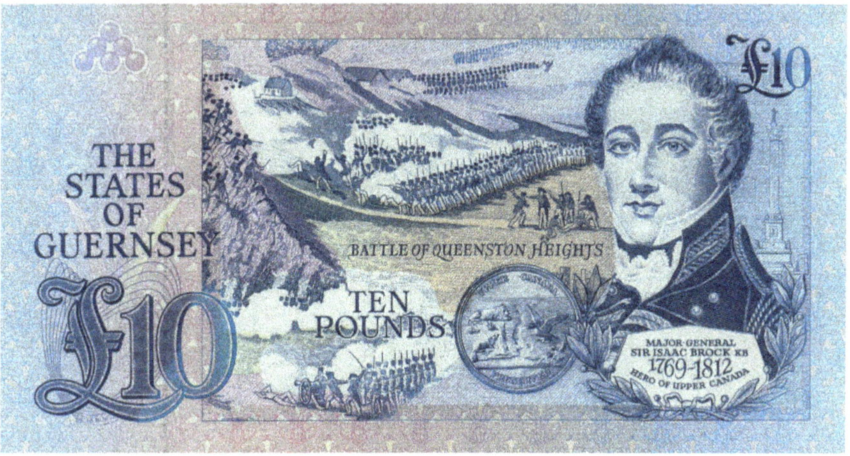

Plate 29 A–B.

A. Bradbury, Wilkinson and Company (after J. Hudson, 1816), *Lieutenant George Dunn* (misidentified as "Major-General Sir Isaac Brock KB"), 1975–80, banknote, 8.9 x 14.9 cm, Treasury and Resources Department, States of Guernsey.

B. Thomas de la Rue and Company (after J. Hudson, 1816), *Lieutenant George Dunn* (misidentified as "Major-General Sir Isaac Brock KB"), 1980/1992–95, banknote, 8.5 x 15.2 cm, Treasury and Resources Department, States of Guernsey.

Between 1975 and 1995, the States of Guernsey paid homage to one of its most famous sons on not one, but three issues of the island's ten-pound note. Unfortunately, the officer immortalized was not Major General Sir Isaac Brock, but rather Lieutenant George Dunn of the 23rd Regiment (pl. 11). The third issue is not illustrated here because it differs from the second only in size, being slightly smaller. © Treasury and Resources Department, States of Guernsey. Reproduced with permission.

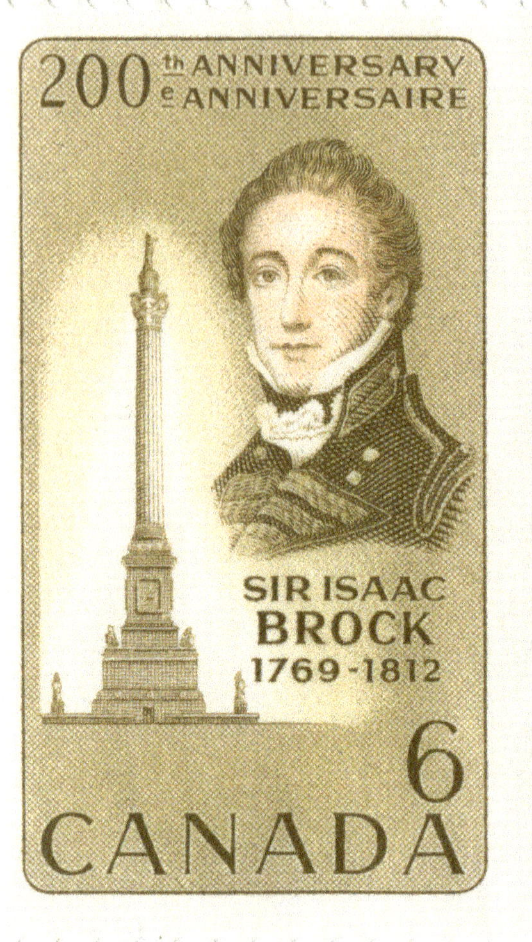

Plate 30. Imre Von Mosdossy/Canadian Post Office Department (after J. Hudson, 1816), *Lieutenant George Dunn* (misidentified as "Sir Isaac Brock"), 1969, postage stamp, 4 x 2.5 cm, author's collection.

In 1969, the Canadian Post Office commemorated the 200th anniversary of Major General Sir Isaac Brock's birth with the issue of this six-cent stamp. The officer portrayed, however, is actually Lieutenant George Dunn of the 23rd Regiment (pl. 11). © Canada Post Corporation. Reproduced with permission.

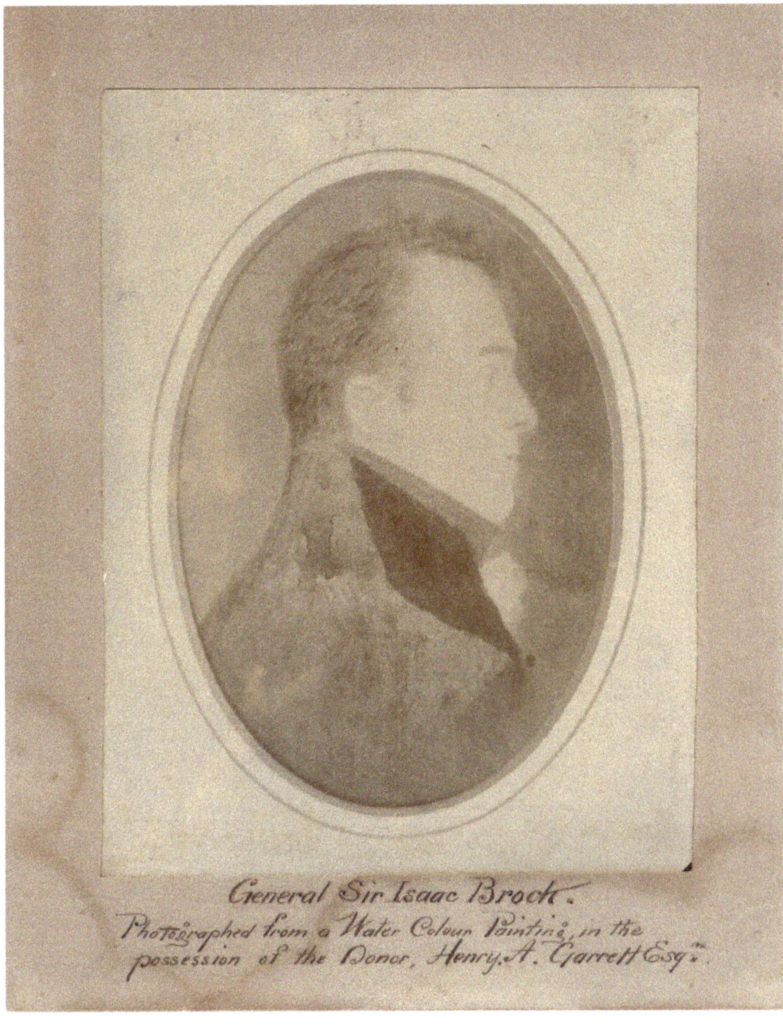

Plate 31. William Quinn (after unknown photographer, date unknown; after Hills and Saunders, 1881; after Gerrit Schipper, 1809/1810), *General Sir Isaac Brock*, circa 1891, photograph in cabinet card format, 25.3 x 20.2 cm, Niagara Historical Society Museum (accession 984.1.127).

The caption of this alleged watercolour painting of "General Sir Isaac Brock" is misleading. It appears to be nothing more than a poor copy of the photograph taken by Hills and Saunders in 1881 (pl. 7), and one that was clumsily overpainted with watercolours. This botched enhancement probably explains the confusion.

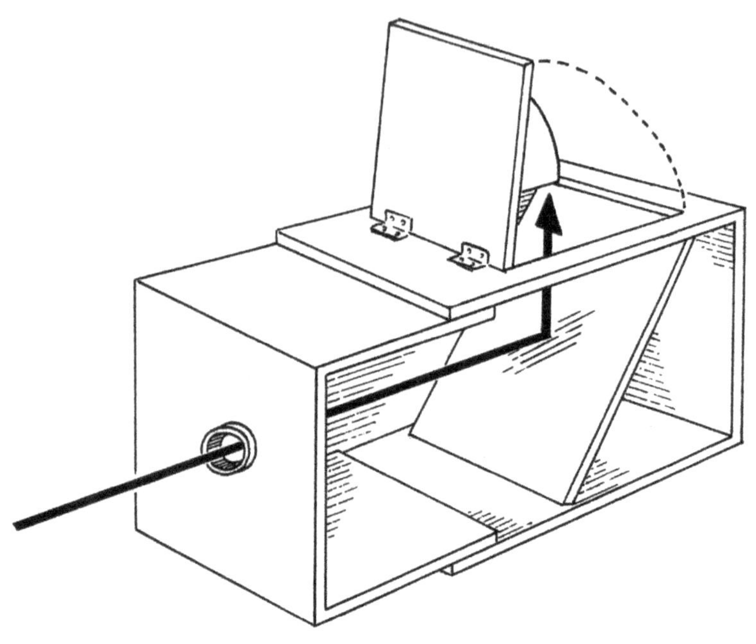

Plate 32. Robert Turner, *Camera Obscura*, 2011, ink diagram on paper, 21.3 x 21.7 cm, author's collection.

In 1804, Gerrit Schipper was still using an achromatic camera obscura to reduce the profiles of his sitters. The term achromatic referred to the lens, which was corrected to produce a sharper image. It was still effectively a camera obscura, however, and probably looked much like the one in this cut-away diagram. Through the aperture, the image was projected into an angled mirror, reflected on a ground glass plate, and then traced by the operator. © Author's collection.

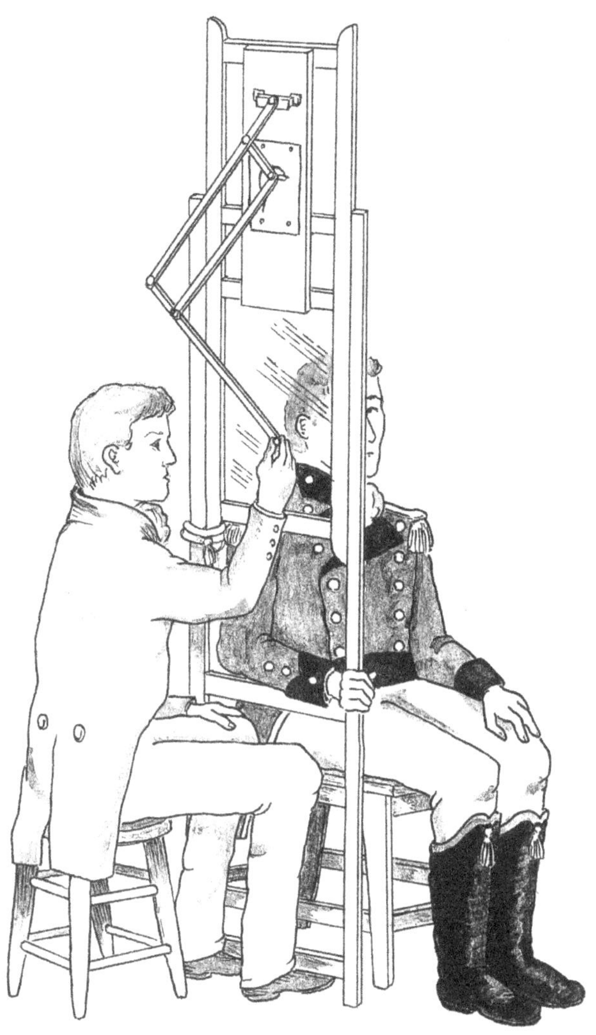

Plate 33. Robert Turner, *Physiognotrace*, 2011, ink and wash diagram on paper, 30.5 x 22.9 cm, author's collection.

This diagram illustrates the probable means by which Gerrit Schipper began work on Brigadier General Isaac Brock's profile portrait (pl. 3). Using a modified version of the physiognotrace, Schipper quickly transferred the sitter's reduced profile onto a piece of paper. He then enhanced the outline with his artistic skills—a process that occupied about three-quarters of an hour.

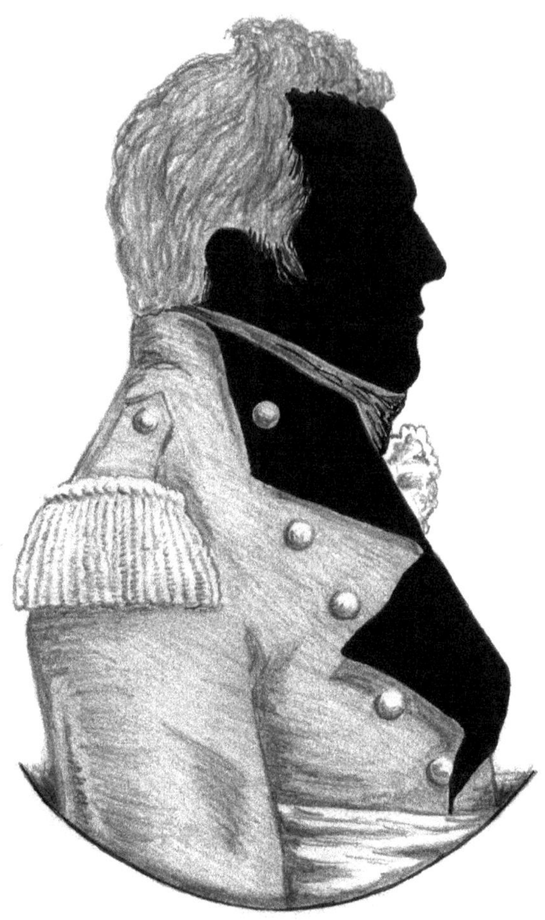

Plate 34. Robert Turner, *Brigadier General Isaac Brock's Bronzed Silhouette*, 2011, ink and graphite drawing on paper, 23.3 x 21.5 cm, author's collection.

This ink and graphite drawing replicates a traditional bronzed silhouette photographed in black and white. The outline was derived from the profile portrait of Brigadier General Isaac Brock by Gerrit Schipper (pl. 3). Given that Schipper used a physiognotrace to transfer Brock's facial features onto paper, the delineation can be regarded as highly accurate—illustrating what the bronze profile (pl. 8) and the Jarvis silhouette (pl. 18) should have looked like, had they been intended to represent the future "Hero of Upper Canada." © Author's collection.

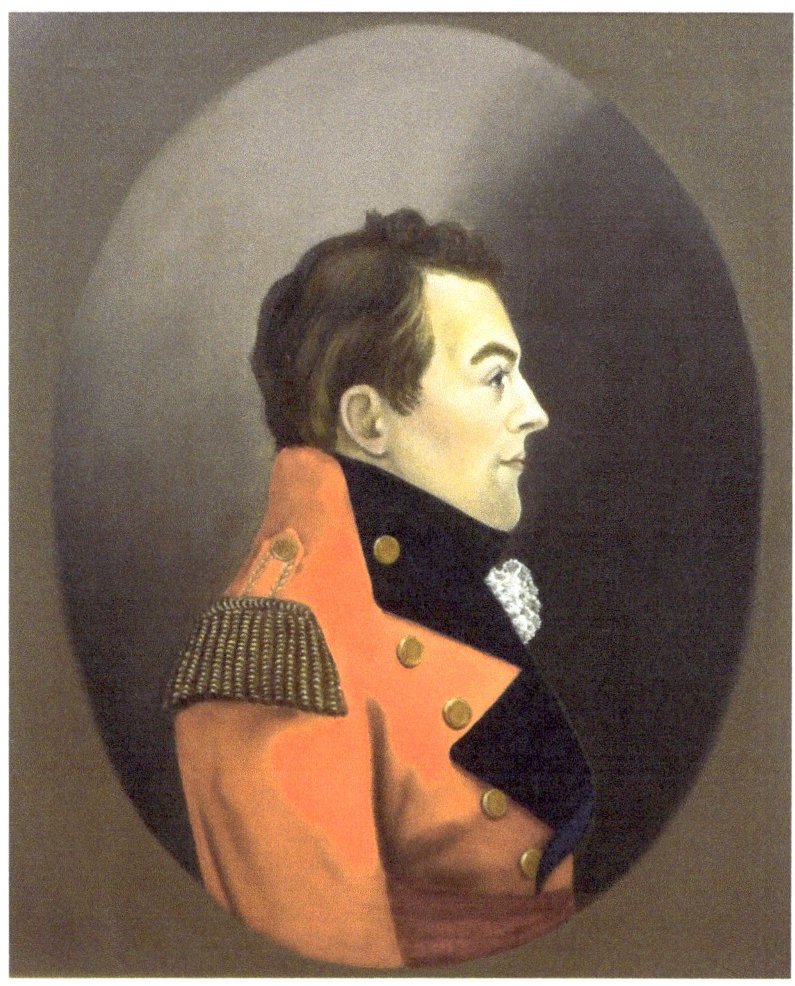

Plate 35. Philippa Abrahams (after Gerrit Schipper, 1809/1810), *Major General Sir Isaac Brock*, 1985, oil painting on canvas, 66 x 56 cm, Archives and Special Collections, James A. Gibson Library, Brock University (catalogue BC-029).

After Captain Michael H.T. Mellish declined to sell the portrait of his famous collateral ancestor, the Weir Foundation commissioned Philippa Abrahams to paint two copies of it. Working from a colour photograph of Gerrit Schipper's profile portrait of Brigadier General Isaac Brock (pl. 3), Abrahams completed her paintings in 1985. One of them went to what is now the RiverBrink Art Museum in Queenston, Ontario. The other painting, illustrated here, was donated to Brock University in nearby St. Catharines.

Introduction

Of the many portraits depicting Sir Isaac Brock, most were painted long after his death. Just two are known to have been done from life, and only one shows him at about the time he achieved everlasting fame. Things might have been different had he survived the War of 1812, assuming that he did so with his reputation intact. As Brock the conquering hero, he was likely to have enjoyed sittings with some of the leading artists of the early nineteenth century. But he was killed only a few months after the Americans declared war. Consequently, Brock's likeness was the inspiration for numerous artists' impressions—all of which were accepted as bona fide. To understand how Brock's portrait became something of a cottage industry for artistic license, it is first necessary to examine the significance of heroic iconography in commemorating his legacy.

As the military commander of Upper Canada, Brock was responsible for defending what is now southern Ontario against the threat of American invasion. His capture of Detroit in August of 1812 secured the colony's western region in spectacular fashion, but in October of that same year, while attempting to repel an American attack on the Niagara frontier, he met with an untimely death. Despite his loss, Upper Canada emerged from the War of 1812, if not unscathed, then at least geographically intact. And rightly or wrongly, it was Brock who was praised for the colony's salvation. In 1814, the government of a grateful province unanimously resolved to commemorate his sacrifice with a monument on Queenston Heights.[1] While inadequate funding caused long delays in the monument's construction, the necessity for an ongoing subscription drive actually helped to immortalize Brock through the occasional reiteration of his worth. Eventually, in October of 1824, the "Hero of Upper Canada" was ceremoniously re-interred in the crypt beneath a rising column of the Tuscan order.[2] By the time of its completion in 1826, Brock's Monument had become emblematic of Upper Canada's strong attachment to Great Britain. But there was one disgruntled Upper Canadian who would take exception with all the symbolism.

In 1840, a miscreant by the name of Benjamin Lett shattered the monument with a blast of gunpowder.[3] This heinous act, one of a number Lett committed in Upper Canada, was met with calls for a new monument. The proposal received an overwhelming show of support.[4] But as was the case with the first monument, money was scarce. Work was finally commenced in 1853, completed in 1856, and in 1859—once the grounds were suitably landscaped—the second Brock Monument was at last inaugurated.[5] There were throngs of spectators and a full complement of aging dignitaries, some of whom were invited to recount their fond memories of Brock for the assembled multitudes.[6] Ironically, Lett's villainy served to strengthen the ties of loyalty to the mother country. It also helped to shape a destiny quite apart from that of the United States. Canadian nationalism, which was even then beginning to take hold, would become a recurring theme after the confederation of Britain's North American colonies in 1867. And because the new Dominion of Canada was still part of the British Empire, Sir Isaac Brock was just as relevant to the nation builders as he had been to their colonial antecedents.

Given the length of time required to build Brock's first monument, it seems extraordinary that no one thought to enquire after his portrait. Had the monument been built according to the original design, the question of a likeness might have become a more pressing issue. But the bronze statue of Brock planned for the top of his monument never materialized, as there was simply no money for such an elaborate finial.[7] Subsequently, when work began on Brock's second monument, it was generally assumed that his portrait did not exist.[8] As the Canadian historian Gilbert Auchinleck observed in July of 1853: "we are unacquainted with the preservation of any portrait, public or private, of Gen. Brock in this country."[9] Auchinleck was right. There was no portrait of Brock—not in Canada, at least.

Auchinleck made his observation while publishing a serialized account of the War of 1812, and he was probably disappointed at not being able to find a portrait of Brock to use as an illustration.[10] But whereas

Auchinleck was quick to admit defeat, other Brock enthusiasts were not so easily daunted. Whether imperialists, nationalists, or some combination of the two, these patriotic individuals recognized the value of historical portraiture in forging a unique Canadian identity. They were also intrigued by the possibility that a portrait of Brock might still be found in Guernsey, if for no other reason than he was known to have relatives there. But while the search for Brock's portrait was lauded as a matter of national importance, the responsibility for finding it fell to a few private individuals who acted independently of one another. Unfortunately, their efforts met with repeated failure. However, just as Canadian nationalism helped to keep Brock's memory alive, it also fostered a determination to know his face.

By the time a small profile portrait (pl. 3) was finally brought to light in the mid-1870s, it was too late to be used in conjunction with Brock's second monument. This imposing fluted column was completed nearly fifteen years earlier, and in grand style. Among other things, there was a fanciful relief depicting his death, inaccurate renderings of his heraldic shield, and a larger-than-life statue that bore not the slightest resemblance to Brock—certainly not as he appeared in his newly discovered portrait.[11] The sculptor's liberty is perhaps understandable, given that no portrait of Brock was thought to exist. Even if the profile portrait had been discovered earlier, it hardly lent itself to heroic art on a monumental scale. After all, it was a modest little composition painted mainly in pastels. But to enterprising artists, a less-than-heroic portrait could still be used as the basis for more impressive and profitable replicas—the sporadic demand for which was a by-product of the same sense of nationalism that had prompted the search for Brock's portrait in the first place. While none of the duplicates succeeded in capturing the essence or integrity of the original likeness, the differences were subtle enough to avoid controversy. In time, any similar-looking portrait with a label bearing Brock's name was accepted as such, with little or no regard for historical accuracy.

This lax attitude towards Brock's likeness was further exacerbated by a number of misidentified portraits, one of which (pl. 11) was copied almost as much as the original. Nor was there any attempt to clarify the confusion, as Canada's art historians tended to be more interested in artists than sitters.[12] And the indifference of mainstream academic historians did nothing to mitigate the problem. By the mid-twentieth century, most of these arbiters of past events were careful to avoid Brock as much as possible.[13] Their condescending attitude can be traced to the professionalization of Canadian history, which began to take place in the newly formed history departments of Canada's leading universities at the turn of that same century.[14] Disdaining any association with the over-glorified biographical commemorations of Victorian times, this new breed of academic historians also shunned antiquarian pursuits and connoisseurship.[15] Opportunistic artists took advantage of the situation and began painting Brock's portrait in a manner to suit themselves. Since an accurate likeness was presumed to be the point of the exercise, none of these fictitious portraits were ever questioned. Encouraged by the prospect of not having to defend their increasingly imaginative portraits of Brock, these same opportunistic artists became especially active around the time of important anniversaries. In a cycle that continues to this day, the number of spurious likenesses began to grow ever larger. Yet, this highly dubious and rather fraudulent practice might have been halted, or at the very least curtailed, had some eminent Canadian historian been sufficiently roused to publicly challenge the abuse at an early date. But the academic types preferred to remain aloof, and they became ever more indifferent with the passage of time.

By the late 1960s, a new historiographical approach was all the rage. Favouring the people over their leaders, it further marginalized great men such as Brock. Beyond academe, however, there was still a lingering fascination with Brock's life, as one of Canada's most successful writers discovered when he wrote a popular history about the War of 1812. It was 1980, and *The Invasion of Canada* by Pierre Berton was enjoying a great deal of critical acclaim.[16] While most academic historians were privately derisive of Berton's lack of scholarly qualifications, one openly expressed his misgivings about the writer's inconsistent treatment of historical evidence.[17] Perplexed but unfazed, Berton followed up with *Flames Across the Border* in 1981, which was no more rigorous in its analysis than *The Invasion of Canada*, and yet no less popular.[18] There can be no doubt that many of Berton's academic detractors simply resented his phenomenal success, especially as he was seen to be impinging upon their own area of expertise. In reality, however, Berton was simply filling a void left by the academic historians themselves, and in the process he very ably demonstrated that

Canadians had not forgotten the War of 1812. Neither had they forsaken Sir Isaac Brock.

When *The Invasion of Canada* began to take shape in 1979, there was already a large supply of Brock likenesses on hand. Nearly all of them were bogus, but nobody writing about Brock or the War of 1812 bothered to check the authenticity of the pictures they used to illustrate their books. Unwittingly, Berton managed to get it right, and he was one of the few who did.[19] Ignorance being bliss, the misrepresentations of Brock continued unabated. Yet, the tide was slowly beginning to turn. In the late 1970s, Ludwig Kosche took it upon himself to authenticate several portraits reputed to be of Brock. Kosche, who was then librarian at the Canadian War Museum, went on to publish a substantial article in which he presented his findings.[20] In it, he concluded that only two of the portraits were genuine, or painted from life. One of them was a miniature, which showed Brock as a young ensign (pl. 27). The other portrait, a half-length profile facing right, presented a more mature likeness (pl. 3). This was the portrait brought to light in the 1870s. It was also the most historically appropriate, having been painted only a few years before the War of 1812 and Brock's meteoric rise to fame.

The article by Kosche was a commendable attempt to alert his fellow scholars to the many pitfalls associated with Brock's portraits, and he certainly looked to be the indisputable authority on the subject. But while his article initially impressed me as a shining example of dedicated historical research, its shortcomings soon became all too apparent. In running afoul of Kosche, I vowed to carry on where he left off. However, like Kosche, I first had to contend with a certain lieutenant governor of Ontario and his own obsession with the true face of Sir Isaac Brock.

I

The Viceregal Legacy

In 1880, the people of Ontario learned that their next lieutenant governor was to be John Beverley Robinson, whose father and namesake had been a prominent lawyer, politician, and chief justice of earlier times.[1] Soon after his appointment, the new lieutenant governor struck upon the idea of a portrait gallery dedicated to his predecessors and all those who would come after him—a Gallery of Governors, as it were.[2] This pet project was largely motivated by the lieutenant governor's keen sense of Ontario's history, and his family's influential standing among the upper echelons of the province when it was still known as Upper Canada. But patriotism and posterity were also major considerations. The portraits were intended to be a source of pride among all classes of people—not only in Ontario, but in the rest of Canada as well. At a time when nationalism was on the rise, and when the imperial connection to Great Britain was still of paramount importance to a large segment of the Canadian population, it was perfectly reasonable for Lieutenant Governor Robinson to think that the collected portraits of his antecedents would inspire a devotion to the Crown for generations to come.

Lieutenant Governor Robinson's method of assembling his collection of viceregal portraits quickly became well established. In each case, he began by looking for a suitable likeness, which was then borrowed or photographed so that George Berthon, a renowned Toronto-based artist, could work up an appropriately dignified copy in oils.[3] By the spring of 1881, the lieutenant governor was anxious to track down a portrait of Major General Sir Isaac Brock, who served as president (or acting lieutenant governor) of Upper Canada prior to his death in 1812. The logical place to begin such a search was Guernsey, the Channel Island where Brock was born and raised. To aid in the search, the lieutenant governor enlisted the assistance of a brother who was then living in London. But Colonel Charles W. Robinson was not optimistic. He recalled that some years earlier he had attempted to find a portrait of Brock for the Royal Hospital at Chelsea and been told that none existed.[4] The lieutenant governor was not deterred, however, and it appears that a journalist-turned-historian gave him reason to hope.

In 1880, the same year that Lieutenant Governor Robinson began his mandate, John Charles Dent published the first volume of his *Canadian Portrait Gallery*, which was followed by three additional volumes chronicling the lives of Canada's leading personalities. The popularity of these illustrated books coincided with the emergence of a culture in which the enhancement of text with images was becoming increasingly common. Not surprisingly, Brock's entry in the *Canadian Portrait Gallery* warranted a lavish colour portrait using the chromolithography process (fig. 1). The resulting illustration, a profile in muted tones, was similar to a wood engraving (fig. 2) that had appeared several years earlier in the *Globe*, a Toronto newspaper edited by Dent.[5] Both interpretations were based on a portrait owned by Brock's relatives in Guernsey, who had only just recently allowed it to be photographed for Dr. John George Hodgins of Toronto.[6] As Ontario's deputy minister of education, Dr. Hodgins wanted to have the photograph for a display in the Educational Museum, where Brock's likeness would serve to evoke a heightened sense of pride in being Canadian.[7] As noted, the latter part of the nineteenth century was a period of nation-building. And since the central theme of this movement was a love of one's country, heroic iconography became a mechanism for instilling patriotism among the citizenry of the new nation. Having recognized the significance of such pictures, Dr. Hodgins enquired after Brock's portrait. His efforts were rewarded with a photograph featuring the portrait of a pleasant-looking British officer in profile facing right. Dent used this same photograph as the basis for his illustrations, one or both of which likely convinced the lieutenant governor that a portrait of Sir Isaac Brock did in fact exist.

With the help of his brother, Lieutenant Governor Robinson managed to locate Brock's profile portrait, which also brought about a complication—as there were two such portraits from which to choose. One (fig. 3)

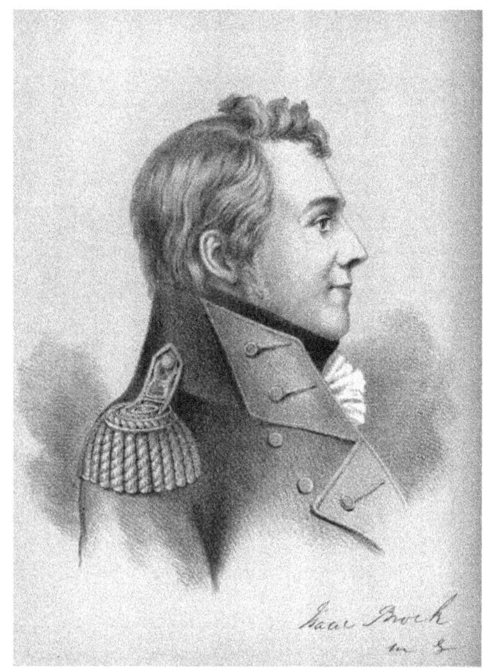

FIGURE 1.

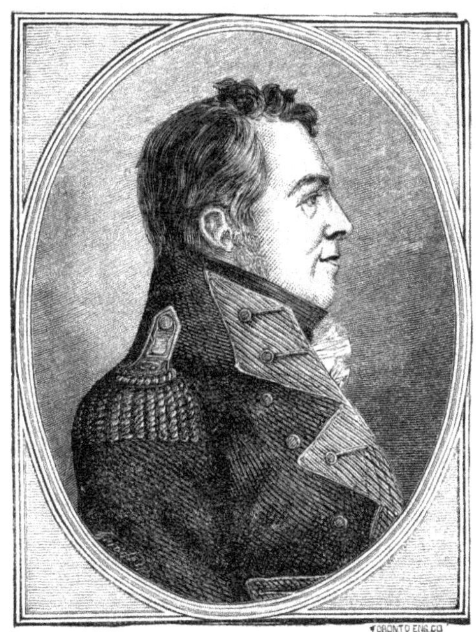

FIGURE 2.

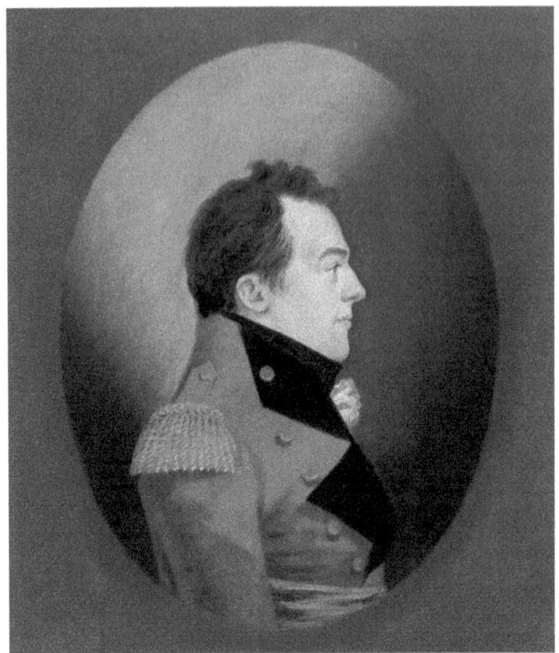

Figure 3.

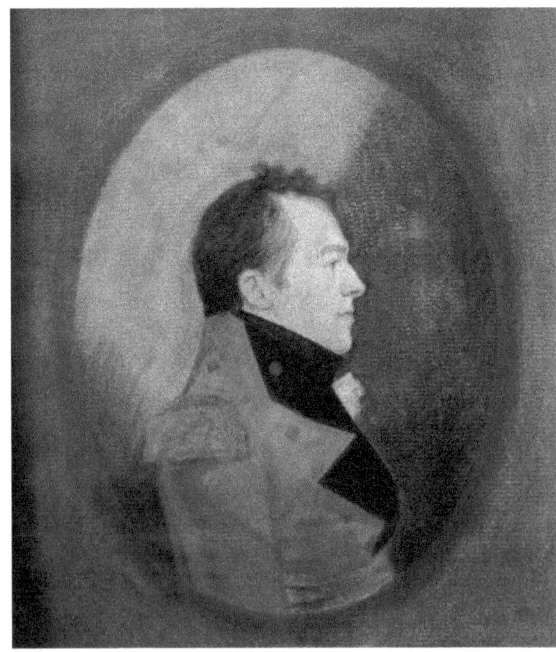

Figure 4.

was owned by Mrs. Henry (Mary Ann Collings) Tupper, whose deceased husband was a nephew to Brock through his mother, Mrs. John Elisha (Elizabeth Brock) Tupper. The other (fig. 4) was the property of Mrs. George Huyshe, the former Miss Rosa Brock and a daughter of Brock's brother, John Savery Brock. The discovery of two portraits called for a clarification, especially since what the lieutenant governor was really looking for was a full-faced likeness. He hoped that one of the two profile portraits might have been incorrectly described, and that one of them might in fact be closer to what he wanted. Dutifully, Colonel Robinson applied to Mrs. Huyshe for additional information.

The portrait belonging to Mrs. Tupper was found to be finely executed. But the one owned by Mrs. Huyshe was rendered in a somewhat cruder fashion, although the face was very well done.[8] What Mrs. Huyshe never mentioned, however, was that both portraits were done in profile and nearly identical. Moreover, hers was obviously a copy. Because it was known to have belonged to her father, this reproduction was likely commissioned by him as a memento of his deceased brother.[9] And since the original was considered more appropriate for the lieutenant governor's purposes, Mrs. Tupper very reluctantly allowed it to be sent to London to be copied—not only by a photographer, but an artist as well. Colonel Robinson thought the latter means of reproduction might suffice for his brother's gallery. With this in mind, he made arrangements for the portrait, measuring only some eight inches by nine (20.3 x 23.4 cm), to be duplicated twice that size in oils.[10] The colonel also arranged for a smaller watercolour copy in sepia tones, which he planned to donate to the Royal Hospital at Chelsea (fig. 5).[11] The artist commissioned for both works was Miss Alice Kerr-Nelson, "a lady with a great deal of talent" whose straitened circumstances forced her to turn to painting for a livelihood.[12] Fortunately for Colonel Robinson, Miss Kerr-Nelson was not so destitute that she required an advance, just sufficiently cash-strapped that she agreed to do the work subject to approval. Miss Kerr-Nelson wasted no time, and before long she had both portraits done and ready for the colonel's inspection.

Finished in a competent and robust manner, the oil painting Miss Kerr-Nelson presented to Colonel Robinson (fig. 6) portrayed Brock as a young officer with an intense gaze. The colonel was pleased with the results, preferring Miss Kerr-Nelson's portrait of Brock even to Mrs.

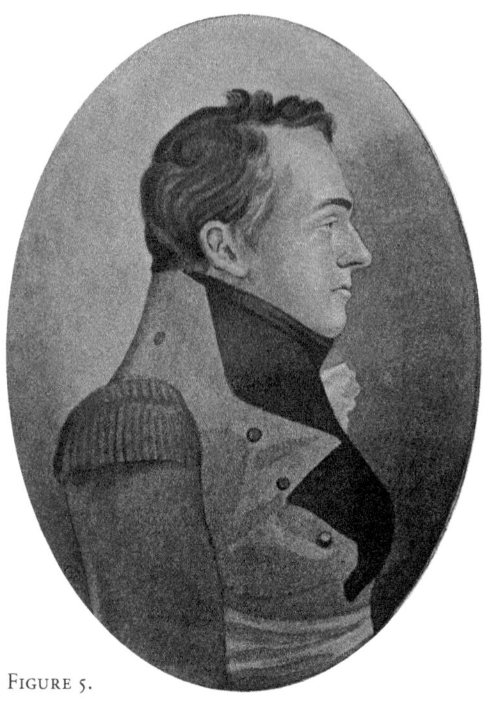

FIGURE 5.

Tupper's original (fig. 3), which he found "a rather wishy washy production."[13] Colonel Robinson thought, erroneously, that the weak effect of the Tupper original was due to the use of a combination of chalk and watercolour. Actually, it was mainly pastel with some chalk and graphite, but no watercolour. Although Colonel Robinson was partial to Miss Kerr-Nelson's copy, it remained to be seen whether or not it would receive the viceregal nod. Colonel Robinson was fairly confident that his brother would recommend the purchase of Miss Kerr-Nelson's painting, but he was also well aware that the lieutenant governor might insist on having Berthon paint Brock's official portrait. Therefore, Colonel Robinson had the original portrait photographed—just in case Berthon chose to work from it.[14] If nothing else, Miss Kerr-Nelson's painting could be used as a colour guide, since the photograph was only available in black and white (fig. 7). And if the lieutenant governor decided against the purchase, Berthon could still make good use of the painting before it had to be returned or sold to someone else.[15]

Having settled on this strategy, Colonel Robinson thought it best

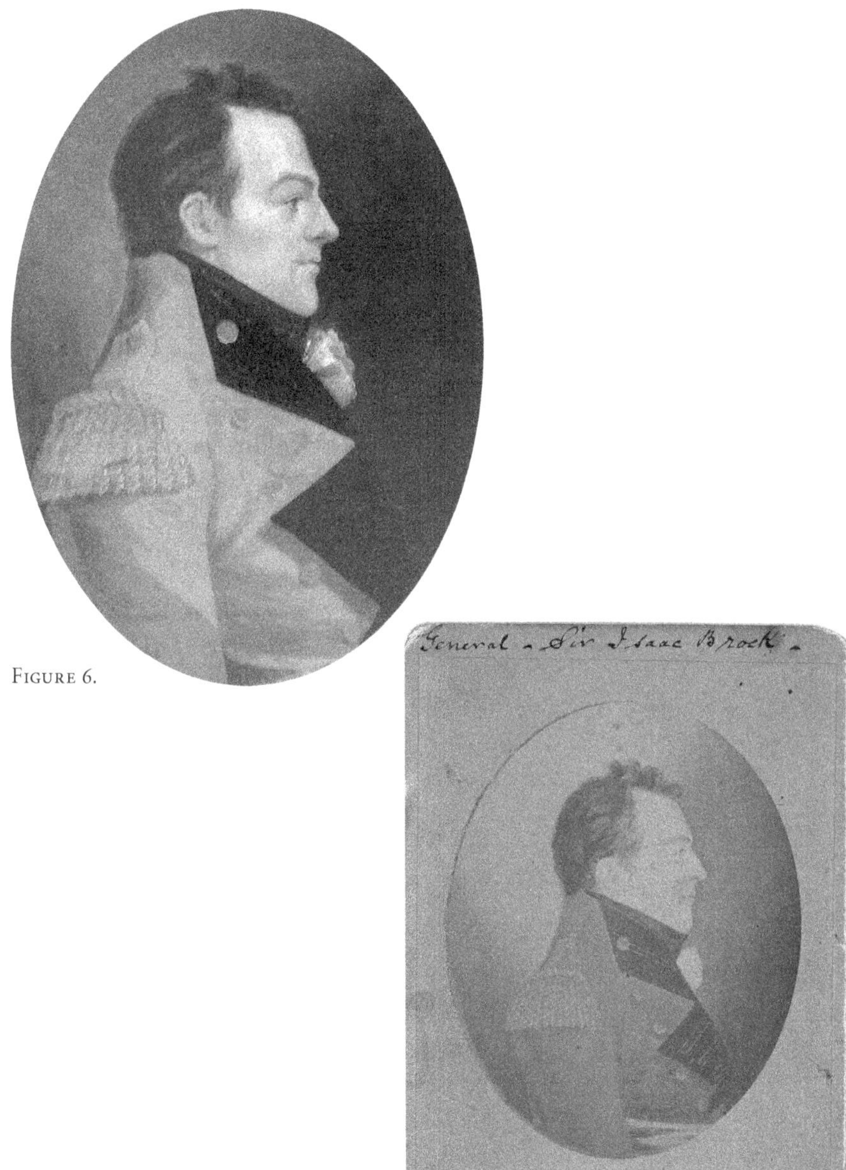

Figure 6.

Figure 7.

to have the painting by Miss Kerr-Nelson sent to Canada in the care of Miss Augusta Robinson, one of the lieutenant governor's daughters. Miss Robinson happened to be in England, and so the timing must have seemed nothing short of providential.[16] But Colonel Robinson's well-laid plans were soon upset. His brother was becoming uneasy about the commission and his skepticism focused squarely on the original profile portrait, which the colonel had just gone to great lengths to have reproduced.

Lieutenant Governor Robinson, still mindful of his brother's earlier and unsuccessful attempt to find Brock's portrait, became more than a little concerned after reading a short passage in *The Life and Correspondence of Major-General Sir Isaac Brock, K.B.*[17] The author of this work was Brock's nephew, and Ferdinand Brock Tupper related a very disconcerting story in one of the footnotes. Apparently, when the officers of the 49th Regiment requested a portrait of Brock in order to have it copied for their mess room, they were disappointed to learn that the family "possessed no good likeness of the general."[18] The lieutenant governor was understandably dismayed, as Tupper seemed to imply that there was no portrait of Brock—but now there were two! Troubled by this discrepancy, the lieutenant governor wrote to his brother early in January of 1882, explaining the situation.[19] Colonel Robinson promptly mailed off a letter to Mrs. Tupper, and he soon had a message back. Mrs. Hubert Le Cocq, who was the former Miss Victoria Tupper, replied for her ailing mother by assuring the colonel that there had simply been a misunderstanding.

As Mrs. Le Cocq pointed out, the officers of the 49th Regiment were disappointed not because the family possessed no likeness of Brock but rather because they "possessed no *good* likeness."[20] In other words, the profile portrait was not considered good enough for the officers' mess. Colonel Robinson accepted what Mrs. Le Cocq told him, surmising that it was animosity that accounted for the confusion surrounding the profile portrait's existence. "Guernsey," he remarked, "is a small place and very likely one branch of Tuppers and Brocks doesn't get on with another branch and so on. I know that there are differences among them. I can only suppose my explanation to be true, for I do not pretend to have any certainty about it."[21] It never occurred to Colonel Robinson that someone might have been trying to suppress the profile portrait, and that Ferdinand Brock Tupper himself was the most obvious culprit.

In addition to writing Brock's first biography, Tupper also took on the added responsibility of safeguarding his uncle's image, which he did by keeping the two profile portraits under wraps. Conspiratorial though it might seem, Tupper had both the motive and the means. He was undoubtedly Sir Isaac Brock's greatest admirer, and had a tendency to present his hero in the best possible light.[22] As for Brock's profile portraits, Tupper seems to have disapproved of both, possibly because they showed only one half of the noble countenance.[23] Whatever Tupper's rationale, he was evidently determined to conceal them by denying their very existence. Despite the fact that neither portrait was in his possession, he was still capable of keeping them a closely guarded secret. His status as Brock's biographer was the key to his success. With the publication of his *Family Records* in 1835, and *The Life and Correspondence of Major-General Sir Isaac Brock, K.B.* in 1845, which was soon followed by an enlarged edition in 1847, Tupper became the contact person for anyone wanting to track down a portrait of his uncle.[24] As such, he was able to intercept and deflect any request that threatened to reveal the truth. The number of times Tupper was approached is unknown, but there is a sample of what likely became his typical response. In 1861, a Canadian historian by the name of Henry J. Morgan wrote to Tupper expressing an interest in Brock's portrait.[25] Tupper replied by saying: "I cannot tell you where you can obtain a portrait of the late Sir Isaac Brock, nor am I aware of any such being in existence."[26] Yet, the original profile portrait was owned by his younger brother Henry Tupper, just as it had been for more than twenty years.[27]

This peculiar behaviour on the part of Ferdinand Brock Tupper became routine, and whenever someone enquired after a portrait of Sir Isaac Brock, that person invariably met with the same fate as Morgan—such as when Colonel Robinson asked on behalf of the Royal Hospital at Chelsea.[28] And Dr. Hodgins might have been the next victim, except that he had the good fortune to initiate his search after Tupper's death in December of 1873.[29]

At the same time that Colonel Robinson wrote to query Mrs. Henry Tupper about the disappointed officers of the 49th Regiment, he also asked how the profile portrait had come to be in her husband's possession.[30] Unfortunately, when Mrs. Le Cocq replied for her mother she could offer little in the way of provenance. She was able to report that an aged relative, a niece to Sir Isaac Brock, always remembered "seeing the two portraits in the houses of her uncles" (by which she meant to say that each uncle owned one).[31] But perhaps sensing that Colonel Robinson would require something more definitive, Mrs. Le Cocq called on the assistance of her cousin.[32] Miss Henrietta Tupper was knowledgeable in such matters of family history, as she was Ferdinand Brock Tupper's daughter. But unlike her hero-worshipping father, Miss Tupper had no agenda and nothing to hide. She was happy to elaborate on the meagre provenance supplied by Mrs. Le Cocq. The profile portrait belonging to Mrs. Henry Tupper (fig. 3) was a bequest to that lady's husband from his uncle, Irving Brock. The other one, which was thought to be a copy (fig. 4), formed part of the inheritance Mrs. Huyshe received from her father, John Savery Brock.[33]

Thanks to Colonel Robinson and Miss Tupper, the lieutenant governor had a much better understanding of the confusing provenance of the two profile portraits of Sir Isaac Brock. While there was no indication as to the identity of the artist responsible for either of them, it was of little consequence.[34] The lieutenant governor was satisfied that the portrait copied for him by Miss Kerr-Nelson was an authentic likeness, which was all that mattered, but he could not help but dwell on the portrait owned by Mrs. Huyshe. Since she had not specified that it was a close copy of the profile portrait, the lieutenant governor was left wondering if it could yet be the kind of full-faced portrait he sought.

Once again, Colonel Robinson wrote to Mrs. Huyshe. If her portrait happened to be full-faced, then he wished to have it photographed for his brother's consideration.[35] But Mrs. Huyshe was on vacation in Malta when the colonel's letter arrived, and so she referred it to Miss Henrietta Tupper for reply.[36] In her answer to Colonel Robinson, Miss Tupper enclosed a photograph of the portrait owned by Mrs. Huyshe (fig. 4).[37] Disappointingly, it too was a profile portrait and clearly a facsimile of the one owned by Mrs. Tupper. Perhaps as consolation, Miss Tupper mentioned a third likeness of Brock, "also a profile, in bronze" (fig. 8).[38] This mysterious portrait was actually a bronzed silhouette, meaning a silhouette with painted highlights of gold. But as Colonel Robinson assured his brother, "it is pretty clear that we have already got the best likeness possible of Sir Isaac and that no full faced one *undoubtedly* is to be obtained."[39]

By August of 1882, Miss Kerr-Nelson's portrait of Brock (fig. 6) arrived

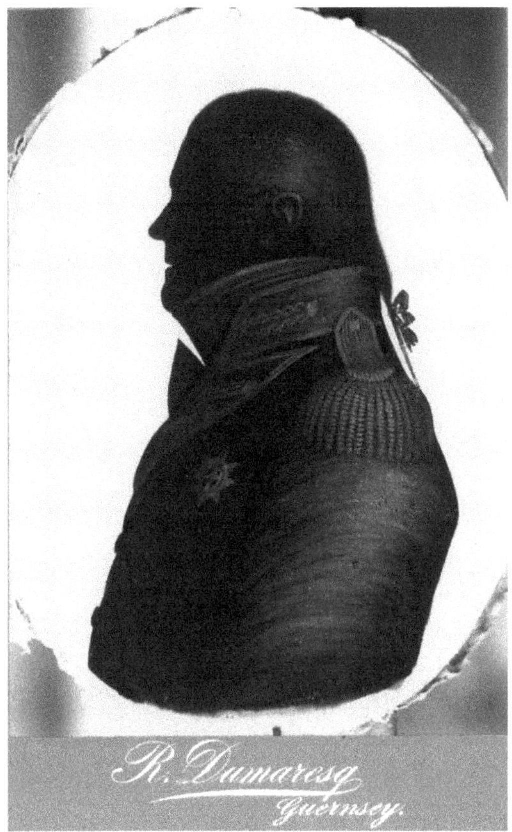

FIGURE 8.

in Toronto.[40] While there is no record of the lieutenant governor's reaction to it, he must have been favourably impressed as it was retained and put in an elaborate gold frame.[41] But, just as Colonel Robinson feared, Miss Kerr-Nelson's artistic abilities were not deemed suitable for Government House. The lieutenant governor preferred the style of George Berthon's portraiture, and that artist was soon commissioned to paint the official portrait of Sir Isaac Brock. Berthon worked diligently on his assignment, which appears to have been completed sometime before the end of that same year.[42] Judging from the finished canvas (fig. 9) he relied almost exclusively on the photograph of the original profile portrait (fig. 3). It would seem that Miss Kerr-Nelson's bold brush strokes, while they may have suited Brock's character, were not compatible with Berthon's more

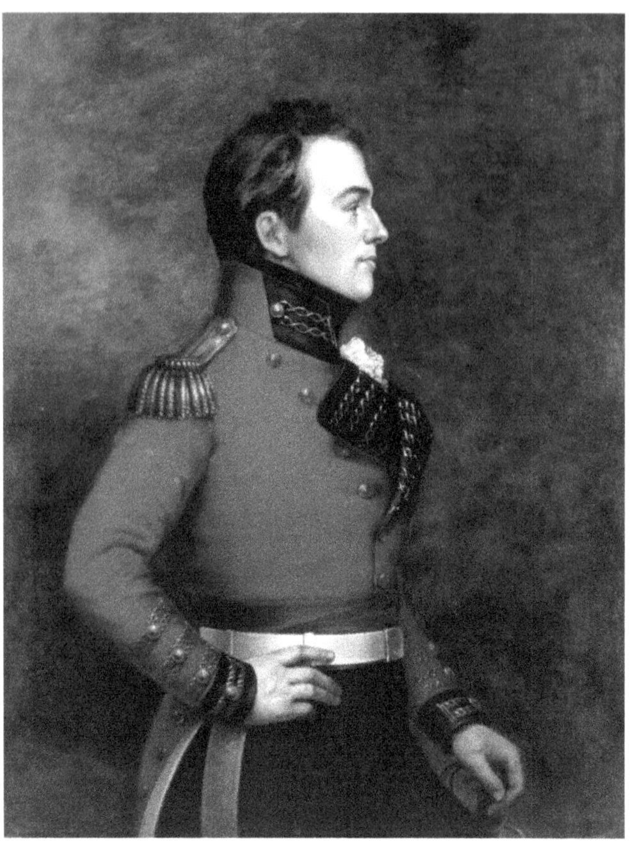

Figure 9.

refined style of painting.

Berthon was careful to make a faithful copy of Brock's profile portrait, but only in terms of the facial features. In painting the rest of the portrait, he allowed himself considerable latitude. The uniform, for example, was upgraded to reflect Brock's ultimate promotion to major general. Moreover he was shown in a dress uniform—the formality of which was more in keeping with the stately decor of Government House.[43] Brock was also represented in three-quarter length, as opposed to the half-length of the original portrait, which allowed Berthon's subject to strike a more dignified pose (albeit still in profile).

One of the official portrait's early admirers was the Canadian historian William Kingsford, who was also one of the few people to recognize the importance of Lieutenant Governor Robinson's Gallery of Governors. As Kingsford observed, Ontario was singularly fortunate in possessing authentic portraits of its lieutenant governors from the earliest date, "not fanciful works of art, christened [as authentic] by auctioneers and dealers."[44] Kingsford then went on to predict the rich benefits to be derived from one of the portraits in particular: "The veneration felt in Canada for the memory of the illustrious Brock, is general in every sense. His name is a household word with our youth, and it will be a matter of common satisfaction to know that the portrait we possess is genuine and undoubted."[45] It would have been more prophetic, however, had Kingsford foretold of a general apathy, as none of the portraits could have much of an impact on the public sequestered deep within Government House. As a result, Lieutenant Governor Robinson's good deed went largely unnoticed.

Apart from Kingsford, no one else took much interest in Berthon's portrait of Brock until 1894, when a Toronto artist suddenly asked about it. To the Honourable John Beverley Robinson (who was no longer the lieutenant governor), it might have seemed that perhaps a fitting recognition of his good deed was finally in the offing.[46] But if so, it soon became obvious that John Wycliffe Lowes Forster was driven more by self-interest than by any appreciation for Robinson's efforts in procuring Brock's portrait.[47] Having been commissioned to render his own version, Forster wanted to make use of the same reference material Berthon had utilized, including the portrait by Miss Kerr-Nelson (fig. 6).[48] Robinson graciously complied with the request, no doubt because Forster's client—like Robinson himself—hailed from one of Ontario's old Conservative dynasties. This client was John A. Macdonell, a lawyer from eastern Ontario, a published historian, and a relative of Lieutenant Colonel John Macdonell—Brock's courageous provincial aide-de-camp.[49]

Such a famous association was certainly justification enough for John A. Macdonell to commission a portrait of Brock, but there might have been another consideration as well. Soon after the portrait (fig. 10) was completed (in December of 1894) a contributor to the *Week*'s "Art Notes"—possibly Forster himself—apprised the paper's readers that it was "to form the frontispiece of Mr. D[avid] B. Read's 'Life and Times of General Brock,' now in press."[50] While this reference seems to suggest that the commission was undertaken to provide Read with an illustration, it is

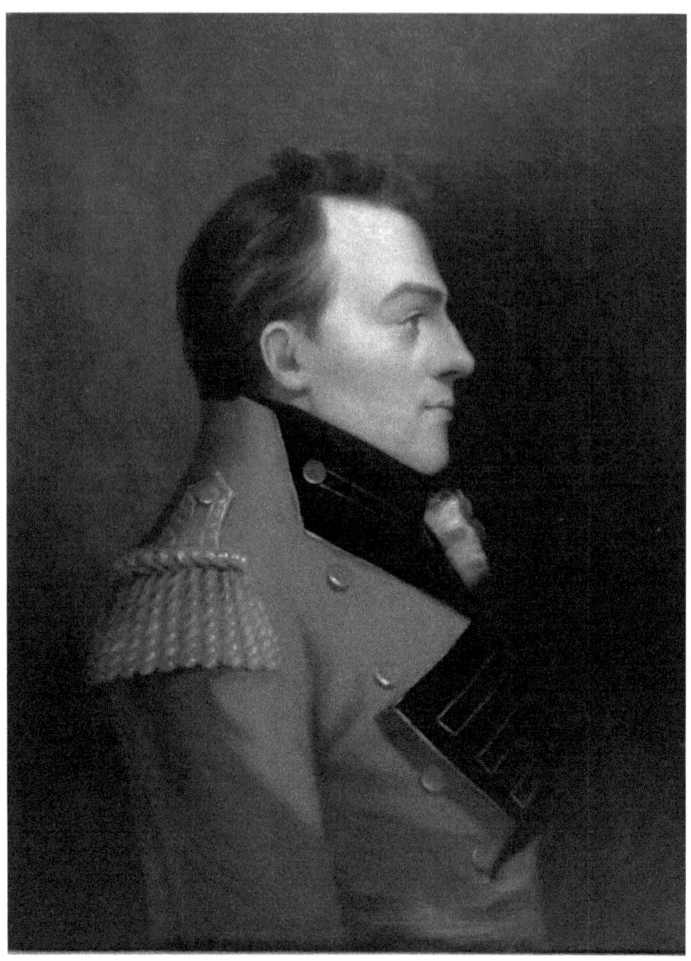

FIGURE 10.

also possible that the arrangement was merely coincidental. Whatever it was that motivated Forster, the end result was nothing short of striking. One observer described the new portrait of Brock as "powerful," in the sense that it conveyed an impression of the "great intellectual and physical features which characterized the man."[51] This assessment must have been extremely gratifying to Forster, who was known to boast about his ability to capture "the character and prevalent moods" of his sitters.[52] Yet, Forster owed much of his success in this instance to Mrs. Carl Hirschberg, the former Miss Alice Kerr-Nelson, as it was her painting he had copied.[53]

Forster's portrait of Brock was a highly successful commission, both for its artistic merit and also for its effectiveness as a marketing tool. Thanks to the obliging nature of John A. Macdonell, the portrait was reproduced in a number of publications and even borrowed for the occasional exhibit.[54] It was all good advertising—and very timely, given the potential for lucrative repeat business in the not-too-distant future. The centenary of Brock's death was less than a decade away, and thanks to the Macdonell commission Forster was poised to capitalize on the dead general's heroic image. But before he was able to corner the market, a couple of historically minded ladies threatened his bottom line with a new and improved portrait of Sir Isaac Brock.

2

By Way of a Discovery

Miss Agnes FitzGibbon and Miss Sara Mickle were both founding members of the Women's Canadian Historical Society of Toronto.[1] While Miss FitzGibbon considered herself an author first and foremost, she never achieved the same degree of recognition as her maternal grandmother, Mrs. Susanna (Strickland) Moodie, of *Roughing it in the Bush* fame. Nevertheless, Miss FitzGibbon did her part to carry on the Strickland family's literary tradition. By the early 1890s her inspiration had become historical in nature, and in 1894 she published the story of her grandfather, Colonel James FitzGibbon, a veteran of the War of 1812 who went on to become a staunch defender of the Upper Canadian establishment.[2] As for Miss Mickle, she too inherited a literary disposition. Her great-grandfather, the Scottish poet William Julius Mickle, was celebrated for his translation of *The Lusiads*, an epic poem of Portuguese discovery in the New World. Like Miss FitzGibbon, Miss Mickle also developed a strong interest in Canadian history, which would come to find expression in her tireless dedication to heritage preservation.[3] In 1895, however, Miss Mickle was content to fulfil her responsibilities as an executive member of the historical society she helped to establish.

Miss Mickle and Miss FitzGibbon worked well together, and by the spring of 1896 they were collaborating on a project. With Miss FitzGibbon acting as her assistant, Miss Mickle began compiling a calendar to commemorate the 400th anniversary of John Cabot's discovery of North America in 1497.[4] The title, however, was somewhat misleading. *The Cabot Calendar* was never meant to be devoted exclusively to the exploits of the great explorer. Nor was it intended to be a calendar in the conventional sense. What Miss Mickle envisioned, rather, was a chronology of significant events in Canada's history, organized by month and brimming with line drawings illustrating the glorious past. She also planned to have several full-page monochrome portraits of the country's most outstanding historical figures, including such famous names as Cabot, Champlain, Frontenac, Wolfe, and Brock.[5]

Miss Mickle had little difficulty obtaining suitable copies of the first four portraits, but that of Sir Isaac Brock presented something of a challenge. She was well aware of the profile portrait in John Charles Dent's *Canadian Portrait Gallery* (fig. 1), and also the one by John Wycliffe Lowes Forster in David B. Read's *Life and Times of Major-General Sir Isaac Brock, K.B.* (fig. 10).[6] But neither of these portraits met with her approval, simply because they could not be reproduced to appear consistent with those she had already assembled for her calendar.[7] George Berthon's official portrait of Brock (fig. 9) was also rejected, as it was thought to have lost much of the "intellectuality and personality of the man."[8] More likely, Miss Mickle was simply unable to find a portrait to her liking, and so she continued to search for something better. Eventually, she remembered having heard that someone in Toronto possessed china and possibly other items that had once belonged to Brock. Thinking that this mix might include a more desirable portrait of Brock, Miss Mickle pursued the lead through her informant—who happened to be James Bain, Toronto's chief librarian.[9]

Bain directed Miss Mickle to George C. Taylor, a local broom and brush manufacturer.[10] It was Taylor's mother who had the heirlooms, and Taylor believed that a portrait of Brock might be among them, as there was a distant family connection to the famous general.[11] Obligingly, he wrote to his mother, Mrs. Heber (Lucy Short) Taylor of Franklin, New Hampshire, explaining Miss Mickle's interest and asking for further particulars. Word soon came back that there was indeed a portrait of Brock. It was a miniature on ivory, and a most excellent likeness, which Mrs. Taylor was willing to lend for reproduction in Miss Mickle's calendar.[12] This was an exciting development, but the death of one of Mrs. Taylor's other sons caused an unavoidable delay in arranging the loan.[13]

Since there was no delicate way to prompt action on Mrs. Taylor's part, Miss Mickle occupied her time by inquiring into the miniature's authenticity. This she did by investigating all the earlier owners, and also the relationship between Mrs. Taylor's ancestors and Sir Isaac Brock. After

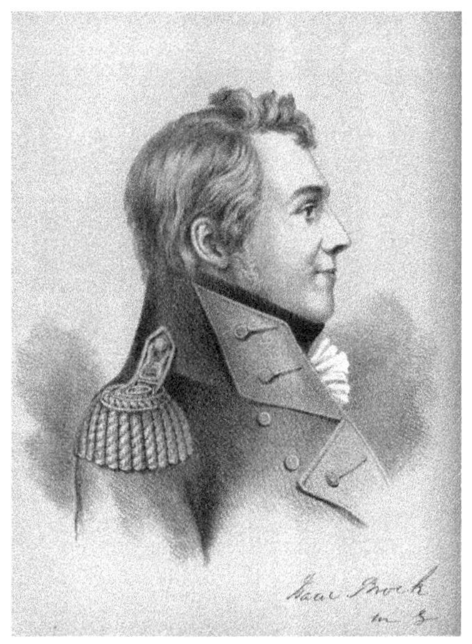

Figure 1.

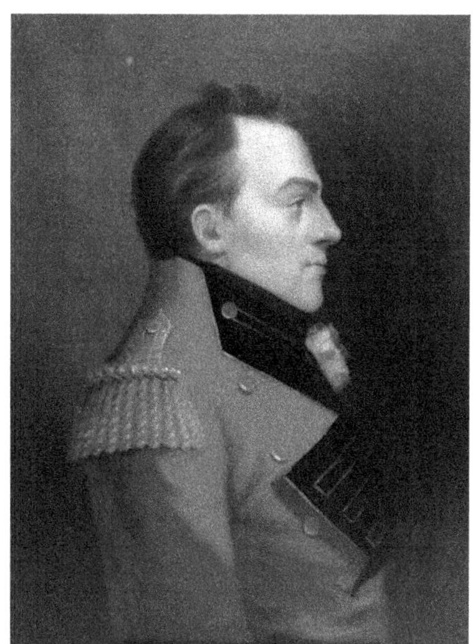

Figure 10.

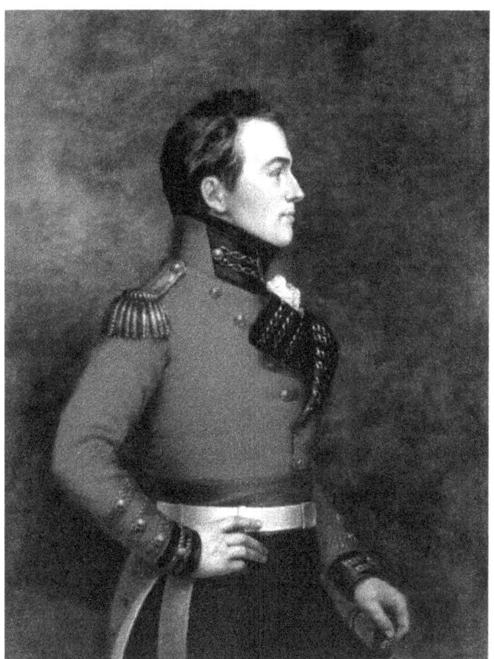

Figure 9.

consulting a book, possibly David B. Read's biography of Brock, and communicating further with George C. Taylor, Miss Mickle followed up by seeking the advice of Mrs. Robert (Sarah Anne Vincent) Curzon, a friend from Toronto who had written about the Battle of Queenston Heights. Mrs. Curzon advised a letter to James Le Moine of Quebec City, as he was a tireless scholar of French Canadian history and someone who might have information on Brock's Canadian relatives—given that they hailed from la belle province.[14] While Le Moine seems to have been limited in the assistance he was able to provide, Miss Mickle tended to believe the family tradition that described how the miniature passed from Brock's cousin down through his Canadian and American descendants. As Miss Mickle understood it, Mrs. Taylor inherited the miniature from her great-aunt, Mrs. George (Matilda Short) Dunn of Three Rivers, or Trois-Rivières, Quebec. The miniature had been left to Mrs. Dunn by her sister, who was the widow of Captain James Brock, and who had in turn obtained it from the estate of his cousin, Major General Isaac Brock. Reinforcing this provenance was Mrs. Taylor's recollection that Mrs. Dunn had identified the sitter as Sir Isaac Brock.[15] Miss Mickle was favourably inclined, but no matter how much she wanted to believe that the miniature was actually Brock, it remained to be seen whether or not this much-anticipated likeness would be appropriate for *The Cabot Calendar*.

In June of 1896, after more than a month, Miss Mickle finally received the miniature (fig. 11).[16] It was well worth the wait, as this new portrait of Brock was positively enchanting. The officer it portrayed was young, handsome, and noble looking. Miss Mickle was overjoyed, and so too was her associate. Miss FitzGibbon had nothing but praise for the miniature. "It is an unmistakable likeness," she asserted, "a face showing power and strong determination, loveableness and straightforward manliness of character; a face which explains why his soldiers obeyed him, loved him so dearly and followed him so devotedly, and why he has won so high a place in the hearts of the people of Upper Canada, a veritable Sir Isaac Brock."[17]

The miniature was perfect, possessing as it did all the characteristics one would expect of a heroic figure like Brock. It was also perfect for *The Cabot Calendar*, and Miss Mickle wasted no time in having it photographed (fig. 12) in order to begin the process of lithographic reproduction.[18] She was rather disgusted, however, when the artist making the halftone thought he

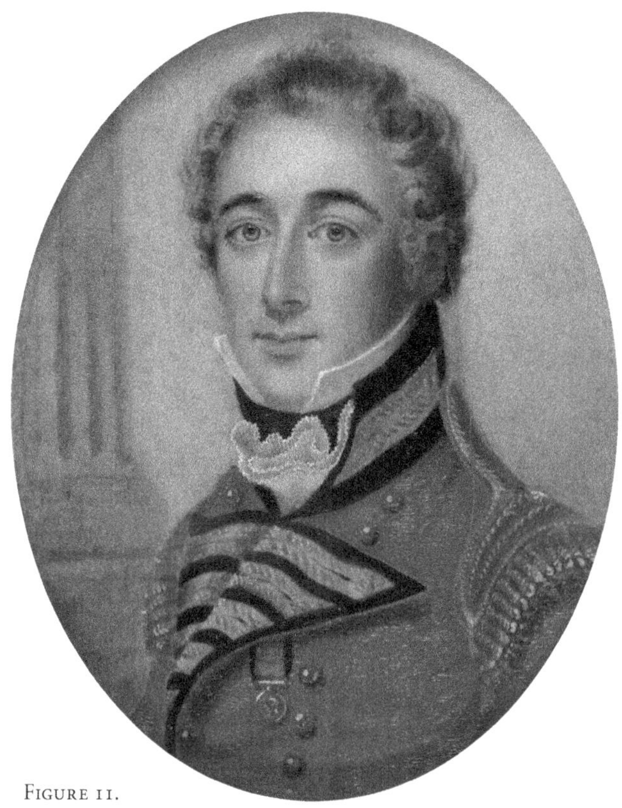

Figure 11.

recognized the likeness.[19] The Misses Mickle and FitzGibbon were hoping to keep the discovery "quiet," in order to boost sales by having the announcement of a newly discovered miniature of Brock coincide with the release of *The Cabot Calendar*. But word of the miniature was spreading fast. It was already the main topic of conversation at the Toronto Public Library, where George C. Taylor had shown it to librarian Bain. But as much as Miss Mickle and Miss FitzGibbon were annoyed by all this unwelcome attention, they themselves were partly to blame—having allowed Mrs. Curzon the same indulgence of a personal viewing.[20]

As work progressed on the calendar, the miniature was restored by Gerald S. Hayward, a prominent American miniature painter who was then visiting Toronto.[21] Hayward's home was on New York's Long Island, but he was born in Canada and still made the occasional trip back to his native land.[22] Earlier, after examining the miniature, he agreed to

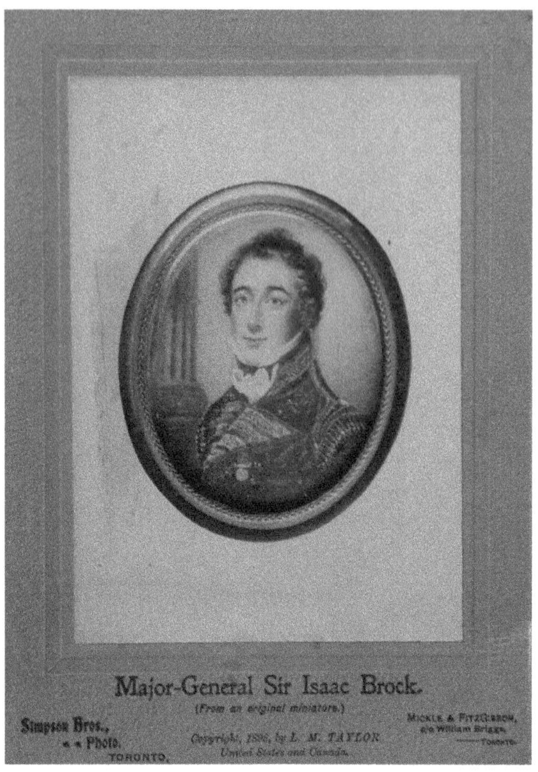

Figure 12.

undertake the restoration, which was done at George C. Taylor's expense. However, it was Miss Mickle who did all the negotiating, and it was during this interaction that Hayward offered to paint her a copy.[23] Miss Mickle readily agreed to the proposal, although it was only a short time later that she managed to purchase the original.[24] While the date of this transaction is not known, it likely came about after Hayward completed his copy, as such a duplicate would have been pointless once Miss Mickle became the proud owner of the original miniature. And whether or not she regretted her haste in commissioning Hayward, Miss Mickle did get value for the money she handed over to him.

In addition to Hayward's artistic services, Miss Mickle made good use of his expertise in assessing the miniature, which was the work of an elusive artist known only as J. Hudson. Specifically, she wondered if he could explain the peculiar manner in which the miniature had been dated. It looked to be "18X6," and according to Hayward the "X" was meant to represent zero, "as we often do now on cheques."[25] This interpretation seemed logical enough, since Brock was known to have been in England during 1806. The miniature could also have been painted in London, as it was likely there that such an exquisite portrait would have been commissioned. Moreover, Brock was then in his mid-thirties, and the sitter appeared to be roughly the same age. Hayward also thought the medal, which was prominently displayed on the sitter's chest, must have been awarded to Brock for his service at the Battle of "Egmont-op-Zee" in 1799.[26] It all seemed quite plausible to Miss Mickle, and she was not about to second-guess Gerald S. Hayward when he was arguing her case.

Although the copy of the miniature (fig. 13) and the restored original were both delivered by mid-August of 1896, Miss Mickle was becoming impatient.[27] She was anxious to announce her great discovery and launch the pre-Christmas sales of *The Cabot Calendar*, but there was someone else she wanted to consult. It was Allan Cassels, a Toronto lawyer whose opinion mattered a great deal to Mickle.[28] However, in showing him the miniature (fig. 11), she was dismayed to find his reaction more critical than congratulatory. Upon scrutinizing the uniform, Cassels noticed that it looked as though it was rapidly filled in, which indicated the work of a less talented artist. Oddly, nothing was known about the quality of Hudson's portraiture, and so the criticism was probably meant to cast doubt on the miniature and thus diminish its importance. As Miss Mickle recalled, Cassels "thought the miniature had been probably painted after death from another picture, [and] that it would be found to be a copy."[29] Miss Mickle was not at all pleased with this critique, but she knew how to neutralize it.

In returning to Hayward, Miss Mickle repeated the concerns expressed by Cassels. Yet, Hayward remained firm in his convictions. While he admitted that the uniform might have been painted rapidly, he saw no reason to believe that it had been done by a "different hand." Nor was the miniature a copy, as it was obviously done from life. And just because Miss Mickle and Miss FitzGibbon could find no record of J. Hudson, it did not automatically make him a less talented artist as Cassels suggested. There were many good artists who never managed to make a name for themselves. But in order to be absolutely sure, Hayward compared the

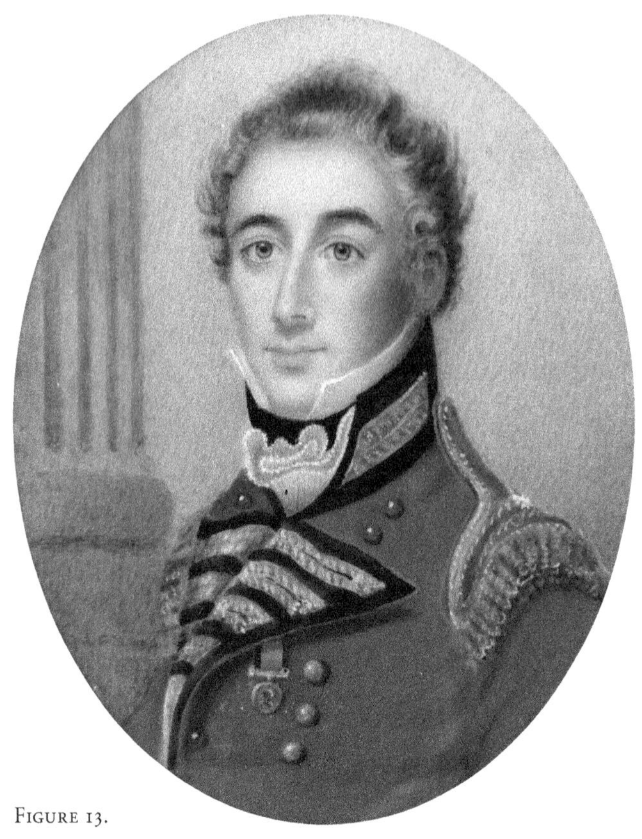

Figure 13.

miniature with every other portrait of Brock he could find, and in each case he judged the face to be the same. The only difference was the superior workmanship of the miniature discovered by Miss Mickle.[30]

When Miss Mickle presented Cassels with a copy of Hayward's opinion, the lawyer promptly conceded. "I am very glad to hear from you about the Brock miniature," Cassels wrote early in September of 1896. "Whatever Hayward says about its being taken from life is sure to be correct and you bring it at once within historic interest. All these memorials will some day or other be of great value, and I hope you will be duly acknowledged as its discoverer and preserver for it was certainly in great need of restoration."[31] Although Cassels was not completely won over, he was by no means prepared to engage in a heated debate over a questionable miniature of Sir Isaac Brock. Miss Mickle was very pleased with this outcome, and also with herself.[32] She held her ground, not her tongue, and in the process proved herself capable of standing up to a man—and not just any man, but a prominent lawyer. It was an empowering experience for a Canadian woman in the late nineteenth century, but despite Miss Mickle's newfound confidence, she was hardly a publicity seeker.

In the end, it was agreed that Miss FitzGibbon should be the one to break the news about the miniature. Accordingly, she chronicled Miss Mickle's discovery in a long letter to the editor of the Toronto *Globe*.[33] Then, after a bit of free advertising for *The Cabot Calendar*, Miss FitzGibbon turned her attention to Berthon's portrait of Brock (fig. 9), which she criticized in an unnecessarily severe manner. "Whether taken from a good original or not," she declared, "the copy [by Berthon] is not a masterpiece, and the copies from it as well as photographs taken at various times, the negatives of which have been touched up to suit the ideas of the photographer, are even less so."[34] In further denouncing Berthon's portrait as a "lifeless presentment," Miss FitzGibbon was no doubt trying to enhance the importance of the miniature discovered by Miss Mickle. At the same time, however, she must have also known that any attack upon the official portrait of Brock was bound to cause a stir.

Sure enough, Miss FitzGibbon's letter drew the ire of someone writing from Toronto, and under the cover of a nom de plume. "Historian" took offence with the harsh remarks about Berthon's portrait of Brock, and assumed that Miss FitzGibbon was critical of the portrait simply because it was painted in profile. Yet, "Historian" came to this erroneous conclusion even though Miss FitzGibbon merely made reference to the lithographic artist's opinion, namely that Berthon's portrait of Brock could not be reproduced in a manner consistent with those of Cabot, Champlain, Frontenac, and Wolfe.[35] Evidently, "Historian" had yet to see a copy of *The Cabot Calendar*, with its profile portraits of both Frontenac and Wolfe. In fact, Miss FitzGibbon's complaint had nothing to do with the pose Berthon used for his portrait of Brock. Rather, it was the portrait's quality, which Miss FitzGibbon found lacking. Yet, judging from Berthon's very fine rendering, she probably only saw photographs of the portrait and not the portrait itself.

There was a great deal of confusion on both sides, and misconceptions were lobbed back and forth across the columns of the *Globe*. For

"Historian," who still had the floor (so to speak), it was unfair to judge the quality of a portrait based on the pose of its sitter. As for the allegation of retouched negatives, "Historian" defended the photographs taken of the portrait of Brock by Forster—which was commissioned by John A. Macdonell in 1894 (fig. 10). While these were not in fact the photographs Miss FitzGibbon had in mind, "Historian" used them to argue that the "intellectuality and personality" of the portrait, supposedly lost in the dark room, was actually "most noticeable," even if it was a profile portrait. Finally, in response to Miss FitzGibbon's criticism that Berthon's portrait was a "lifeless presentment," "Historian" simply excused it as "a pardonable [or understandable] enthusiasm under the circumstances."[36] And far from resenting Miss Mickle's discovery, "Historian" welcomed the miniature of Sir Isaac Brock . . . in so much as it complemented the official portrait by Berthon.

"Historian" was very likely one of the Robinsons; however, not the former lieutenant governor, as the Honourable John Beverley Robinson was dead.[37] Neither was it Colonel (now Major General) Charles W. Robinson, since he was still living in England whereas "Historian" wrote from Toronto.[38] That city, however, was also home to another Robinson brother. As a gifted lawyer with a highly developed sense of diplomacy, Christopher Robinson could very well have been responsible for a carefully worded protest.[39] He was also a very retiring sort of gentleman, and just the type of person who might have made use of a pseudonym.[40] And he most assuredly would have objected to Miss FitzGibbon's trouncing of Brock's official portrait, if for no other reason than it was commissioned by his late brother.

In her reply, Miss FitzGibbon began by chastising people such as "Historian" for not having the courage to identify themselves when expressing their opinions. And yet she herself also became fairly guarded, refraining from further comment on Berthon's portrait of Brock. Instead, she changed the subject by giving Miss Mickle credit for noticing subtle differences among the several profile portraits of Brock. Similar findings were reported by Miss Janet Carnochan, a teacher and historian from what is now Niagara-on-the-Lake, Ontario, which led Miss FitzGibbon to speculate that there were other portraits of Brock waiting to be found.[41] What she failed to consider, however, was the possibility that most of Brock's portraits were merely variations on the original profile portrait (fig. 3).[42]

Regarding the retouched negatives, Miss FitzGibbon appears to have thought the photographs discussed by "Historian" were duplicates of the one Berthon used for his portrait of Brock or, in other words, the photographs of the original profile portrait owned by Mrs. Tupper in Guernsey. As already noted, however, it was actually the portrait of Brock painted by Forster that "Historian" visualized when he penned his own letter to the editor. Miss FitzGibbon, however, was none the wiser and readily confessed that the "half dozen photographs taken for private gifts from the original miniature in the possession of Mrs. Tupper" were not available to Miss Mickle and herself when they began work on *The Cabot Calendar*.[43] Despite this minor concession, she had no intention of retracting her allegation of retouched negatives—not when she recalled how the doctored pictures were sold as souvenirs at the Lundy's Lane Observatory (a scenic look-out tower near Niagara Falls). Whether or not these cheap productions were really "touched up" photographs of the original profile portrait of Brock, Miss FitzGibbon remained defiant. But there was no rebuttal from "Historian," who seems to have given up the fight. Perhaps it had something to do with a low tolerance for frustration. Whatever the case, Miss FitzGibbon must have derived great satisfaction from having silenced her newsprint opponent.

Notwithstanding "Historian's" interference, *The Cabot Calendar* was well received.[44] So too was the new portrait of Sir Isaac Brock it contained (fig. 14). No one else took exception with Miss Mickle's discovery, at least not publicly. It might have been out of fear, as even the most innocent query could unleash the fury of Miss FitzGibbon's very public wrath. Such an apprehension may have influenced a perplexed lawyer from Montreal, whose suspicions were aroused by this new portrait of Brock.[45] David Ross McCord was an avid collector of Canadiana. He was also an occasional correspondent of Miss Henrietta Tupper in Guernsey, as she possessed a number of Brock-related artifacts that he had a mind to acquire for his collection. Years earlier, she kindly supplied him with the profile portrait of Brock, or rather a photograph of the copy owned by Mrs. Huyshe (fig. 4), which seemed authentic until *The Cabot Calendar* was published in 1896.[46] When McCord saw the new likeness of Brock, he dispatched one of the calendars to Miss Tupper in hopes that she might be able to enlighten him.

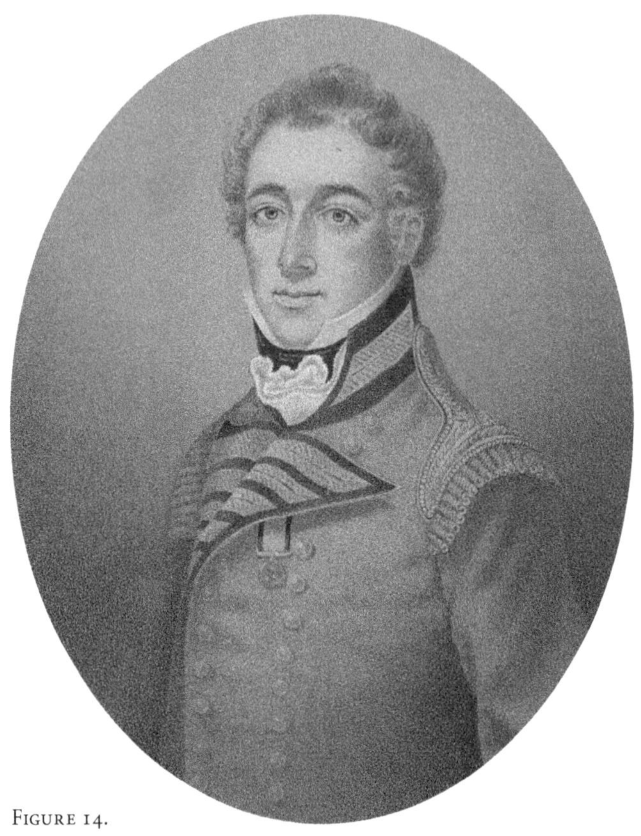

FIGURE 14.

She could only agree that "the supposed portrait of Sir Isaac differs very considerably from that which was painted from the miniature [meaning the profile portrait]."[47] But if Miss Tupper had misgivings about the authenticity of this new portrait, she kept them largely to herself. McCord did likewise. The Robinsons, however, were not nearly so discreet.

In April of 1897, disturbing rumours began to circulate about Miss Mickle's discovery. This scuttlebutt began in England, where Major General Charles W. Robinson had good reason to doubt that the miniature actually featured Sir Isaac Brock. Much of the general's uncertainty had to do with the uniform. Brock was known to have been a full colonel at the time the miniature was ostensibly painted in 1806; yet the uniform suggested that of a lower ranking officer.[48] The medal, which the miniature painter Gerald S. Hayward linked to Brock's service at the Battle of

Egmont-op-Zee in 1799, was also suspect. General Robinson believed it to be the Military General Service Medal of 1847, which to the best of his knowledge was not awarded posthumously.[49] Therefore, it could not have been an honour bestowed upon Brock, as he was killed in 1812—some thirty-five years earlier. In trying to come up with a rational explanation for this discrepancy, the general decided that someone must have altered the miniature at a later date.[50] While such an alteration did not rule out Brock as the sitter, General Robinson remained skeptical. It was very difficult for him to believe that Miss Mickle could succeed in finding such an important portrait, especially when Brock's regiment had failed in the same endeavour.[51] The fact that the miniature had been copyrighted was also very telling, and General Robinson thought he knew the truth behind Miss Mickle's discovery. The whole affair was nothing more than "an attempt to foist a false portrait on the public and make money out of it."[52]

Disregarding all the mean-spirited gossip, Miss Mickle remained calm and even philosophical. As for the general, he was just upset that another portrait of Brock had come to light. Yet, he also seemed "very anxious not 'to be dragged into any controversy' over it."[53] Miss Mickle was right. General Robinson had no desire to spar with a woman in one of Canada's leading dailies. Such behaviour on the part of a gentleman would have been unseemly, and probably explains why the general decided on a more devious course of action. It was a letter-writing campaign involving his brother, Christopher Robinson, and his sister, Mrs. James (Augusta Robinson) Strachan. This low-key approach suited the general, who knew he could count on his siblings to cast doubt on the miniature's authenticity. Before long, Miss Mickle was made aware of General Robinson's poison pen letters, which goaded her so much that she boldly asked Mrs. Strachan for copies of them. Not surprisingly, the general's sister declined the request.[54]

Miss Mickle appears to have been genuinely astonished by the refusal, as it was no secret that Mrs. Strachan had shown the letters to others of their mutual acquaintance. Both Miss Mickle and Miss FitzGibbon suffered hurt feelings as a result, but Miss FitzGibbon was particularly wounded, as she and Mrs. Strachan had been life-long friends.[55] The slight also confirmed Miss Mickle's fear that General Robinson was trying to build a case against the miniature. While it was unclear whether or not he would go public with his rumours of fraud, the Misses Mickle and FitzGibbon thought it best to prepare for that eventuality. They resolved to counteract any effort by the general to denounce the new likeness of Brock, and they had good reason to be apprehensive: it appeared that John Wycliffe Lowes Forster was on the general's side.

Having ingratiated himself with the late lieutenant governor for the sake of obtaining props and other materials by which to paint his own portrait of Brock (fig. 10), Forster was firmly embedded in the Robinson camp.[56] But even if Miss FitzGibbon and Miss Mickle were unaware of this arrangement, there were other indicators of Forster's allegiance to the Robinsons. The first ominous sign came soon after Miss Mickle's discovery was first announced in September of 1896, when the Toronto *Globe* suddenly carried an article highlighting Forster's artwork. Included was a large picture of the Brock portrait commissioned by John A. Macdonell, along with a careful accounting of its authenticity.[57] Forster's partiality to the Robinsons was evident throughout the write-up, and things only got worse several months later when a troubling report came to hand: Forster was preparing for a trip abroad to continue his studies in Paris, and he was also planning to visit Guernsey, where he expected to "fulfil a commission."[58] With this news, Miss Mickle and Miss FitzGibbon became convinced that Forster was in the employ of General Robinson, and that his unspecified commission would somehow serve the Robinson interests to the detriment of their own.

Miss Mickle reacted by making it her mission to find an ironclad confirmation, and by whatever means necessary, that her newly discovered miniature (fig. 11) was actually a portrait of Sir Isaac Brock. This she did by means of several letters to various people asking pointed questions about the miniature's provenance. But in striving to find supporting evidence for her discovery, Miss Mickle happened upon a sizeable complication. Mrs. Dunn, who bequeathed the miniature to her great-niece (Mrs. Heber Taylor), apparently also had another portrait of an officer (fig. 15) said to be a "picture of a general in uniform."[59] This other portrait—apparently a medium sized oil painting—belonged to Mrs. Taylor's sister, Mrs. Alfred (Matilda Short) de Beaumont of Montreal, and Mrs. de Beaumont was quite insistent that it portrayed Sir Isaac Brock. She was also convinced that the miniature owned by her sister was a portrait of their great-aunt's

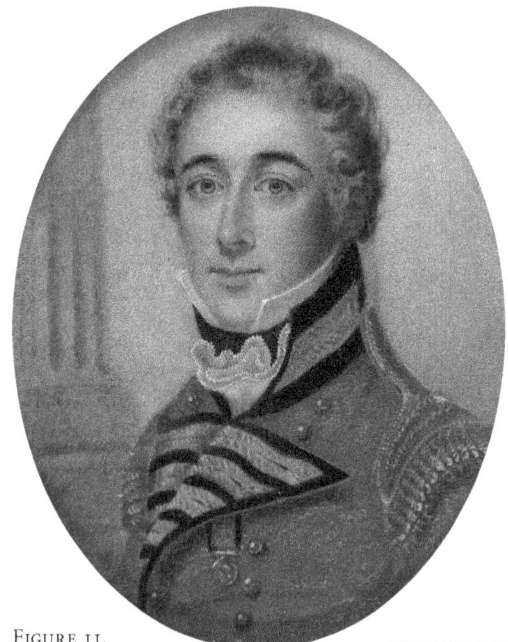

Figure 11.

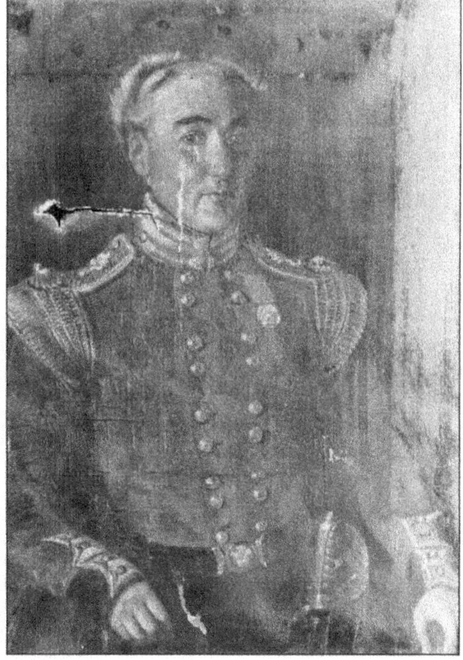

Figure 15.

late husband, Captain George Dunn. This unwelcome news was quite a shock to Miss Mickle, as it disputed the identification of the miniature she had purchased from Mrs. Taylor. The resulting dilemma was potentially far more damaging than all of the gossiping Robinsons combined. And since *The Cabot Calendar* featured one of the two portraits under discussion, Miss Mickle could only hope that it was hers that proved to be authentic.

Exactly how Miss Mickle became aware of Mrs. de Beaumont's so-called portrait of Sir Isaac Brock is not known. It may have been mentioned in one of the letters she received while attempting to confirm the authenticity of the miniature. However, by the end of April 1897, Miss Mickle raised the matter of Mrs. de Beaumont's portrait of Brock with the Reverend Henry C. Stuart of Trois-Rivières. She had already communicated with him some months earlier regarding the relatives of Captain James Brock, presumably while conducting due diligence on the miniature.[60] In taking up her cause once again, Rev. Stuart wrote to one of Captain Brock's nephews, an old gentleman in Montreal by the name of George S. Carter.[61] Anticipating that Mrs. de Beaumont might know something about the portrait, Carter took the liberty of paying that lady a visit. Mrs. de Beaumont repeated her story and provided other information as well, all of which Carter passed on to Rev. Stuart. In addition, Carter described the portrait, pronouncing it to be a "beautiful miniature [or rather a small painting] of the General in full regimentals, and as bright and fresh looking as when it was turned out of the hands of the artist who painted it."[62]

Having enquired after the portrait, which he was led to believe was that of Sir Isaac Brock, Carter thought there might be some interest on Miss Mickle's part in purchasing it. "Mrs. De Beaumont has promised to hold the picture subject to my wish and pleasure, but plainly hinted that she would not part with it without a *quid pro quo*."[63] Rev. Stuart, however, questioned Carter's investigative skills, thinking instead that the portrait might be of Captain James Brock or perhaps even Lieutenant Colonel William C. Short (who was killed at the Battle of Fort Stephenson in 1813).[64] But Miss Mickle completely disregarded Rev. Stuart's speculations. She was far too fixated on the authenticity of her miniature, now that the collateral descendants of Captain James Brock appeared to be in the business of selling portraits of Sir Isaac Brock.

After skirting the issue as much as possible, Miss Mickle had no choice but to seek clarification from the lady who sold her the miniature in the first place. But Mrs. Taylor did not appreciate the tone of Miss Mickle's letter, which insinuated that the identity of the sitter may have been misrepresented for financial gain. "I assure you, Miss Mickle, my [great] Aunt [Mrs. Dunn] had no interest in making a *false statement* relative to the Portrait of Sir Isaac Brock, and I may also say neither had I."[65] Mrs. Taylor was adamant that the miniature she sent to Toronto was authentic, and while she was on the topic of miniatures, she closed her letter by observing: "I think it very likely Sir Isaac had more than *one*."[66] Miss Mickle, however, was not interested in any and all miniatures of Brock—just the one she had come to cherish.

In mid-May of 1897, Miss Mickle carried on with her interrogations by addressing a letter to Frederick M. Short. Like George S. Carter, Short was an aged nephew of Captain James Brock. He was also Mrs. Taylor's uncle, and it just so happened that he lived with her in Franklin, New Hampshire.[67] In complying with Miss Mickle's request for information about the miniature, Short recounted a painful incident from his childhood. "When I first came to Canada, Mrs. James Brock (my Aunt) was shewing me the Pictures in her Parlor and told me that [miniature] was the Portrait of Sir Isaac Brock and that he was a famous Soldier and cast up to me that if I had accepted the Commission in the British Army, which she had got the promise of for me, I might have been some day a famous man too, but as I had refused I need not expect any favours from her."[68] The boy never forgot the reproach, and he had no hesitation in stating that the miniature at the centre of this odd story (fig. 11) was the same one his niece had sold out of the family.[69] Unfortunately for Short, he appears to have been either mistaken or mendacious. But on a more positive note, he also claimed to be familiar with the portrait owned by Mrs. de Beaumont (fig. 15), which he positively identified as his elderly uncle: Captain George Dunn. Since he supposedly knew his uncle's features from personal experience, Short might have been well qualified to dispute Mrs. de Beaumont's portrait of Sir Isaac Brock. But Miss Mickle was not overly impressed with Short's story, and she reacted to it by seeking further assurances from him.

In his reply, Short tried a new tack by vehemently expressing his low opinion of Mrs. de Beaumont's painting. "That Picture to my mind represents a wild Harum Scarum man." While Short was quick to apologize for his use of this expression, which was rather inappropriate for a lady, he knew "of no other that will so aptly describe the Picture in question."[70] After all, the sitter gave the impression of "a man more fitted for a Lunatic Asylum than one to command the love and Esteem of his men."[71] This line of reasoning was utterly ridiculous, of course, but it probably helped sway Miss Mickle into thinking that Mrs. de Beaumont's portrait might not be Brock after all. Mrs. Taylor came up with an even more compelling argument: "As for the Portrait which Mrs. de Beaumont has, I most *emphatically* say [it] is the Portrait of Capt. Dunn. I think I have a good right to know, as I had it to *veil* & *unveil* twice a day for Mrs. Dunn to lament over."[72] Years earlier, Mrs. Taylor had been responsible for taking care of her bedridden great-aunt, and one of her duties included a very peculiar ritual.[73] Every night, she took the portrait down from the wall and placed it near the foot of the old lady's bed, while at the same time having to endure her aunt's repeated cries of "Dunn! Dunn! Why did you leave me?"[74] Given this bizarre behaviour, Mrs. Taylor had no doubt as to the identity of the officer in this portrait.[75] Without a doubt, it was Captain—or more accurately Lieutenant—George Dunn.[76]

As far as Mrs. Taylor and her uncle were concerned, the miniature sold to Miss Mickle was now effectively authenticated as being that of Sir Isaac Brock. Miss Mickle, however, was still not entirely persuaded, and so she must have been thankful for Miss FitzGibbon's generous offer to seek out the opinions of some art experts in London. If these specialists could agree that the likeness in the miniature was the same as those in the profile portraits, it would serve to validate Miss Mickle's discovery. This strategy might have been inspired by the comparisons made by Gerald S. Hayward, who assured Miss Mickle that the miniature she purchased compared favourably with every other portrait of Brock he could find. In any case, it was a happy coincidence that Miss FitzGibbon was planning to set out for England only a few weeks after Forster took his leave.[77] Although Miss FitzGibbon's trip had nothing to do with Brock, she was determined to assist Miss Mickle in authenticating the miniature—even if it meant adjusting her itinerary.

Miss FitzGibbon's first stop was New York City, where she made a detour in order to visit Gerald S. Hayward on Long Island. Over tea, she told her host all about General Robinson's hostility towards Miss Mickle's discovery. Hayward was "intensely amused," and confidently ruled out the possibility that there had been any tampering with the miniature (fig. 11). He was also certain that the medal was not a later addition, and even if he had failed to notice it as such, "the lens would have done so when it was photographed." With regard to the uniform, it was absurd to think that "any such minor changes in the style or cut of the trimmings" could be assigned a specific date. Furthermore, "no critic whose authority was worth having on such a question could avoid recognizing the fact that the profile and the miniature were one and the same person."[78] Hayward's unshakable faith in the miniature was encouraging, and Miss FitzGibbon parted company with him feeling very optimistic.

Arriving in London at the end of April 1897, Miss FitzGibbon found the city "full to over flowing" with people from all over the British Empire.[79] They had come to celebrate Queen Victoria's Diamond Jubilee, which greatly annoyed Miss FitzGibbon as it forced her to go in search of lodgings beyond the capital. After getting herself settled in, she returned to London and eventually made her way to the Royal Colonial Institute—a learned society that promoted discourse on a wide range of subjects.[80] The main attraction for Miss FitzGibbon was a fairly impressive library, and it was there that she began her search by consulting James R. Boosé, the Institute's librarian. During their conversation, Miss FitzGibbon stopped short of saying anything about General Robinson or the newly discovered miniature of Brock. She simply voiced a desire to verify the "authentic data" (or compelling evidence), which she and Miss Mickle already possessed.[81] Miss FitzGibbon was thinking in terms of the uniform and medal in the miniature, both of which General Robinson seemed to doubt. Boosé, however, could do little more than offer a referral to his counterpart at the Royal United Service Institution, as Major Robert M. Holden was known to have made a comprehensive study of uniforms and medals.

A few days later, Miss FitzGibbon paid a visit to the Royal United Service Institution, an organization dedicated to the study of military and naval science. In asking for Major Holden, she was disappointed to learn that he was out. She returned several hours later, only to find that he had gone off to a lecture. Miss FitzGibbon was becoming extremely frustrated.[82] Nor did her mood improve when she went to register for mail delivery at the Canadian High Commission. While there, she discovered that Forster had put in a request to have his mail forwarded to Guernsey. As she rhetorically asked in her next letter to Miss Mickle, "what has brought Forster to Guernsey if not to get ahead of us about the portrait—prove his & disprove ours[?]"[83] Paranoia was getting the better of Miss FitzGibbon, and Major Holden's continued absence only made it worse.

The next morning, Miss FitzGibbon returned once again to the Royal United Service Institution. And once again, she was told that Major Holden was out. This time, she left him a note requesting a meeting for later that afternoon. It was perhaps a test to determine if she was being ignored, as she was given to believe that he would be back by three o'clock. But upon her return, Miss FitzGibbon finally managed to catch up with the elusive major, who enthusiastically asked what he could do for her. "I have a miniature here," she bluntly rejoined, "that I wish to show you and ask what the uniform in it is. I think that perhaps will be the shortest and most straightforward way of arriving at the information I want." Somewhat taken aback, Major Holden could only answer "certainly, you are right." As soon as he saw the miniature (fig. 11), or rather a photographic copy, he recalled having seen it before. When Miss FitzGibbon demanded to know where, the major replied "General Robinson brought it to me." And when Miss FitzGibbon insisted on knowing in what form, she was told a "pamphlet or circular, or something of the kind," which could only be taken to mean one thing: *The Cabot Calendar*. "Yes," said Miss FitzGibbon, "and what was your opinion?" The major confessed he was unable to make out the medal, which General Robinson specifically enquired about, although he suspected that it "probably had been painted on the miniature later."[84]

With this brief exchange, Miss FitzGibbon suddenly realized that she had located the chief source of General Robinson's information. Now it was her turn to exploit Major Holden's good-natured willingness to help, and this time to Miss Mickle's advantage. Unfortunately for Miss FitzGibbon, the major could not venture an opinion regarding the miniature's authenticity. But eager to be of some assistance, he helpfully intimated that artists often painted uniforms "to suit their artistic fancies."[85] Suddenly, the uniform was no longer an issue, and neither was the medal.[86] The major's insight was most gratifying, as it completely dispelled General Robinson's contention against the miniature.[87]

Having finally met Major Holden, Miss FitzGibbon developed a favourable opinion of the gentleman. While he was not as helpful as she would have liked, neither did he appear to be on the side of General Robinson. It was a great relief, and when the major offered to do anything he could to help her, Miss FitzGibbon took him at his word.[88] In dropping her guard, she told him all about General Robinson's objections, and how she and Miss Mickle were "perfectly well satisfied" with the authenticity of the miniature, but thought it "only right" to make further enquiries. Miss FitzGibbon also let it be known that she was going to Guernsey, "to learn if there were any other members of the [Brock] family who could by any possibility have sat for this miniature." Before parting company with Major Holden, she felt the need to explain why the miniature had been copyrighted, which she claimed was only done to prevent it being reproduced in all sorts of "horrible newspaper prints."[89] Miss FitzGibbon added that the legal protection was vested in Mrs. Taylor.

This last revelation was intended to dispel any notion that Miss Mickle and Miss FitzGibbon hoped to make money out of Brock's new portrait. Nevertheless, the prospect of turning a profit from Miss Mickle's discovery had been a consideration right from the start—although the miniature was beginning to look much less lucrative than it first appeared. The costs associated with proving the identity of the sitter were beginning to mount and, as Miss FitzGibbon explained to Miss Mickle soon after her meeting with Major Holden, "even if we do prove its authenticity to such men as General Robinson, the doing so will be so expensive that it will be years before we get even interest on the outlay."[90] However, Miss FitzGibbon also thought a financial disappointment in the meantime would at least "prove that we are—perforce perhaps—honest in saying that we do not expect to make money out of it."[91]

On the same day that Miss FitzGibbon met with Major Holden, she received a letter "most kind" from Guernsey. In it, Miss Henrietta Tupper invited her to visit, adding that Forster had already introduced himself to the Tuppers and other Brock relatives. As Miss Fitzgibbon noted for Miss Mickle's benefit, "they find him interesting—but say no more."[92] Faced with such ambiguity, Miss FitzGibbon was very discreet in her reply to Miss Tupper and careful not to say anything untoward about Forster.

Rather, she feigned a desire that "he will be still there when I arrive, as I know him slightly."[93] Forster's head start gave Miss FitzGibbon cause to be wary. She had no idea what he might have said about Miss Mickle's discovery, or how it might be perceived in Guernsey. Ultimately, there was only one way to find out.

3

All to Prove a Point

It was sometime around the middle of May 1897 when Miss FitzGibbon stepped onto the pier at St. Peter Port, the capital of Guernsey and birthplace of Sir Isaac Brock. She was on her way to visit Miss Henrietta Tupper, whose friendly reception must have come as a great relief. Far from being unduly influenced by John Wycliffe Lowes Forster, Miss Tupper was well disposed to the idea of another portrait of Brock. Much of her indulgence had to do with the claim that Captain James Brock owned the miniature at one time. Miss Tupper was well aware that Captain Brock was a first cousin to Sir Isaac Brock, and that he had served in Canada as paymaster to the 49th Regiment. It was therefore conceivable that Captain Brock might have owned a miniature of his cousin, and that his family in Canada would have preserved such a prized heirloom. With her curiosity thus piqued, Miss Tupper was only too happy to help Miss FitzGibbon with the investigation.[1]

The first order of business was to enquire after Lieutenant Colonel J. Percy Groves of the Royal Guernsey Militia, who was also librarian of the Candie Library in St. Peter Port and a military historian of some renown. Because Miss Tupper and the rest of her family valued his opinion, Miss FitzGibbon thought it best to ask him for his interpretation of the uniform and medal worn by the officer in Miss Mickle's miniature.[2] However, there were no expectations on her part, as Major Robert M. Holden had already decided that both of these attributes were merely "artistic fancies." Despite a thorough search, Colonel Groves was unable to be of much assistance—although he did raise the possibility that the medal might have been awarded for the Battle of Waterloo.[3] Considering that this battle took place in 1815, nearly three years after Brock's death, Miss FitzGibbon dismissed the suggestion . . . and the colonel himself.[4]

Believing that Colonel Groves had been tainted by Forster's bias, Miss FitzGibbon tended to ignore his expertise.[5] However, if the colonel was a disappointment, then Miss Guille more than made up for it. Miss Mary Elizabeth Guille was a septuagenarian whose maternal grandfather was one of Sir Isaac Brock's first cousins.[6] She was very smart for her age, and she had a vivid recollection of Brock's brothers—Daniel de Lisle Brock and John Savery Brock. Miss Guille was therefore an important witness to history, and one who happened to tell Miss FitzGibbon exactly what she wanted to hear. Upon seeing one of the photographs of the newly discovered miniature (figs 12, 17), Miss Guille did not hesitate in pronouncing the sitter to be a Brock. Miss FitzGibbon presumed that she meant Sir Isaac Brock.[7]

Miss Guille's conviction prompted an acceptance of the miniature by the other Brock relatives, and of the charming Canadian lady who brought the pleasing miniature to their attention. Miss FitzGibbon was careful to cultivate a good relationship with Brock's extended family, and one of their number—a Mrs. Bubb—was "very much impressed by the clear, precise manner in which Miss FitzGibbon explained everything. She has the subject not only at her finger's ends, but at her heart, and I did wish like you, that our dear Fathers and Aunt de Lisle could have met her—they could have told her so much more than we can, in fact I believe she knows more than we do. She is certainly a woman one does not meet every day, and I felt much drawn to her. I hope to see more of her."[8] Miss FitzGibbon had a knack for winning people over, but she also knew that no amount of charisma could guarantee the entire Brock family's support for Miss Mickle's discovery. And she still had to contend with the objections of Major General Charles W. Robinson, which Forster was sure to raise whenever possible. The most effective means of countering Forster's negativity would have been for Miss FitzGibbon to reveal his complicity in the general's scheming, but she worried that such a bold disclosure might reflect badly on herself. In a stroke of good luck, however, the general soon became his own worst enemy.

One morning during breakfast with Miss Tupper, Miss FitzGibbon saw an opportunity to enlighten her new friend.[9] As the two ladies sat enjoying each other's company, the post arrived with a packet addressed to "F. Brock Tupper Esq."—the sight of which gave Miss Tupper such a shock that she dropped it on the table. "Who," she exclaimed, "can be writing to me who does not know my father is gone!"[10] In picking up the packet, Miss FitzGibbon found a clue written on the back, which she read out: "Gen[eral] R does not want the enclosed picture back, so please do not trouble to return it."[11] Miss Tupper was intrigued that General Robinson had something to do with the packet, and inside she found a letter from a Mrs. Lewin—who years earlier had acted as something of an agent for Miss Alice Kerr-Nelson. It was Miss Kerr-Nelson who had made the copy (fig. 6) of Mrs. Henry Tupper's profile portrait of Brock (fig. 3) for Lieutenant Governor John Beverley Robinson.[12] Also enclosed was a page from *The Cabot Calendar* with the lithographic illustration of Miss Mickle's miniature (fig. 14), and a letter from General Robinson to Mrs. Lewin enquiring if the Brocks in Guernsey had any knowledge of this additional portrait. For Miss FitzGibbon, it was the perfect setup.

The timely arrival of Mrs. Lewin's packet allowed Miss FitzGibbon to broach the subject of General Robinson's objections to the miniature, by which she hoped to lower Miss Tupper's now diminished estimation of him. By making his request through Mrs. Lewin, instead of going directly to Miss Tupper, General Robinson appeared to be acting in a clandestine manner. Miss FitzGibbon further capitalized on the general's misstep by expressing her disapproval of his having written "in so underhand a way," which she judged to be very "ungentlemanly."[13] She then proceeded to blurt out all the problems she and Miss Mickle were having with him, and how he was surreptitiously undermining the credibility of the newly discovered miniature of Brock (fig. 11).

Miss Tupper was sympathetic and promised to write a fitting reply, which led Miss FitzGibbon to believe that General Robinson would soon have his comeuppance.[14] She also expected him to get the message that Miss Tupper was firmly on Miss Mickle's side. But in writing to tell Miss Mickle about her good fortune, Miss FitzGibbon became somewhat defensive as she recounted how she had manipulated Miss Tupper. In downplaying her own bad behaviour, Miss FitzGibbon claimed that Miss Tupper knew how carefully she was conducting the investigation, and how it would always be carried out "honestly and in search of the truth."[15] In fact, Miss FitzGibbon's perception of the truth in this instance was more than a little slanted in favour of Miss Mickle's discovery. And yet she was absolutely convinced that this new portrait of Sir Isaac Brock was genuine and that its case could be argued successfully. She had already persuaded most of the Brock relatives that Miss Mickle's miniature was authentic, which was reassuring . . . until it became evident that there was still a holdout in the person of Kentish Brock.

This gentleman, besides having important connections in Guernsey, was also an influential member of the Brock family.[16] As such, his views held sway—and he was more than a little inclined to entertain Forster's opinions. Miss FitzGibbon was not overly perturbed when she learned of this dissenter, as she still had the backing of both Miss Guille and Miss Tupper. These ladies were highly respected in Guernsey, and their approval of Miss Mickle's miniature was sure to quash any interference on the part of Kentish Brock. And by the first week of July, even he was suddenly found to endorse Miss Mickle's discovery.[17] In relaying the good news to Miss Mickle, an overjoyed Miss FitzGibbon asked: "What do you think of that, my cat?"[18] As Miss FitzGibbon would come to realize, however, Kentish Brock's acceptance of the miniature did not lessen his appreciation for the artistic talent displayed in Forster's artwork. He was toying with the idea of having a painting of Brock for Guernsey's Royal Court House, and whether it was the profile portrait or the miniature that was replicated in oils, Kentish Brock was determined that Forster should be the one to do it.[19]

Not long after her breakfast intrigues, Miss FitzGibbon was back in London.[20] Forster remained in Guernsey, lingering just long enough to finish his mysterious commission before heading off to Paris. It was a study for a portrait of Brock (fig. 16). He also made a nuisance of himself, just as Miss FitzGibbon had predicted.[21] Based on his many years of experience as a portrait painter, Forster considered himself completely justified in voicing his concerns about certain aspects of the miniature—or, more precisely, the illustration reproduced in *The Cabot Calendar* (fig. 14). Most notably, he made an issue of the arch of the eyebrow and the shape of the nose, neither of which compared very favourably with the two profile portraits (figs 3, 4) in Guernsey.[22] Forster's pronouncements were damaging, but Miss FitzGibbon knew that they would have little bearing on the Brock relatives. However, she also knew that their favourable opinion

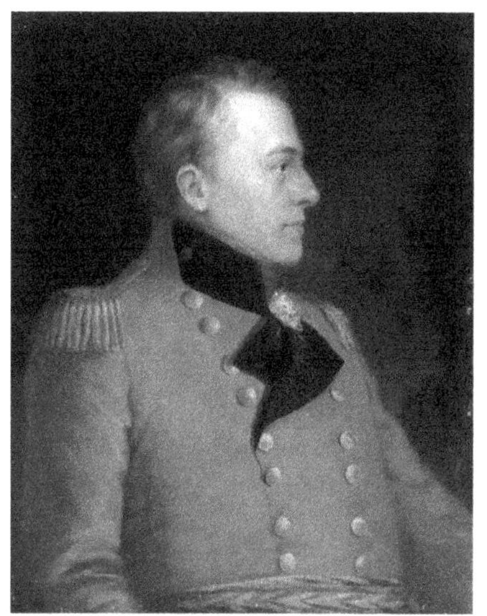

FIGURE 16.

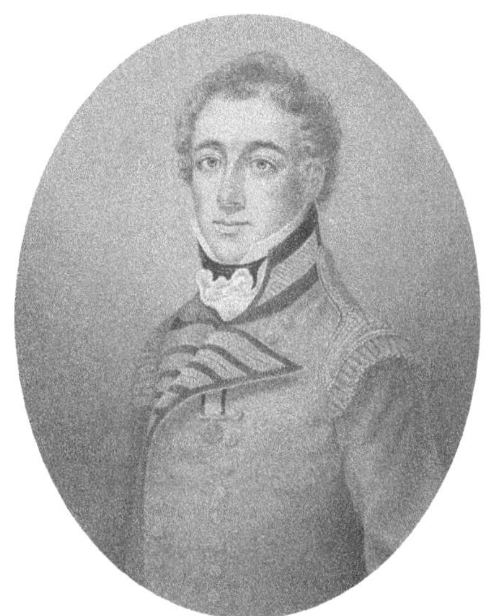

FIGURE 14.

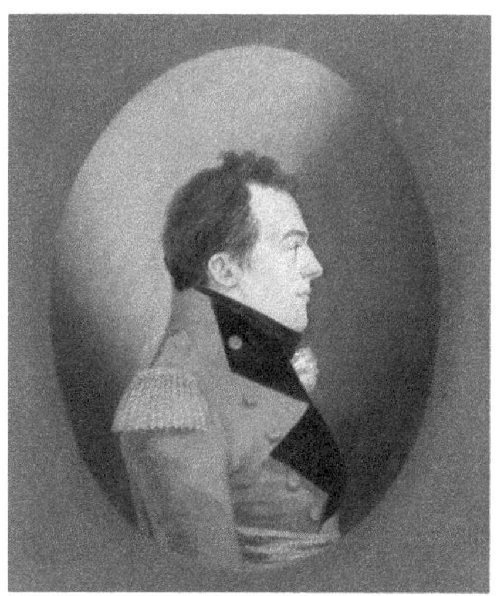

FIGURE 3.

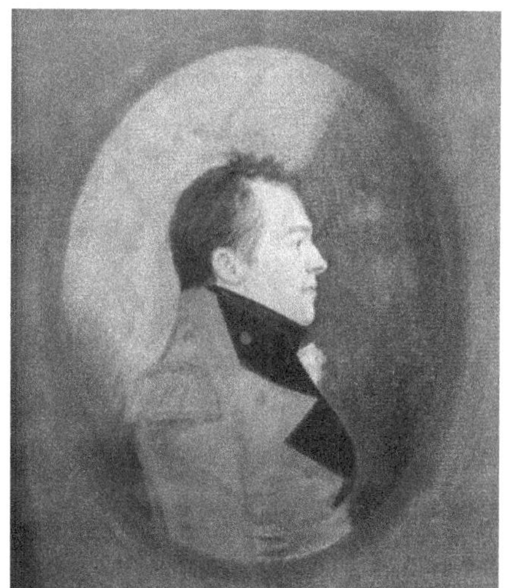

FIGURE 4.

would be no match for the States of Guernsey (the island's parliament). Miss FitzGibbon had good reason to worry about the possibility of a political intervention. There were reports that Forster was offering to sell the States a portrait of Sir Isaac Brock, which was likely to be an elaboration on one of his copies of the profile portrait. Such a commission, she feared, would give him and the Robinsons "this card to defeat us."[23] Yet, Miss FitzGibbon was not quite ready to throw in her hand.

Encouraged by her visit to see Gerald S. Hayward, whose attitude towards the miniature was so utterly agreeable, Miss FitzGibbon became all the more intent on seeking out some further expert opinions in London. Two or three positive reports would be more than enough to neutralize Forster's opposition, just in case his doubts regarding Miss Mickle's discovery were ever given credence.[24] If so, a forceful rebuttal could be quickly and easily deployed by way of the press.[25] All it required was a careful comparison. Miss FitzGibbon was confident that the art experts would see an unmistakable resemblance between the sitter in the miniature and the profile portraits, despite what Forster had to say. To this end, she asked Miss Tupper to bring her both versions of the profile portrait (figs 3, 4). While Miss Tupper was happy to oblige, as she was going to London anyway, it would require considerable effort to negotiate the loan of these treasured heirlooms, and she simply could not fathom why two copies of the same portrait were required.[26] They were virtually identical, and so Miss Tupper decided to ask for the loan of only one—which happened to be the copy (fig. 4), and the one that Forster used as the model for his own portrait of Brock.[27]

This new arrangement greatly displeased Miss FitzGibbon, as she expected Miss Tupper to do her bidding, and also because she believed that no self-respecting art expert would give her an opinion without seeing the original profile portrait (fig. 3). For this same reason, Miss FitzGibbon regretted not having the miniature (fig. 11), which remained back in Toronto with Miss Mickle.[28] Clearly, her plans had not been fully developed when she set out for England and now the situation was becoming dire. But in giving the matter some further thought, she decided it might be possible to make do. After all, she still had her photographs of the miniature (figs 12, 17), as well as the copy made by Hayward (fig. 13), and before long she would also have the copy of the profile portrait (fig. 4). Therefore, a facial

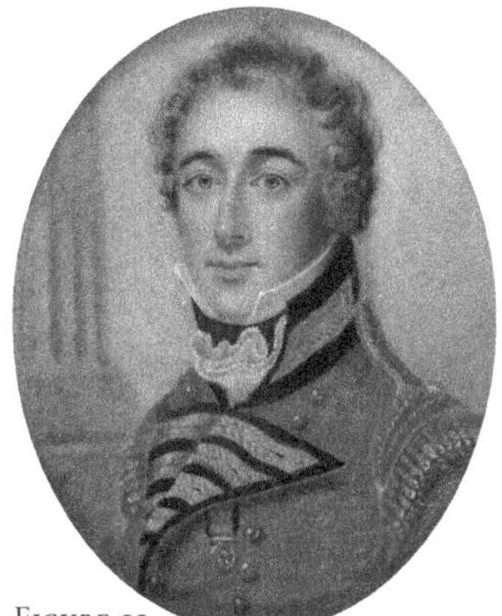
Figure 11.

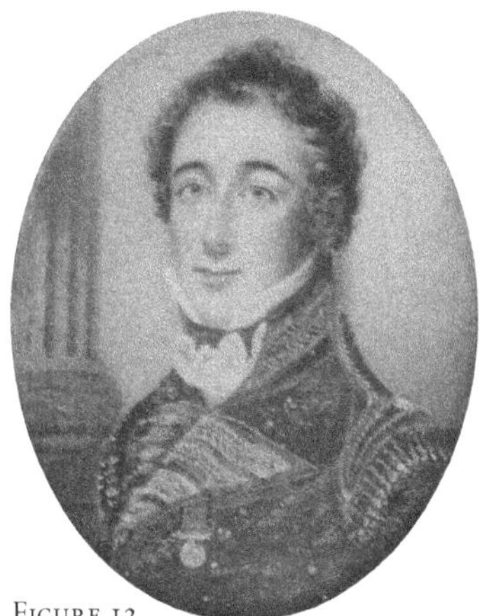
Figure 12.

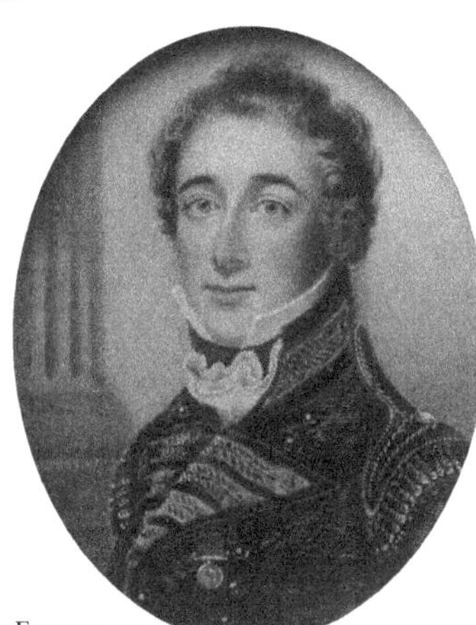
Figure 17.

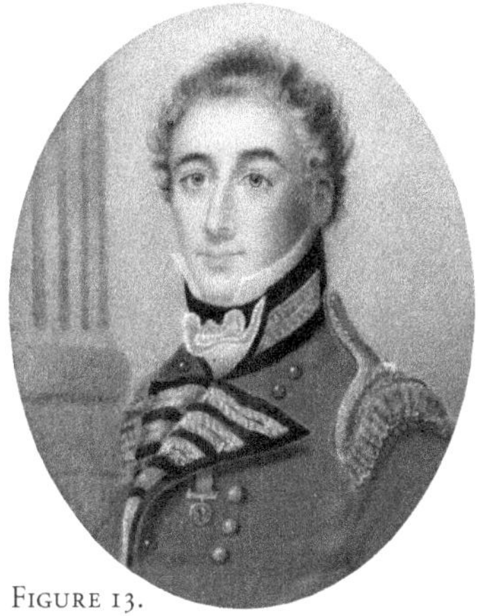
Figure 13.

comparison was still feasible—even if the effort was becoming something of a struggle.

As much as Miss FitzGibbon wanted to participate in the miniature's authentication, her resolve was severely tested by Queen Victoria's Diamond Jubilee and all the disruption that went along with it. Going in search of art experts was extremely difficult, and unsettled personal affairs caused additional stress.[29] Along with worrying about an ailing sister back home in Canada, Miss FitzGibbon was also burdened with the responsibility of having to sell a family property in England.[30] The pressure was intense, and a harsh criticism would prove to be last straw.

In mid-June of 1897, Miss FitzGibbon received a letter from Miss Mickle scolding her for having been in an "excited state," presumably because she had been overly talkative with Major Holden. Losing her temper, Miss FitzGibbon angrily replied: "You have always, to judge by your letters, been in a more excited state than I have been over it, so do not throw stones—and do not waste postage, time and paper telling, nay urging me to do what I am doing to the best of my ability. I have given it the first place in time and thoughts, so do not scold any more. I have many other things to do and think of, and can only do the best I can."[31] More hurt than offended, Miss FitzGibbon made use of the same letter to make amends. "Now do not run away with the thought I have ever intended to give up," she assured her dear "pardner."[32] There was no reason to let a slight misunderstanding come between them, and Miss FitzGibbon was sure everything would turn out right in the end.

Although the copy of the profile portrait had been available since the second week of June, the Queen's Jubilee continued to complicate matters.[33] A fatigued Miss FitzGibbon therefore decided to forgo her pursuit of art experts, but only long enough for a brief respite in Bristol.[34] She hoped to find London back to normal by the time of her return a few days later. But much to her chagrin, there were still hordes of people everywhere she went. Compounding the problem was Miss FitzGibbon's own growing sense of inadequacy, which found expression in her correspondence with Miss Mickle. "I have worried myself nearly into brain fever over my failure to do all you require," she confessed. It was then that she explained: "I dare say all the anxiety and . . . other things coming all at once has left me more incapable than I otherwise might have been. I go over it again & again until I wish I had never come to England at all. I believe now we could have done better about it all by letter."[35] Miss FitzGibbon was beginning to doubt her ability to assist Miss Mickle, and in the process she became seriously depressed over it. Yet, she also had every reason to believe that the miniature could in fact be authenticated, and this belief helped to improve her disposition.

A re-invigorated Miss FitzGibbon was soon looking for guidance at George Rowney and Company, the world-famous artist supplies manufacturer.[36] In speaking to one of Rowney's sons, possibly Walter Rowney, she asked him if he knew of any artists who might offer their opinions on "vexed or unknown portraits."[37] Miss FitzGibbon elaborated by saying that she had two such portraits "purporting to be of the same person, one a profile, the other a full face," and she wanted an expert opinion to confirm that they were one and the same. The response was unequivocal. Only a miniature painter could answer such a question, "as they knew the correct measurements by which to judge."[38] Miss FitzGibbon was then given the address of Frank Nowlan, a miniature painter in Soho Square who also specialized in the restoration of these diminutive portraits.[39] But before she had a chance to see Nowlan, Miss FitzGibbon met up with Henry F. Rawstorne.

Rawstorne was a solicitor who also happened to be a friend of Lionel Cust, the director of the National Portrait Gallery.[40] How Miss FitzGibbon became aware of Rawstorne is not known, but upon hearing of her interest in finding some art experts, he very kindly offered to invite Cust's participation. Miss FitzGibbon accepted Rawstorne's suggestion and gave him the pictures Cust would require to make a comparison. One of them was Baker's photograph of the miniature discovered by Miss Mickle (fig. 17), but instead of the profile portrait supplied by Miss Tupper (fig. 4), Miss FitzGibbon substituted the proof print of a silhouette she had just received from Canada (fig. 18).[41] It was only after Miss FitzGibbon set out for England that Miss Mickle obtained a photographic copy of this silhouette from Aemilius Jarvis, a prominent Toronto banker and financier. According to the story related by Jarvis, the silhouette came down through several generations of his family via his grandmother, Miss Mary Boyles Powell. She was the supposed fiancée of Lieutenant Colonel John Macdonell, who was Brock's ill-fated provincial aide-de-camp.[42] This

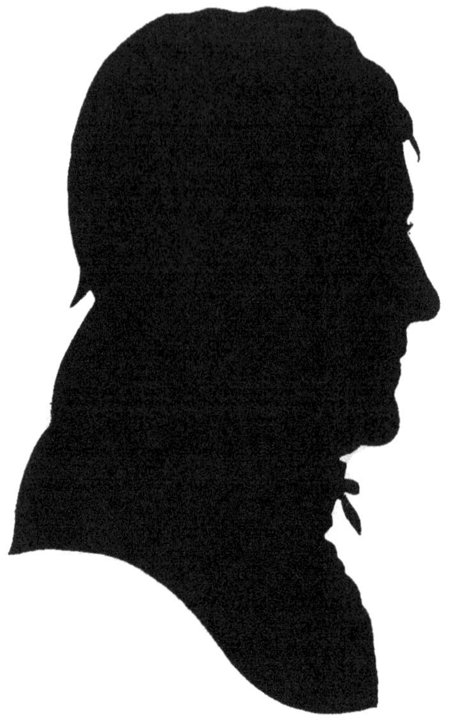

FIGURE 18.

provenance convinced Miss Mickle that the Jarvis silhouette was a reliable indicator of Brock's profile, and that it would serve as an accurate gauge of her miniature's authenticity. Just as Miss FitzGibbon advocated, a careful comparison was all it would take to settle the question. But in order to achieve a result that would silence the naysayers, the comparison had to be conducted by art experts of the type only to be found in London. Accordingly, Miss Mickle hastened to send off the proof print to England. The delivery was made just in a nick of time, and Miss Mickle took it for granted that Miss FitzGibbon would embrace this new approach to authenticating the miniature. But the awful truth soon became all too apparent: Miss FitzGibbon had an agenda of her own.

Regardless of the seemingly unassailable family traditions validating the Jarvis silhouette, Miss FitzGibbon was not entirely satisfied that it was actually Brock's profile. But against her better judgement, she proceeded as per the new instructions from Miss Mickle, who made it abundantly clear that they had "no interest in proving Miss Tupper's portrait."[43] Miss Mickle actually meant the profile portrait brought over from Guernsey by Miss Henrietta Tupper, which was the copy then belonging to John Savery Carey (fig. 4). In any case, now that Miss Mickle had the Jarvis silhouette, she wanted nothing to do with the portrait supplied by Miss Tupper—fearing that it might lead to some advantage for General Robinson. Miss FitzGibbon, however, was not prepared to abandon the profile portraits, as there was always the possibility that the art experts might refuse to consider the Jarvis silhouette for some unknown reason. If so, she wanted them to compare the copy of the profile portrait (fig. 4) with the miniature (fig. 11). That way, if the sitter proved to be the same in each case, then Miss Mickle would still have confirmation of her miniature's authenticity—as the profile portrait was widely accepted to be the very image of Sir Isaac Brock.

At the National Portrait Gallery, Director Cust seemed to think that the photographs of Miss Mickle's miniature (fig. 17) and the Jarvis silhouette (fig. 18) both featured the same man, but he was far too shrewd to put it in writing. Instead, he recommended that Miss FitzGibbon consult Algernon Graves, a print publisher who was known to have compiled a list of portrait painters from years past.[44] Rawstorne took it upon himself to set up a meeting, and it was agreed that Graves would see Miss FitzGibbon the next day at five o'clock in the afternoon. The following morning, Miss FitzGibbon made good use of her free time by calling on Frank Nowlan, the miniature painter in Soho. She found him to be "a clever, keen-faced Irishman of about sixty in a dusty, rather crowded study—with lovely old furniture and a real art look about it."[45] Just as she had done for Cust, Miss FitzGibbon provided Nowlan with Baker's photograph of the miniature and also the proof print of the Jarvis silhouette. Arranging them side-by-side, she asked Nowlan if he thought they portrayed the same man. After a careful study lasting some ten or fifteen minutes, Nowlan finally agreed. "Yes," he said, "I have no hesitation in saying they are of the same man—the lock of hair over the forehead in the silhouette is the only doubtful point, but nose, eyes, eyebrows, mouth, chin are alike."[46] The silhouette (fig. 18) appeared to portray an older man with a full head of hair, while the miniature (fig. 17) featured a young man with a thinning hairline. Without labouring the point, Miss FitzGibbon asked Nowlan for his opinion in writing. The old artist complied, and for a small fee Miss FitzGibbon had the first of her expert opinions.[47]

Miss FitzGibbon then made her way to Pall Mall, where she hoped to get a second opinion from Algernon Graves. But this gentleman had to decline, as he did not consider himself qualified to judge likenesses. His interest was mainly historical, but he agreed to look through his lists for the obscure artist who signed his name to the miniature. Try as he might, Graves was unable to find any reference to a J. Hudson.[48] When his pressing and persistent visitor happened to drop Gerald S. Hayward's name, Graves finally saw an opportunity to be of assistance. "There you may get an opinion," he replied. As was the case at Rowney's, Graves advised that "a miniature painter would be the best to consult."[49] He then very graciously offered to escort Miss FitzGibbon to a nearby exhibition of miniatures, which had only recently opened, and where he thought she might find someone able to help. Thinking this an excellent idea, Miss FitzGibbon agreed to set out for the gallery hosting the Society of Miniature Painters.[50] Upon entering, Graves introduced her to the secretary of the society who, after learning the nature of her request, advised that she speak to the president. As a miniature painter himself, that gentleman "could speak with [more] authority than any one else in the artist world of London."[51] Finding that Miss FitzGibbon was agreeable, the secretary began writing out a letter of introduction. Just then, however, two men walked into the gallery, one of whom happened to be Alyn Williams—the president who was just described to Miss FitzGibbon.[52]

When Williams offered to help the lady from Canada, Miss FitzGibbon produced Baker's photograph of the miniature (fig. 17) and also the proof print of the Jarvis silhouette (fig.18). Although Williams expressed regret at not being able to see the originals, he was still willing to offer an opinion. Such a question as Miss FitzGibbon wished to have answered, he assured her, could be just "as readily if not better judged from a photograph than from the original or from a painting," and this because "the photograph was sure to have the lines clear and correct."[53] When Williams questioned the silhouette for the same reason as Frank Nowlan, namely the protruding lock of hair over the sitter's forehead, Miss FitzGibbon immediately offered up a photograph of the original profile portrait of Brock (fig. 3).[54] She had been holding this forbidden likeness in reserve, waiting for just one more expert to question the Jarvis silhouette. And now, released from any further obligation to Miss Mickle, the real test could begin. After judging the resemblance between the profile portrait and the miniature, Williams gave his verdict. "Those two," he declared, "are of the same man—there is no doubt whatever about it—but I should doubt the silhouette."[55]

With two art experts casting doubt on the Jarvis silhouette (fig.18), it could hardly be regarded as an accurate gauge of the miniature's authenticity. Miss FitzGibbon was not at all surprised. Yet, Frank Nowlan thought it bore some resemblance to the miniature discovered by Miss Mickle, and so too did Lionel Cust. But all that mattered was what Alyn Williams, in his capacity as president of the Society of Miniature Painters, had to say. And by thinking the likeness in the miniature (fig. 11) matched that of the original profile portrait (fig. 3), he provided the confirmation Miss FitzGibbon's needed without having to resort to the Jarvis silhouette.[56]

Miss Mickle was not happy that her instructions had been blatantly disregarded, or that Williams had cast doubt on the Jarvis silhouette. Although his comparison actually served her purpose, Miss Mickle found his low opinion of silhouettes galling in the extreme. It was an inadvertent offence, and one Williams committed while examining the Jarvis silhouette for Miss FitzGibbon. Despite recognizing it to be the work of a professional, he recounted his experience that even the most skillfully cut silhouettes were often "quite unlike the man or face they are supposed to represent."[57] Miss Mickle, however, had no patience for Williams, or his "theories about the humbler sister art of silhouette-making."[58] She preferred to believe that the Jarvis silhouette was "surely a good one." And given Miss Mickle's unyieldingly attitude, it was just as well that Williams had his dealings with Miss FitzGibbon—as she was more favourably inclined to his opinion and therefore more susceptible to the salesmanship he was about to unleash on her.

When Miss FitzGibbon asked Williams for a written statement of his opinion, he readily complied and she must have thought herself ahead of the game.[59] But it was Williams who got the better of Miss FitzGibbon

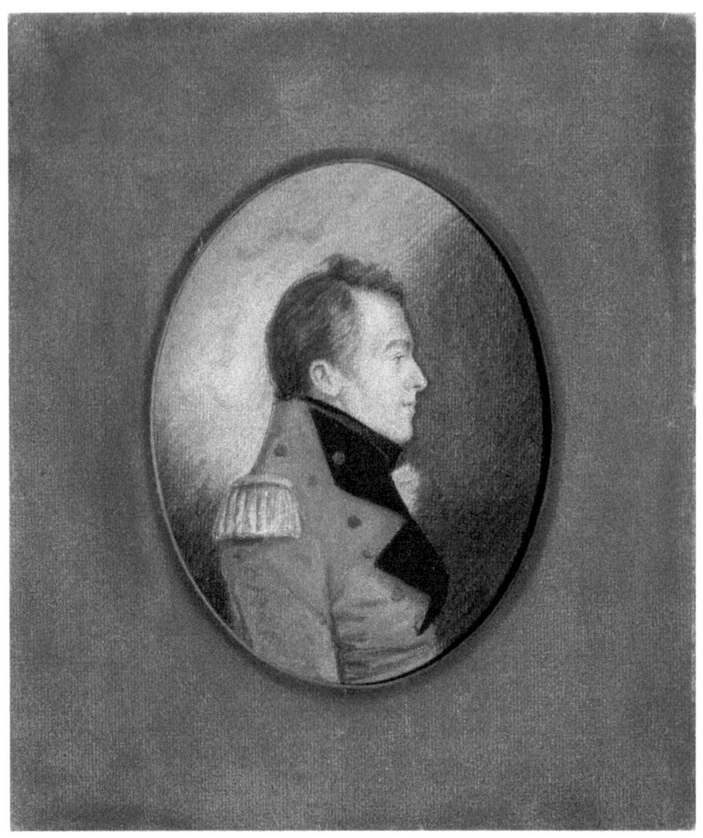

Figure 19.

when he persuaded her to commission a copy of Brock's profile portrait (fig. 19). What he proposed, in effect, was a copy of a copy—as the profile portrait brought to London by Miss Tupper was not the original. And while Miss Tupper may have been put to a lot of trouble for nothing, Williams was certainly able to profit by her inconvenience. Upon learning that the portrait was close at hand, he "advised a facsimile." Miss FitzGibbon fell for the sales pitch, and as she reported back to Miss Mickle, "I see the advantage as it will confound the bad copyists."[60] Back in Canada, Miss Mickle was baffled as to which portrait Williams had copied, and in asking Miss FitzGibbon for a clarification, she was told in no uncertain terms that it was the original. "The other is the *copy!*"[61]

Unfortunately for Miss FitzGibbon, she had it backwards. The profile portrait borrowed from John Savery Carey (fig. 4) was generally thought to be a copy, as it was weaker in style.[62] Miss Tupper and Mrs. Huyshe had concluded as much in 1881, and Miss FitzGibbon saw no reason to doubt them. That is, until Williams convinced her otherwise by declaring it to have been "done from life originally and by a good hand."[63] An artist of Williams's stature was not likely to have ventured such an opinion without seeing the other portrait, had he known of its existence. But Miss FitzGibbon was rather selective in the material she presented to the art experts, and so Williams might have been unaware of the original profile portrait belonging to Henry Bingham de Vic Tupper (fig. 3). Whatever the case, Miss FitzGibbon went along with Williams and began treating the copy of Brock's profile portrait as though it were the original. As far as she was concerned, the judgement of the president of the Society of Miniature Painters was incontrovertible (so long as it upheld Miss Mickle's discovery). Miss Tupper, no doubt, would have disagreed with this revisionist approach had she any knowledge of it. But it appears that Miss FitzGibbon kept this new development to herself, and with some justification. Although Miss Tupper was an enthusiastic supporter of the newly discovered miniature of Brock (fig. 11), she also had an annoying habit of speaking her mind—as in the case of a certain bronzed silhouette.

What Miss Tupper called the "bronze profile" (fig. 8) was really just a silhouette with gold highlights. As for the sitter, he looked to be a heavy-set army officer with his hair tied back in a queue and a badge conspicuously displayed on his chest.[64] Miss Tupper and her relatives treasured the bronze profile as a faithful likeness of Sir Isaac Brock. But when it was shown to Miss FitzGibbon, she was immediately suspicious. Privately, she expressed her belief that the officer portrayed "a very much older looking party" than Brock, who did not live beyond the age of forty-three.[65] Moreover, there was also a problem with the insignia, which Miss FitzGibbon thought was meant to represent the Order of the Bath. She knew that Brock had been knighted, and furthermore that he was killed before the news could reach him. Consequently, it was impossible for him to have worn any such badge of honour. A confident Miss FitzGibbon summarily rejected the bronze profile by telling Miss Mickle: "I do not think it is Brock at all."[66]

It was obvious to Miss FitzGibbon that the bronze profile portrayed someone other than Sir Isaac Brock, and she probably should have been

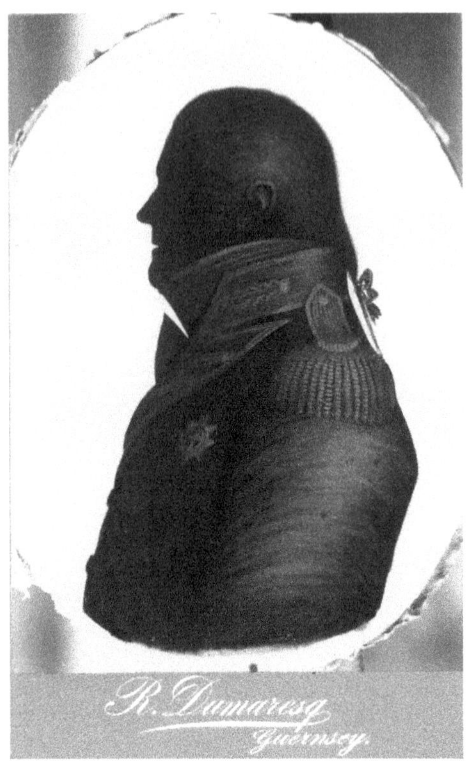

FIGURE 8.

content in this knowledge. But curiosity got the better of her. In trying to account for the misidentification, she began to look upon the bronze profile as a "posthumous production."[67] A mourning keepsake also suggested itself, which led her to think that the bronze profile might have been inspired by the statue of Brock in his memorial at St. Paul's Cathedral (fig. 20).[68] But then she decided that the bronze profile must have been devised in advance of Brock's memorial. This seemed a more plausible sequence, as it allowed for the bronze profile to have served as a guide in sculpting the hero's face. Daniel de Lisle Brock was the logical choice for a model, since he was known to resemble his famous brother. Of course, it would have been more logical for the sculptor to work directly from a sitting with Daniel de Lisle Brock—except that it would have rendered the bronze profile unnecessary. It was a sticking point that apparently never occurred to Miss FitzGibbon, perhaps because she had become obsessed with the

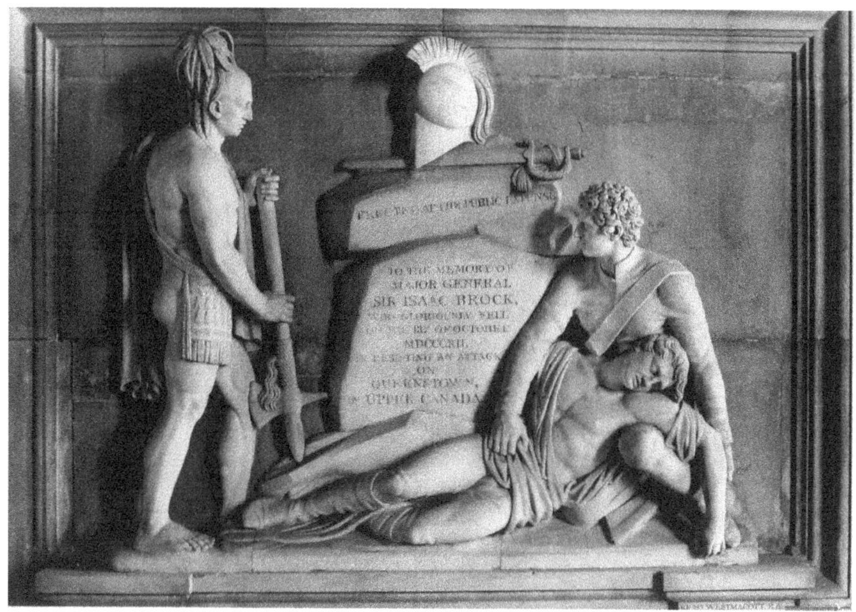

FIGURE 20.

queue evident in the bronze profile. Although she seems to have known that this hair style was outdated by the time of Brock's death in 1812, Miss FitzGibbon simply assumed that a queue was added to the bronze profile at some point—and for no better reason than Brock may have worn one during his last visit home in 1806.[69] Miss FitzGibbon had a grand time letting her imagination run wild, but this much was certain: the bronze profile was not Brock. It must have come as quite a nasty surprise, however, when Miss Tupper steadfastly refused to agree.

Miss Tupper had grown up believing that the bronze profile represented her famous great-uncle, and she would not be told otherwise—certainly not by an outsider who seemed to think that family traditions in Canada were more reliable than those in Guernsey. If the authenticity of the miniature discovered by Miss Mickle could rest on the Short family tradition, then there was no reason why Miss FitzGibbon should doubt the Tupper family tradition regarding the bronze profile. "No clue," Miss Tupper urged, "is more to be relied on, than well authenticated and substantiated tradition coming down from those *who knew the man*."[70] Miss Tupper was uncompromising in her stance on the bronze profile, which left Miss FitzGibbon no choice but to acquiesce. The bronze profile was merely a side issue, and it certainly did not warrant an acrimonious debate, or the possible loss of Miss Tupper's support for the miniature discovered by Miss Mickle.[71] Still, Miss FitzGibbon must have thought it fortuitous that she decided to exclude Miss Tupper from her sessions with the art experts.[72] She was simply too outspoken, and Miss FitzGibbon was not about to risk losing control of the proceedings. But with the miniature authenticated, Miss Tupper was less of a concern. Forster, however, still remained a threat.

By the second week of August, having finished attending to her personal affairs in England, Miss FitzGibbon was on her way home.[73] In the meantime Forster had returned to Guernsey for the sole purpose of painting a larger portrait of Brock (fig. 21).[74] And just as Miss FitzGibbon suspected, he was hoping to make a sale to the States of Guernsey.[75] He was no doubt prodded by Kentish Brock, who Miss FitzGibbon mistakenly believed had been brought onside. As Forster recalled nearly thirty years later, he had only just completed his study when a deputation from the States: "waited upon me, and said they hoped that I would consent to the portrait I had made remaining on the Island, their belief being that his native home had first claim. I expressed appreciation of their desire, and said, 'My country, Canada, claims Sir Isaac Brock as her particular hero, because his great master achievements for the defence of Canada and the Empire were performed within our borders. And as the portrait, if satisfactory, may be regarded as a commission from the Ontario Government, therefore this first portrait must go to Canada. I offered, however, to paint for Guernsey a portrait in larger half-length from the original material, which included authentic documents and data. The proposition was referred to the States and approved, and the resulting portrait of General Brock now hangs in the States [or Royal Court] House."[76] Actually, it was several members of the Royal Court who were "waited upon," and by Kentish Brock. His purpose was to determine if they might be interested in purchasing Forster's study (fig. 16), but it was thought too small and so the offer was declined. It was only then that Forster suggested a larger portrait, although Kentish Brock claimed it was he who proposed the enlargement.[77]

Forster definitely preferred his own view of the past, probably because the impression of an unsolicited interest in his work was a far greater

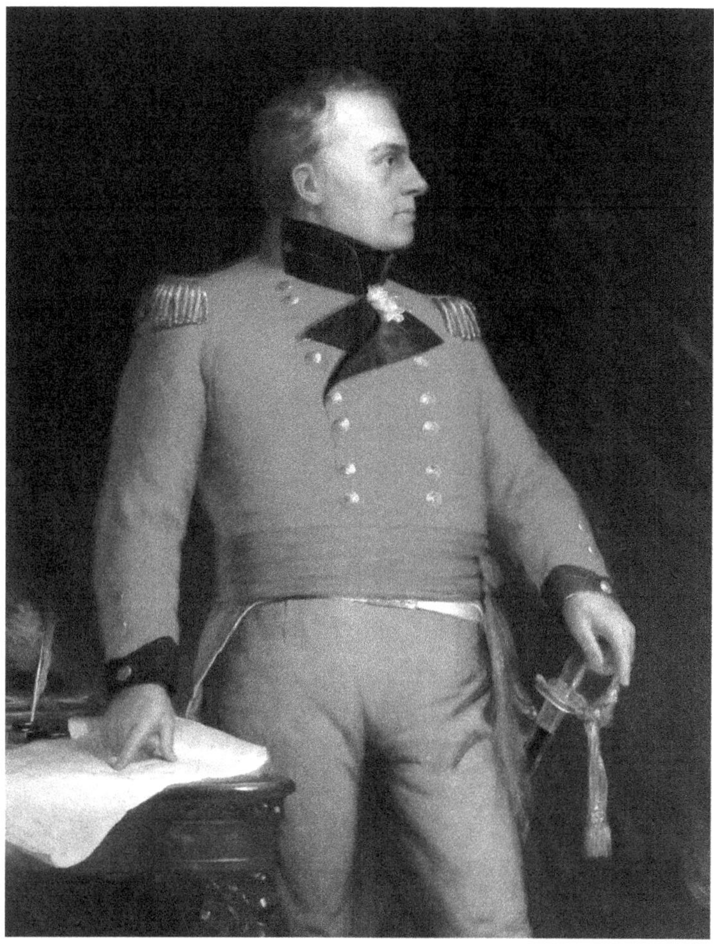

FIGURE 21.

testament to his talent. The artist as patriot was another concept that appealed to Forster's rather inflated ego, which demanded nothing less than a legacy of unanimous approval for his new portrait of Brock. It is no wonder, then, that Forster left the world a record of himself designed to perpetuate the myth of his own importance. His was a grand deceit, which might never have come to light . . . had it not been for a debate by the States of Guernsey.

On the first day of September 1897, some two weeks after Forster arrived back in Toronto, the States met to deliberate a number of different proposals, including his offer to sell them a portrait of Sir Isaac Brock.[78] Under consideration was whether or not to vote £40 for the purchase of the smaller portrait (fig. 16), or £60 for the larger one (fig. 21). The debate really centred on the deluxe canvas, however—it having already been decided that a larger portrait would be more suitable for display in the Royal Court House. The president of the States, Bailiff T. Godfrey Carey, was not averse to the idea of a memorial to Brock in the form of a portrait, and in his opening remarks he emphasized the significance of such an undertaking: "We ought to be proud of Sir Isaac Brock, a compatriot who has so distinguished himself." Then the bailiff asked: "Should we not seize this opportunity of perpetuating his memory by placing his portrait in the Royal Court?" There were already several memorials to Brock, especially in Canada, and "there ought to be one in Guernsey." It seemed the bailiff was ready to support the purchase, but then he did an about-face. Not convinced that Forster was the best artist for such an important commission, Bailiff Carey cautioned the assembled deputies, jurats, and rectors. Before casting their votes, they first had to ask themselves: "Is the portrait good enough?"[79]

The bailiff's warning was due in large measure to the meddling of Miss FitzGibbon. During her short stay in Guernsey, she did her level best to defame Forster's reputation as an artist.[80] But Miss FitzGibbon's greatest meddling involved a lady who was introduced to her as Mrs. Nathaniel Stevenson, the wife of Guernsey's lieutenant governor.[81] When Mrs. Stevenson casually asked about the level of esteem for Forster's artwork in Canada, Miss FitzGibbon found herself momentarily at a loss for words. But her awkward hesitation seemed to have the desired effect, as she later heard it said that Forster failed to sell the States his study for Brock's portrait because the lieutenant governor would not consent to its purchase.[82] However, Miss FitzGibbon's informant was seriously mistaken as to the extent of viceregal influence over the States. While Lieutenant Governor Stevenson held an exalted position as the Queen's representative in Guernsey, he possessed no legislative authority. Even if Mrs. Stevenson had induced her husband into believing that Forster's work was inadequate, the lieutenant governor could not have interfered with the purchase of the study. Nor is there any evidence to suggest that he had any intention of doing so. Granted, the lieutenant governor may have thought the study too small, but it does not appear that he went so far as to publicly voice his disapproval of Forster's work.[83] Bailiff Carey, however, had no such qualms—and he had no hesitation in expressing his reservations about the calibre of Forster's artistic abilities.

Kentish Brock reacted by providing the bailiff with a list of the eminent Canadians whose portraits had been painted by Forster.[84] But despite this attempt to reverse the damage done by Miss FitzGibbon, the bailiff remained skeptical. Unable to challenge Forster's popularity in Canada, the bailiff turned his attention to the original likeness of Brock by questioning its authenticity. He made enquiries of Miss Tupper, who asserted that the copy of Brock's profile portrait (fig. 4), which Forster used for his own rendition, as well as the original (fig. 3), "have been always known in the family as Sir Isaac."[85] Thwarted once again, the bailiff decided that the best way to sabotage the purchase of Forster's painting was to question his artistic merit at a meeting of the States. By planting the seed of doubt in his opening remarks, the bailiff hoped his fellow members would decide on their own that Forster's portrait of Brock was not "good enough" for the Royal Court.

The debate began with another Carey addressing the cost of the larger painting (fig. 21). In keeping with a Guernseyman's high regard for economy, Deputy William Carey argued that "it was essential to get proper value for one's money." He then proceeded to read a letter from a well-known artist, who stated his belief that the States "would have a good bargain at £60."[86] Based on this recommendation, Deputy Carey thought the "picture did great credit to Mr. Forster, the artist." The Very Reverend Thomas Bell was not so sure. He thought it advisable to send the matter to committee and wait for a report.[87] But before his fellow members of the States had a chance to weigh the pros and cons of such a motion, the proceedings were upset by yet another Carey.

Jurat De Vic F. Carey was a retired major general in the British army, and one who now took on the additional role of art critic. As he bluntly pointed out: "Sir Isaac Brock is represented with a neck large enough for two."[88] This was not the portrait's only flaw. Brock appeared to be about six inches too short. His head was too big and not properly positioned. The right arm was not long enough, and it was also badly painted—as were the hands. As for the uniform, it was all wrong. Jurat Carey spoke

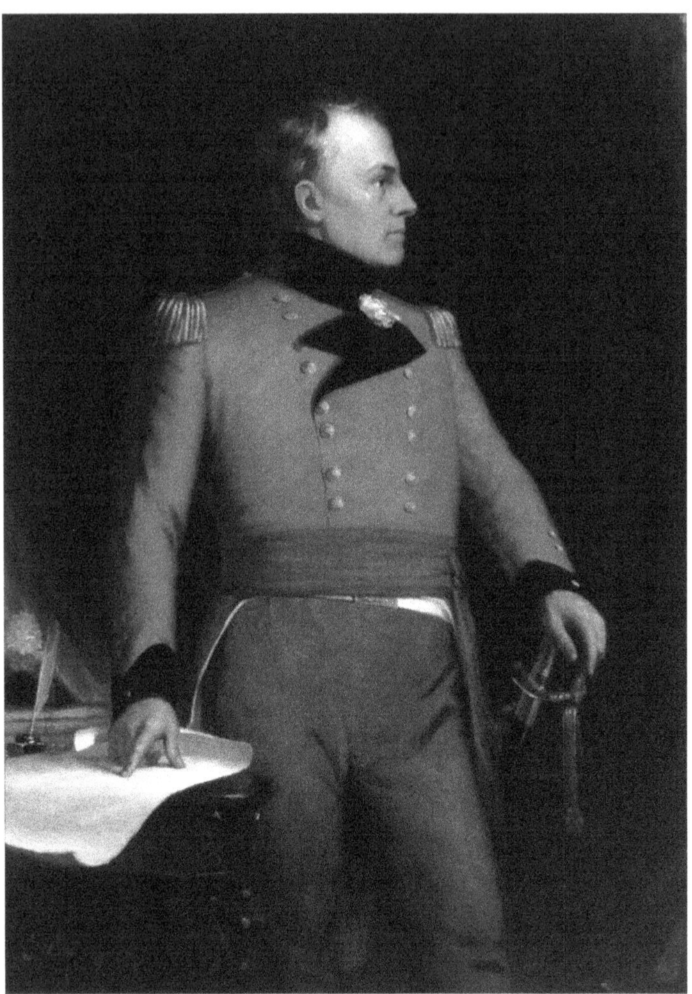

FIGURE 22.

with confidence, as he "was backed up" in what he had to say. But notwithstanding his severe critique, there was soon a more balanced view of Forster's work.[89]

Jurat Jean T.R. de Havilland suggested that perhaps "the faults might have been in the original [portrait]." Deputy James Le Page agreed, adding that "Sir Isaac Brock might have looked just as he is depicted, in which case the artist had only done his duty in representing him with all the deformities mentioned." Forster's support continued to grow, with several of the members echoing Rev. Bell's call for a committee. Bailiff Carey, however, thought they should simply choose an expert to decide, "as people differ in questions of art." But when Deputy Edouard Valpied alerted the assembly that such an "expert would charge a fair [or high] price for his opinion," the debate suddenly became rather subdued. It was then that the cost-conscious Deputy Carey warned the States about discussions on art, and how they "never came to an end." Faced with this frightening prospect, Jurat Jean Tardif proclaimed Forster to be a competent man, and so "there was no need to go further for an opinion."[90] The amendment for a committee was then withdrawn and the question put to a vote, which was carried by an "overwhelming majority" in favour of purchasing Forster's larger portrait of Brock.[91] The deed was done.

Despite the best efforts of Miss FitzGibbon and Bailiff Carey, Forster was still able to make a lucrative sale to the States of Guernsey. With it came the formal recognition that threatened to mitigate Miss Mickle's discovery. Yet, this advantage was never put to good use. Like General Robinson, Forster was leery of controversies. They were bad for business, and he was not about to alienate customers who might be interested in his line of Brock portraits. There was only one such sale, however, and that was to the Government of Ontario in 1900 (fig. 22).[92] As for the Robinsons, they finally decided to call off their crusade against the miniature (fig. 11)—mainly because the painting by George Berthon (fig. 9) was still recognized as the official portrait of Sir Isaac Brock.[93] And while Miss Mickle was never rewarded with great fame or fortune for her discovery, both she and Miss FitzGibbon derived great satisfaction from the miniature's acceptance as authentic and also in having browbeat their opponents—with the exception of one who was yet to be born.

4

Of Uniforms and Portraits

Ludwig Kosche was an unlikely Brock enthusiast. Having grown up in Germany during the 1930s, much of his childhood was dominated by Nazi ideology. Such an upbringing was hardly conducive to fostering an interest in the Canadian exploits of a long dead British general, and yet it was the rise of the Third Reich that ultimately brought Kosche into contact with the heroic story of Sir Isaac Brock. As a young man struggling to make his way in a ruined post-war economy, Kosche realized that he would have to seek out his future elsewhere and so in 1950 he immigrated to Canada. But after several years spent working on the railways of northern Ontario, he gave up a good and steady job for the uncertain life of an academic. In 1964, he began his undergraduate studies and two years later received a bachelor of arts degree in history. Kosche then went on to earn a master's degree in the same discipline—history, but not Canadian history. Preferring the familiarity of the German national experience, he chose an aspect of the First World War for his thesis topic. After successfully defending his research in April of 1969, Kosche might have pursued a doctorate and established himself as a professional historian.[1] He chose to become a librarian instead.[2]

By 1974, Kosche managed to land a job at the Ottawa Public Library.[3] Within a few years, however, he found employment more to his liking as the new librarian at the Canadian War Museum.[4] It was in this capacity that he began to develop an appreciation for Sir Isaac Brock, as one of the museum's most prized artifacts was Brock's undress or plain coatee (fig. 23)—the short close-fitting uniform coat he allegedly wore at the Battle of Queenston Heights.[5] The coatee had never been fully authenticated and so Kosche, a dedicated scholar, rose to the challenge. Eventually he concluded

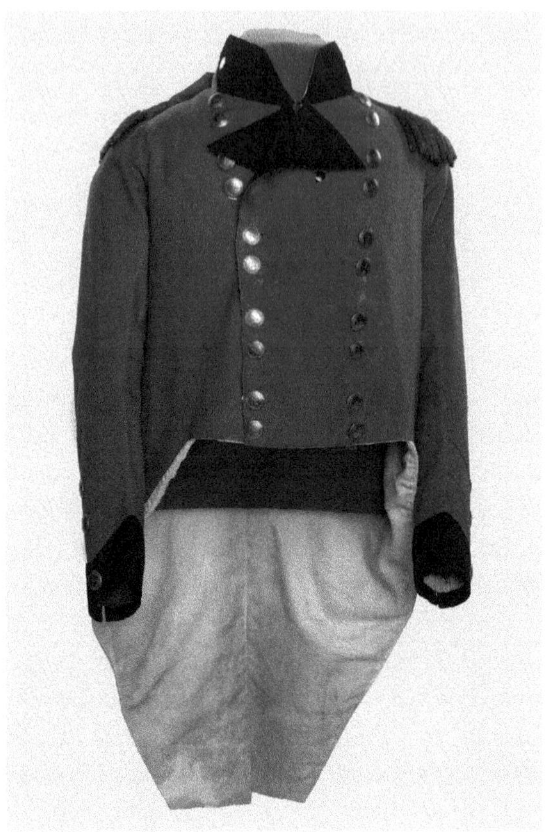

FIGURE 23.

that this coatee was in fact the one worn by Brock at the time of his death.[6] As part of his research, Kosche made a careful inspection of Brock's portraits by John Wycliffe Lowes Forster, including those in St. Peter Port and Toronto (figs 21, 22), as well as the study in Ottawa (fig. 16). Since Forster was thought to have worked from the actual brigadier general's coatee in which Brock was killed, Kosche treated these artworks as primary sources.[7] He also began investigating other portraits of Brock—initially for the sake of the uniform, and then for Brock's likeness itself.

This evolution began in April of 1978, when Kosche wrote to Captain Michael H.T. Mellish of St. Peter Port, Guernsey. He did so thinking that Captain Mellish, a collateral descendant of Sir Isaac Brock, might have documentation relating to the coatee. There was good reason to be

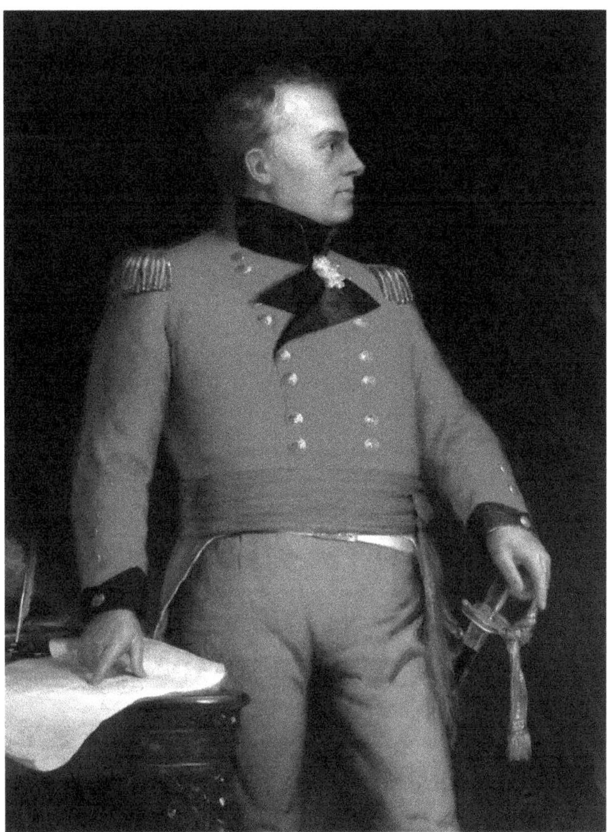

FIGURE 21.

optimistic. Captain Mellish was known to possess a profile portrait of his famous ancestor (fig. 3), not to mention certain other inherited heirlooms. Kosche thought there might also be an archival component as well. It was an intriguing possibility, and since he was planning a research trip to Guernsey for early the next month, Kosche hoped a visit to Captain Mellish might be added to his itinerary.[8] The captain was agreeable, but unfortunately had nothing in the way of old family papers—although he was happy to let Kosche come and view his Brock heirlooms. Kosche took up the invitation, mainly because he wanted to discuss the brigadier general's coatee.[9] He had already decided that the uniform in the profile portrait represented a lower rank, and so that artwork was of little interest. But there was another attraction in Guernsey. Forster's portrait of Brock at the

Royal Court (fig. 21) held great appeal, as it contained an abundance of visual information regarding the coatee—all of which Kosche anticipated putting to good use back in Ottawa.

Before taking his leave of the Royal Court, Kosche requested a colour photograph of Brock's portrait. But nearly five months later, he was still waiting for action on the part of the deputy greffier (or deputy registrar). While the necessary arrangements were even then being made, the process was proving far too slow for Kosche. Having given up on the deputy greffier, an exasperated Kosche wrote to Captain Mellish in hopes that it might be possible to have the photographic work done more quickly by someone else.[10] The captain, however, preferred to use a gentler approach in trying to move things along. As secretary and aide-de-camp to the lieutenant governor of Guernsey, Captain Mellish thought he could bring about the desired result simply by mentioning it to the deputy greffier. He was right. A few weeks later, the captain was able to report that the request was "in hand."[11] A grateful Kosche reciprocated by sharing his research with Captain Mellish, who in turn became a source of much encouragement. This moral support meant a great deal to Kosche, especially as he was beginning to feel underappreciated at the Canadian War Museum.[12]

In December of 1978, Kosche wrote to Captain Mellish about some minor differences he noticed in two of Forster's portraits of Brock. While comparing photographs of the painting at the Ontario Legislature (fig. 22) with its study (fig. 16), he saw that the stock around Brock's neck and the sash at his waist differed from one artwork to the other.[13] An inscription on the back of the study indicated that Forster had used the "original portrait in the possession of John Savery Carey" as a reference, which was reason enough for Kosche to suspect that the artistic representation of Brock's uniform might not be entirely accurate. Although he assumed this "original portrait" was the profile portrait Captain Mellish had hanging in his sitting room (fig. 3), it was actually Carey's copy (fig. 4).[14] The likenesses, however, were essentially the same, and Kosche noticed that the uniforms in the profile portraits were very similar to those depicted in Forster's portrayals. This was a cause for concern, as it suggested that Forster might have relied too heavily on the profile portrait—the portrait that showed Brock as a colonel. But in the end, Kosche appears to have satisfied himself that Forster's interest in the profile portrait was limited to Brock's face.[15]

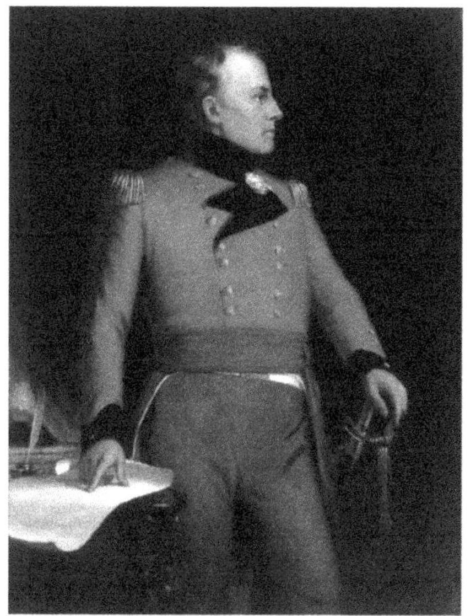

FIGURE 22.

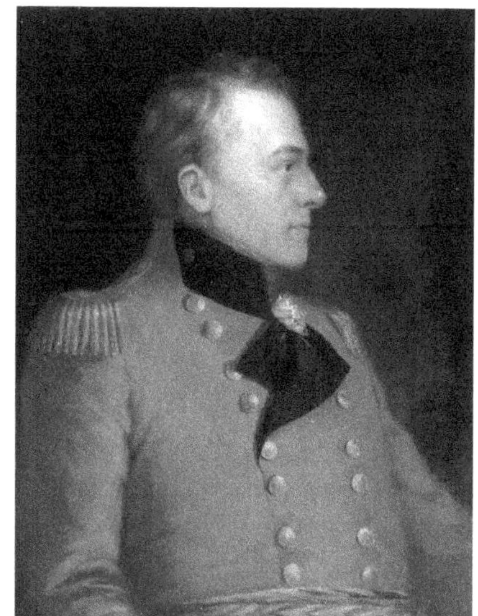

FIGURE 16.

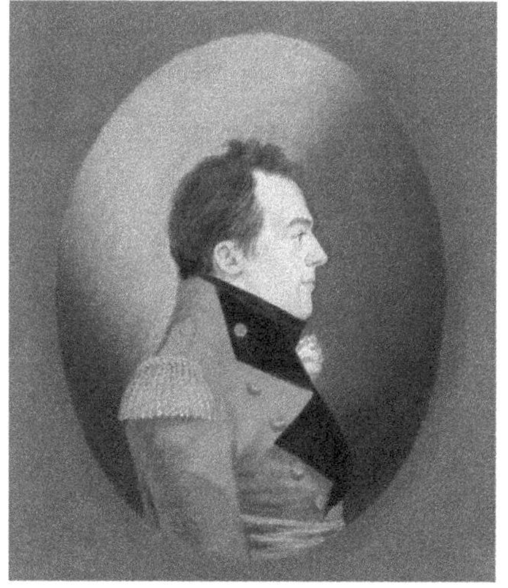

FIGURE 3.

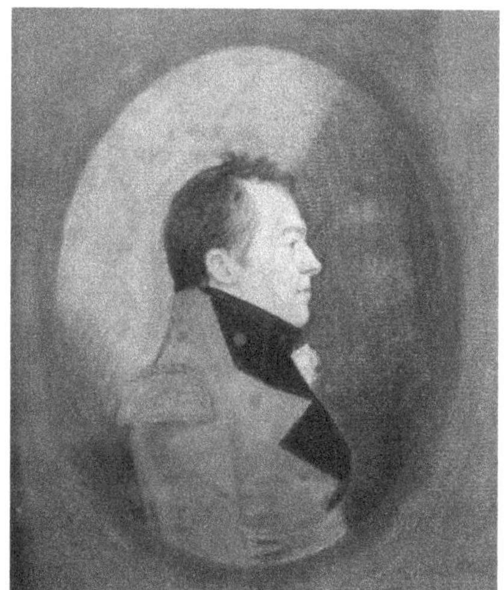

FIGURE 4.

Presumably, he came to this conclusion after taking the portrait's age into consideration. It stood to reason that if the profile portrait was painted earlier than 1808, when Brock was appointed brigadier general, then the uniform it featured could not be the coatee at the Canadian War Museum (which was very definitely that of a brigadier general). But in attempting to eliminate the profile portrait by means of its age, Kosche came across a date of 1811. This made "no sense," however, as Brock was known to have been in Canada by that time, and the profile portrait was supposed to have been commissioned in England sometime earlier.[16] Captain Mellish was asked for the date from his sources, which he provided by way of the following reply: "The portrait I have between the windows in my sitting room has been attributed by the British Museum authorities to [James] Sharples, and the date is around 1806 when Sir Isaac was a colonel and it is thought to have been done in London."[17] While much of this information was obviously based on family tradition, the attribution itself appeared to be well sourced. What Kosche could not have known, however, is the extent to which the attribution was influenced by a pleasant trip to Canada.

In June of 1965, Captain and Mrs. Mellish were the guests of honour at the opening of a new branch of the Royal Trust Company in St. Catharines, Ontario. As Brock's nearest relative, the captain was fêted with much pomp and ceremony.[18] He was also treated to a tour of the newly chartered Brock University, which was named in honour of his highly regarded ancestor. It was in the library there that Captain Mellish was "shown a book about Sir Isaac," with what appeared to be Brock's profile portrait serving as the frontispiece.[19] However, the artist was listed as Alyn Williams, which suggests the copy of the profile portrait he painted for Miss Agnes FitzGibbon in 1897 (fig. 19). For Captain Mellish, this duplication and the reference to Williams came as a surprise—or rather the latest surprise. Two days earlier, during a visit to the Niagara Historical Society Museum in Niagara-on-the-Lake, the captain had seen a photograph of Brock's portrait.[20] Strangely, it was nothing like the one he had back in Guernsey; the caption identified the artist as a J. Hudson. This was the same artist who painted the miniature discovered by Miss Sara Mickle in 1896 (fig. 11).[21] But Captain Mellish had no knowledge of any portraits of Brock other than his own profile portrait of a middle-aged officer (fig. 3) and the miniature featuring a young ensign (fig. 27). The

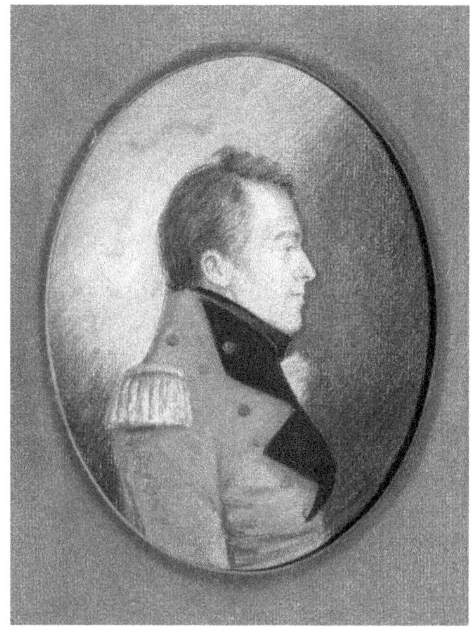

Figure 19.

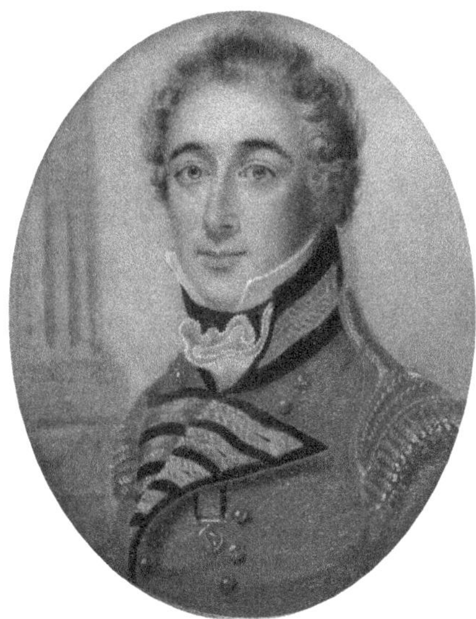

Figure 11.

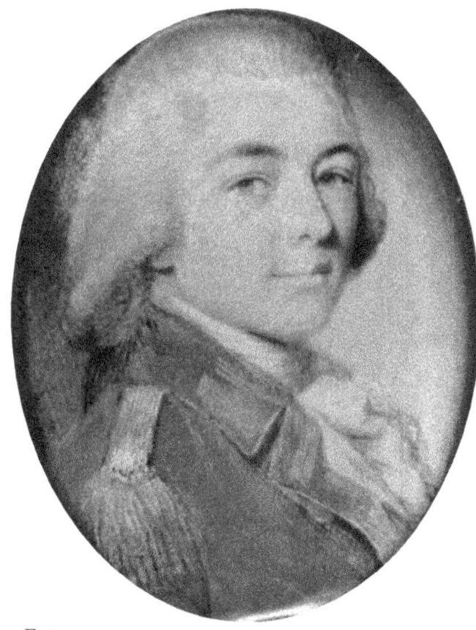

Figure 27.

sudden complication was extremely vexing, and although the captain became somewhat confused as to which of these new renderings was most like the unsigned profile portrait owned by him, he became determined to know the artist's true identity.

Not long after he departed Canada, Captain Mellish addressed a letter to the Keeper of Prints and Drawings at the British Museum, hoping that it might result in an attribution for the unsigned profile portrait.[22] But the reply he received from the senior research assistant, Reginald Williams, was disappointing. Williams had no records that might help to establish the name of the artist.[23] However, since the portrait described by Captain Mellish seemed to be an oil painting, he thought it might be worthwhile contacting the National Portrait Gallery, as the staff there were specialists in that medium. Before closing, Williams offered to make further enquiries on the captain's behalf—provided the portrait was actually a drawing. But Captain Mellish, either misunderstanding or ignoring the stipulation, went ahead and asked Williams "to get in touch with [the] National Portrait Gallery."[24]

An indulgent Williams consulted one of the curators at the National Portrait Gallery, but the meeting was unproductive and so there was nothing further he could do . . . unless Captain Mellish was willing to send the profile portrait to London for a personal examination. As Williams explained, it was the only way to attempt an identification of the artist.[25] Captain Mellish readily agreed to the proposal, but he also took the added precaution of making the delivery himself.[26] Several months later, in January of 1966, there was finally news of an attribution. Williams thought he saw a strong similarity with the work of James Sharples, an English itinerant artist who travelled extensively in the United States. "I am not saying that your portrait is certainly by him," Williams clarified, "but it is close enough to make an attribution."[27] The curator at the National Portrait Gallery came to the same conclusion, as did another curator on the staff of the City Art Gallery in Bristol. But Captain Mellish, now more observant, noticed a discrepancy.

In a biographical sketch supplied by Williams himself, it was recorded that Sharples went to the United States in about 1796 and that he was still there at the time of his death in 1811. This information (which was later found to be incorrect) contradicted what Captain Mellish had come to understand, namely that Brock sat for his portrait in London during his last trip home in 1806.[28] Some other artist must have painted Brock's profile portrait, as the biographical sketch placed Sharples squarely in the United States when Brock took his leave of absence. Although rather a sizeable discrepancy, Captain Mellish merely wished to voice his concern over it. As he pointed out to Williams: "It is possible of course that [Sharples] may have visited Canada, and painted the picture there, but bearing in mind the political feeling between the United States [and] Great Britain . . . at that time, I wonder if this could be so."[29] Obviously, the captain was not entirely comfortable with the attribution to Sharples, but he never suggested a follow-up—nor did Williams offer one.

Perhaps because a more eligible artist was lacking, the attribution to James Sharples was allowed to stand. However, this tenuous state of affairs was soon put to the test after a certain librarian came on the scene in the late 1970s. Initially, Kosche was only mildly interested in the profile portrait (fig. 3), and primarily because he wanted to eliminate the complication it posed to his study of Brock's uniform. When he learned from Captain Mellish that this portrait was painted five years earlier than his unidentified source claimed, there was no containing his happiness. "It is exactly what I was looking for," he informed the captain, "and it fits the facts."[30] Since Brock was a colonel when he supposedly sat for his portrait in 1806, and the coatee in the Canadian War Museum reflected Brock's appointment to brigadier general in 1808, Kosche was able to dismiss the profile portrait for being too early. But these facts were soon contested.

Towards the end of May 1979, Kosche shared an interesting tidbit with Captain Mellish. It was discovered in a letter at the Public Archives of Canada penned by John Andre, a deputy clerk with the planning board for the Borough of York (now part of Toronto).[31] In his letter, Andre pronounced the profile portrait to be the work of William Berczy, a Bavarian artist, architect, and settlement agent who was active during the early years of Upper Canada.[32] There was absolutely no doubt in Andre's mind: "my qualifications entitle me to such an opinion, officially."[33] These official qualifications, it would seem, were linked to his status as Berczy's biographer.[34] One of the illustrations Andre used in his book was Brock's original profile portrait, which the caption dated to 1811.[35] This was the same year Kosche had come across earlier, suggesting that his unidentified source might very well have been Andre's biography of Berczy. Although Kosche preferred the date of 1806 (as assigned by Captain Mellish), he nevertheless thought that Andre's attribution held potential. If Berczy actually painted the profile portrait, then it might perhaps allow for a confirmation of the date as Berczy was a well-documented early Canadian artist.

With his research into the coatee completed and ready for publication, Kosche was free to satisfy his curiosity about Brock's profile portrait. Armed with a colour photograph, courtesy of Captain Mellish, he set out to test Andre's attribution to Berczy.[36] It was late in 1979 when Kosche secured the help of his friend, Dr. Alan McNairn, who was then an assistant curator of European art at the National Gallery of Canada. Using the photograph of Brock's profile portrait, Dr. McNairn compared it with other known works by Berczy and Sharples. By the end of January 1980, Kosche was able to share the results with Captain Mellish. Dr. McNairn had no doubt that the portrait was the work of William Berczy.[37] Upon receiving this confirmation, Kosche decided to ask Andre how he had come up with Berczy as the artist. The answer he received was both evasive and vague. Andre recalled that his attribution was based in part on tradition, but he was unable to be more specific.[38] However, he promised to go back over his notes. In the meantime, Kosche waited on the captain's reply. Bolstered by Dr. McNairn's credentials, he fully expected that Captain Mellish would welcome the news of an attribution to Berczy, as well as yet another date for the profile portrait.

When Kosche wrote to Captain Mellish about the new attribution, he also let it be known that he now thought 1809 was the most likely date for the profile portrait. The captain must have been astonished, as Brock sat for his portrait while wearing his colonel's uniform. This rank, of course, was more in keeping with a date of 1806 as Brock remained a colonel until appointed a brigadier general in 1808. But in light of the new attribution, Kosche decided that 1809 seemed more credible because "both Berczy and Brock were at that time in Quebec [City]."[39] Obviously, Kosche was trying to make the new attribution fit Brock's military career and he tried to do so by citing a flaw in the attribution to James Sharples, namely his residence in Bath during the first half of 1806.[40] Such an abode, Kosche reasoned, would not have allowed for the profile portrait, as Brock apparently never made it beyond London during his leave in 1806, except to visit family in Guernsey.[41] Kosche seemed to think that by ruling out any possibility of a sitting with Sharples, he could safely disregard a date of 1806 for the profile portrait, which was necessary in order to accommodate the 1809 attribution to Berczy. What Kosche failed to take into account when writing to Captain Mellish, however, was the uniform Brock wore at the time of his sitting.

When Captain Mellish replied to the letter from Kosche early in March of 1980, he was inclined to go along with the new attribution to William Berczy because it was endorsed by a curator at the National Gallery of Canada.[42] Besides which, the captain had long-standing doubts about the attribution to Sharples. From what Captain Mellish was led to believe, Sharples was living in the United States during Brock's leave in 1806. Therefore, an attribution to him was unlikely. And it remained no less doubtful once Kosche established that Sharples was known to have been at Bath for a portion of that year.[43] But as for the revised date, there was no comment from Captain Mellish. Perhaps it was just an oversight, or perhaps he was trying to avoid being disagreeable. Then again, perhaps the captain saw no good reason to reject 1806 just because it was now thought that a Canadian artist painted Brock's profile portrait. After all, there was always the possibility that the sitting took place upon Brock's return to Canada.[44] Moreover, Brock was portrayed as a colonel and he was indeed known to have held that rank in 1806. Since Brock remained a colonel until his appointment to brigadier general in 1808, and because the uniform in the portrait was that of a colonel, the revised date of 1809 was simply too late. But while the captain probably thought 1806 was a better choice, he seems to have preferred keeping that opinion to himself. If so, the time was fast approaching when he would have to take a stand.

As Kosche awaited the captain's reply, he finally got word back from John Andre. But far from providing a definite reason for having attributed Brock's profile portrait to Berczy, Andre sidestepped the issue by raising a new one. Picking up on Kosche's earlier observation, namely the similarity between several of Berczy's portraits in terms of backgrounds and uniforms, Andre now agreed that they might have been "pre-drawn," or rather pre-painted, and he went so far as to produce documentation of it.[45] This documentation was a letter from Jacques Viger to Berczy's son in 1827. Viger, a sort of Québécois Renaissance man from Montreal, expressed his belief that a portrait of Frontenac by the senior Berczy had been unsaleable because it reminded too many people of the former British governor Sir James H. Craig (who did nothing to endear himself to the French Canadian population).[46] Andre took Viger's remark to mean that Berczy's portraits looked similar to one another because they were mass-produced, just as Kosche seemed to suggest. But whereas Viger's criticism was directed against only one portrait, Andre implicated the entire body of Berczy's work—including the profile portrait of Brock owned by Captain Mellish (fig. 3). In the end, it was nothing more than a red herring.

Andre was stalling for time, and not only for the sake of an attribution. He was desperate to find some means of justifying the date he ascribed to Brock's profile portrait, as Kosche wanted a source for that as well. But Andre was having trouble coming up with the necessary paperwork. No doubt fearing that his reputation as Berczy's biographer would suffer because of it, Andre suddenly found a novel way to save face. In agreeing with Kosche about the possibility of "pre-drawn" backgrounds and uniforms, Andre speculated that Berczy might have painted Brock's portrait without the benefit of a sitting.[47] Berczy was known to have met with various officials in the Canadas, both civil and military, and so Andre thought it entirely possible that Berczy had a recollection of Brock from some earlier encounter in Lower Canada. Such a meeting would have allowed Berczy to become familiar with Brock's features, giving the artist sufficient knowledge of his subject to paint a portrait from memory. As for Berczy's need to engage in such clandestine portraiture, it stemmed from his claims against the Upper Canadian government. Plagued by considerable difficulties in procuring tracts of land for his settlement scheme, the advent of Brock's administration of Upper Canada in October of 1811 offered Berczy renewed hope for a resolution. This change of leadership coincided with the date Andre gave Brock's profile portrait. Knowing that Berczy had wasted little time in restating his case, Andre assumed that he did so with a petition to Brock. Neither did Andre think it unreasonable that Berczy might have sent along a small portrait of Brock, done from memory on a pre-painted background, "just to stress the fact that he had met him previously in Montreal"—and presumably to curry favour.[48]

Unfortunately, there is no such petition—and no grounds for thinking there ever was one.[49] Berczy probably submitted his case to Brock by means of a less formal letter, which he called his "application," and which Andre took to mean a petition.[50] But even if Andre knew of Berczy's misleading nomenclature, it is unlikely that it would have caused him the slightest concern. Judging from the manner in which he interpreted historical evidence, he would have taken some other liberty with the facts.[51] However, he could have saved himself all the trouble by simply admitting that he should have given Brock's profile portrait a date of circa 1811. But as Berczy's official biographer, Andre could not acknowledge that he had guessed incorrectly. Instead, he devised an outlandish explanation for his choice of 1811 "as the most probable date."[52]

Kosche, however, was not impressed with John Andre's overwrought explanation, especially with regard to the date of Brock's profile portrait. He also doubted that it was painted from memory, or that Berczy made use of pre-painted backgrounds and uniforms—even though it was Kosche himself who first suggested the idea. He now knew something about the portrait that exonerated Berczy of prefabrication. It was the stock around Brock's neck. Unlike the regulation black silk prescribed for general officers, this one appeared to be fashioned out of a dark green fabric with a "tartan-like" (or plaid) design.[53] Actually, Kosche had the wrong impression, but the variation he perceived convinced him that Brock's profile portrait was in fact "the result of an actual sitting."[54] And since Andre's date of 1811 was obviously lacking in solid evidence, Kosche simply replaced it with his own reckoning of 1809. There was just one problem. If Brock sat for his portrait in 1809, then—strictly speaking—he should have been wearing his brigadier general's uniform. After all, he was appointed a brigadier general early in 1808. But the coatee shown in the profile portrait (fig. 3) certainly appeared to be that of a colonel.[55] This was the rank Brock held in 1806, which—according to the family tradition related by Captain Mellish—was the same year that Brock sat for his portrait. Kosche could not abide such an early date, as it did not allow for a meeting between Berczy and Brock in 1809. The chronology was a problem, indeed—and one that demanded a solution.

Kosche began by wondering if Brock's uniform was simply outdated, possibly because of a delay in the arrival of his new wardrobe.[56] While officers of the British army stationed in distant outposts did have to wait inordinate lengths of time for their outfits to arrive, Kosche had to explain why a recently appointed brigadier general would not have delayed sitting for his portrait until such time as he could be portrayed in the latest fashion. Kosche found what he thought to be a perfectly good excuse in Brock's fortieth birthday, which was celebrated in October of 1809. In a move highly reminiscent of Andre's self-serving approach to historical analysis, Kosche jumped to the conclusion that Brock must have marked the occasion with a portrait—without bothering to wait for the arrival of his replacement uniform. In sharing this insight with Captain Mellish, Kosche asked: "Is it not possible that [Brock] had a portrait of himself done at this time to send home for this very reason?"[57] With this goading, the captain finally had to assert himself by replying: "I believe it will be difficult to establish the date."[58]

Although subtle, the rejection was unequivocal. A deflated Kosche was mystified, "given all the factors" which pointed to 1809 as the most likely date for the profile portrait.[59] But he also had to agree that dating the portrait was not going to be easy, as there was no obvious means by which to establish its age. Yet, he was still hopeful that it could be narrowed down "on the basis of indirect, rather than direct data [or evidence]."[60] There the matter stood until early May of 1980, when Kosche sent Captain Mellish his research into the coatee. It came in the form of an article entitled "Relics of Brock," and while the captain did not receive his copy until late in June, the arrival of this offprint proved to be very well timed.[61]

Having turned his attention to several other research projects, Kosche was beginning to lose interest in Brock's profile portrait. One of the distractions was a gold pocket watch, said to have belonged to Sir Isaac Brock. There was also a Nazi staff car, which was reputed to have been used by Adolf Hitler on his various tours of the Third Reich.[62] Both of these artifacts numbered among the collections of the Canadian War Museum, and Kosche spared no pains in going after their respective provenance. Either one of them could have occupied most of his time for much of the foreseeable future. Consequently, his research into Brock's portraits might have been put on hold indefinitely. But then he received a letter from Guernsey. At the end of June 1980, Captain Mellish wrote to thank him for the "Relics of Brock" article, which he described as a "splendid effort." The captain's "generous words" had a profound effect on Kosche, whose interest in Brock's portraits became firmly established as a result—despite a major hurdle.[63]

As Kosche tried to restart an earlier investigation into the miniature discovered by Miss Mickle (fig. 11), which he originally undertook for the sake of Brock's coatee, his request for a colour reproduction of the little portrait went nowhere.[64] Unable to prevail upon its owner, the Women's Canadian Historical Society of Toronto, Kosche resumed work on his other projects. In August of 1981, he published an article on the pocket watch in which he argued against any association with Brock.[65] He then focused much of his energy on the Nazi staff car, during which time his research into Brock's portraits began to languish again.[66] But towards the end of that same summer, Kosche had his interest renewed when he happened to make the acquaintance of a Brock descendant living in Toronto. Robert Arthur was at best a distant relative, but he told a captivating story. It involved a miniature he sold to the Province of Ontario in 1964.[67]

This new miniature (fig. 24) was said to portray Sir Isaac Brock, and when Kosche learned that it had been presented to Brock University in St. Catharines, he promptly enlisted the aid of Dr. Wesley Turner in obtaining a copy. Dr. Turner, a history professor whose research interests included the university's namesake, was agreeable and soon had colour photographs of the miniature sent to Kosche for his inspection.[68] Considering all the frustration Kosche encountered with the Women's Canadian Historical Society of Toronto, he must have been very pleased with the prompt service. But while an elaborate label on the back of the miniature identified the sitter as "Major Gen. Sir Isaac Brock," the uniform was definitely not one that Brock would have worn. The miniature could not be a portrait of him. Nevertheless, a barely distinguishable number in one of the buttons gave Kosche hope that it might be possible to identify the regiment and perhaps the sitter.[69] It was a tantalizing prospect, but Kosche had to resist the temptation. He was far too busy finishing other research projects. The new miniature, however, gave him further reason to believe that Brock's various portraits might make for an interesting study.[70] And once again, it was Captain Mellish who encouraged the endeavour.

During another trip to Europe in April of 1982, Kosche spent a few days in Guernsey and conferred with Captain Mellish about Brock's portraits. Much of their conversation was spent discussing a photograph of the new miniature of Brock (fig. 24), which Kosche sent to the captain in advance of his visit. But it was only after he departed that Captain Mellish noticed something unusual. The sitter in this new miniature bore an uncanny resemblance to Brock's older brother. The captain's suspicion was confirmed by another miniature he owned, which was long held to be that of John Brock as an officer in the 8th (or King's) Regiment (fig. 25).[71] Captain Mellish was rather cautious in breaking the news, perhaps because the label on the back of the new miniature was so elaborately designed that it seemed incontrovertible. Kosche, however, was quite excited by the captain's observation, and soon arranged for another meeting with Robert Arthur in August of 1982. Knowing that Arthur had a pencil sketch of his ancestor, John Savery Brock (fig. 26), Kosche wanted to see how it compared with the new miniature.[72] Unfortunately, Kosche mistook John Savery Brock for John Brock. It was easily enough done, as there were two Brock brothers named John.[73] One was the eldest son of the family, who was known simply as John Brock. The other was John Savery Brock, who usually went by his middle name and thereby avoided much confusion. Kosche was unaware of this peculiarity, but he knew something was amiss when he saw that John Savery Brock looked nothing like the sitter in the new miniature.

Kosche checked the published army lists (in essence, a directory of British army officers), but there was no Captain John Savery Brock. However, there was a paymaster named Savery Brock, although he had served with the 49th Regiment and not the 8th Regiment.[74] Also, the facings of the 49th were full (or bluish) green, while those of the officer in the new miniature were a pale yellow.[75] This was an important point, because some of the army lists made reference to a Captain John Brock of the 81st Regiment, and that regiment's facings were buff (or pale yellow).[76] Once again, the number in the button became noteworthy. If it was eighty-one, then the sitter was probably Captain John Brock—just as Captain Mellish presumed.

The question was finally decided in favour of the 81st Regiment, and with this outcome Kosche concluded that the new miniature had been mislabelled.[77] While not a portrait of Captain Isaac Brock, the extra likeness of his older brother was still a nice find. It complemented the miniature of Lieutenant John Brock (fig. 25), which portrayed him as a younger looking officer in a uniform with blue facings. As Kosche was able to verify, these

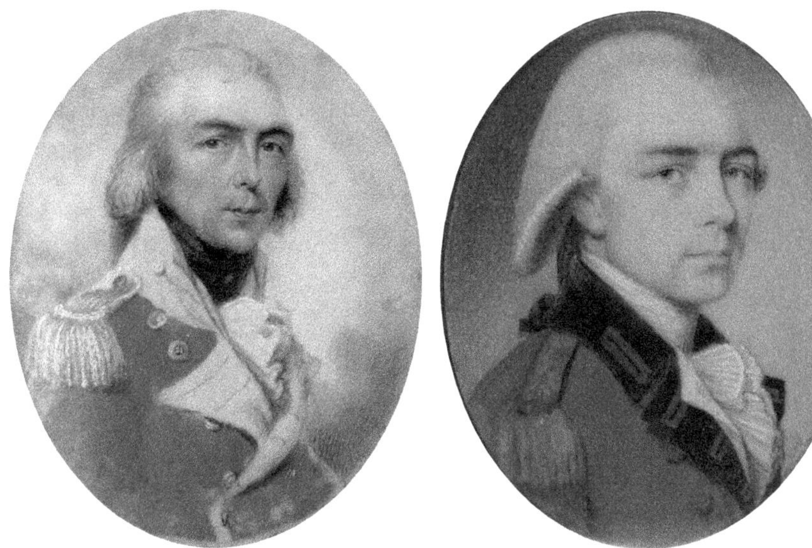
FIGURE 24.

FIGURE 25.

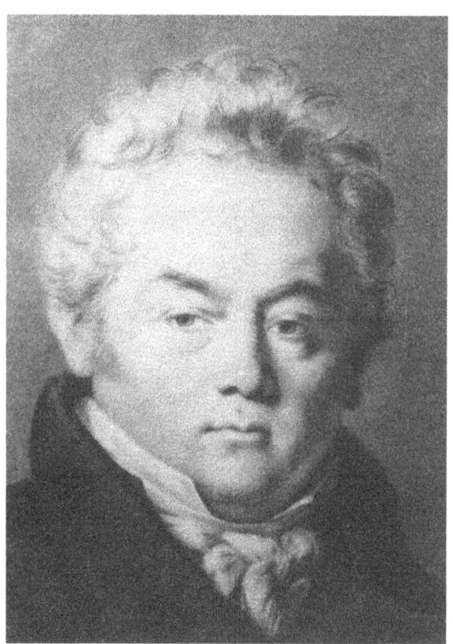
FIGURE 26.

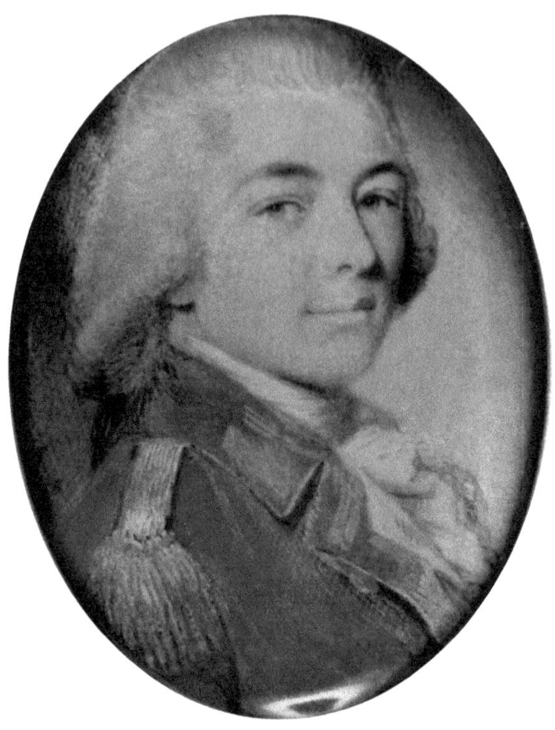

FIGURE 27.

were the facings of the 8th Regiment—the same regiment in which John Brock began his military career.[78] These facings also matched those in another miniature owned by Captain Mellish, which was confidently said to portray Isaac Brock as a young ensign in the 8th Regiment (fig. 27). Family tradition linked these latter miniatures to Philip Jean, a renowned portrait painter from the nearby Channel Island of Jersey.[79] And based on Brock's youthful appearance, it was taken for granted that Jean painted his miniature soon after he received his ensign's commission in 1785.[80]

Kosche was heartened by these findings, and also by those resulting from his interactions with Robert Arthur. In the course of their second meeting, Kosche produced a colour photograph of a full-length portrait (fig. 28). It was believed to show Brock as a captain in the 49th Regiment, circa 1792.[81] Kosche had known of this portrait since the early months of 1980, but it was proving extremely difficult to trace.[82] Much to his amazement, however, Arthur remembered the elusive portrait from his

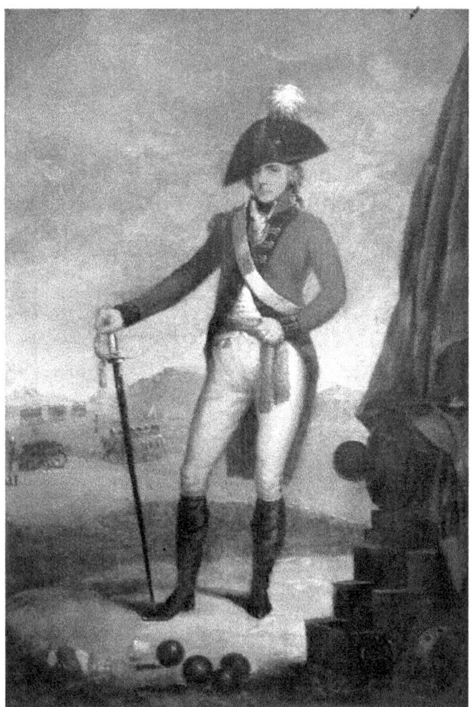

FIGURE 28.

childhood in Guernsey. The owner was a relative of his by the name of Mrs. Sowels, and upon her death the portrait was bequeathed to the States of Guernsey.[83] With this intelligence, Kosche promptly enlisted the assistance of Captain Mellish in searching the Royal Court's art collection. But the full-length portrait was not to be found there, and it soon became evident why.[84]

In late September of 1982, Kosche had a visit from Dr. Alan Earp, who was then president of Brock University. Dr. Earp had come to deliver the miniature that had formerly belonged to Robert Arthur, and was now thought to portray Captain John Brock of the 81st Regiment (fig. 24). Kosche had requested this loan as part of his effort to decipher the number painted in one of the buttons on the sitter's chest.[85] The conscientious Dr. Earp also brought along a small collection of other Brock-related items, thinking they might be of some interest. Among the assembled items were two photographs, one of which Kosche instantly recognized.

It was Brock's profile portrait, or rather one of the painted copies.[86] For this reason, it did not elicit much of a reaction. But the other photograph was nothing short of riveting, since it featured the full-length portrait. As Dr. Earp explained, the original painting was owned by the Honourable P. Michael Pitfield, clerk of Canada's Privy Council and secretary to the cabinet of Prime Minister Pierre Elliott Trudeau.[87] It was a marvellous find, and Kosche soon entered into communication with Pitfield—"a rather high-powered bureaucrat."

Although Kosche was determined to investigate this new lead, he had to wait until the summer of 1983 before finally receiving permission for a detailed examination of the full-length portrait. René Chartrand was asked to help, and as a curator from Parks Canada who specialized in the history of military uniforms, he quickly came up with a number of troubling discrepancies. Most notably, the colour of the facings was not consistent with those of a captain in the 49th Regiment. Instead of green, the colour designated for that regiment, the lapels, cuffs, and even the lining of the skirts all looked to be blue.[88] There was no mistaking the implication. If the facings were any colour other than green, then the officer in the full-length portrait could not possibly be Captain Isaac Brock. Another examination, more scientific in nature, was conducted at the National Gallery of Canada. Using both ultra-violet and infra-red light, assistant curator Michael Pantazzi was able to detect evidence of a selective cleaning and a repositioning of the right arm. Unfortunately, there was no sign of an inscription or signature to help in identifying either the artist or his sitter. But Pantazzi did succeed in verifying the colour of the facings. They were blue.[89]

René Chartrand was vindicated, but in trying to establish the actual regiment according to the blue facings, he was stymied.[90] Still, he did succeed in revising the age of the full-length portrait from its former approximate date of 1792 to sometime between 1801 and 1803. While the style of sword and hat both pointed to the latter 1790s, he doubted that the painting could have been commissioned prior to 1801. Chartrand drew this conclusion from the draped flag displayed in the portrait, which he identified as the Union Flag of Great Britain—or the Union Jack, as it is commonly known. This flag, redesigned to include the Irish cross of St. Patrick, was first unfurled in 1801.[91] But Brock was already a lieutenant colonel by then, and in a regiment with green facings.[92] Therefore, as Kosche realized, the officer in the full-length portrait had to be someone else, perhaps even his older brother. In returning to the army lists, Kosche found several entries for John Brock between 1802 and 1804, all of which listed him as the captain of an Independent Company of Invalids in Jersey. When a dress regulation was found for the officers commanding these units, the blue facings it described seemed a perfect match for the uniform in the full-length portrait (fig. 28).[93] With this apparent meshing of evidence, Kosche was convinced that the officer was none other than Captain John Brock . . . regardless of some annoying evidence to the contrary.

As Ferdinand Brock Tupper revealed as far back as 1845, his uncle—then lieutenant colonel—John Brock was killed in a duel at the Cape of Good Hope in July of 1801.[94] But Kosche chose to put his faith in the army lists, which recorded John Brock as a captain of the Jersey Invalids until at least 1804, and so Tupper was blamed for having gotten the date wrong. But had Kosche done some fact checking, he might have seen that Tupper was right.[95] While John Brock had been appointed a captain of the Jersey Invalids in April of 1801, the transfer did not take place before he was killed the following July—at which time he was still serving as a brevet lieutenant colonel of the 81st Regiment.[96] The army lists, however, continued to publish the appointment as if it had actually taken place. It was a misprint, of course, and one that went unnoticed until somebody at the War Office finally began to comprehend that Captain Brock was dead. Due in part to this unfortunate slip-up, Kosche incorrectly identified the officer in the full-length portrait as Captain John Brock of the Jersey Invalids, circa 1801–04. Certainly, the uniform and its blue facings seemed to confirm Captain Brock's new posting to the Jersey Invalids.[97] But if the truth be known, Lieutenant Colonel John Brock was still wearing a uniform with buff facings when he went off to fight his duel.

At the same time that Kosche was trying to make sense of the full-length portrait (fig. 28), there were a couple of very interesting developments. In January of 1983, Captain Mellish uncovered the copy of Brock's profile portrait (fig. 4). It was found in the Bailiff's Office as the captain followed-up on Kosche's earlier and now unnecessary request for information on the full-length portrait.[98] Unfortunately, the full-length portrait itself could not be located, as none of the "authorities" in Guernsey "have ever seen a picture like that here."[99] Kosche was not surprised, as he had already learned that the painting was in fact owned by the Honourable P. Michael Pitfield. The other development originated with a renewed attempt to obtain a colour photograph of the miniature Miss Sara Mickle had discovered (fig. 11). In February of 1983, several years after his first request, Kosche finally met with an encouraging response from the Women's Canadian Historical Society of Toronto. Like Kosche, the society's secretary harboured doubts about the authenticity of this miniature. But while Miss Lorna R. Procter was sympathetic, she remained silent for fear of causing a rift among the membership. By 1983, however, she was ready to take a chance for the sake of historical accuracy. The society was dying out, and an aged Miss Procter sensed the urgency in having certain outstanding matters resolved—the most pressing of which was the miniature.[100]

In complying with Kosche's request for a colour photograph, Miss Procter became overly protective of the resulting print. It took some very careful packaging before she would relinquish the picture to the care of the post office. But upon seeing the canvas bag into which the mail was thrown, she beat a hasty retreat for home.[101] Then she hit upon the idea of a bus trip to Ottawa, so that she could make the delivery in person. Fortunately for her, Kosche was planning his own trip to Toronto. Just as Miss Procter expected, Kosche was becoming impatient to have the photograph. Yet, her distrust of the postal system actually worked to his advantage. By going to meet with Miss Procter, Kosche was able to negotiate the loan of Miss Agnes FitzGibbon's notebook.[102] This notebook was really compiled by Miss Sara Mickle, who used it as a record of her efforts to test the authenticity of the miniature she discovered.[103] Kosche had known about the notebook for some three or four years, and he was curious to see if it might offer any clues about the miniature's provenance.[104] As it turned out, there was much useful information—so much, in fact, that he began transcribing it for his files.[105]

In working his way through the notebook, Kosche was alerted to the objections raised by Major General Charles W. Robinson.[106] There were some very troubling anomalies associated with the miniature, such as a wing where there should have been an epaulette, and a medal that Brock was never awarded. For these reasons, Kosche began to think that the

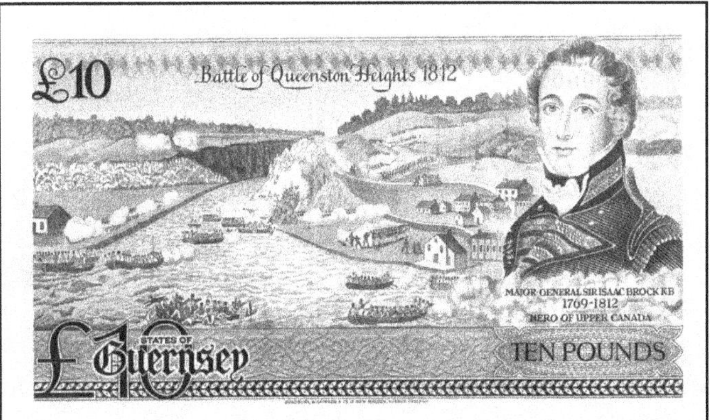

Figure 29a.

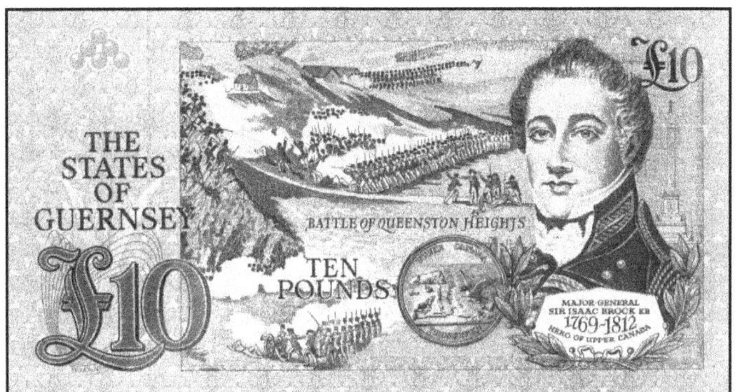

Figure 29b.

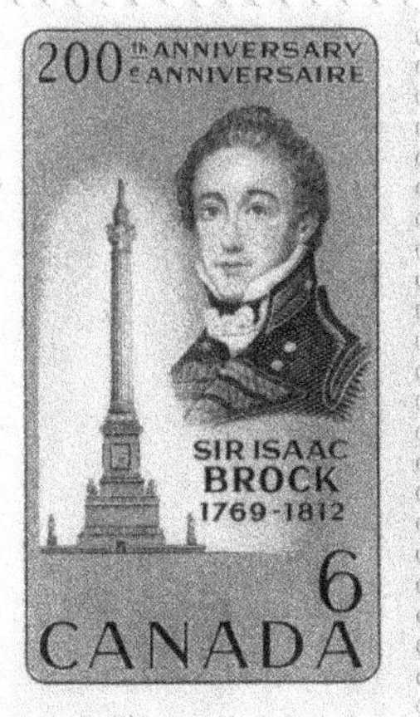

Figure 30.

miniature portrayed someone other than Brock. He also became obsessed with the idea of debunking Miss Mickle's discovery, and he knew exactly how to go about it. A minute examination of the colour photograph from Miss Procter was sure to yield overlooked details about the uniform, details that Kosche had no doubt would reveal a regiment completely unrelated to Brock's military career. The only thing better would be to unmask the impostor's true identity—and certain passages in Miss Mickle's notebook provided Kosche with valuable clues toward that end. When she documented the provenance of the miniature, Miss Mickle also included some very useful information regarding Captain George Dunn of the 23rd Regiment (the Royal Welch Fusiliers). Captain Dunn rated inclusion because he was the second husband of Mrs. James Wallace, the former Miss Matilda Short, who was said to have inherited the miniature from her sister, the wife of Captain James Brock.[107] Captain Brock was Sir Isaac Brock's cousin, and it was this relationship that Mrs. Heber Taylor used to vouch for the miniature she inherited from her great aunt (Mrs. Dunn).[108] But as Kosche sifted through the myriad details contained in Miss Mickle's notebook, he became convinced that Captain George Dunn had been mistaken for Sir Isaac Brock.[109]

In setting out to prove his hypothesis, Kosche confirmed that Captain Dunn served in the 23rd Regiment, not as captain, but rather first lieutenant and paymaster. Next came a thorough review of the uniform, which was conclusively shown to be that of the 23rd Regiment—a regiment with which Brock had no affiliation. An examination of the medal provided further evidence of a miniature portraying Captain Dunn. Just as Colonel Groves proposed in 1897, it was the Waterloo Medal—an award bestowed on every British soldier who participated in the defeat of Napoleon's army, including Lieutenant George Dunn.[110] Of course, the Battle of Waterloo was fought in June of 1815, nearly three years after Brock's death, and this chronological impossibility utterly disproved the miniature.[111] It did not portray Sir Isaac Brock as a junior officer. Rather, the likeness was that of an obscure but handsome young veteran of the Napoleonic Wars, whose image was mistakenly embraced as the "Hero of Upper Canada." Having been perpetuated in countless books, articles, three issues of a Guernsey banknote (fig. 29A–B), a Canadian postage stamp (fig. 30), and all manner of printed ephemera, the misconception was firmly entrenched in the Canadian psyche.[112] But no matter how deeply rooted the blunder, Kosche was determined to blow the whistle. Then he began to have second thoughts.

5

An Evolving History

The officer in the miniature discovered by Miss Mickle (fig. 11) portrayed Lieutenant George Dunn after the Battle of Waterloo, and not Major General Sir Isaac Brock as a junior officer. There was no doubt about it—yet Ludwig Kosche worried that any attempt to correct such a long-standing mistake would be highly contentious. It was therefore imperative to make the strongest case possible for Lieutenant Dunn. In order to do so, Kosche had to establish the miniature's date, confirm the sitter's identity, and supply a provenance. Only then would he feel comfortable in rewriting Canadian history. While Kosche was certainly up for the task, he soon found himself becoming overly dependent upon Miss Mickle's notebook. There was simply no other source for most of the information he required. And despite her bias in favour of the miniature being a portrait of Sir Isaac Brock, Miss Mickle's research was still quite useful.

The miniature's date had not been an issue previously, but now Kosche recognized the importance of being able to prove that it was painted subsequent to Brock's death in 1812. The miniature, however, was generally accepted to date from 1806, based on the curious 18X6 inscription it bore. Although he was unable to find any dating system which combined both Roman and Arabic numerals, Kosche was impressed by the cheque-writing analogy of Gerald S. Hayward—whose interpretation found a prominent place in Miss Mickle's notebook.[1] According to Hayward, it was a long-held banking practice to use XX to represent 00 or no cents. In like manner, an X had been substituted for a zero when the miniature was dated.[2] Kosche could see Hayward's point; unfortunately, it did not serve his purpose as there was a sizeable problem with such an early date—and it had to do with the sitter. He looked rather young to be an officer with

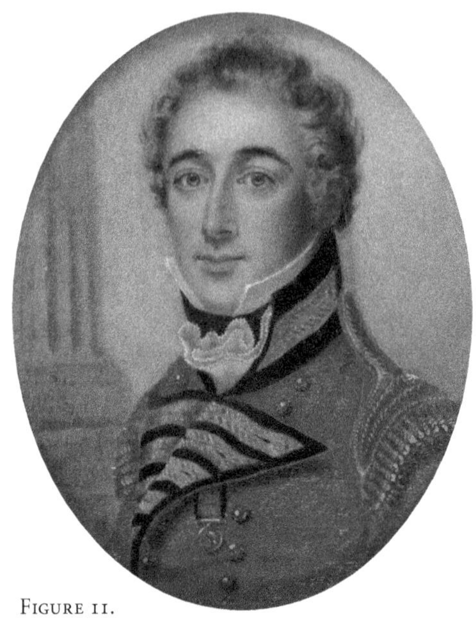

FIGURE 11.

some twenty years' worth of service, as was the case with Brock by 1806.[3] In mulling over this disparity, it occurred to Kosche that instead of a zero, perhaps the X was meant to represent a Roman numeral ten. Interpreted this way, the date suddenly became 1816. It was quite the eureka moment for Kosche, as 1816 was the first year in which the Waterloo Medal was awarded.[4] But to be absolutely sure of himself, Kosche had to find some viable explanation for the additional ten years.[5]

Various art experts were consulted in May and June of 1983, but none of them had ever encountered such an unusual method of dating a painting.[6] Eventually Kosche found what he needed in the judgement of a long-dead artist. Many years earlier, John Wycliffe Lowes Forster had dismissed the X as nothing more than the slip of a brush.[7] Kosche thought the idea compelling—even more so than Hayward's cheque-writing analogy or his own Roman numeral theory. A more objective source might have been preferable, given Forster's close association with the Robinsons, but Kosche was still satisfied that he had the right date for the miniature. And having established 1816 as the year it was painted, he was more at ease with the sitter's new identity. Before long, however, there would be a far better indicator that it was really Lieutenant George Dunn.

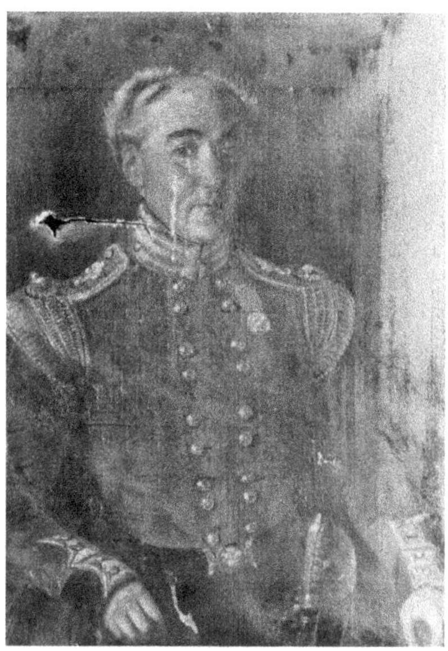

FIGURE 15.

Earlier, in January of 1983, Kosche was put in touch with a gentleman in Toronto who was said to have a portrait of Sir Isaac Brock. The gentleman, John Short, was a descendant of the same Short family with the connection to Captain James Brock.[8] This distinction lent a great deal of credibility to Short's claim and Kosche was anxious to see the portrait he possessed. Kosche became all the more eager in March, once he began poring over Miss Mickle's notebook. It was then that he learned of Mrs. Heber Taylor, the lady who owned the so-called miniature of Sir Isaac Brock (fig. 11), and how she too descended from the Short family. Suddenly the odds for yet another portrait of Brock seemed vastly improved. But when Kosche finally had a chance to view the portrait in November of 1983, he saw that it featured an elderly looking British officer (fig. 15). Since Brock was barely middle-aged at the time of his death, it was impossible that he could have been depicted as an old man. Thus Short's portrait did not depict Sir Isaac Brock. Yet, upon closer inspection, Kosche noticed something about the sitter's uniform that gave him pause. It looked very similar in style to the uniform in the miniature of Lieutenant George Dunn. There was also what appeared to be the Waterloo Medal. After securing a photograph of the portrait and conducting further research, Kosche was able to identify the uniform as that of the 23rd Regiment, the Royal Welch Fusiliers.[9] And once he established that the sitter was in fact wearing the Waterloo Medal, Kosch was confident that he knew the identity of the elderly officer. It was none other than Lieutenant George Dunn.

During his investigation, Kosche might have derived some benefit had he known about the "wild Harum Scarum man" incident. Unfortunately for him, his research did not extend much beyond Mickle's notebook and she chose not to make mention of it.[10] As a result, Kosche never knew the significance of Frederick M. Short's vehement argument against Mrs. de Beaumont's supposed portrait of Sir Isaac Brock (fig. 15). However, by delving deeper into the entire set of papers preserved by the Women's Canadian Historical Society of Toronto, Kosche almost certainly would have uncovered Short's original letter and his derogatory remarks about the elderly Lieutenant Dunn's portrait—including the one describing the poor old officer as having a wild harum-scarum look about him. Instead, Kosche was left to deal with a severely edited transcript in Miss Mickle's notebook.[11] The upshot, however, was essentially the same. Short, who was Mrs. Taylor's uncle, was positive that the sitter in the harum-scarum portrait was not Sir Isaac Brock, and Kosche had—quite independently—come to the same conclusion. But whereas Short insisted that the miniature (fig. 11) portrayed Sir Isaac Brock, Kosche now doubted it as well.

Even before he came face-to-face with the harum-scarum man, Kosche was becoming ever more convinced that the miniature owned by the Women's Canadian Historical Society of Toronto was really that of a youthful Lieutenant George Dunn. He was so sure of himself that he shared his findings with Miss Lorna R. Procter in September of 1983, just prior to his setting out on a month-long vacation. But Kosche received some very disagreeable news not long after he arrived back in Ottawa.[12] As Miss Procter feared, her fellow executive members were not entirely accepting of Lieutenant George Dunn. Many of them simply ignored Kosche and his research, preferring to believe what they had always believed—namely, that the miniature portrayed Sir Isaac Brock.[13] While Miss Procter was firmly on side with Kosche, she agonized over how best to share his disappointing conclusion with the general membership. Kosche, for his part, was more concerned with the wider world; if the apathy of the Women's Canadian Historical Society of Toronto was any indication, he could count on being brushed off by the nation at large. Worse yet, he might be forced to endure much resentment and hostility. Although he remained undaunted, Kosche also saw the need for additional evidence to neutralize the skeptics. And because he wanted to start writing up his research before the end of the year, he was under considerable pressure to move as quickly as possible.[14] But the article he envisioned still required a thorough investigation of the miniature's provenance.

Sometime earlier, Kosche happened upon a brief historical record of the miniature (fig. 11). The "Chronology," as it was called, contained a preamble in which Miss FitzGibbon outlined the following ownership: "This miniature of Gen. Sir Isaac Brock formerly belonged to his brother [cousin], James Brock, captain and paymaster of the 49th Regiment of Foot. It was left to his widow, a daughter of the Rev. Robert Shortt, Rector of Trois-Rivières. She left it, with other valuable relics, to her sister Matilda, widow of George Dunn, Captain [Lieutenant] and Paymaster of the 23rd Welsh [Welch] Fusiliers. Mrs. Dunn, by codicil dated Nov. 14th 1867, bequeathed it to her niece, Mrs. Heber Taylor, daughter of the late Mr. John Shortt."[15] On the surface, Miss FitzGibbon appeared to have drawn her information from credible sources. But when Kosche reviewed Miss Mickle's transcription of Mrs. James Brock's will, as well as the codicil to Mrs. George Dunn's will, he could find no mention of a miniature purporting to be that of Sir Isaac Brock. Miss FitzGibbon's misrepresentation, whether intentional or not, was a caution against her research, and alerted Kosche to the necessity of going back to the original records. Thus motivated, Kosche arranged for copies of the relevant testamentary documents. While he had no expectation that they would authenticate the miniature in Brock's favour, he was curious to know if one or the other of them made reference to Lieutenant George Dunn.

Kosche began by seeking a copy of the will of Mrs. James Brock, who died at Montreal in 1859, but there was no provision for a miniature of any kind.[16] Nor was there any mention of Lieutenant George Dunn. The same held true for the codicil to Mrs. George Dunn's will.[17] Kosche was not surprised, given what he had already seen of Miss Mickle's transcripts. There was nothing in the probate record to substantiate the Short family tradition that Mrs. Brock left a miniature of Sir Isaac Brock to her sister, Mrs. Dunn, or that Mrs. Dunn then left it to her niece, Mrs. Taylor.

Kosche was thoroughly disillusioned with Miss FitzGibbon, and her lack of historical rigour.[18] She had just assumed that the miniature was passed down through the Short family according to the provenance provided by Mrs. Taylor. She also took it for granted that Mrs. Brock's will and Mrs. Dunn's codicil provided for these bequests without actually stipulating as much.[19] Kosche, however, was more careful in his analysis. He concluded that since no provision was made for the miniature in Mrs. Brock's will, then she probably never owned it. Such an heirloom was not likely to have been overlooked, not when numerous other small items had warranted a special mention.

While Kosche could use this absence of evidence to argue against the miniature being a portrait of Brock, he still wanted confirmation that it portrayed Lieutenant George Dunn. A timely—if somewhat indirect—validation came in November of 1983, when another Short descendant positively identified the portrait of Lieutenant Dunn as an old officer (fig. 15).[20] And because H. Douglass Short of Kingston was an avid genealogist, Kosche deemed his identification to be reliable. Having thus established that this portrait was in fact Lieutenant George Dunn, it should have been fairly obvious that the miniature of the younger officer was the same man, as they both looked much alike. Kosche nevertheless had trouble making the connection, despite the nearly matching uniforms. In the end, it was these same uniforms—or rather his uncertainty about them—that prompted Kosche to go after an expert opinion. Norman Holme, the assistant curator of the Royal Welch Fusiliers Museum, was happy to be of service and was unequivocal in his response: "the subject is undoubtedly wearing the uniform of an officer in the Royal Welch Fusilers." Furthermore, Holme was able to observe that "the facial similarities are clearly apparent."[21] Kosche remained undecided, although he did grant that there appeared to be "the same longish face."[22] Somehow, he appears to have overlooked Dunn's most striking facial feature, and that which resulted in the poor old lieutenant being described as a "wild Harum Scarum man": his distinctively high eyebrows.

Given the circumstantial evidence Kosche managed to assemble, no reasonable person would disagree that the miniature long thought to portray Sir Isaac Brock was really Lieutenant George Dunn. And yet Kosche was still very nervous about going public with what he knew. In February of 1984, he admitted his reticence to Captain Mellish. Having finished that section of his article on Brock's portraits dealing with the miniature discovered by Miss Mickle (fig. 11), Kosche sent a copy to the captain. In his covering letter, Kosche commented on his choice of wording when discussing the sitter's identity, and his unwillingness to "definitely state" that the miniature was of Lieutenant George Dunn. Kosche thought it better to say "a high degree of probability," since he had given up all hope of ever finding the absolute proof he required to ward off the naysayers. "To my mind," he explained, "the evidence does not permit stronger language, nor do I think it advisable to push the case more strongly, lest the effect be exactly the reverse." Kosche was also doubtful that one article, no matter how well documented or forcefully written, would be sufficient to undo a misconception that had been allowed to stand uncontested for almost a century. "One has to enlist time as one's ally," he philosophized.[23]

There was little reaction from Captain Mellish, other than to agree that using stronger language might have "the reverse effect."[24] This nonchalant attitude was understandable, as he was not terribly concerned about a misidentified miniature of Lieutenant George Dunn. The captain was more interested in what Kosche had to say about his own portraits of Brock, and so he looked forward to the delivery of future instalments. The one that arrived in mid-March of 1984 held the most appeal, as it dealt with the profile portrait of Brock (fig. 3).[25] While much of the information contained in this instalment was familiar to the captain, notably the revised attribution from James Sharples to William Berczy, there were also a couple of new—and rather troubling—revelations. The first seemed to call the profile portrait's very existence into question, while the second proposed that this seemingly non-existent portrait may have gone to Guernsey in 1818! Poor Captain Mellish was more than a little perplexed. What he could not have known, however, is that Kosche had become too reliant on the research of Miss Agnes FitzGibbon, and the analysis of Miss Sara Mickle.

The first revelation came about as Kosche was making his way through Miss Mickle's notebook. In reading one of her many transcripts, he encountered a brief but unnerving passage from a letter dating to 1813. Written by Major John B. Glegg, Brock's former aide-de-camp, it was addressed to the dead general's brother and heir. Before closing his missive, Major

Glegg assured William Brock that he did not have a portrait of his lamented brother. But by devoting just one short sentence to the subject, Major Glegg allowed considerable latitude for anyone wishing to second-guess its meaning. Miss FitzGibbon took the lead by misquoting the major in a letter she wrote to Miss Mickle:

> I am quite sure that the General did not sit for any portrait in this country and I do not know of there being any likeness of him.[26]

Actually, what the major wrote was this:

> I regret to say that I never possessed a good likeness of your Brother, nor did he ever sit for it being taken in this Country.[27]

It was not quite the same thing, but the paraphrasing was close enough for Miss FitzGibbon to play devil's advocate. As she hypothesized, perhaps the miniature discovered by Miss Mickle portrayed someone else . . . perhaps even Captain James Brock.[28]

Miss Mickle was horrified. "I [would] never have dreamed of James Brock," she confided to her notebook. The "internal evidence of the portrait was dead against it."[29] Unfortunately, Miss Mickle did not expand on what she thought constituted this "internal evidence." She may have meant that since the miniature was dated 1806, and because Brock was known to have been on leave in England during that year, then it was probably he who sat for the artist J. Hudson. Or perhaps it had something to do with the youthful appearance of the officer, which was thought to be compatible with Brock's age in 1806 (he was thirty-six years old for most of that year).[30] Whatever her rationale, Miss Mickle was convinced that the sitter was the future Sir Isaac Brock. The very notion that her miniature might portray Captain James Brock was extremely aggravating. If, as Miss FitzGibbon believed, the sitter were Captain James Brock, "we must then believe that Mrs. Brock did not know her own husband . . . nor Mrs. Dunn her own brother-in-law."[31] As for Major Glegg's assurance that the general did not sit for any portrait in this country, he "*did not know* what he was saying."[32] After all, there was Mr. Garrett's watercolour portrait

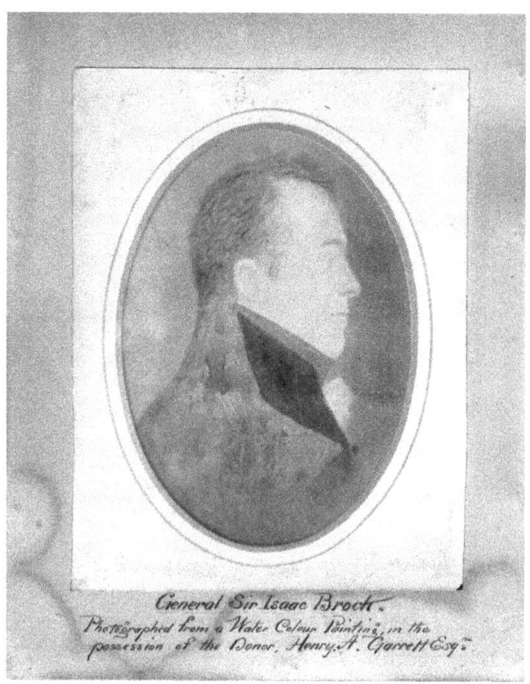

FIGURE 31.

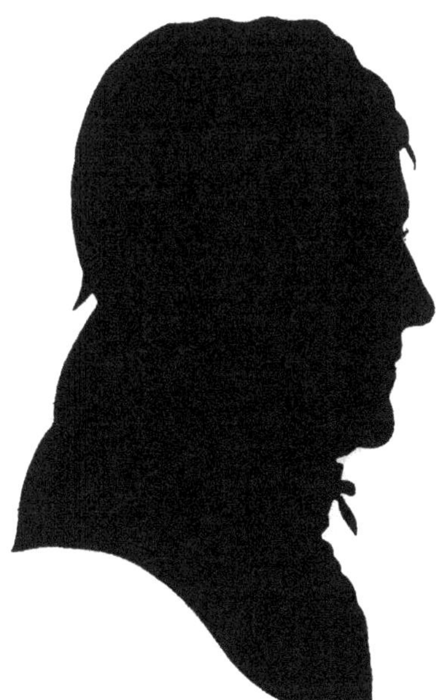

FIGURE 18.

of Brock (fig. 31), which was almost certainly produced in Canada, and also the Jarvis silhouette (fig. 18)—"perfectly authentic and taken in Canada."[33] But Miss Mickle was a little too hasty in disposing of Major Glegg, as his assertion that Brock never sat for his likeness being taken "in this Country," which she took to mean Canada, could have been used with great effect to reinforce her claim that the miniature had been painted in England.

Miss Mickle, however, remained hostile towards Major Glegg, mainly because she thought he implied that there was no portrait of Brock. To suggest such a thing was absolutely ridiculous, because it would "cut out the Guernsey portraits" as well as the miniature.[34] Miss Mickle was unyielding: Major Glegg was not to be trusted. But surely, all he meant was that Brock never sat for a portrait while he was posted to Upper Canada.[35] The major ventured no opinion as to portraits that might have been painted elsewhere, and so nothing he said could be construed as ruling out those such as the profile portraits (figs 3, 4), or even the miniature (fig. 11). Yet, because Major Glegg's statement had a negative connotation, Miss Mickle felt the need to dispute it. Kosche, however, was not so quick to condemn. Unlike Miss Mickle, he had great respect for Major Glegg. Besides having been Brock's military aide-de-camp, Captain Glegg (as he then ranked) was one of the general's closest friends and a co-administrator of his estate. In this latter capacity, it was his sad duty to pack up Brock's personal effects and send them off to William Brock in England.[36] If anyone could shed light on the question of Brock's portrait, it was Major John B. Glegg. Unfortunately, his statement regarding Brock's likeness was far from encouraging . . . unless, of course, it was taken out of context.

Kosche decided to go back and review the original source of Major Glegg's statement, and conveniently enough he just happened to have a copy of the major's letter to William Brock.[37] As he searched his files for it, Kosche must have hoped for a better understanding of what the major had to say about Brock's portrait. If so, he was disappointed. The letter offered nothing in the way of an elaboration. And since it was unlikely that more of the same type of correspondence would ever be found, Kosche was forced to work out the meaning of Major Glegg's cryptic message for himself.[38] After pondering the terminology, he finally resolved that "a good likeness" equated with a formal portrait requiring several sittings.

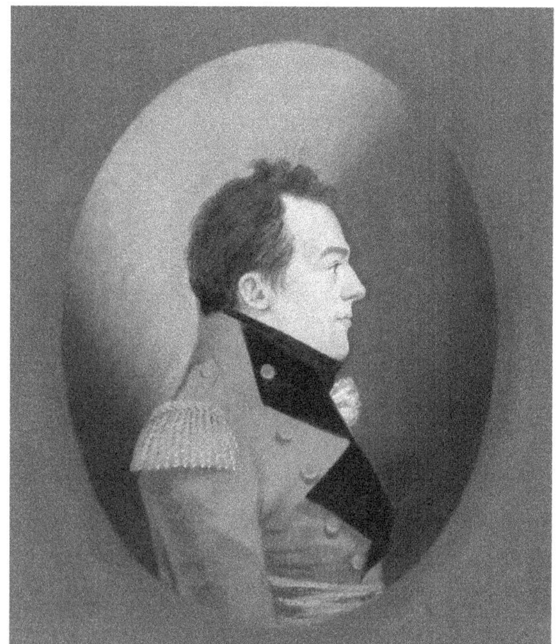

Figure 3.

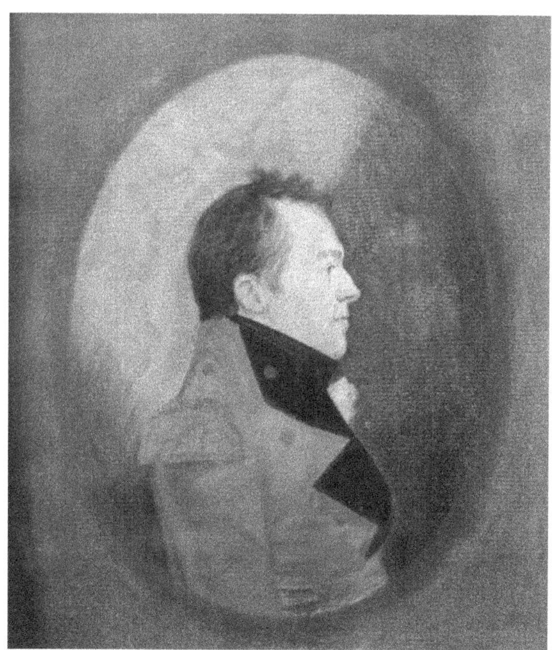

Figure 4.

The major's statement, therefore, was something more along the lines of an affirmation that Brock never commissioned an oil painting of himself while in Canada.[39] It still allowed for a small profile portrait in pastels, however, as Major Glegg only referred to there being no "good likeness" or formal portrait of Brock. And there was still the possibility that perhaps Major Glegg "knew less than he thought he did."[40]

Kosche was beginning to rethink the extent of Major Glegg's familiarity with Brock, and he was influenced to a large extent by Miss Mickle. Having checked for the major's entries in *The Quebec Almanac*, she found that he was frequently absent prior to his appointment as Brock's aide-de-camp in 1810.[41] In light of these duties elsewhere, there was bound to be a sizeable gap in Major Glegg's knowledge of Brock's private affairs. Kosche tended to agree, but he still had great faith in the man who effectively acted as Brock's personal assistant.

While Major Glegg might not have been privy to every detail of Brock's private affairs, Kosche found it difficult to accept Miss Mickle's contention that he must therefore have been ignorant of the profile portrait (fig. 3). For Kosche, this was an unreasonable assumption, especially given the major's close association with Brock towards the end of his life. Kosche further contemplated the possibility that Major Glegg might have owned this portrait at one time. Such an acquisition might explain how Captain Mellish ultimately came to possess it. Although pure speculation on his part, Kosche had a hunch that Major Glegg sent the profile portrait to William Brock and from him it passed to his family in Guernsey, which put Captain Mellish in line to inherit it. But as Kosche himself acknowledged, there was "nothing" to substantiate this sequence of events or even Major Glegg's ownership.[42] Oddly enough, Kosche was far less circumspect regarding the portrait's arrival in Guernsey, as another old letter seemed to confirm its delivery there. The peculiar insights Kosche gained from this contemporary source would form the second troubling revelation for Captain Mellish to entertain, and once again it involved Miss FitzGibbon.

Upon her departure from St. Peter Port in 1897, Miss FitzGibbon was given the letter Major Glegg wrote to William Brock. It was a gift from Miss Henrietta Tupper, as were a number of other old letters. One of them dated to January of 1818 and was written by Brock's brother. After returning from a tour of Upper Canada, Savery Brock had allowed himself some time in London before continuing on to Guernsey.[43] His baggage having been sent ahead, a nephew was given special instructions regarding one of the items Savery brought back from Canada. Ferdinand Brock Tupper was to "tell Mrs. Charles de Jersey to be particular in looking over every book for a miniature, that I fancy is placed between the leaves in one or other of them, and to give it with my compliments to the sister of the gentleman."[44] The keyword was "miniature," of course—and Miss FitzGibbon instantly thought of the profile portrait.

That Savery Brock neglected to describe the miniature in any detail was immaterial. Like it, the profile portrait (which was painted on a letter size sheet of paper) could easily have fit between the pages of a not overly large book. Savery Brock was obviously visualizing the profile portrait, and Miss FitzGibbon was anxious to share this new information with Miss Mickle. Writing in early June of 1897, Miss FitzGibbon introduced the topic by way of some new background information on the bronze profile (fig. 8).[45] She had already persuaded herself that this bronzed silhouette was modelled after Daniel de Lisle Brock—if only because he bore a close resemblance to his brother, Isaac.[46] But after reading Savery Brock's letter, Miss FitzGibbon further posited that until Mrs. de Jersey delivered the miniature, the bronze profile was the closest thing to a portrait of Brock his family had.[47] This want of a portrait seemed to be in keeping with Savery Brock's concern for the miniature he ensconced in a book. It all made perfect sense.[48]

Miss Mickle, however, was not nearly so taken with Miss FitzGibbon's conjectures. Much of this indifference was linked to Miss Mickle's fixation with the miniature she discovered. To her, the other miniature was nothing more than an unwelcome distraction. But Miss Mickle soon had a change of heart, once she began to toy with the idea that Savery Brock might have been writing about her miniature. Perhaps, she speculated, he "heard when in Canada that the miniature (mine) still existed—had not been destroyed at Ft George or the taking of York. That he knew he had not seen it among the things and he hopes that for safe packing it may have been removed from its frame and put between the leaves [of a book]."[49] Ironically, this severe bout of wishful thinking followed Miss Mickle's reprimand of Miss FitzGibbon, who was derided for suggesting

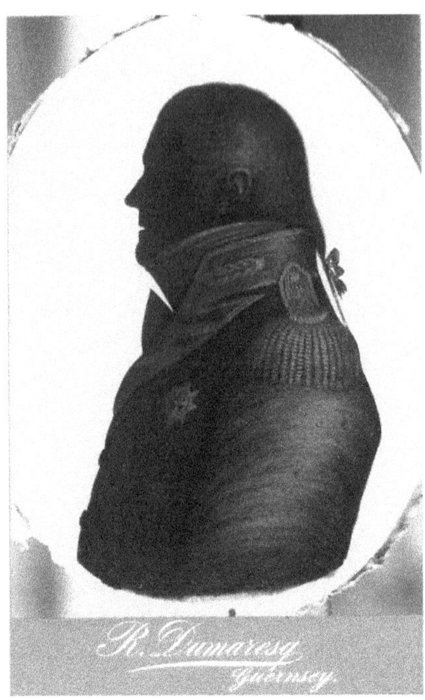

FIGURE 8.

that the miniature might have portrayed Captain James Brock. Yet, Miss Mickle's subjective reading of the evidence was no less reckless, especially as it negated any opportunity for her own discovery of Brock's miniature. Had the miniature (fig. 11) actually been sent to Guernsey in Savery Brock's baggage, it probably would have remained there. But Miss Mickle duly recorded her slanted impression and when her notebook was lent to Ludwig Kosche many years later, it made for fascinating reading.[50]

Initially, Kosche treated Savery Brock's instructions to Mrs. de Jersey with a healthy dose of skepticism.[51] Unlike Miss FitzGibbon and Miss Mickle, he saw the futility in trying to determine which miniature Savery Brock had in mind. Nevertheless, he was intrigued by the potential connection between it and the profile portrait owned by Captain Mellish. A Canadian origin for the profile portrait certainly meshed with the attribution to William Berczy, and Savery Brock's instructions might very well explain how it ended up in Guernsey.[52] Still, there was no way of telling if the miniature in Savery Brock's baggage was the profile portrait owned by Captain Mellish—although Kosche seems to have grown comfortable with Miss FitzGibbon's conclusion that they were one and the same item.[53]

Captain Mellish was not inclined to say much about these various revelations, except that they were "very interesting."[54] There was not the slightest hint of incredulity in the captain's reply, probably because the revelations—although troubling—were also inconclusive. So, even if Brock never sat for a good or formal likeness in Canada, and whether or not it was the miniature delivered to Guernsey 1818, the captain still had a very fine profile portrait of his famous ancestor. And just as the revelations were "very interesting," so too were all the observations Kosche sent along with them.

Among these observations, there was a misleading description of Brock as a relatively young-looking officer "with a full mop of hair." Actually, he was approaching middle age with a receding hairline. There was also a "wart" on his right cheek, by which Kosche really meant a mole. The size of Brock's head was also given due consideration, although it did not appear exceptionally large to Kosche (in spite of Brock's own description). Neither did there seem to be a weightiness to his physique, which Ferdinand Brock Tupper had characterized as "perhaps too portly."[55] Brock's uniform was discussed as well, with Kosche remarking that there was no medal or any other insignia. These missing "decorations" were reassuring to Kosche, knowing as he did that Brock died before receiving any.[56] As for the portrait's date, he adjusted it once again, this time from his earlier reckoning of 1809 to the last quarter of 1808.[57] It was necessary in order to accommodate a possible meeting between Brock and Berczy in Montreal, a detail which John Andre had brought to light.[58] Kosche also tried to account for the copy of the profile portrait (fig. 4), but he was unable to do anything more than confirm that it was a weaker rendition.[59] Being able to distinguish it from the original was good enough, however.

Captain Mellish was just as content, and he thought the article in progress to be "most thorough."[60] With this vote of confidence, Kosche began to think about a publisher. Someone willing to print the illustrations in colour was to be preferred, but he knew the added expense would be difficult to justify.[61] In late March and early April of 1984, he had hopes that the Women's Canadian Historical Society of Toronto might be willing to take on his project. Unfortunately, his negotiations with Miss Lorna

R. Procter were compromised by an increasingly paranoid demand for secrecy. As Kosche became ever more agitated by the prospect of having to share his research before it was published, he rather bluntly told Miss Procter that he did not want other people sticking their noses into his business. He was especially bothered that some of these other people might be history professors, who he regarded as being overly critical of antiquarian pursuits. Sensing that Miss Procter might be offended by this injunction, Kosche apologized by claiming that he only wanted to maintain an element of surprise.[62] But it was too late. Miss Procter, while she remained supportive, was not in good health and lacked the stamina to cope with the darker side of Ludwig Kosche. Not surprisingly, his proposal involving the Women's Canadian Historical Society of Toronto was unsuccessful.

After a failed attempt to interest the Toronto Historical Board, Kosche went back to a former publisher. His article on the "Relics of Brock" had been featured in *Archivaria*, the journal of the Association of Canadian Archivists, and Kosche was fairly confident that its editor would be receptive to another Brock-related submission.[63] The only disadvantage with *Archivaria* was its usual practice of printing illustrations in black and white. If authors wanted them in colour, they had to foot the bill for the extra cost. Kosche, however, was optimistic that he would be able to find a source of funding. Unfortunately, his optimism was unwarranted and he soon had to resign himself to a less elaborate presentation. While Kosche might have gone in search of another journal, an article on Brock's portraits seemed a good fit for *Archivaria*. Moreover, he just wanted it done and out of the way.[64]

Kosche submitted his manuscript to *Archivaria* in the summer of 1984, which eventually brought a favourable assessment from the journal's editor, Thomas C. Nesmith. Looking beyond his concerns about the manuscript's length and complexity, Nesmith made allowance for its obvious significance.[65] In due course, the manuscript was sent out for peer review. Remarkably, Kosche no longer seemed the least bit perturbed by having to share his research in advance of publication. Perhaps he expected the anonymous readers to be agreeable archivists, as opposed to overly critical history professors. In any case, and by the end of September 1984, both readers recommended publication.[66] As one of them stated: "It will be a valuable reference for any scholar or archivist concerned with Brock and the iconography of Brock. It is as well a very interesting demonstration of the use of military costume to authenticate portraiture."[67] This same reader also appended nearly three pages of questions and comments, all of which were forwarded to Kosche at the end of January in 1985. After the better part of a month spent in making revisions, there was nothing left for him to do but wait for the offprints.[68]

Six months later, during a visit to the Public Archives of Canada, Kosche happened upon the recently released summer issue of *Archivaria*. In it, he found the long-awaited article.[69] Much to his delight, the illustrations reproduced "quite well" in black and white.[70] Kosche was very pleased, and he wasted little time in getting copies for all the people who had supported his endeavour. Foremost among them was Captain Mellish, who responded with considerable praise.[71] Kosche received similar accolades, and like the "Relics of Brock" article, his "Contemporary Portraits of Isaac Brock" was well received.[72] It would also be his crowning achievement at the Canadian War Museum.

A few weeks later, Kosche took early retirement. In sharing this news with Captain Mellish, the fifty-six-year-old librarian cited a number of reasons for his departure, including a desire to pursue his own interests.[73] Kosche quickly adapted to his newfound freedom, much of which he spent in travelling and researching.[74] While Sir Isaac Brock did not figure into this new routine, Kosche continued to correspond with Captain Mellish. Gradually, however, the letters ceased and eventually the captain lost touch with Kosche, as did former colleagues. By the time Kosche died in 2000, his professional legacy was all but forgotten at the Canadian War Museum.[75] Yet, his name lived on as the author of several important artifact studies. His last submission to *Archivaria*, "The Contemporary Portraits of Isaac Brock," was long held to be an important piece of original research. But while Ludwig Kosche was an honest historian who did some very good work, he was not destined to have the last word on Brock's portraits.

6

For Want of a True Face

By the time I began researching Sir Isaac Brock, Ludwig Kosche had been dead for the better part of two years. It was then the spring of 2002, and nearly seventeen years had passed since his article on the "Contemporary Portraits of Isaac Brock" was published. Having leafed through it on more than one occasion, I was well aware of the contribution Koche made to the study of Brock iconography. Yet, most of my energy was still devoted to Tecumseh, or rather the mystery surrounding his bones. For this reason, I had to put my growing fascination with Brock's portraits on hold. One day, however, I took a much-needed break from Native history and went in search of Kosche's article. Recalling a thorough study, I expected a definitive conclusion. Disconcertingly, however, it appeared that Kosche was not entirely comfortable with some of his own findings. Still, his article was not a complete disappointment.

Kosche was able to identify the two portraits most likely to be authentic likenesses of Brock (figs 3, 27). He also convincingly argued that a miniature long thought to portray a young Isaac Brock was actually Lieutenant George Dunn (fig. 11). But he failed to stress these significant breakthroughs, and this because he was unable to find the documentation necessary to prove his points. Thus constrained, Kosche presented his findings in rather ambiguous language, as if the reader was expected to come around to his way of thinking. Nor did it help that he wrote in a convoluted and sometimes condescending manner. The end result was a lingering uncertainty, which led some War of 1812 historians to question whether any of Brock's portraits were authentic.[1]

To be fair, a cautious approach was recommended by one of the readers who took part in the peer review of Kosche's article.[2] But Kosche was

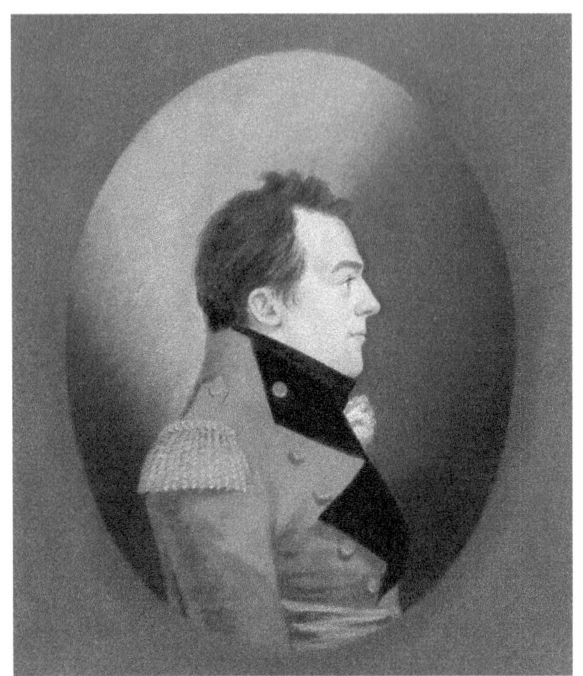

Figure 3.

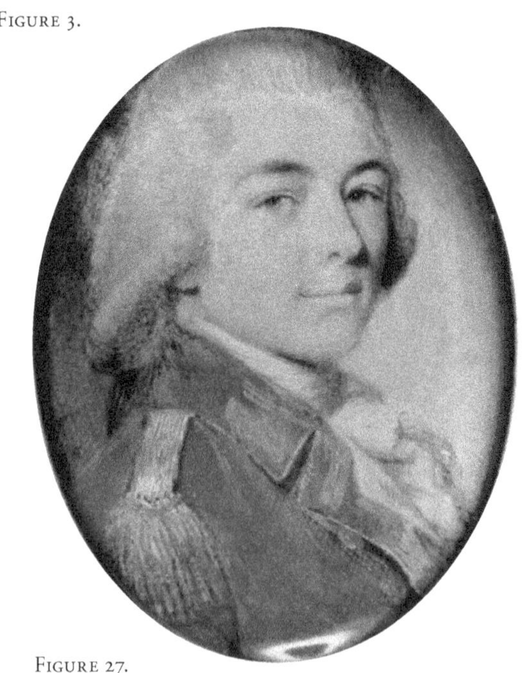

Figure 27.

overly cautious, mainly because he feared being abused for alerting the world to the misidentification of Lieutenant George Dunn's miniature. He was also convinced that the first angry outburst would come from the Women's Canadian Historical Society of Toronto, where certain members refused to give up their long-held belief that the miniature was of Sir Isaac Brock.[3] But as the weeks and months passed, the dreaded backlash failed to materialize. No doubt, it was stifled by the society's ongoing decline, which in the summer of 1985 forced the ladies of the executive to debate the sale of their most valuable asset—their club house.[4] They were far too occupied with that unpleasant business to take much, if any, notice of Kosche's article. Neither were there any complaints voiced beyond this shrinking sphere of influence. However, it was not a lack of interest that allowed Kosche to make his bold claim without recrimination. It had more to do with the fact that most Canadians were unaware of the revision he made to their pictorial heritage.

Because the circulation of *Archivaria* was, for the most part, limited to members of the Association of Canadian Archivists, it is not surprising that Kosche's article drew little attention. Had he published his findings on the Dunn miniature (fig. 11) separately, and as a feature article in one of the country's leading newspapers, they would have been more widely known. Of course, there was also likely to have been a greater reaction—which probably would have been largely negative, just as Kosche dreaded. And since he did not take well to criticism, it was perhaps best that his exposé on Lieutenant George Dunn's miniature was published without much fanfare.

In rediscovering Kosche's article, I was optimistic that his research would facilitate my own. I was keen to find an authentic likeness of Brock, and it was reassuring to know that Kosche was able to establish that there were at least two credible portraits in existence.[5] The first showed Brock as a young ensign in the 8th (or King's) Regiment (fig. 27), and the sitter's youthful appearance corresponded with Brock's age when he entered the British army in 1785. As well, the facings of the uniform were blue—the correct colour for the 8th Regiment.[6] The second portrait, otherwise known as the profile portrait (fig. 3), featured an older Brock only a few years prior to his death in 1812. This was exactly the image I wanted: a mature Brock near the height of his fame. Yet, Kosche seemed unsure of

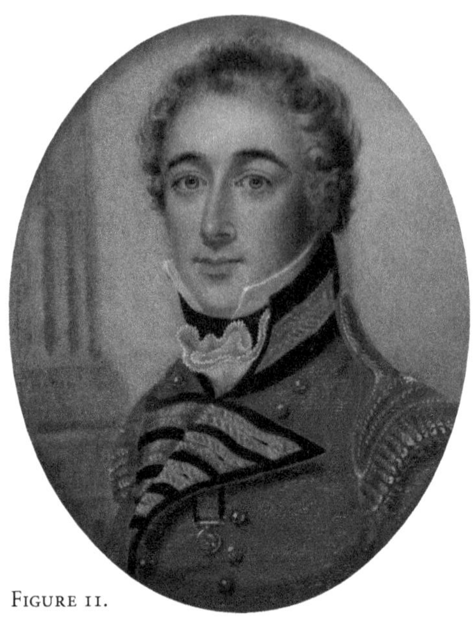

FIGURE 11.

himself when it came to the profile portrait, even hinting that someone should undertake further research to back him up.[7] Although the suggestion seemed a bit peculiar, as Kosche was supposed to be the expert on the subject, I had no reason to doubt the article's scholarship—not until December of 2002. It was then that my faith in Kosche began to waver.

Quite by accident, I stumbled upon an art catalogue that was published in conjunction with an exhibition at the National Gallery of Canada in 1991. It showcased the artwork of William Berczy, who Kosche named as the artist responsible for Brock's profile portrait.[8] Well do I remember my anticipation as I began flipping through the pages of the catalogue, expecting at any moment to catch a glimpse of the distinctive portrait. But it was nowhere to be found.[9] This omission struck me as being very odd, given that Kosche published his article six years prior to the publication of the catalogue. Therefore, it was difficult to imagine that the catalogue's authors would not have known about Brock's portrait and its attribution to Berczy. I blamed myself for having gone through the catalogue too quickly, and so I began another round of flipping . . . albeit more slowly this time. In reaching the appendices, I was stopped in my tracks by an illustration that looked remarkably similar in style to Brock's profile portrait. I carried on, hoping that Brock's likeness would jump out at me, but there was no sign of it. In going back to the beginning of what proved to be appendix B, I discovered it was an essay by Mary Macaulay Allodi entitled "Pastel Profiles," which looked promising enough.[10] If nothing else, I expected to find Brock's portrait mentioned somewhere in the text. But I was disappointed for a third time—although I soon began to understand why.

As Allodi observed, these profile portraits were not consistent with Berczy's portraiture. For one thing, he was not known to have used pastels. Nor were his portraits ever "as rigid and formula-bound as the pastel profiles."[11] Allodi therefore concluded that the profile portraits had been mistakenly attributed to Berczy, and she had a pretty good idea as to who really painted them.[12] It was Gerrit Schipper, a Dutch itinerant artist who was known to have travelled extensively throughout the United States in the first decade of the nineteenth century. Allodi's first clue came courtesy of the Art Gallery of Ontario, where a profile portrait of Governor Sir James Henry Craig, also done in pastels, provided a very close match to the profile portraits thought to have been painted by Berczy. Like them, the portrait of Governor Craig was unsigned. While there was no indication as to the artist's name, Allodi was able to make the connection to Schipper based on his very public displeasure with an unscrupulous publisher.[13]

In March of 1810, a brazen John D. Turnbull of Montreal had Schipper's portrait of Governor Craig engraved without the artist's permission.[14] Schipper, who was then residing in Quebec City, responded to this shameless misappropriation by taking his case to the Lower Canadian press—including the *Quebec Gazette*. It was in the pages of this newspaper that Allodi became aware of the dispute with Turnbull. In a good-sized advertisement, Schipper charged that Turnbull's print was an inferior copy of his own portrait of the governor. Such an imposition was not to be tolerated, particularly when there was a considerable amount of money at stake. Schipper's art was his main source of income, which explains why he did not take kindly to someone like Turnbull cutting in on his profits, and using one of his own portraits to do so. In retaliation, Schipper pledged to deliver a far superior print from a mezzotint engraver in London. By utilizing Turnbull's own marketing strategy and selling these prints through subscription, Schipper was determined to beat the plagiarist at his own game.[15]

It is impossible to know if Schipper profited from his attempt to exact revenge, but this much is certain: his response to Turnbull's infringement was a great boon to Mary Allodi. Thanks to all the press coverage generated by this controversy, she was able to identify Schipper as the artist who painted Governor Craig's portrait. And because there was such an obvious similarity between this profile portrait and those thought to have been done by Berczy, she was able to assign them a mass attribution to Schipper.[16] Consequently, they were excluded from his exhibition at the National Gallery of Canada. The implication resulting from the downsizing of Berczy's body of work seems to have been lost on Kosche, perhaps because he had become engrossed with other projects. But while Kosche might have been oblivious to Allodi's revisionism, her idea of an attribution to Schipper appears to have begun taking hold soon after his article on the "Contemporary Portraits of Isaac Brock" was published in 1985. The following year, John Andre acknowledged the possibility, but apparently without telling Kosche.[17] As for Dr. Alan McNairn, he had no further involvement with Brock's profile portrait until 2009. It was then, in a decision heavily influenced by Allodi's essay, that he revised his attribution from Berczy to Schipper.[18]

Mary Allodi's revelation was profound, and had she used Brock's profile portrait (fig. 3) to illustrate her argument in favour of an attribution to Schipper, I would have rejoiced at my good fortune. It was clear to me that she was fully justified in giving him credit for all the portraits previously thought to have been the work of Berczy. Brock's portrait, however, was still in need of its own attribution—a problem I hoped to rectify with Allodi's help. In January of 2003, after viewing some very indifferent photographs (and the only ones I had at the time), she agreed that the profile portrait owned by Captain Michael H.T. Mellish "could certainly be by Schipper."[19] This assessment, while heartening, was not as conclusive as I would have liked. But I presumed she was willing to make a more formal attribution at some later date, once I managed to get a better photograph. It soon became apparent that she had more pressing concerns, although she did encourage me to get in touch with an American art historian whose area of specialization was the portraiture of Gerrit Schipper. I could not have asked for a better referral.

Jeanne Riger developed an interest in Gerrit Schipper through her affiliation with the Museum of American Folk Art in New York City. In 1990, having made Schipper's life her specialty, Riger published an article about it in an issue of the museum's magazine.[20] After reading the piece, I was eager to ask Riger for an attribution. But I hesitated to contact her, as I was still lacking a good photograph of Brock's profile portrait. When nothing better turned up by the end of October 2003, I became impatient and decided to go ahead with a letter to Riger.[21] My gamble paid off with a kind offer of assistance, which was all very fine and well—except that Riger was indeed hesitant to judge Brock's portrait until she saw a high-quality photograph.[22] This requirement did not bode well for an attribution, and left me in rather a desperate situation. As such, it called for a desperate measure.

In May of 2004, I made a trip to Guernsey for the express purpose of visiting Belvedere House at Fort George. There, hanging between the windows in the sitting room, was Brock's profile portrait (fig. 3). It was still the prized possession of Captain Mellish, who was by then nearing his ninetieth year.[23] Yet, in spite of his great age and rather fragile health, he had readily consented to a photoshoot including myself, a professional photographer, and a couple of friends acting as assistants. I feared that our group might overwhelm the poor old gentleman, but Captain Mellish soon put me at ease. Still, I was careful not to push my luck by asking too many questions about the portrait's provenance. My earlier correspondence with the captain had warned me against it, and one of his comments was especially revealing. After writing to him about the possible attribution to Gerrit Schipper, Captain Mellish pessimistically replied: "I don't know if we shall ever find out who did the picture of Sir Isaac Brock."[24] He did not seem up to rehashing the same old question, and so a photographic copy of the profile portrait became the sole object of my visit. But ultimately there was no avoiding the subject of attribution.

Soon after my arrival, Captain Mellish began to speak about his military service during the Second World War. He then deviated somewhat by relating an incident touching upon Brock's profile portrait. It had to do with the Nazi occupation of Guernsey between 1940 and 1945, when German officers were liable to billet themselves with whomever they pleased. At that time, the portrait was in the possession of Miss Edith Tupper, a cousin of the captain's who lived in a house next to St. Stephen's

Church in St. Peter Port.[25] As it transpired, the portrait was never in any real danger of being carried off as a war trophy, for the simple reason that none of the enemy wanted to take up residence with Miss Tupper. As Captain Mellish gleefully blurted out, it was because she "didn't have the electric!" Her inability to provide this basic amenity compelled the Germans to look elsewhere for their accommodations. It was just as well for the profile portrait, given that Miss Tupper took no precautions to safeguard it or any of her other mementos of Sir Isaac Brock. These heirlooms simply did not rate as highly in her estimation as the family's silver, which she carefully packed away in cake tins and secretly buried in her garden.[26]

After hearing this story, I was all the more relieved when the photographs and their negatives came back in perfect order, and I would soon come to appreciate the importance of having secured the best reproduction of the profile portrait then available. Earlier, and just prior to my departure for Guernsey, I happened upon what I considered to be a pretty good snapshot of the portrait, which I hurriedly sent off to Jeanne Riger. Although I had every intention of providing her with a professional grade photograph after my return, I was hoping for a tentative attribution in the meantime. I was surprised, however, when she deferred any opinion whatsoever until she had the optimal image. Happily for me, I was able to meet her exacting standards.[27]

The photograph was mailed to Riger in mid-June of 2004, and by the end of that same month I had my reply. "The pastel portrait of Isaac Brock is beautiful," she enthused, and "I do think that the portrait is by Gerritt Schipper." In elaborating upon her decision, Riger emphasized the identifying characteristics of the portrait: "The flesh tones and the treatment of the [eye] and mouth, the use of the oval spandrel with light above the head and darker shadings below, the button detailing on the uniform, which is almost identical to that in his portrait of Sir James Henry Craig, all seem to indicate Schipper's hand."[28] I was immensely gratified by this attribution. Kosche might not have been quite so thrilled by the outcome, had he lived long enough to see it. And yet it was Kosche himself who stressed the importance of further research. "Establishing the identity of the artist," he advised, as well as the portrait's age, "would be welcome additional evidence for the purpose of underpinning as strongly as possible the authenticity of this profile as a genuine portrait of Brock."[29] This was the same suggestion I had studiously ignored at the outset of my investigation into Brock's portraits. But now that Berczy had fallen out of favour, I had a new appreciation for the advice Kosche offered.

With Gerrit Schipper established as the artist who painted Brock's profile portrait, I wanted to determine—if only approximately—the date of the work. Knowing as I did, that Schipper ordered all his papers to be destroyed upon his death in 1825, I had no expectations of finding a record of Brock's profile portrait in something like a sitters' notebook.[30] But I also knew that itinerant artists often announced their comings and goings in the local press, which I thought might be useful in tracking Schipper's movements. Likewise, there was also a good chance that Brock's military correspondence would allow me to place him in his various postings. By collating all this data, I planned to narrow down the date of Brock's sitting with Schipper. It was just a matter of determining when the two men were in the same place at the same time.

Initially, I thought the search could be limited to the period between 1808 and 1810, when Schipper was known to have been in Montreal and then Quebec City. It seemed unlikely to me that Brock could have met up with Schipper during any of the artist's extensive tours of the United States—although I did recall that Brock had it in mind to partake of the healing waters at Ballston in upstate New York, and this at about the same time that Schipper was in nearby Albany. But in consulting my sources, I saw that Brock was thinking of a jaunt to Ballston in January of 1811, by which time Schipper had already sailed for England.[31] I then undertook a more exhaustive search beginning with 1802—the same year in which both Schipper and Brock set out for North America. Eventually, I discovered that it was Schipper who crossed paths with Brock, and not the other way around.

In May of 1802, Schipper disembarked at New York City. After spending several weeks there, he began making his way down the eastern seaboard. By the end of March 1803, he was in Charleston, South Carolina, and the following autumn found him at Boston, Massachusetts.[32] In the spring of 1804, he travelled to nearby Salem. Later that summer, he went back to Boston and then on to Worcester, Massachusetts.[33] Then, in October of 1804, Schipper introduced himself to the citizens of Albany.[34] In the spring of 1805, after short stays in Schaghticoke and Hudson, New

York, he made his presence known in Hartford, Connecticut.[35] At the beginning of 1806, there was another stint in New York City for several months. By August of that year, he was back in Hartford and making preparations for the opening of a drawing academy.[36] Before embarking on this new venture, however, Schipper made a sudden appearance in Amsterdam, New York, where he was married in late October of 1806.[37] He then promptly returned to Hartford with his new wife, who no doubt shared in the management of the academy. Schipper seems to have preferred Hartford as his place of residence, and he might have been ready to settle down there permanently. However, any designs he had on Hartford were soon dashed.

To quote Jeanne Riger, Schipper "was bucking the times" by trying to start a business in New England at the end of 1806.[38] The region's prosperity, which had been adversely affected by the economic warfare being waged between England and France, suffered a further decline after President Thomas Jefferson's general embargo was enacted in December of 1807. In response, Schipper once again pulled up stakes for the wandering life of an itinerant artist. By the spring of 1808, he was back in Albany; but it was no haven from the hard times. There was little money in upstate New York for such niceties as portraits, and so Schipper had no choice but to seek out fresh markets beyond the Empire State's borders . . . and the reach of his creditors.[39]

With late October of 1808, Schipper and his family were heading north to the British province of Lower Canada (now Quebec).[40] Upon their arrival in Montreal, they found a merchant class prospering from its lucrative commercial ties with the mother country. There was also a thriving illicit trade with New England, thanks to the many smugglers who traversed the border without much difficulty.[41] Business was good, and Schipper took full advantage of the situation to pursue his artistic vocation.[42] However, Brigadier General Isaac Brock was not among his Montreal clientele. Although Brock had been posted to Montreal in March of 1808, he was transferred to Quebec City the following September—nearly two months before Schipper arrived.[43] And once Schipper established himself in Montreal, he was content to remain there until the demand for his services began to wane.[44] The following spring, in May of 1809, Schipper finally decided it was time for a change.[45] His next destination was Quebec

City, and it was there that he would meet with the most famous of his Lower Canadian sitters.[46]

Sir James H. Craig was governor-in-chief of the several colonies comprising British North America, and also captain general (or commander-in-chief) of the military forces therein. Unquestionably, he held the most exulted position in the land, and his patronage surely gave a boost to Schipper's reputation.[47] It can only be speculated as to how this commission originated, but the resulting profile portrait was well received by Governor Craig, and his favourable opinion of Schipper's work must have brought in other people looking to have their portraits painted. Perhaps it was the governor's influence that prompted Brock to sit for his own profile portrait. There is also the possibility that it was a gift from Sir James. The governor is known to have been fond of Brock and exceedingly generous towards him.[48] But regardless of how it came about, Brock's profile portrait could only have been painted in Quebec City.

As my research had shown, Brock was already in Quebec City when Schipper arrived there in late May of 1809. I also ascertained that both Schipper and Brock remained in relatively close proximity with one another until the summer of 1810. Brock was the first to take his leave, and by mid-July of 1810 he was en route for his new posting at Fort George in Upper Canada.[49] As there was no other opportunity for a sitting with Schipper, I was confident that Brock's profile portrait (fig. 3) dated to sometime between late May of 1809 and early July of 1810. Schipper intended to set out for England in June of 1810, but his plans were considerably delayed.[50] He was still in Quebec City during the first part of August, when he received a letter of introduction from the governor.[51] However, it must not have been long afterwards that Schipper and his family departed, as they arrived at Portsmouth near the end of September 1810.[52]

Despite my confidence in having narrowed down the date of Brock's profile portrait, I began to feel the need for verification. And thanks to Kosche, I believed a test was possible. His analysis of the uniform Brock wore to his sitting gave me reason to believe that I could use a similar means to test the accuracy of my own time frame. I envisioned a fairly straightforward exercise, as I knew there were dress regulations for officers of the British army during Brock's time.[53] But unlike Kosche, who made use of the same source, I had the benefit of a correct attribution.

To Kosche, the portrait's age was "naturally of the greatest interest to determine," especially if it was shown to be more accurate than John Andre's date of 1811—or even Captain Mellish's date of 1806.[54] Kosche was convinced that he could make a better job of it by interpreting the dateable attributes of the uniform, or the coatee as it was more properly known. The dark blue facings and collar patch, for example, were emblematic of Brock's elevated status as a general officer, and also his appointment to brigadier general on the staff of Governor Craig, both of which came early in 1808.[55] But the buttons were not so easily understood. In fact, they were downright confusing. As decreed by a general order of 1804, the buttons on a brigadier general's uniform were to be set in pairs. And yet Schipper depicted the buttons in Brock's profile portrait as being evenly spaced.[56] This was the arrangement for lower ranking regimental officers in the 49th Regiment, whose buttons were placed "as for the regiment" (or according to established usage). With evenly spaced buttons evoking Brock's former rank as a colonel and a date prior to 1808, Kosche was understandably confused. In the end, he had to accept that Brock's old uniform must have been altered—at least to the extent that it was given new facings, collar patches, and epaulettes.[57]

Initially, Kosche surmised that anything less than a proper brigadier general's coatee meant that Brock's profile portrait must have pre-dated the arrival of his new uniform, a delivery that might not have taken place until 1809 or 1810.[58] This "time-lag" was an important consideration, as Kosche had to accommodate the attribution to Berczy. However, 1810 was too late, given the possibility of an earlier meeting between Brock and Berczy at Montreal in late 1808, or at Quebec City sometime in 1809.[59] The year 1809, it will be remembered, was singled out for another reason: Brock's fortieth birthday. This was a milestone that warranted a portrait, no matter the state of Brock's uniform.[60] Thus, the period between late 1808 and sometime in 1809 looked right for an attribution to Berczy, and also the altered colonel's uniform.

Like Kosche, I believed that Brock had reused his colonel's uniform by replacing the full green facings with new ones of dark blue, adding collar patches of the same colour, and substituting new epaulettes.[61] There was really no other explanation, and alterations such as these could have been made by any competent tailor.[62] I could also accept that the buttons were left in their original settings because the corresponding buttonholes made them too difficult to move, and so they remained a vestige of Brock's colonelcy—just as the profile portrait suggested.[63] It was perfectly logical, and so too was the "time-lag" used to explain the slow delivery of Brock's new brigadier general's uniform. Unfortunately for Kosche, and as Brock's new uniform revealed, he was far too accommodating of Berczy.

Although Brock was appointed a brigadier general early in 1808, Kosche thought it unlikely that he could have received his new uniforms before the end of that same year.[64] This was a reasonable enough assumption. An officer's wardrobe was ordered from England, and given the closing of navigation on the St. Lawrence River each winter, Brock might have been kept waiting for his new uniforms until well into 1809 or even 1810, depending on when the order was placed. Eventually, I found a reference to the delivery of the new uniforms, which Brock acknowledged at the beginning of the second week of July in 1810.[65] The date of this delivery was significant, as it completely overturned the period Kosche assigned to the profile portrait—namely late 1808 or 1809.

While I had evidence to show that it had taken nearly two years for Brock's new uniforms to be delivered, it did seem an awfully long time. Nagged by self-doubt, I felt obliged to go after some additional evidence. I began by checking to see when Brock received confirmation of his appointment to brigadier general, as he was not likely to have ordered a new set of uniforms in advance of it.[66] As I soon discovered, Brock got his official notification by early September of 1808.[67] Consequently, he had sufficient time to place an order for his new uniforms before the close of navigation. In which case the tailors in England should have been able to complete their work by the summer of 1809, with plenty of time for a consignment to Quebec City. But there must have been a glitch somewhere, as the delivery was not made for another year. Given the great expense of a new set of uniforms, I could well imagine that Brock was in no hurry to place his order. The delay, therefore, was not necessarily the fault of some lax tailoring, but more likely the result of procrastination on the part of Brigadier General Brock.

During the course of my impromptu study of early nineteenth century British army uniforms, I began to think that Kosche was far stricter in his reading of the dress regulations than even Governor Craig.[68] Admittedly, some commanders were sticklers for proper attire, but Brock appears to have enjoyed a fair leeway—as witnessed by the muddled uniform he wore to his sitting with Schipper. As Brock himself would have understood, new uniforms were an inescapable component of his new status as a brigadier general and staff officer. But since this appointment was limited to Upper and Lower Canada, he must have been loath to purchase expensive new uniforms and accoutrements, knowing that his rank would revert to that of a colonel once he left the Canadas.[69] Governor Craig was probably sympathetic to Brock's plight, perhaps even to the point of ignoring the dress regulations for as long as possible. Such a favour would have allowed Brock to put off doing anything about his new uniforms until the spring or summer of 1809, thereby delaying their arrival—as it turned out—until July of 1810. Ironically, such an end date would have agreed with Kosche's "time-lag," had he not tried to make allowance for Berczy. But in doing so he effectively undermined his own research.

After clarifying the fine points of Brock's brigadier general's uniform, I turned my attention once again to the profile portrait. Now that I knew when, where, and by whom it was painted, I found myself becoming interested in the artist's style and technique. As Mary Allodi observed, there was a "rigid" and "formula-bound" appearance to Schipper's profile portraits, which was evident in the surviving examples of his work.[70] Accordingly, she proposed that Schipper might have used a physiognotrace.[71] I was taken with the idea, as there was a definite draftsman-like quality to Schipper's work that seemed to suggest a drawing instrument of some kind. But whereas Allodi had a feeling it was a physiognotrace, Jeanne Riger had evidence of something else. Citing a newspaper advertisement dating to January of 1804, she could point to Schipper's endorsement of the camera obscura for "imitating Nature correctly."[72]

In Schipper's day, the camera obscura was a well-known optical device. Some versions were as large as a good-sized room or marquee. But given that Schipper was an itinerant, his camera obscura would have been much smaller and portable. It was most likely a rectangular wooden box with a small opening at one end (fig. 32). As light passed through this opening, or aperture, the image was inverted and reversed. An angled mirror reflected the image upwards to the bottom of a ground glass plate. Viewed from above, it appeared right side up and could be traced onto a sheet of

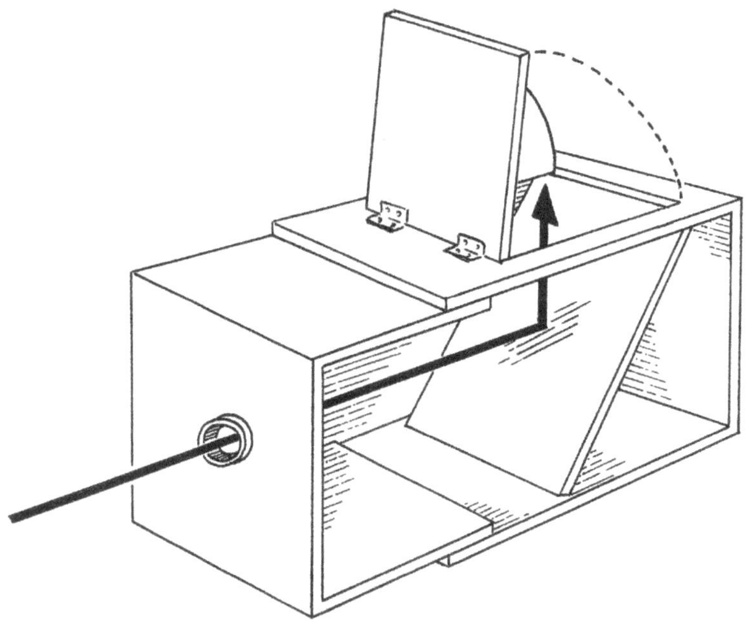

FIGURE 32.

paper. Schipper's camera obscura was also achromatic, meaning that the lens was corrected to diminish chromatic aberration (or colour distortion), thus producing a sharper image.[73] With the better optics of the achromatic camera obscura, Schipper was able to expeditiously trace the sitter's profile in a proportionally reduced size. He then used his artistic ability to finish off the portrait, all of which took about three quarters of an hour.[74] This melding of technology and art combined for a striking likeness, which was so true to life that Schipper was willing to guarantee it. On the off chance that the sitter disapproved of his handiwork, no payment was required.[75] As a cocksure Schipper boasted, the achromatic camera obscura was "highly valued by the first Artists in *Europe*."[76] In effect, he adapted an early form of photography to his artistic pursuits.

When Schipper first arrived at Boston in October of 1803, the physiognotrace was all the rage.[77] Invented some twenty years earlier by a French court cellist named Gilles-Louis Chrétien, the physiognotrace was essentially an easel with a vertically mounted pantograph. By looking through an eyepiece attached to the pantograph and carefully tracing the sitter's profile, Chrétien was able to draw a reduced outline onto an attached piece of paper.[78] The profile was then completed freehand, with Chrétien drawing in the sitter's face and attire. Some physiognotrace operators made quite a profitable business out of this invention, which they accomplished by engraving the finished profiles. This innovation allowed them to reproduce multiple copies for increased sales.[79] Theoretically, anyone could use the physiognotrace to make a faithful outline of a sitter's profile, but a pleasing portrait still called for a talented artist and Gerrit Schipper was just such an artist.

As noted, Mary Allodi was the first person to propose that Schipper might have used a physiognotrace. This she inferred from an advertisement, which Schipper placed in the *Montreal Gazette* at the end of November in 1808. In it, he informed his readers of a "new experiment adopted to take likenesses."[80] But unlike Allodi, who interpreted Schipper's "new experiment" as a veiled reference to a physiognotrace, I thought it had something to do with the way he prepared his pastels. Notwithstanding this difference of opinion, Schipper's use of a physiognotrace was soon confirmed. During a search of the *Quebec Mercury*, I caught sight of the following auction notice from August of 1810: "On THURSDAY, the 9th, at the house of Mr. G. HUOT, No. 7, St. John street, The Household furniture of Mr. G. Schipper, a new fashionable Stove for coal, a Phisiognotrace upon a new construction, a quantity of picture-frames gilt and plain, a few boxes of Crayons, and a variety of other articles."[81] Needless to say, Allodi was delighted with my find, as it provided strong evidence that Schipper's Lower Canadian profile portraits were made using a physiognotrace. For me, there was also the very real possibility that Schipper began his portrait of Brock with one of these drawing instruments. It looked to be a given, but then I began to contemplate the disturbing possibility that he might have gone back to using his camera obscura.

Making sense of the mechanized nature aspect of Schipper's portraiture was proving to be far more complicated than I had anticipated. Did he use a physiognotrace, or a camera obscura? There seemed to be no way to tell, at least not until the spring of 2009. By then, Schipper's profile portrait of Brock (fig. 3) had been sold to the Guernsey Museum and

Art Gallery.[82] This sale could not have come at a better time, as I hoped to verify Kosche's assertion that Brock had a "wart," or mole, on his right cheek.[83] Because this mark was not visible in any of the old photographs of the profile portrait, I concluded that Kosche was mistaken. But wanting to be sure, I looked to a friend in Guernsey for some help. I expected that Gillian Lenfestey would be permitted to scrutinize the so-called wart, if only through the antique glass protecting the portrait's fragile surface. But upon enquiry, Gillian was informed that the portrait had been removed from its frame for some much-needed conservation work. With word of this development, she was able to arrange for a complete "non-destructive" examination of the portrait. It was conducted by Helen Conlon, the Guernsey Museum and Art Gallery's fine art curator, and Gillian was invited to watch.

As Gillian later reported, the mole was actually nothing more than a discolouration in the pastels.[84] As well, a search for the artist's signature failed to produce a specimen of Schipper's "spindly handwriting."[85] Neither was there an inscription to confirm the sitter's identity. However, a certain amount of smudging was detected in the pastels. This damage was thought to have occurred gradually over time, after the mat supplied by Schipper had been discarded.[86] Otherwise, the portrait was in a good state of preservation. There was some migration of the red pigment from Brock's uniform into the upper right background, possibly the result of some injudicious swipe of a hand, but fortunately the blurring missed his face.[87] In examining the four sheets of laid paper used as a backing for the portrait, one of them was seen to have a few test marks of various colours—as if Schipper was trying out his pastels. There was nothing else worthy of note, other than a pinhole in each of the portrait's upper corners. Gillian thought they were probably made by Schipper himself, and that he must have pinned the sheet down while working on Brock's portrait.[88] I saw the pinholes in much the same way, but more in keeping with a physiognotrace. While I knew there were variations in its construction, one feature of the physiognotrace remained constant. The sheet of paper had to be held firmly in place, and from what I had seen in various illustrations, the preferred method was to use tacks or pins.

To my mind, the pinholes held great potential as evidence of a physiognotrace. But I also recognized the need for additional evidence, and there was one course of action that suggested itself almost immediately. Riger first suggested an X-ray of the portrait. In December of 2005, about a year and a half after she made this attribution, Riger recommended the use of electromagnetic radiation "to see if there is the telltale profile outline over which [Schipper] blended the pastels."[89] Although I could well appreciate the importance of an underdrawing, I was reluctant to ask Captain Mellish for the loan of Brock's profile portrait. But I had no hesitation in seeking the same indulgence of the Guernsey Museum and Art Gallery, once I had word that the portrait was liberated from its frame. Helen Conlon was receptive to the idea, although she thought an ultraviolet lamp might work just as well. When its black light proved ineffective, she tried a specialized hand-held "torch"—or flashlight. The pencil line delineating the profile then became "as clear as day."[90] Without all the bother of an X-ray, Conlon had come up with the additional evidence of a physiognotrace—or so I thought. Before long, I had to admit that Schipper could also have traced Brock's profile using a camera obscura, as pencil lines were not exclusively a by-product of the physiognotrace. I was back to square one.

In returning to the pinholes, I decided to contact the process historian at George Eastman House in Rochester, New York. As an authority on pre-photographic imaging processes, Mark Osterman was well qualified to offer an opinion. But instead of agreeing that the pinholes were indicative of a physiognotrace, Osterman countered with a disheartening "Hmmm." He then described the different ways in which the sheet of paper could have been held in place, and how they were "completely variable." Whether it was a physiognotrace or a camera obscura, "people used whatever worked."[91] Osterman thought it more likely that thin metal straps might have been installed to stabilize the paper—although pins or tacks could have functioned just as well, and possibly along with the metal straps.[92] It looked as though it would be impossible to say what caused the pinholes in Brock's portrait, but then I recalled the auction sale notice. Prominently mentioned among the more outstanding items up for offer was Schipper's "Phisiognotrace upon a new construction." Suddenly, I realized that it was the best evidence I was ever likely to find, because if Schipper had a physiognotrace to sell in August of 1810, then he was probably still using it when Brock sat for his portrait a short time earlier (sometime between late May of 1809 and early July of 1810). Moreover, the physiognotrace was just the type of technology that Schipper would have found most serviceable.

While Schipper was an accomplished profile artist, his talent was not well suited to full-length portraits requiring larger formats—as evidenced by the few surviving samples.[93] In each of these larger works, Schipper's awkward treatment of anatomy and perspective is reminiscent of early American folk art. While such naivety is now looked upon as charming and desirable, it was a serious handicap for an artist in the early nineteenth century striving to produce accurate likenesses of his sitters. Challenged by the complexities of form and depth, Schipper opted for half-portraits in profile. But achieving the correct proportions of a sitter's head and shoulders appears to have required more time than he could afford. By resorting to a camera obscura, Schipper was able to reduce a profile more quickly. However, distortion and a lack of focus made for poor images that were difficult to trace. The achromatic camera obscura corrected these problems to a degree, although the image it produced was still far from ideal. Schipper nevertheless considered it to be a vast improvement, and so the achromatic camera obscura became the tool of his trade. In time, however, it would be superseded by a slight variation on Chrétien's physiognotrace.[94]

In the United States, the physiognotrace was frequently converted into a silhouette-making machine. It was easily done, and required very little in the way of new materials. The frame was simply reworked to hold a pane of glass, which was covered on the outer side with gauze or oiled paper. With the light from a nearby window, or perhaps even a candle, the sitter's shadow was cast upon on the translucent coating. Then, by means of a stylus connected to a vertically mounted pantograph, the shadow was traced from the other side of the glass, which remained uncovered and smooth. As in the case of Chrétien's original physiognotrace, the sitter's profile was simultaneously reduced and drawn onto a piece of paper attached near the top of the instrument. The profile was then cut out, and because the paper's reverse side had been blackened, the sitter received a proper-looking silhouette. It was certainly a quick and easy way of making these desirable little keepsakes, but Schipper had no need of a silhouette-making machine. However, he must have seen the advantage in a further reconfiguration of the physiognotrace.

By removing the covering from the pane of glass, Schipper had a clear view of the sitter's profile (fig. 33).[95] With this minor modification, he was able to do his tracing in short order—as there was none of the distortion and lack of focus inherent with the camera obscura.[96] After retrieving the sheet of paper with the reduced profile outlined on it, Schipper sketched in the sitter's features. He then painted the background, contrasting it between light and dark for the best effect. Next came the hair, which was completed in advance of the face to safeguard against any contamination by darker pigments. Once Schipper had achieved an accurate likeness, the portrait was finished with a depiction of the clothing.[97] If the sitter was pleased, then the portrait was matted and framed under glass.[98] Most sitters were very pleased. Regardless of the blank expression that signified his style, Schipper's "mastery of facial modeling and natural flesh tones" gave his profile portraits a presence seldom achieved by itinerant artists.[99] That there was an element of mechanization to his art was of no consequence, although Schipper himself seems to have been more than a little self-conscious about his use of a physiognotrace.

Schipper was slow to embrace the greater utility of the physiognotrace. By late January of 1804, he still employed an achromatic camera obscura—and this at a time when the physiognotrace was becoming a sensation in the United States.[100] While Schipper did eventually abandon his old ways, it appears that much of his resistance to change was the result of an unfortunate association. Many physiognotrace operators worked alongside carnival-like attractions, and the vulgarity of these entertainments might explain why he never acknowledged his own physiognotrace.[101] Although he was by no means a famous artist, Schipper took great pride in being a man of respectability.

Having concluded that Brock's profile portrait (fig. 3) started out as a mechanically traced outline, and that it was therefore a reliable delineation, I began to conceptualize a modern rendering of his silhouette (fig. 34). My goal was to test the authenticity of the bronze profile (fig. 8) and the Jarvis silhouette (fig. 18). But even before the new silhouette was finished, I could see that there was no comparison between it and the bronze profile. As for the Jarvis silhouette, it fared somewhat better except that the sitter appeared to be wearing civilian clothing. This tends to rule out Brock, and so neither of the original silhouettes can be trusted to convey an accurate representation of Brock's profile. That distinction falls to the

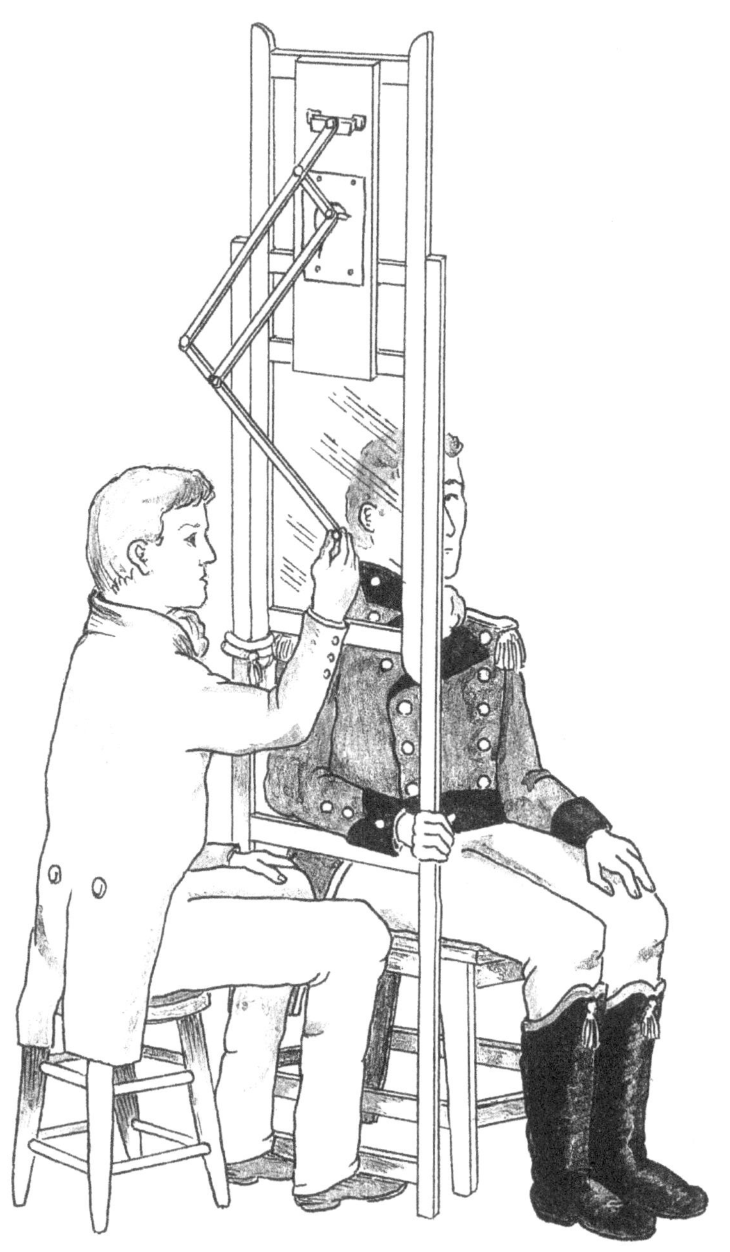

Figure 33.

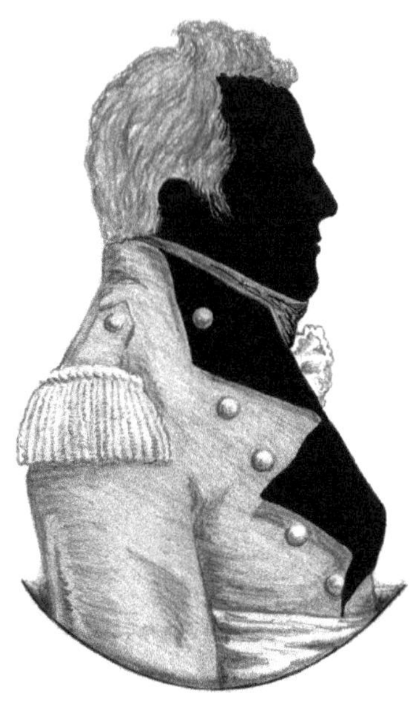

FIGURE 34.

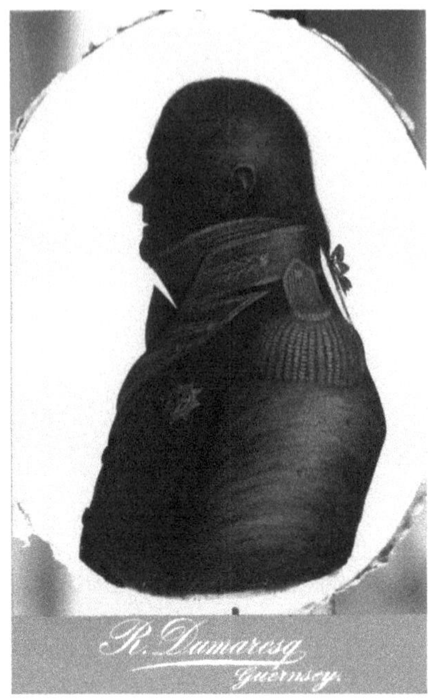

FIGURE 8.

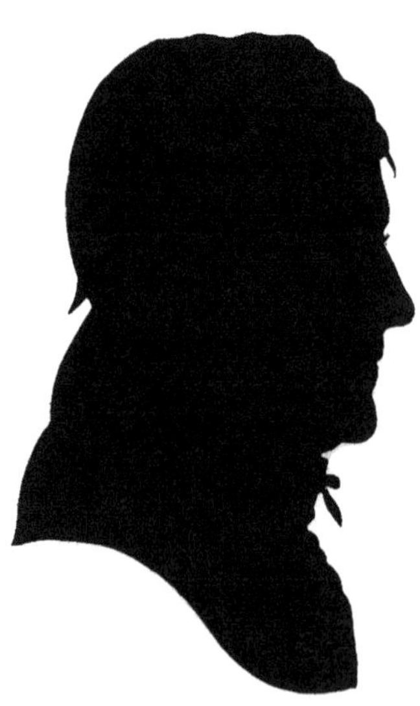

FIGURE 18.

recreation derived from the profile portrait. Although commissioned nearly two hundred years after Brock's death, the precision that went into the making of Schipper's portraiture ensures an accurate silhouette.

My exploration of the largely forgotten world of the physiognotrace was a very rewarding experience, as it brought me to a better understanding of the probable means by which Gerrit Schipper painted his profile portraits—including that of Brigadier General Isaac Brock (fig. 3). With the attribution provided by Jeanne Riger and my investigation into the date of Brock's sitting (not to mention various other asides), I thought every detail surrounding the portrait's creation had been fully considered. But despite my best efforts, one issue remained unresolved. It arose from research carried out by Kosche in which he attempted to explain how the profile portrait made its way to Guernsey.

7

A Very Close Call

Although Ludwig Kosche was convinced that Brock's profile portrait (fig. 3) had been painted in Montreal or Quebec City, he struggled to find the evidence necessary to account for how it ended up in Guernsey. Kosche regarded Major John B. Glegg's statement that he "never possessed a good likeness" of Brock as potentially relevant, if only because it did not rule out the possibility that the profile portrait was sent to William Brock. But even this clue was ultimately dismissed for being "anything but explicit."[1] Admittedly, Major Glegg's statement was vague; however, I was not prepared to reject it out of hand. Instead, I steeled myself for yet another in-depth analysis. While I knew my diligence might result in more confusion than clarification, the major's close association with Brock justified the extra effort.

I started off by checking to make sure that Kosche had copied Major Glegg's statement verbatim. It squared perfectly: "I regret to say," the major wrote, "that I never possessed a good likeness of your Brother, nor did he ever sit for it being taken in this Country."[2] After several readings, not only of this passage but also the entire letter in which it was contained, I began to wonder what had suddenly prompted Major Glegg to raise the matter of Brock's portrait. With a few more readings, I realized that the major was answering a question posed by William Brock after he inherited his brother's personal effects. This query was originally contained in a letter written to Major Glegg in early June of 1813. But by the following September, William Brock had reason to believe that his letter had been lost to an enemy privateer on the high seas, and so he wrote again, enclosing a copy of his first letter with the second—both of which Major Glegg acknowledged in his reply.[3] I knew full well that any attempt to locate these additional letters would be futile. However, by reading between the lines of Major Glegg's letter, I could see that William Brock had not only thanked him for the delivery of his brother's personal effects, but also asked if there might be a better portrait. Such a request would account for Major Glegg having to admit in his reply that he never possessed a "good likeness" of Brock, by which he simply meant to say that had nothing better to offer. There was no doubt in my mind that William Brock had received a portrait of his brother from Major Glegg, but for some unknown reason it was found wanting.

In trying to account for the profile portrait's whereabouts, Kosche had uncovered what he thought was better evidence that Brock's profile portrait had been sent to Guernsey at an early date. It was Mrs. De Beauvoir de Lisle's recollection, which was written down for Colonel Charles W. Robinson in 1882. According to Mrs. de Lisle, who was the former Miss Caroline Tupper, there were two portraits of her uncle Isaac, and these portraits were the property of his brothers, Irving and Savery Brock, respectively.[4] Considering Mrs. de Lisle's longevity and relationship to Brock, her recollection was welcomed as evidence "of a slightly more solid quality" than Major Glegg's statement.[5] That Mrs. de Lisle remembered two portraits was easily explained: one was the original (fig. 3), and the other was the copy (fig. 4). Kosche thought it was feasible enough, but he was still unable to definitively link either one of them to the profile portrait owned by Captain Mellish.[6]

While searching for a viable solution to this dilemma, Kosche happened upon the footnote in Ferdinand Brock Tupper's biography of his famous uncle. In it, Tupper recited an attempt by the officers of the 49th Regiment to obtain a portrait of Brock for their mess room. When they approached the family in 1845, these officers were disappointed to learn that Brock's relatives "possessed no good likeness of the general"—suggesting that there was no such portrait.[7] This, of course, was the same misconception that had given Lieutenant Governor John Beverly Robinson so much cause for concern. But as Kosche learned from the lieutenant governor's experience, which he found published in an old magazine article, the officers of the 49th Regiment were disappointed not because the family possessed *no likeness* of Brock, but rather because they "possessed *no good likeness*."[8] This latter wording was suspiciously similar to Major

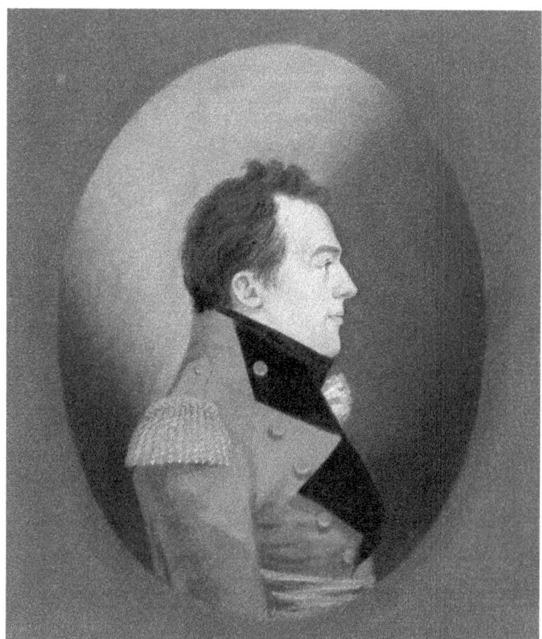

Figure 3.

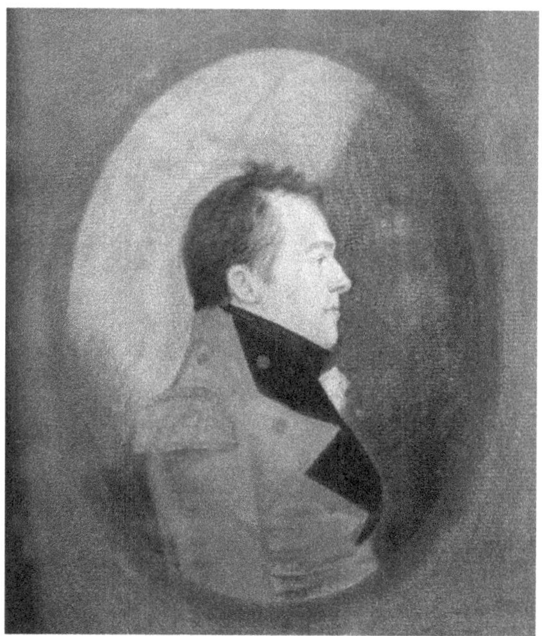

Figure 4.

Glegg's statement that he "never possessed a good likeness" of Brock, and so it appeared to Kosche that Tupper was influenced by what he must have thought was the major's low opinion of the profile portrait.[9] Kosche might not have been any further ahead in terms of making a connection, but thanks to Mrs. de Lisle's recollection, he could argue that whether good, bad, or indifferent, one of the portraits she remembered was the profile portrait owned by Captain Mellish. Then, just when Kosche was beginning to think the matter well enough resolved, the question of quality came back to haunt him.

From what Kosche could tell, the profile portrait was of a very fine quality—and its copy, of which he was aware, was nearly as good. Why Tupper should have considered either one of them to be "no good" was a great mystery, and so Kosche tried to determine why the copy was made in hopes that it might somehow explain Tupper's negative attitude. Unfortunately there were no revealing records. Yet, because the profile portrait owned by Captain Mellish excelled in "clarity, precision of execution, and strength of colour," it was obviously the original and the version that warranted the most attention.[10] This determination, however, did nothing to bring about closure, as Kosche soon began to question whether Tupper referred to the profile portrait (fig. 3) or the bronze profile (fig. 8).[11] In the end, he decided that Tupper must have been thinking of something other than the bronze profile, or bronzed silhouette, as it could not possibly depict Brock. The sitter was wearing the Garter Star, and Brock was never a Garter knight. And to think that Tupper might not have been able to differentiate between the insignia of the Order of the Garter and that of the Order of the Bath, the honour which was actually bestowed upon Brock, would have been "straining credulity."[12] In eliminating the bronze profile, Kosche was left with the profile portrait owned by Captain Mellish and the very real likelihood that it was one of the two portraits Mrs. de Lisle remembered seeing when she went to visit her uncles.[13]

I had to agree with Kosche as to the validity of Mrs. de Lisle's evidence, and I also judged him correct in his rejection of the bronze profile as a possible silhouette of Brock. But I was not satisfied with his interpretation of Tupper's footnote. While I gave him much credit for having recognized that Tupper's reference to Brock's family was really an allusion to Tupper himself, it was surprising to me that Kosche did not suspect

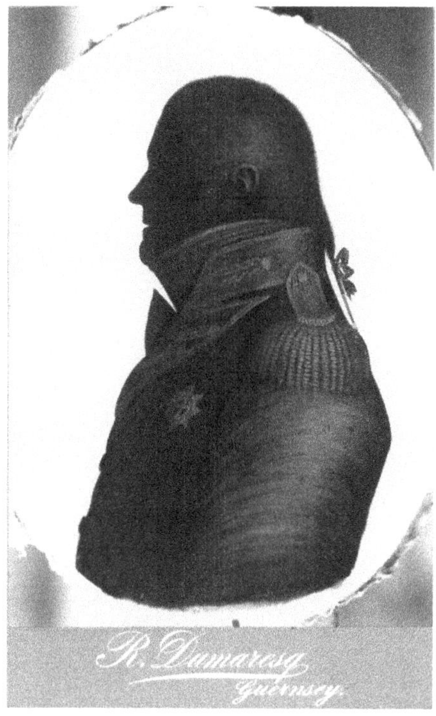

FIGURE 8.

any other chicanery on the part of Brock's nephew and biographer. As already mentioned, he seemed to think that Tupper was echoing Major Glegg's supposedly low opinion of the original profile portrait.[14] It was clear to me, however, that the major did not disparage the quality of the portrait he sent to William Brock. I had already established that person was Tupper himself, and that he was motivated by a desire to suppress a portrait he thought to be no good—a possible characteristic of his obsessive hero-worship, and one that Kosche failed to notice. Kosche, however, redeemed himself somewhat by emphasizing Mrs. de Lisle's recollection that a portrait of Brock was known to have been in Guernsey from the time of her youth.[15] His review of this evidence was spot on. But he also thought he knew how the profile portrait made its way to Guernsey, and in that regard he was decidedly wide of the mark.

A Canadian origin for the profile portrait required a transatlantic crossing for the person entrusted with delivering it, and Kosche could find

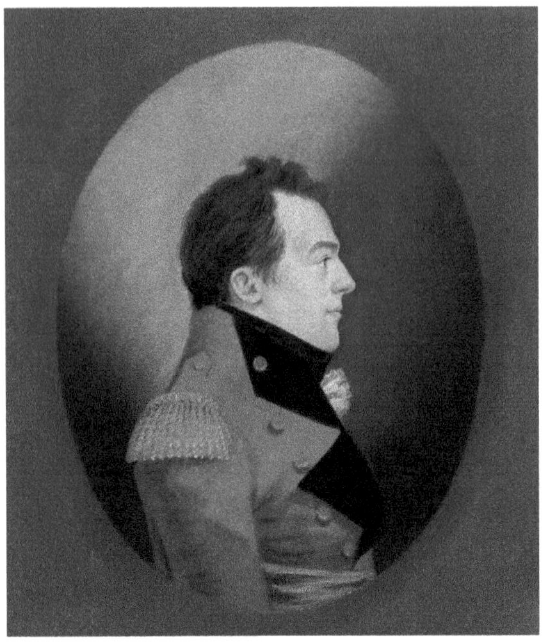

FIGURE 3.

no evidence that it was Major Glegg.[16] However, one of Brock's younger brothers soon became a more likely candidate. Among the transcribed letters Kosche read in Miss Sara Mickle's notebook, one was written by Savery Brock early in January of 1818. This was the letter he addressed to his nephew, Ferdinand Brock Tupper. Much of it dealt with his uncle's tour of Upper Canada, but there were also these instructions: "tell Mrs. Charles de Jersey to be particular in looking over every book for a miniature, that I fancy is placed between the leaves in one or other of them, and to give it with my compliments to the sister of the gentleman."[17] Intrigued by the idea that this miniature could have been the profile portrait of Brock (fig. 3), Kosche readily embraced Miss FitzGibbon's assumption that it was acquired by Savery Brock and brought back to Guernsey with him.[18]

It all made perfect sense to Kosche, especially as the profile portrait was a relatively small item. Unframed, it was only about the same size as a modern sheet of letter size paper.[19] Still, there was no way of knowing if the miniature Savery Brock described in his letter to Ferdinand Brock Tupper was actually the profile portrait. But despite the inherent risk of making a mistake, Kosche suppressed his doubts because of the "simple fact that John Savery thought, rightly or wrongly, that there was a miniature which was presumably a portrait of Brock; why else the excitement?"[20] Unlike Kosche, I did not perceive that Savery Brock was in an excited state when he penned his instructions for Mrs. de Jersey, and my reading of the situation also differed markedly from that of Miss FitzGibbon. While I concurred with her in so much as the unidentified "gentleman" mentioned in the letter was probably the sitter, I was not willing to accept that the miniature Savery Brock wanted Mrs. de Jersey to retrieve was necessarily Brock's profile portrait.

I had my reasons for being a doubting Thomas, not least of which was all the effort it would have required to make the profile portrait more compact. I simply could not understand why anyone would have gone to the trouble of removing a small portrait from its frame, only to make it fit in a book of about the same size. Even with its frame, the profile portrait was still small enough to be packed away in a trunk.[21] I also had to reject Miss FitzGibbon's insistence that the "sister of the gentleman" who figured so prominently in Savery Brock's instructions was Mrs. John Elisha Tupper.[22] True enough, Mrs. Tupper was the only one of Brock's sisters who was still alive when Savery Brock returned from Canada at the end of 1817, but it did not follow that she was the lady he intended to receive the miniature. Miss FitzGibbon, however, had not the slightest hesitancy in assigning this identification to the mystery woman, as Brock's profile portrait (which she assumed to be the miniature mentioned in Savery Brock's letter) was handed down through several generations of the Tupper family. To Kosche, Miss FitzGibbon's argument was credible, but I was having none of it. The miniature could have portrayed anyone, although I suspected it was some gentleman from Guernsey who, along with his sister, was not especially well known to Savery Brock. Thus, a lack of familiarity set the tone for his instructions that the miniature be delivered "with my compliments to the sister of the gentleman."

While the language of polite society during the Regency was governed by a strict etiquette, it was not so formal as to be utterly devoid of feeling. Close friends and relatives could be quite intimate, while still maintaining the necessary level of decorum. But instead of referring to his supposed brother and sister on a first name basis, Savery Brock wrote of them as if they were strangers, albeit esteemed strangers. Granted, there was no reason for him to have mentioned Elizabeth by name, as she was his only surviving sister. Yet, I thought it very peculiar that he should have described her as "the sister of the gentleman," rather than "my sister," and that he could have treated his late brother in such a detached and emotionless manner. Miss FitzGibbon might have scored more points had Savery Brock instructed Mrs. de Jersey to be particular in looking over every book for a miniature of "my ever-to-be-lamented brother," or something to that effect.

Having rejected Savery Brock as the person who conveyed the profile portrait to Guernsey, I turned my attention once again to Major John B. Glegg. I had already gathered that in replying to William Brock's request for a better portrait of his brother, Major Glegg was merely admitting that he had nothing else to offer. I took the major at his word. He did not have a "good likeness," or a better portrait of Brock, and neither was such a portrait ever painted in "this Country," or Upper Canada.[23] It was as simple as that, and Major Glegg's statement in no way compromised the profile portrait attributed to Gerrit Schipper. In fact, the major's statement agreed with my findings, namely that the profile portrait had been painted in Lower Canada, that Brock must have taken it to Upper Canada, and that it remained in his quarters at York (now Toronto) until Major Glegg sent it off to England. Much to my surprise, this sequence of events also included a very close call on Lake Ontario.

On 8 November, 1812, Commodore Isaac Chauncey boarded the brig *Oneida* at Sackets Harbor and sailed out into Lake Ontario. Along with a flotilla of six schooners, he led the way through storms of sleet and snow towards the Upper Canada shore. The shipping season was rapidly coming to an end, and Commodore Chauncey was eager to wrest control of the lake from the British naval force known as the Provincial Marine. The commodore decided on this bold action after receiving intelligence that several British warships were making their way back to Kingston from York. Running before the wind, the British fleet had the advantage of speed as it raced down along the lakeshore. But Commodore Chauncey was optimistic that he might "fall in" with some of the enemy's ships before they reached their destination.[24] This was all the inducement he needed to ignore the dangers of a boisterous lake.

After an overnight anchorage at the Duck Islands off Prince Edward Point, Commodore Chauncey's flotilla began cruising early the next morning. Eventually, the Americans caught sight of the corvette *Royal George* and gave chase, but in the evening they lost track of the British warship during a squall in the Bay of Quinte. Early on the tenth, after another overnight anchorage, the Americans descended upon Ernestown—today's Bath, Ontario—where they captured the merchant schooner *Two Brothers*. But the slow sailing prize was soon ordered burned. This drastic action was taken because the *Royal George* had come into view for a second time. There was a quick pursuit, but the British ship succeeded in reaching Kingston harbour. Disregarding the shore batteries and adverse winds, Commodore Chauncey's flotilla followed after the *Royal George* and gave it a severe pounding. After nearly two hours of battle, and with darkness descending upon them, the Americans were obliged to break off the attack. The commodore planned to return the next day from an anchorage close by, but with the wind threatening to blow a gale, he decided that any further attempt against the *Royal George* would be imprudent. However, in beating out for the open lake during the morning of the eleventh, the American flotilla encountered the *Governor Simcoe*, a merchant schooner in the employ of the Provincial Marine. As before, the American guns inflicted heavy damage, but the *Governor Simcoe* made its escape—only to sink within sight of the wharf at Kingston.[25] Later that same day, another opportunity resulted in the seizure of the merchant schooner *Mary Hatt*.[26] It was a nice prize, but there would soon be a better one.

On the afternoon of 11 November, as Commodore Chauncey's flotilla menaced the eastern end of Lake Ontario, the merchant sloop *Elizabeth* sailed out of York harbour bound for Kingston.[27] On board was Captain James Brock, paymaster to the 49th Regiment, and a cousin to Major General Isaac Brock. Captain Brock was heading home with his wife, along with their trunks and other baggage. But there was considerably more than the usual impedimenta of a travelling officer and his lady.[28] Stowed away in the *Elizabeth*'s hold was all the silverware that Captain Brock had just bought from his deceased cousin's estate.[29] And while he would later deny it, Captain Brock also appears to have been transporting the general's personal effects as well.

Although Captain Brock's posting was at Kingston, the death of his cousin prompted a sudden and unexpected trip to York. As Brock's only relative in the Canadas, Captain Brock was appointed a co-administrator of the dead hero's estate. It was a temporary measure, until such time as Brock's next-of-kin could apply for letters of administration.[30] The other administrator was Major Glegg (then a captain), who must have been deemed eligible because he was Brock's military aide-de-camp. Under this co-operative arrangement, Captains Brock and Glegg were allowed to proceed with a settlement of Brock's affairs, thereby avoiding any unnecessary delays in the midst of an escalating war. And there was no question as to who was the rightful heir. More than once, Brock was heard to say: "I have no occasion for a will, for all and much more than I have belongs to my brother William."[31] It was only fair, given that William Brock provided the funds necessary for the purchase of his brother's commissions.

On 5 November, 1812, Captain Brock petitioned the Probate Court on behalf of himself and Captain Glegg for the administration of his late cousin's estate.[32] The two men then sailed to Niagara(-on-the-Lake), where they accounted for the remainder of Brock's chattel property. They returned to York on 7 November, no doubt having paid their respects at Brock's grave in Fort George.[33] Three days later, the Probate Court granted them letters of administration. With his testamentary duties completed, Captain Brock was free to take his leave. On the eleventh, he and his wife embarked for Kingston.[34] They had little to dread, as the *Elizabeth* sailed in convoy with the *Earl of Moira*—one of the British warships dominating Lake Ontario.[35] But back in York, there was a growing unease and Brock's successor was especially apprehensive. On 14 November, after receiving dispatches informing him of the attack on the *Royal George*, Major General Roger Hale Sheaffe began to worry that the *Earl of Moira* might become the enemy's next target. However, he took some comfort in gauging the weather, which had begun to worsen soon after the *Earl of Moira* and the *Elizabeth* set out for Kingston. Strong winds from the northwest were sure to hasten the ships into the occasional and concealing flurry of snow. Major General Sheaffe also reassured himself that the rising tempest might even force the prowling American flotilla to seek shelter in their own port.[36] What he could not have known, however, was that Commodore Chauncey paid little heed to the weather.

During that same night of 11 November, Commodore Chauncey

was compelled to anchor off the Duck Islands because his pilots "refused to keep the sea." But conditions improved the next morning, allowing the American flotilla to tack against the wind for another adventure at Kingston. Hoping to lure the *Royal George* out from beneath the British batteries, Commodore Chauncey ordered the *Growler* to take the prize *Mary Hatt* in convoy and sail past the harbour. But the decoy failed, and so the American ships anchored for the night in the lee of a nearby island.[37] The following day, which was the thirteenth, Master Mervine Mix of the *Growler* sent the *Mary Hatt* to Sackets Harbor.[38] He then got underway to meet Commodore Chauncey at the Duck Islands. En route, Master Mix had the great good fortune to capture the *Elizabeth*. The commodore was immediately apprised of this development, and also that the British sloop was intercepted while sailing nearly two miles (or just over three kilometres) behind the *Earl of Moira*.[39] Without hesitation, Commodore Chauncey "weighed and stood for Kingston," hoping that his flotilla might succeed in gaining another victory. But the wind and heavy snow worked against him. When he finally spied the *Earl of Moira*, late in the morning of 14 November, it was entering Kingston harbour. Reluctantly, Commodore Chauncey called off the pursuit and signalled a return to port.[40]

Back in Sackets Harbor, word quickly spread that one of the prisoners taken in the *Elizabeth* was a relative of the famous General Brock—but there was a great deal of confusion as to the exact relationship. Some people thought that Captain Brock was a nephew, while others believed him to be a brother. In fact, he was a first cousin—not that it made much difference to Commodore Chauncey. He was happy to make the acquaintance of anyone related to such a well-respected foe. This favourable opinion was a great benefit to Captain Brock. As an officer, he could expect a certain level of civility from his American counterparts. However, as General Brock's cousin, he was shown a much greater degree of courtesy. Gratified and rather unguarded, Captain Brock reciprocated with considerable intelligence about the strength of Kingston's defences.[41] Soon after, and not surprisingly, the commodore issued a parole for Captain Brock.[42] The captain was also allowed the return of his baggage, all of which was understood to be the private property of General Brock.[43] It was a very noble gesture—but the consent of the *Growler*'s crew was also required, as all the baggage under discussion was partly their prize. Fortunately, the American tars were just as high-minded as their commodore.[44] Within a few days of their capture, Captain Brock, his wife, and most of the other British prisoners were sent to Kingston under a flag of truce.[45] Things had turned out much better than Captain Brock could have imagined, but he would not emerge from the ordeal completely unscathed.

In meeting with Lieutenant Colonel John Vincent, the commanding officer at Kingston, Captain Brock shared what he knew about the naval preparations at Sackets Harbor.[46] Of course, there was no need to confess what he had blabbered to the Americans, including his indiscreet assurance that they now had "command of the lake."[47] Captain Brock should have been a little less forthcoming in what he told the enemy, but Commodore Chauncey's genial nature was hard to resist. And Captain Brock knew what was likely to happen if he were to spurn his captor's hospitality and friendly overtures. For one thing, he could count on having his baggage confiscated. A parole might also be denied (as was the case with the *Elizabeth*'s captain, who angered Commodore Chauncey by concealing his ship's papers).[48] Captain Brock avoided the same misstep, and in the process he recited everything he knew about Kingston's defences. There was no harm in it . . . not until his deceit began to appear in print.

The taking of the *Elizabeth* necessitated an addendum to the report Commodore Chauncey had just finished writing for Paul Hamilton, the Secretary of the Navy. But because the commodore was in a hurry to go after the *Earl of Moira*, the extra paperwork fell to his own secretary, Samuel T. Anderson. Dutifully, Anderson wrote out a covering letter informing Secretary Hamilton that the *Growler* had "returned with a prize, and in her captain Brock, brother [sic] to the late general of that name, with the baggage of the latter."[49] In addition, Anderson cited Captain Brock's remark that Kingston was strongly defended, which was harmless enough. But then Anderson went on to describe Captain Brock's astonishment at being told that the American flotilla held its own against the defences of Kingston, as the 49th Regiment was "quartered there, 500 strong, besides other regulars and a well-appointed militia."[50] Inadvertently, Captain Brock had provided valuable intelligence to the enemy. Yet, his unfortunate slip of the tongue might have gone unnoticed, had it not been for Anderson's letter and its publication in the American press. Consequently, and within a matter of weeks, the incriminating document was communicated far and wide throughout the United States. Eventually, the news of Captain Brock's indiscretion reached Upper Canada, where it caused a sensation—most notably in Kingston.

Near the end of December 1812, a suitably embarrassed Captain Brock took up his pen to offer a public explanation, and he was in no mood to mince words. In response to Anderson's offensive letter, he flatly denied having given the Americans any information about the strength of the British forces at Kingston. "Indeed," he angrily retorted, "Commodore Chauncey, had he even expected any such communication, was too much the Gentleman to ask any questions on the subject." Instead, Captain Brock blamed Anderson for having made a false statement, "as the Commodore knew that I was neither General Brock's Brother *nor had any of the General's baggage with me.*"[51]

Captain Brock's vehement denial about the military intelligence he passed to Commodore Chauncey seemed logical. Nor was it unreasonable to think that the captain would have wanted to refute Anderson's incorrect assertion that he was a brother to General Brock. But the bit about the general's baggage was mystifying, as it implied that neither one of the trunks containing Brock's personal effects—including the profile portrait—was consigned to the *Elizabeth*.[52] This unnerving discrepancy called for a further investigation, but first I wanted to see if Captain Brock's letter to the editor had prompted a reaction from the American side. It had not, which led me to conclude that the captain was able to salvage his good name without causing any offence to Commodore Chauncey. The commodore's secretary, however, must have felt unfairly besmirched. As the author of Captain Brock's embarrassment, and a person of no particular consequence, Anderson could be maligned with impunity. It was fortunate for Captain Brock that he did so without alienating Commodore Chauncey, given an incident that occurred a short time later. After the British retreat from Fort George in May of 1813, the commodore very decently let Captain Brock's wife board an American vessel so that she could be safely evacuated.[53] Evidently, Commodore Chauncey was still favourably inclined towards the Brocks, despite the gratuitous abuse inflicted upon his secretary.

It appeared to me that Anderson had accurately represented Captain

Brock's statement about the strength of Kingston's defences. As for the captain's claim that he had none of his cousin's baggage with him when he was captured, I had ample evidence to show that Anderson was correct on that head as well. Most of this evidence came in the form of contemporary newspaper accounts, all of which contradicted Captain Brock. Nevertheless, I was careful to scrutinize these sources—given one news item claiming that Brock's body had been discovered in the hold of a British ship, embalmed "*in a hogshead of spirits*."[54] But apart from this absurdity, and a few minor errors here and there, the main points relating to the *Elizabeth*'s loss were consistent. The general consensus, both in and around Sackets Harbor, was that Brock's baggage had fallen into American hands.[55] Commodore Chauncey thought as much, according to his letter books, and his secretary was of the same mind. So too was Henry Murney, the *Elizabeth*'s master.[56] The only person who disagreed, so it seems, was Captain Brock.

At first, I thought Captain Brock's angry denial vis-à-vis his cousin's baggage had something to do with the intelligence he passed on to Commodore Chauncey. However, it soon became clear that Brock's baggage was its own sore point. In contemplating Captain Brock's reaction, or overreaction, I became curious to know how the American sailors had come to believe that General Brock's baggage was included among their spoils of war. Eventually, I found the answer in an issue of the *Buffalo Gazette* dating from December of 1812, which included an interesting account of the generosity manifested by the *Growler*'s crew.[57] Their decision to relinquish Brock's personal effects was unanimous, and based entirely on Captain Brock's claim that all the baggage he had on board the *Elizabeth* was the property of his dead cousin.[58]

Yet, Captain Brock then went on to disavow any responsibility for the safekeeping of his cousin's baggage. This attempt to distance himself from Brock's personal effects struck me as being very odd, as it was not likely a fluke that Captain Brock just happened to embark in the same sloop assigned to transport his cousin's baggage to Kingston.[59] I also found it hard to believe that Captain Brock, as one of the administrators of Brock's estate, would not have been in charge of his cousin's baggage during the voyage. The captain's dodgy behaviour was more than a little suspicious, and it was beginning to look as though he had something to hide—such as all the silverware in his baggage.

Ferdinand Brock Tupper certainly believed that this silverware, or plate as it was called, formed part of his uncle's personal effects, and obviously so too did the Americans.[60] But while Brock was known to have owned a good deal of plate at the time of his death, none of it went to his brother in England. Like most of his chattel property, these items were sold at York to settle Brock's estate. One of the people making purchases was Captain Brock, and among his various acquisitions was a quantity of silverware.[61] The captain might have thought his plate was as good as lost when the *Elizabeth* was first captured, but he later managed to secure his recent purchase by letting on that it comprised part of Brock's personal effects. This ploy probably explains why Captain Brock was so adamant that he had nothing to do with his cousin's baggage. It was unfortunate that Commodore Chauncey had to be duped in such an underhanded manner, but Captain Brock must have known that his plate was more likely to be restored by the Americans if they thought it belonged to the estate of the dead British general they had come to admire. The captain was guilty of bad form, but his transgression was minor and there was little fear of it being exposed—that is, until Anderson's letter was published.[62]

While the duplicity by which Captain Brock preserved his property would have been viewed as distasteful by many of his contemporaries, he stood a good chance of being forgiven in light of the wartime circumstances. But the exploitation of a dead soldier's fame would have been considered most ungentlemanly, and given that an unblemished reputation was of paramount importance to a British officer in the early nineteenth century, a scandal—even one emanating from the enemy's camp—threatened to impair a promising military career. It is not surprising, then, that Captain Brock was so anxious to distance himself from his cousin's baggage. And there can be no question that he deceived Commodore Chauncey into believing that it belonged to Brock in order to secure his own property as well. Yet, were it not for this artifice, Brock's profile portrait would have been lost.[63] Thankfully, however, there was more than enough plate in the *Elizabeth*'s hold to alter this outcome.

Upon his return to Kingston, Captain Brock did not participate further in the conveyance of his cousin's personal effects, other than possibly arranging for them to be sent on to Quebec City. Although winter was closing in, there was still time to ship the trunks by means of a batteau (one of the many flat-bottomed coasting vessels used for heavy transport). And if the trunks got no farther than Montreal before the freeze, they could still be sent overland by wagon the rest of the way, perhaps even by sleigh once the roads were sufficiently snow covered. While the trunks were unlikely to arrive in Quebec City before the close of navigation, they would at least be ready for shipment in the spring.[64] Unfortunately, there are no records to verify any of these conjectures, and yet William Brock acknowledged the receipt of his brother's personal effects in June of 1813.[65] The timing of this delivery meant that Brock's trunks must have been sent to England soon after the opening of navigation at Quebec City, which was in the first week of May 1813.[66] For the trunks to have been dispatched so early in the season, they were likely stored near the wharves of the lower town well in advance of their lading. Despite the absence of detailed shipping records for the period, which made it impossible for me to say anything more definite about the trunks, there was still much to be learned from Brock's servant and the role he played in their delivery.

When Thomas Porter joined the 49th Regiment in 1797, he was just another young recruit.[67] In time, however, he was singled out to be Brock's servant. It was a great honour, and apparently one occasioned by the death of Private James Dobson in 1805.[68] Private Dobson was an earlier servant, and the same one who faithfully nursed Brock back to health in the West Indies (after a near fatal illness almost killed the young officer).[69] Private Dobson's was a hard act to follow, but Private Porter proved himself no less devoted and so he was chosen to accompany Brock's personal effects to England. Upon his arrival at William Brock's residence near London, Private Porter made a very favourable impression. Brock's family were touched by the young man's kindness—so much so, in fact, that they requested his discharge from the army.[70] The Duke of York, as commander-in-chief of the British Army, willingly complied with this "small tribute" to the memory of a gallant officer.[71]

Initially, Private Porter's delivery of Brock's personal effects seemed to substantiate Captain James Brock's claim that he had nothing to do with his cousin's baggage. This was no little complication for me, as Private Porter's involvement suggested that perhaps it was he who accompanied Brock's personal effects on board the *Elizabeth*—and that Captain Brock's passage in the same vessel was nothing more than a coincidence. But as I soon began to appreciate, if Brock's personal effects were in Private Porter's custody at the time of the *Elizabeth's* capture, then he should have been listed as one of the British prisoners at Sackets Harbor. Yet, Private Porter's name was absent. I went back over my sources, but after all was said and done, it still appeared to me that Captain Brock had been assigned the task of looking after his cousin's trunks. As I racked my brain trying to comprehend the arrangements made for the delivery of Brock's personal effects, two scenarios emerged. Either Private Porter was selected for the job right from the outset, or he was a later substitute for Captain Brock.

The muster books and pay lists of the 49th Regiment revealed that Private Porter was in garrison at York until the early spring of 1813.[72] This information precluded the possibility that he was taken prisoner on the *Elizabeth*, or that he was employed in transporting Brock's personal effects to Kingston. Still, it was Private Porter who eventually delivered the general's trunks to William Brock. But as I was beginning to realize, this assignment was not the result of Captain Brock's imprisonment. Rather, it was because the trunks were never intended to go farther than Quebec City until the opening of navigation in 1813, and so Private Porter's services were not immediately required. Since there was no urgency for his departure from the regiment, he remained at York over the winter. The trunks, however, were sent ahead, no doubt in the care of Captain Brock, and in his capacity as a co-administrator of Brock's estate.[73]

While it was Private Porter's sad duty to convey Brock's trunks to England, Captain Glegg had all the worry over their safety. The thought of enemy privateers menacing Britain's transatlantic shipping must have made him extremely anxious.[74] But little did he realize, there was a more immediate peril on the storm-tossed waters of Lake Ontario. And when Captain Glegg received news of the *Elizabeth*'s misfortune, he was surely horrified. Yet, Brock's personal effects would have been subjected to far greater risk had they been left at York. It was a threat that became painfully apparent the following spring. During an American attack at the end of April 1813, Captain—or rather Major—Glegg had no choice but to abandon the few keepsakes he still retained from Brock's estate. As the British army under Major General Sheaffe beat a hasty retreat towards Kingston, these sentimental items were confiscated by the Americans and sold for the relief of their wounded soldiers.[75] Brock's profile portrait would have suffered the same fate, had it not been sent out of harm's way in a timely fashion.

8

In Coming Forward

At the same time that William Brock received his brother's personal effects in June of 1813, a monument to Sir Isaac Brock was being proposed for St. Paul's Cathedral.[1] As its main proponent, William Brock surely recognized the importance of having a good likeness from which to sculpt the hero's face.[2] Unfortunately, the portrait supplied by Major John B. Glegg was not up to snuff—possibly because it was done in profile (fig. 3). While such a portrait might have functioned perfectly well for a modest effigy, William Brock seems to have had his heart set on something more grandiose and in keeping with his late brother's elevation to the pantheon of British heroism. He might even have contemplated a larger-than-life statue, like many of the other monuments in St. Paul's. Whatever the case, William Brock was motivated by the national significance of his endeavour, and so he wrote to Major Glegg hoping to find a more suitable, or full-faced, portrait. Unfortunately, there was nothing better to be had from Canada.[3]

The monument proposal went ahead regardless, and in August of 1814 Richard Westmacott was commissioned to undertake the work.[4] This renowned British sculptor handily compensated for a lack of reference material by means of a highly romanticized neoclassical tableau.[5] With the central figure recumbent in death, eyes closed and head tilted sideways, Westmacott imagined Brock's likeness to conform with the classical motif of the dying warrior (figs 20, 20A). Indeed to anyone who knew Brock intimately, most notably his siblings, the sculpture was merely symbolic. However, given the difficulties Westmacott laboured under, it is unlikely that anyone in the Brock family would have expressed the slightest displeasure with his effort. The resulting memorial was still a great honour, even if it was not quite what William Brock had in mind. And

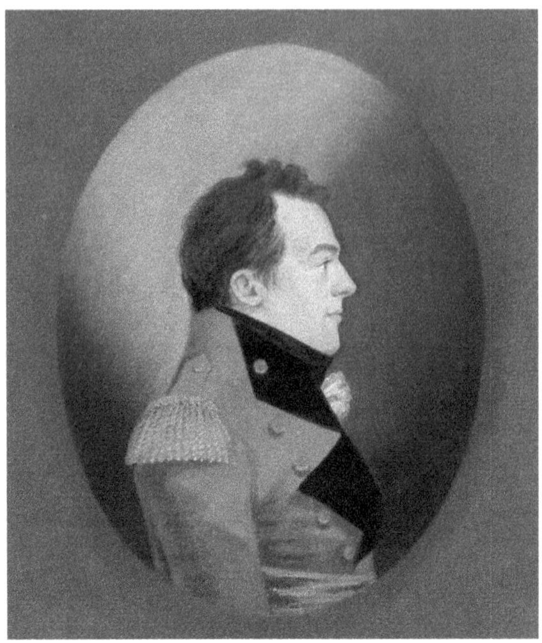

FIGURE 3.

Westmacott's rendition certainly comes closer to the truth than the statue adorning Brock's Monument on Queenston Heights, which could easily be mistaken for the American General Winfield Scott (mutton chops and all).[6]

During the course of my research into Brock's memorial, I could see how Westmacott had made good use of the profile portrait to represent the deceased hero as an alluring young man. However, based on the only two portraits known to be authentic, there is no disputing the fact that Brock was blessed with good looks. In the case of the miniature (fig. 27), he is shown as a handsome young ensign.[7] The profile portrait (fig. 3), which was painted some twenty-four or twenty-five years later, attests to the fact that Brock was still handsome as he approached middle age. But notwithstanding the strong visual evidence contained in these two portraits, I became curious to know how he fared in contemporary eyewitness accounts. There were precious few, however, and none of them actually referred to Brock as having been good-looking. In fact, one went so far as to call him ugly!

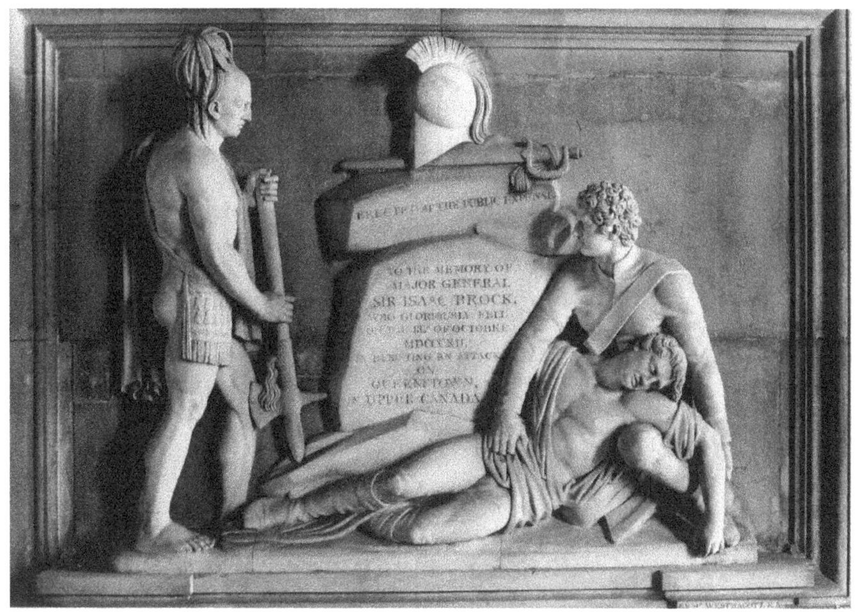

Figure 20.

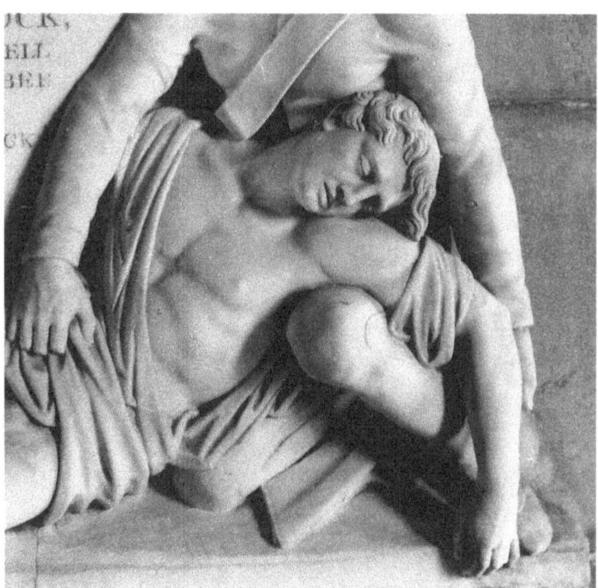

Figure 20a.

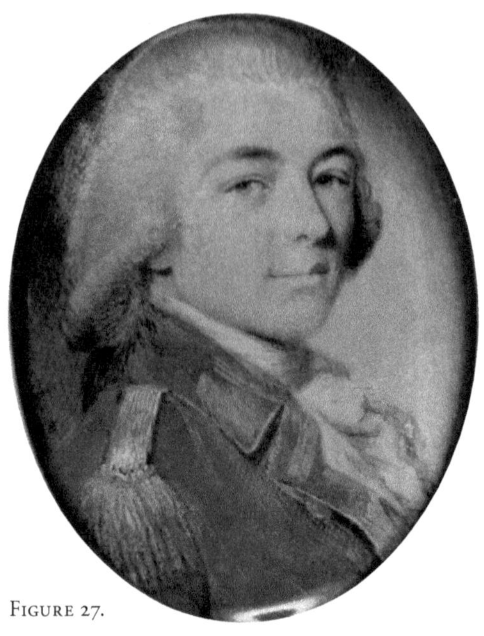

FIGURE 27.

Beginning with Major John Richardson, an aspiring Canadian author who also happened to be a veteran of the War of 1812, I hoped to get to the heart of the matter by establishing some basic facts about Brock's appearance. In 1842, Richardson remembered that Brock "was tall, stout, and inclining to corpulency." He was also "of fair and florid complexion, had a large forehead, full face, but not prominent features, rather small, greyish-blue eyes, with a very slight cast in one of them—small mouth, with a pleasing smile, and good teeth."[8] Tupper's own (and largely inferred) description corresponds with that of Major Richardson, except that it is more specific with regard to his uncle's height. "In stature he was tall (. . . about six feet two inches [1.88 m]), erect, athletic, and well-proportioned, although in his latter years his figure was perhaps too portly."[9] Another Canadian veteran of the War of 1812 was John Beverley Robinson, who went on to become chief justice of what is now Ontario. He supposed Brock to be "not quite so tall" as Tupper claimed, but was willing to concede the point.[10] The acting assistant quartermaster general of the American army at the surrender of Detroit was William Stanley Hatch, and his recollection was that Brock "must have been six feet three or four inches [1.91 or 1.93 m] in height; very massive and large boned, though not fleshy, and apparently of immense muscular power."[11] George Sanderson, the captain of an Ohio volunteer company captured after the surrender, held a much less flattering view.[12] He saw in Brock "a heavily built man, about six feet three inches [1.91 m] in height, broad shoulders, large hips, and lame, walking with a cane." Moreover, one of his eyes, "the left one I think, was closed, and he was withal the ugliest officer I ever saw."[13]

Suspecting that Sanderson's observation may have been tainted by the spite of a sore loser, I decided to focus my attention on the similarities between his and the other descriptions of Brock. In the end, I was left with the impression of a tall, sturdy man whose body type allowed him to carry his weight well. And if Brock became heavy set towards middle age, then he did so without looking fat—as evidenced by his profile portrait.[14] This likeness also soundly refuted Sanderson's contention that Brock was ugly.[15] In attempting to give Sanderson the benefit of my doubt, I considered the possibility that Brock might have been confused with some other British officer who happened to be lame. While it was difficult to imagine such a mix-up, a case of mistaken identity emerged as the most plausible explanation.

The idea of a disfigured Brock was also employed to explain the direction of his pose in the profile portrait. The person responsible for this theory was William Kingsford, a Canadian historian. In 1886, he published an article outlining the most relevant sources then available for research into the nation's past. Kingsford also used the opportunity to acknowledge significant contributions to the study of Canadian history, and Lieutenant Governor John Beverley Robinson was applauded for his good work in commissioning the viceregal portraits for Government House in Toronto. It was during his interactions with the lieutenant governor that Kingsford became aware of the original profile portrait (fig. 3), and a possible secret meaning behind Brock's pose. As Kingsford related in his article, it involved "some scar or mark on the face" which was hidden by having Brock look to the right.[16] While this interpretation might seem suspiciously similar to Sanderson's description, it appears to have originated with the lieutenant governor himself. At any rate, there is no evidence to suggest that the other side of Brock's face was marred or in any way less attractive.[17]

Although I concluded that Brock was uniformly good-looking, I could see how a sculptor like Westmacott might have been disappointed with the profile portrait. It was hardly adequate to the task of carving a three-dimensional statue, which perhaps explains why it was regarded as "no good." This was the same unfortunate attitude that Ferdinand Brock Tupper had taken to extremes. Yet, there is absolutely nothing to indicate that anyone else in Brock's family—including Brock for that matter—thought ill of the profile portrait. Having come to this realization, my next concern became one of provenance.

William Brock retained the profile portrait until his death in December of 1819.[18] It then passed to his brother, Irving Brock, but the particulars of this bequest are unknown.[19] Although William Brock left a will, he made no provision for the portrait.[20] However, as his widow (the former Miss Sarah Maria Putt) was the sole beneficiary, she may have carried out her husband's last wishes by giving the portrait to her brother-in-law. There is also the possibility that William Brock made a gift of the portrait before he died. This much is certain: Irving Brock was the next owner of the profile portrait. Like his brother before him, Irving Brock made no provision for its disposal, at least not in his will.[21] But according to Miss Henrietta Tupper, he bequeathed the portrait to his nephew, Henry Tupper of Guernsey. If so, it was likely Irving Brock's widow, Mrs. Frances (Longley) Brock, who arranged for the bequest after her husband's death in 1838.[22] And there is no reason to suspect that Henry Tupper did not inherit the portrait, just as Miss Tupper claimed.[23] After all, her source was Henry Tupper's widow (formerly Miss Mary Ann Collings), and who better to have known how the portrait came to be his property? Mrs. Tupper owned the profile portrait after her husband's death in 1875, and it was still in her possession when the Robinsons began making their enquiries six years later.[24]

My research had come full circle, and considering that two centuries had passed since Brock sat for his profile portrait, I congratulated myself on having accomplished all of my goals—and then some. But my smug attitude was short-lived, especially once I began to feel the necessity of bringing the record forward. It was then that a certain fiasco came to mind.

Early in 2009, the Weir Foundation of Queenston, Ontario began an urgent fundraising campaign for the purchase of Gerrit Schipper's profile portrait of Brock (fig. 3). It had been offered to the foundation in December of the previous year by Captain Mellish's son, Nicholas T.L. Mellish.[25] Included was Philip Jean's miniature of Brock as a young ensign (fig. 27). The asking price for the pair was a whopping £70,000, which was calculated as follows: £40,000 for Schipper's profile portrait, and £30,000 for Jean's miniature. While the foundation was eager to have both portraits for the RiverBrink Art Museum, its acquisitions budget fell short of the valuations Nicholas Mellish placed on them. Taking a chance, however, the foundation countered with an offer of £60,000, which was quickly accepted. Despite a tight payment deadline, which was set to expire less than two months later at the end of the February 2009, the foundation's executive believed there was ample time to raise the necessary funds. But Mellish was becoming anxious to finalize the sale, and in the second week of February he reopened negotiations with the Weir Foundation by lowering the price to £50,000.[26] There was a sizeable catch, however.

The foundation now had just ten days to come up with what amounted to an estimated $90,000 CAD.[27] A public appeal for financial assistance was immediately launched. But even with the many contributions received, which totalled almost $83,000 in very short order, it was all for naught. With just a few days before the new deadline, the foundation was informed that the portraits had been sold to the Guernsey Museum and Art Gallery.[28] Mellish had sweetened the deal by throwing in the miniature of John Brock as a lieutenant in the 8th (or King's) Regiment (fig. 25), and he let all three portraits go for the drastically reduced price of £36,000.[29] The Canadian equivalent was approximately $64,500, or about $18,500 less than the nearly $83,000 already raised by the Weir Foundation when Mellish reneged.[30] This outcome was extremely frustrating for everyone who wanted to see the profile portrait put on permanent display in Queenston, and it hearkened back to an incident almost half a century earlier.

In January of 1964, Captain Mellish received an extraordinary letter from Canada. It was written by a lawyer in London, Ontario, who wanted to know if the captain would be interested in "disposing" of Sir Isaac Brock's portrait "presently or at some time in the future." The lawyer was Samuel E. Weir, and he had a particular reason for wanting the profile portrait: "I am collecting for a prospective museum of Canadiana on the

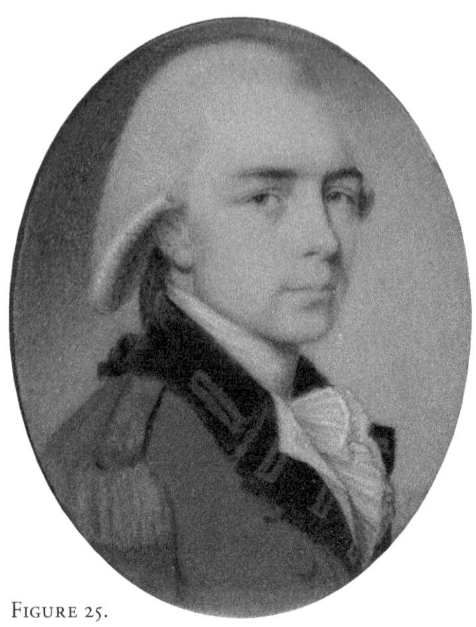

Figure 25.

Niagara River at Queenston, just a few hundred yards from the spot where Brock was killed. The building is now under construction. It will be used by me as a residence until the museum is finally set up, which I expect will be at the time of my death."[31] As Weir further elaborated, it was "probably the most suitable place in the world for this Portrait," and based on this assessment, Captain Mellish was expected to agree.[32] It was an incredibly tactless letter, and one that was all too typical of its author.

Sam Weir was a large, overbearing man whose blunt manner did nothing to endear him to most of the people he met.[33] The severity of these traits showed no signs of moderating as the years advanced—nor did his passion for fine art, rare books, and choice antiques. Weir also had a deep interest in Canadian history, especially the War of 1812 and the Battle of Queenston Heights.[34] Thus, when it came time for him to think about giving up his legal practice, Weir decided to relocate to the sleepy little village of Queenston, Ontario. The retirement he envisioned began to take shape in the early 1960s, with the construction of a colonial style house on the Niagara River named, appropriately enough, River Brink.[35] It was really a museum in the making, and Weir was its sole benefactor. By early 1964, it occurred to the aging lawyer that River Brink should have a portrait of

Sir Isaac Brock—and preferably the original. Somehow or other, he knew there was such a painting. He also knew that it was owned by a Captain Mellish of St. Peter Port in Guernsey. This was all the introduction Weir needed before getting down to business.[36] His letter of enquiry, however, read more like a demand for terms.

Captain Mellish wasted little time in posting his reply. Trusting that the lawyer from Canada would respect his decision, the captain explained that he valued the portrait "very highly indeed," and so he did not feel he would want to "dispose of it either now or in the future."[37] The captain's diplomacy seemed to disarm the brusque old lawyer for a time, but then Weir came up with a plan B. "As you don't feel that you would part with it," he wrote back, "I venture to ask if you would allow me to engage somebody to make a copy of it? I should think there would be an Artist available in Guernsey capable of doing it."[38] Captain Mellish was more than happy to comply with this request, but he also believed a photograph of the portrait would serve the same purpose, and he felt confident that Weir would find one in Ottawa. "I should be glad to know your reaction to this suggestion," the captain added, "and if you take it up, whether or not you have any success."[39] But there were no more letters from Canada. Weir let the matter drop, preferring instead to devote his energies to other, less problematic, acquisitions.

In 1971, Weir finally realized his dream of living in Queenston by completing a gradual move to River Brink, which he then maintained as his principal residence for the rest of his life.[40] After his death in January of 1981, there was a remarkable transformation of the curmudgeonly lawyer's reputation—from misanthrope to philanthrope.[41] This redemption came about through the posthumous donation of his impressive art collection to the people of Ontario.[42] It was exceedingly generous; unfortunately, Weir's gift did not include the likeness of Sir Isaac Brock . . . until an old friend took matters into his own hands.

F. Eugene LaBrie first encountered Sam Weir just after the Second World War, while lecturing in law at the University of Toronto. Despite Weir's long-established career as a barrister and solicitor (having graduated from the Ontario law school in 1920), he had not yet earned a law degree and he was determined to enhance his legal credentials.[43] It was not to be, however, as ill health, the long commute, and a heavy workload forced

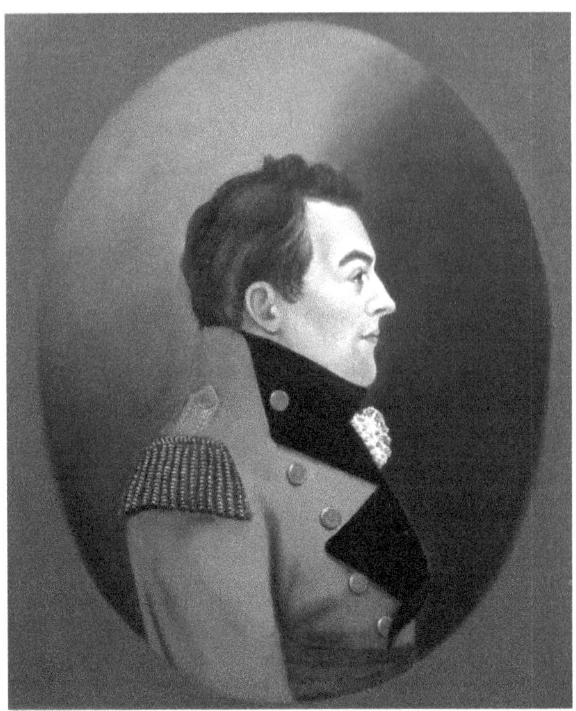

FIGURE 35.

him to abandon his studies—but not before he and LaBrie became good friends.[44] In time, LaBrie took on the additional roles of trusted advisor, close confidant, and finally chairman of the Weir Foundation. And as the person most familiar with Weir's vision for River Brink, LaBrie took it upon himself to obtain a copy of Brock's profile portrait, which he knew had been originally intended but never acted upon. He also planned for a second copy, which would go to Brock University as a donation (fig. 35).[45] Captain Mellish graciously consented to having the portrait photographed, and by the spring of 1984 LaBrie was ready to go in search of an artist.[46]

Someone at the National Portrait Gallery in London recommended Philippa Abrahams.[47] As an art conservator specializing in historical painting techniques, she was thought to be well qualified for the job. Abrahams welcomed the commission, which called for the two portraits to be done in oils as opposed to the pastels of the original. In addition to the medium, the size of the copies was also modified. Abrahams was instructed to make them nearly three times larger, or about twenty-four by twenty inches (61 x 50.8 cm).[48] And while she was encouraged to use her best judgement in representing the uniform, Brock's face was not to be altered. It had to be an exact reproduction. There was one other stipulation. Abrahams had one year in which to finish the portraits. Working expeditiously and using the photographs provided by LaBrie, she was able to finish the commission ahead of the deadline in August of 1985.[49]

Although Weir's intention to grace the walls of River Brink with Brock's likeness was finally realized, it was not before LaBrie himself tried to strike his own deal to purchase the original portrait. But it was to no avail. Captain Mellish valued the profile portrait far too much. Kosche hit the same brick wall in September of 1984, when he casually asked if the captain might consider the possibility of a sale.[50] Kosche was acting on behalf of the Ontario Heritage Foundation, whose executive were looking for ways in which to mark the bicentennial of Ontario's founding in 1784.[51] Even though Kosche knew that Captain Mellish had already decided to pass the portrait on to his son, he saw no harm in testing the waters. In his reply, Captain Mellish mentioned that a Mr. LaBrie had been making overtures about buying the portrait for the past two years, and that he did so in his capacity as chairman of the Weir Foundation. But whether it was the Weir Foundation or the Ontario Heritage Foundation, the captain was still not prepared to entertain the idea of a sale . . . unless, of course, the interested party was willing to hand over £250,000![52]

This grossly inflated price was derived—in part—from LaBrie's unguarded remark that the profile portrait was a national treasure.[53] It is no wonder that Captain Mellish was impressed with the idea that his portrait of Brock was historically significant and therefore extremely valuable.[54] But not even he believed it to be worth a quarter of a million pounds. The captain simply did not wish to part with a prized family heirloom, and by insisting on a small fortune, he was able to deflect irksome enquiries. This strategy certainly had the desired effect on the executive of the Ontario Heritage Foundation, who were quick to acknowledge that they lacked the means for such an extravagant purchase.[55] The same held true for the Weir Foundation. But like Sam Weir before him, Eugene LaBrie had a plan B.

While the Abrahams copy of Brock's profile portrait was meant to put the finishing touch on the collection at RiverBrink, it was a poor substitute for the original. Over time, this pastiche became a constant reminder of what was still lacking in Weir's vision for his museum. After LaBrie's replacement as chairman of the Weir Foundation and the passage of nearly twenty-five years, there was a commendable attempt to repatriate what is arguably a Canadian work of art. That it failed is unfortunate, but every cloud has a silver lining. Soon after the Guernsey Museum and Art Gallery acquired the profile portrait, it was given a much-needed restoration and then generously lent to RiverBrink for a major exhibition commemorating the War of 1812.[56] This kind gesture did much to remove the sting of a missed opportunity.

Conclusion

After nearly a decade's worth of research, the true face of Sir Isaac Brock was finally revealed in the profile portrait by Gerrit Schipper (pl. 3). While Philip Jean's miniature of a youthful Ensign Brock (pl. 27) is authentic in its own right, the depiction of an older Brock on the verge of becoming the "Hero of Upper Canada" holds far greater relevance. For many years, however, the existence of the profile portrait was unknown, as Ferdinand Brock Tupper used his influence as Brock's biographer to suppress it. Thankfully, Dr. John George Hodgins was determined to have an accurate likeness of Brock for Ontario's Educational Museum. His persistence was rewarded with a photograph of the profile portrait, which George Berthon used as the model for his own painting of Brock (pl. 9). This grand canvas was intended to be Brock's official portrait, and it soon became the most widely recognized portrait of the great man—but not for long.

The miniature discovered by Miss Sara Mickle (pl. 11) was considered a much better portrayal, mainly because it was painted in three-quarter pose and showed more of the hero's noble countenance than did Berthon's reworking of the profile portrait. It was also more visually appealing, featuring a handsome young officer for the hopeless romantics to moon over. But while the miniature came highly recommended, it did not appear quite right to certain members of the Robinson family. Gossip began to undermine the credibility of this newfound likeness, and, fearing a confrontation with one of Toronto's first families, Miss Mickle readily accepted Miss Agnes FitzGibbon's offer to seek out evidence of the miniature's authenticity. It must have seemed a godsend at the time, especially as Miss FitzGibbon was developing something of a reputation for being a Canadian historian. But in terms of the miniature, at least, her attitude towards historical research had more to do with proving a point than seeking the truth.

Fortunately for Miss FitzGibbon and Miss Mickle, they were never taken to task over the identity of the young officer in the miniature. Miss FitzGibbon certainly tempted fate when she denounced Berthon's portrait of Brock as being a "lifeless presentment," but despite this provocation none of the Robinsons were willing to engage Miss FitzGibbon in an undignified war of words. "Historian," who was likely Christopher Robinson, merely skirted the issue by defending Berthon's portrait against Miss FitzGibbon's unfair criticism. The Honourable John Beverley Robinson would have been far more outspoken, as it was he who commissioned Berthon's portrait. But the former lieutenant governor was dead. And while Major General Charles W. Robinson was convinced that Miss Mickle was trying to foist a false image on the people of Canada, he was unable to disprove the miniature's authenticity and so he kept his silence. Had he been less concerned about his reputation as a gentleman, the general could very easily have undermined Miss Mickle's discovery simply by pointing out the various discrepancies in the miniature. But just as Miss FitzGibbon predicted, General Robinson had no stomach for fighting women and so the misidentification went unchallenged.

For almost a century thereafter, Lieutenant George Dunn was mistaken for Major General Sir Isaac Brock. Ludwig Kosche finally set the record straight in 1985, and it was a significant breakthrough—albeit one that Kosche himself relegated to obscurity. Publishing his findings in a professional journal of limited distribution was by no means conducive to reaching a wider audience. A more popular approach would have had greater effect, provided there was a willingness on his part to deal with the Dunn miniature separately, and either in a newspaper or magazine article. But Kosche was anxious to be done with Brock, so the portraits were left in their original groupings according to medium. It was an unfortunate decision, as this format made it impossible to emphasize the awful truth behind Lieutenant Dunn's miniature.

Apart from the flaws in his presentation, most of Kosche's findings are sound and reliable. But in accepting William Berczy as the artist responsible for the profile portrait (pl. 3), the normally wary Kosche allowed himself to be led astray. Eventually, Jeanne Riger confirmed my belief that

Gerrit Schipper was the artist. With this correct attribution, I was able to pin down the time and place of the portrait's commission. The unorthodox arrangement of Brock's buttons, which was not in compliance with his appointment to brigadier general, remained a vexing problem as it tended to cast doubt on the sitter's identity. But after making sense of the discrepancy, I resolved the question in favour of Brock and no one else. My next challenge was to try to understand the process used in the making of the profile portrait. Having satisfied myself that Schipper probably employed a physiognotrace, I decided to look into the workings of that instrument. During this exercise, it became obvious to me that Brock's portrait was done from life and that no part of it was pre-painted. Another important consideration was the quality of Schipper's portraiture, and whether it was good or bad. While the latter contention was patently ridiculous, refuting the nonsense required a good deal of effort.

It was Ferdinand Brock Tupper who originated the idea that the profile portrait was somehow "no good." Actually, all Tupper ever claimed was that Brock's family "possessed no good likeness of the general." But in doing so, he implied a negative impression of the profile portrait. Tupper might have been influenced by Major John B. Glegg's admission that he never possessed a "good likeness" of his friend and general. While it is likely that Major Glegg simply meant to say that he had nothing better to offer, Tupper appears to have thought that he was passing judgement on the profile portrait. There is also the possibility that because this portrait shows only one side of Brock's face, it was deemed unsuitable as a model for an elaborate memorial in St. Paul's Cathedral. Such a rejection could easily have given rise to a mistaken belief that the portrait was therefore "no good." Whatever his rationale, Tupper judged Schipper's profile portrait of Brock to be unworthy of his famous uncle.

However much Ferdinand Brock Tupper may have disapproved of the profile portrait (pl. 3), there is not the slightest hint that his uncle was unhappy with it—especially as Brock appears to have kept this particular portrait with him until the day he died. Even if the portrait was a gift from Governor Sir James H. Craig, and supposing there was a reluctance to dispose of it for fear of causing offence, any such concern would have been greatly diminished once Brock was posted to Upper Canada in 1810. With Governor Craig's departure in 1811, followed by the news of his death early the next year, Brock was free to do as he pleased with the profile portrait. But since it was not discarded, Brock probably thought the likeness did him justice. His brothers must have agreed, as they carefully preserved both the original profile portrait and a copy as well. Little is known of this copy (pl. 4), except that it was an heirloom in Savery Brock's branch of the family for many years. And the duplication resulted in a very close copy, which suggests that the original was sufficiently true to life as to warrant an exact reproduction.

But regardless of his skill in rendering an accurate representation, Schipper could not compete with the leading portrait painters of his day—and neither did he try. Instead he specialized in small profile portraits, expeditiously painted in pastels and sold at moderate cost. This was portraiture for the masses, and Schipper was undoubtedly one of its great masters.[1] By combining art and technology, it was Schipper the itinerant artist who ultimately succeeded in capturing the true face of Sir Isaac Brock.

Provenance

While Gerrit Schipper's profile portrait of Brigadier General Isaac Brock (pl. 3) was a long-cherished heirloom, handed down from one generation of collateral descendants to the next, the manner of its transfer was usually accomplished without the necessity of a will. Small value items such as Brock's portrait were not, as a rule, enumerated in estate inventories. They were more likely to have been distributed with less formality and only passing regard for Guernsey's ancient legal tradition of primogeniture. Despite this entrenched form of male birthright, practical considerations frequently altered the inheritance of *personalty*—or chattel property. Such was the case with the portrait now recognized as the true face of Sir Isaac Brock.

Isaac Brock, Quebec City, Lower Canada (Quebec), 1809/1810–1812

Sometime between late May of 1809 and early July of 1810, Gerrit Schipper painted a pastel portrait of Brigadier General Isaac Brock in profile, facing right. Brock took this profile portrait to Fort George in Upper Canada (Ontario) when he was posted there in July of 1810, and also to his subsequent postings at Montreal and York (Toronto). After Brock's death in October of 1812, the portrait was sent to his older brother in England.

William Brock, Stamford Hill, England, 1813–c.1819

William Brock received all of his brother's personal effects in 1813, and six years later he died without issue. It was probably due to the lack of an heir that the profile portrait passed to one of William Brock's younger brothers. William Brock's sole beneficiary was his widow, Sarah Maria (Putt) Brock, and she may have conveyed the portrait in accordance with her husband's last wishes. There is also the possibility that William Brock made a gift of the portrait before he died.

Irving Brock, London/Bath, England, c.1819–1838

The profile portrait remained in Irving Brock's possession until his own death in 1838. As was the case with William Brock's estate, all of Irving Brock's worldly possessions were left to his widow, Frances (Longley) Brock. One notable exception, however, was the profile portrait, which passed to a nephew in Guernsey. This transfer was later described as a bequest, and presumably it was Frances Brock who made the necessary arrangements after her husband's death.

Henry Tupper, St. Peter Port, Guernsey, 1838–1875

Henry Tupper was a nephew of Irving Brock through his mother, Elizabeth Brock, who married John Elisha Tupper. Upon Henry Tupper's death in 1875, the portrait became the property of his widow.

Mary Ann Tupper, St. Peter Port, Guernsey, 1875–1882

After the death of Mary Ann (Collings) Tupper in 1882, the profile portrait went to her eldest son.

De Vic Tupper, St. Peter Port, Guernsey, 1882–1892

At the time of his death in 1892, De Vic Tupper was a widower—his wife, Emily Sophia (Bingham) Tupper, having predeceased him in 1890. Therefore, the profile portrait passed directly to their only son.

Henry Bingham de Vic Tupper, St. Peter Port, Guernsey, 1892–1903

Henry Bingham de Vic Tupper died unmarried in 1903, and so the profile portrait became the property of his three sisters. At some point, however, it was lent to their cousins, Emilia and Henrietta Tupper (the daughters of Ferdinand Brock Tupper), who understood that the loan was to be for the duration of their lifetimes.

Beatrice, Constance, and Edith Tupper, St. Peter Port, Guernsey, 1903–1960

With Emilia Tupper's demise in 1920, followed by that of Henrietta Tupper in 1928, the profile portrait was returned to the surviving sisters of Henry Bingham de Vic Tupper (Constance Tupper having succumbed in 1914). After Beatrice Tupper died in 1942, Edith Tupper continued to own the portrait until she passed away in 1960. Prior to her death Edith Tupper willed the portrait to her first cousin, once removed.

Captain Michael H.T. Mellish, St. Peter Port, Guernsey, 1960–2007

As the grandson of De Vic Tupper's sister, Ethel (Tupper) Mellish, Captain Michael H.T. Mellish was deemed to be the next person in line for the profile portrait. In 2006, it was given to his son for safekeeping.

Nicholas T.L. Mellish, Maldon, Essex, England, 2007–2009

Nicholas T.L. Mellish inherited the profile portrait after the death of his father in 2007. The younger Mellish retained the portrait until early in 2009 when, after various attempts to sell it, he finally struck a deal with the Guernsey Museum and Art Gallery.

The Guernsey Museum and Art Gallery, St. Peter Port, Guernsey, 2009–

The profile portrait is now preserved among the collections of the Guernsey Museum and Art Gallery.

List of Figures and Plates

cabinet card format, 14.3 x 10.2 cm, Notman Photographic Archives, McCord Museum of Canadian History (catalogue MP-0000.2251.1).

9. George Berthon (after Gerrit Schipper, 1809/1810), *Major-General Sir Isaac Brock, KB*, 1882, oil painting on canvas, 111.8 x 83.8 cm, Government of Ontario Art Collection, Archives of Ontario (accession 694,158).

10. John W.L. Forster (after Gerrit Schipper, 1809/1810), *Portrait of Maj. General Sir Isaac Brock KB*, 1894, oil painting on canvas, 83.5 x 68 cm, Niagara Falls History Museum (accession 995.D.067.005).

11. J. (James?) Hudson, *Lieutenant George Dunn* (misidentified as "General Sir Isaac Brock"), 1816, watercolour painting on ivory, 8 x 6.3 cm, Canadian Collection, Department of World Cultures, Royal Ontario Museum (accession 996.58.3.1).

12. Simpson Brothers (after J. Hudson, 1816), *Lieutenant George Dunn* (misidentified as "Major-General Sir Isaac Brock"), 1896, photograph in cabinet card format, 19.2 x 14.1 cm, Archives of Ontario.

13. Gerald S. Hayward (after J. Hudson, 1816), *Lieutenant George Dunn* (misidentified as "General Brock"), 1896, oil painting on ivory, 9 x 7 cm, Canadian Collection, Department of World Cultures, Royal Ontario Museum (accession 921.42.2).

14. Thomas W. Elliott (?)/Toronto Lithographing Company (after J. Hudson, 1816), *Lieutenant George Dunn* (misidentified as "Isaac Brock"), 1896, lithograph, 24.7 x 17.7 cm, *Cabot Calendar*.

15. Association of Canadian Archivists (after unknown artist, circa 1840), *Lieutenant George Dunn*, 1985, halftone illustration of oil painting on canvas, dimensions unknown, *Archivaria*.

16. John W.L. Forster (after unknown copyist, date unknown; after Gerrit Schipper, 1809/1810), *Study of Sir Isaac Brock*, 1897, oil painting on canvas, 76.2 x 60.9 cm, Portrait Gallery of Canada, Library and Archives Canada (accession 1991-30-1).

17. William J. Baker (after J. Hudson, 1816), *Lieutenant George Dunn* (misidentified as "Major-Gen'l Sir Isaac Brock"), 1896, photograph in cabinet card format, 16.5 x 10.7 cm, Military History Research Centre, Canadian War Museum.

18. Champlain Society (after unknown silhouettist, date unknown), *Genl. Brock* (otherwise known as the Jarvis silhouette), 1920, halftone illustration of silhouette, 16.5 x 24 cm, *Select British Documents of the Canadian War of 1812*.

Acknowledgments

During my quest for the true face of Sir Isaac Brock, I was fortunate enough to receive the unstinting assistance of a great many people. First among them was Dr. John Sugden, the acclaimed British historian who encouraged me to begin work on a new Brock biography, and who was just as eager as myself to find an authentic portrait for its frontispiece. During the long and tedious undertaking that followed, John remained a constant source of inspiration.

The lady named in the dedication has been a most enthusiastic supporter, and despite my fears that she might become disenchanted as my research became increasingly protracted, Gillian Lenfestey (now Gillian Davies) never lost interest in Brock's portraits. Without her extensive knowledge of Guernsey's history, as well as that of her late husband, Hugh (who happened to be the island's first archivist), many valuable records would have been beyond my reach.

I also enjoyed a good deal of co-operation from other Guernsey islanders. The former bailiff, Sir Geoffrey Rowland, made a concerted effort to find a missing Brock portrait, while Amanda Bennet, formerly in charge of the Priaulx Library, happily complied with one Brock-related request after another. Helen Conlon, the fine art curator at the Guernsey Museum and Art Gallery, enlightened me as to the conservation of Gerrit Schipper's portrait of Brigadier General Isaac Brock, and Tony C. Booth gave willingly of his time by retrieving select materials from the National Archives, Kew. Not to be overlooked is the late Captain Michael H.T. Mellish, who allowed me to examine and photograph the portraits and other Brock family heirlooms in his possession, and who exhibited all the attributes of a most genial host.

Here in Canada, I met with much kind consideration—especially at Brock University in St. Catharines, Ontario, where the Archives and Special Collections of the James A. Gibson Library preserve memorabilia relating to the University's namesake, including some of the portraits reproduced in this book. Department head David Sharron always indulged my numerous demands upon his time, as did Lynne Prunskus before him. In kind, staff members Edie Williams and Jen Boyce were very attentive in helping me navigate the collection.

Elsewhere in the Niagara peninsula, Kevin Windsor, then curator of the Lundy's Lane Historical Museum (now the Niagara Falls History Museum), amazed me by producing a long lost portrait of Brock. At the RiverBrink Art Museum in Queenston, former curators James Campbell and Gary Essar helped me to understand Samuel E. Weir's collecting interests. In nearby Niagara-on-the-Lake, Clark Bernat, former managing director of the Niagara Historical Society Museum, demonstrated an admirable desire to share the society's impressive archival resources—as did his successor, Sarah Kaufman, and the society's administrator, Amy Klassen.

In Toronto, I met with a gracious reception from Gillian Reddyhoff, the former curator of the Government of Ontario Art Collection, who arranged for my inspection of Brock's portraits in the Ontario legislature. With similar courtesy, Carol Baum, a collection technician with the Royal Ontario Museum, scheduled a personal viewing of several Brock miniatures in the Canadian Collection, Department of World Cultures.

At Trent University's Archives in Peterborough, I was given unfettered access to the Bagnani Papers—an essential source for the study of Brock's portraits. For this indulgence, I owe many thanks to Dr. Bernadine Dodge, now university archivist emeritus, and Jodi Aoki, who is the university's current archivist.

In Ottawa, Collections Manager Carol Reid facilitated my research at the Canadian War Museum, where I made good use of the Ludwig Kosche Papers. Equally helpful was Madeleine Trudeau, a curator with Library and Archives Canada, who was extremely diligent in tracking down elusive facts pertaining to the Brock portraits under her care.

Three art experts were instrumental in revising the attribution of Brock's profile portrait from William Berczy to Gerrit Schipper, and I am exceedingly grateful to: Mary Macaulay Allodi of Toronto, Ontario, who was for many years curator of Canadian Art at the Royal Ontario Museum; Dr. Alan McNairn of Charlottetown, Prince Edward Island, a former director of the New Brunswick Museum; and Jeanne Riger of Whitestone, New York, a long-time docent and researcher at the Museum of American Folk Art, now the American Folk Art Museum.

Interpreting the uniform in Schipper's portrait of Brock gave me a new appreciation for the meaning of the word *problematic*. Thankfully, some very well versed gentlemen helped me decode the many complexities of early nineteenth century British military dress, and I am deeply indebted to: Andrew Cormack of London, England, who is a Fellow of the Society of Antiquaries, editor of the *Journal of the Society for Army Historical Research*, as well as a specialist in British army uniforms of the Napoleonic Wars; Donald E. Graves, near Perth, Ontario, a noted Canadian military historian specializing in the War of 1812; Dr. Ray Hobbs of Hamilton, Ontario, the knowledgeable historian of the 41st Regiment of Foot Military Living History Group; and Peter Twist of Orangeville, Ontario, a highly respected military heritage consultant.

I am also obliged to the following individuals: Erika Alexander, Friends of Fort George, Niagara-on-the-Lake, Ontario; Georgia B. Barnhill, formerly of the American Antiquarian Society, Worcester, Massachusetts; Ted Barrow, formerly of the Frick Art Reference Library, New York, New York; Paul Cox, Archive and Library, National Portrait Gallery, London, England; Ron Dale, formerly of Parks Canada, Niagara-on-the-Lake, Ontario; Alan Derbyshire, Victoria and Albert Museum, London, England; Robert C. Fisher, Library and Archives Canada, Ottawa, Ontario; Major Tanya Grodzinski, Department of History, Royal Military College of Canada, Kingston, Ontario; Jim Hill and Ruth Stoner, Niagara Parks Commission, Niagara Falls, Ontario; the late Nevol Huddleston, London, Ontario; David Kean, London, Ontario; F. Eugene LaBrie, Q.C., Oshawa, Ontario; Sandra Lawrence, formerly of the Weir Foundation/RiverBrink Art Museum, Queenston, Ontario; the late Robert Malcomson, St. Catharines, Ontario; Elizabeth Mathew, United Church of Canada Archives, Toronto, Ontario; Dr. Richard D. Merritt, Niagara-on-the-Lake, Ontario; Dr. Peter Moogk, Department of History, University of British Columbia, Vancouver, British Columbia; Dr. Tom Nesmith, Department of History, University of Manitoba, Winnipeg,

Manitoba; Mark Osterman, George Eastman House International Museum of Photography, Rochester, New York ; the late Stephen A. Otto, Toronto, Ontario; the late Honourable P. Michael Pitfield, Montreal, Quebec, and his former secretary, Hazel Lachapelle, Gatineau, Quebec; Chris Raible, Creemore, Ontario; Jane Reed, The University Club Library, New York, New York; Dennis R. Reid, Department of Art, University of Toronto, Toronto, Ontario; and Craig Williams, Hamilton, Ontario.

I am no less beholden to the staff of various institutions, namely: the Art Gallery of Ontario, Toronto, Ontario; Fort Malden National Historic Site, Amherstburg, Ontario; McCord Museum of Canadian History, Montreal, Quebec; National Archives of the United Kingdom, Kew, England; National Army Museum, London, England; National Portrait Gallery, London, England; and the Rifles Museum (Berkshire and Wiltshire Regiments), Salisbury, England.

I wish especially to thank the anonymous readers who appraised my manuscript for the University of Calgary Press. I was delighted when I learned that the editorial board at the University of Calgary Press had agreed to publish my research into the true face of Sir Isaac Brock, and I extend particular thanks to Brian Scrivener, director, Helen Hajnoczky, editorial and marketing coordinator, Alison Cobra, marketing specialist, Melina Cusano, graphic designer, and publishing assistant Keyan Zhang, all of whom entertained my many questions and concerns with much patience and encouragement. My copy editor was Kathryn Simpson, an expert in the field of art history.

I would like to acknowledge funding support from the Ontario Arts Council, an agency of the Government of Ontario. I am also grateful to Lorraine Filyer, the OAC's former literature officer, who guided me through that organization's grant application process.

A special acknowledgment is reserved for Dr. Didier Flament of Portland, Oregon, who clarified many of the passages in this book—and with a degree of honesty I can only now begin to appreciate.

Guy St-Denis
London, Ontario

Notes

PREFACE

1 Charles P. Stacey, "Brock, Sir Isaac," *Dictionary of Canadian Biography* V: 109–15. In 1983, when this particular volume of the *DCB* was published, Stacey was regarded as Canada's pre-eminent military historian.

2 Sir James H. Craig was the governor-in-chief and military commander of British North America between 1807 and 1811. See: Jean-Pierre Wallot, "Craig, Sir James Henry," *Dictionary of Canadian Biography* V: 205–14.

INTRODUCTION

1 In March of 1814, the sum of £500 was appropriated for the purpose of a monument. See: Ontario, Bureau of Archives, *Ninth Report of the Bureau of Archives for the Province of Ontario*, "Journal of the House of Assembly of Upper Canada," 3 (1912): 159.

2 *Upper Canada Gazette* (York, Upper Canada), 21 Oct., 1824, 347, c. 3.

3 *British Colonist* (Toronto, Upper Canada), 29 Apr., 1840, 3, c. 5. Although born in Ireland, Lett was raised in Upper Canada and it was there that he developed his rabid anti-British sentiments. After Lett's death in December of 1858, a sketch of his life was published with a detailed account of his attack upon Brock's Monument. As the Canadian historian Chris Raible observed, the details of this desecration could only have been supplied by Lett himself. See: *Allen County Democrat* (Lima, Ohio), 5 Jan., 1859, 1, c. 6; Chris Raible, "Benjamin Lett, Rebel Terrorist," *Beaver* 84, no. 5 (Oct./Nov. 2002): 13. I am grateful to Chris Raible for directing me to these sources.

4 *British Colonist*, 5 Aug., 1840, 2, c. 5.

5 Glenn McArthur and Annie Szamosi, *William Thomas: Architect, 1799–1860* (Ottawa, Ontario: Archives of Canadian Art/Carleton University Press, c1996), 96–7.

6 *Globe* (Toronto, Canada West), 14 Oct., 1859, 2, c. 6.

7 Library and Archives Canada, Civil Secretary's Correspondence, Upper Canada and Canada West, Upper Canada Sundries (RG 5, A1), vol. 71, Nichol to Brock, 17 Mar., 1815, 37,699–701; ibid., Richard Westmacott, "Estimates for a Statue in honor of the late Major General Sir Isaac Brock KB from a Model & Drawing," 25 Sept., 1816, 37,706–7. The cost for a bronze statue, eight feet (nearly 2.5 metres) in height with a granite pedestal and plinth measuring another ten feet (or just over 3 metres), was estimated at £2,500. A slightly smaller statue would have saved the monument committee £500, but even £2,000 was beyond their limited means.

8 Stephen A. Otto, "Brock's Two Monuments," *Cuesta* (1991/92): 17.

9 Gilbert Auchinleck, "History of the War Between Great Britain and the United States of America, during the Years 1812, 1813, and 1814," *The Anglo-American Magazine* III, no. 1 (July 1853): 16. Auchinleck appears to have been influenced by Major John Richardson, who published a similarly worded statement about Brock's portrait in 1842. See: Major John Richardson, *War of 1812* (Brockville, Canada West: John Richardson, 1842), 68.

10 Auchinleck's articles were later published in book form. While he might have preferred a portrait of Brock for the frontispiece, Auchinleck used one of Lieutenant General Sir John Coape Sherbrooke instead—presumably because he was the lieutenant governor of Nova Scotia during the War of 1812. See: Gilbert Auchinleck, *A History of the War between Great Britain and the United States of America, during the Years 1812, 1813, and 1814* (Toronto, Canada West: Maclear and Company, 1855), frontispiece.

11 With particular reference to the heraldic shields adorning the four corners of Brock's Monument, each is identical and features a fleur-de-lis instead of an eagle. This same mistake was repeated in a memorial window dedicated to Brock, which was installed in the chancel of St. Saviour, the Brock Memorial Church, Queenston, Ontario. As Brock's heraldic shield is derived from that of the Brock family of Guernsey, which also features a fleur-de-lis, the confusion in Canada is understandable. For Brock's armorial bearings, see: College of Arms, Letters Patent Granting Arms to Sir Isaac Brock, 15 Feb., 1813; ibid., Letters Patent Granting Supporters to the Arms of Sir Isaac Brock, 15 Feb., 1813. Furthermore, Brock's arms bear the motto CANADA, and not VINCIT VERITAS as appears beneath the shields on his monument.

12 This, of course, was the most logical approach when the first broad surveys of Canadian art history began to appear. In 1966, John Russell Harper published *Painting in Canada: A History*. It was followed in 1973 by Dennis R. Reid's *A Concise History of Canadian Painting*. See: John Russell Harper, *Painting in Canada: A History* (Toronto, Ontario: University of Toronto Press, 1966); Dennis R. Reid, *A Concise History of Canadian Painting* (Toronto, Ontario: Oxford University Press, 1973).

13 There were exceptions among Canada's military historians, including Dr. J. Mackay Hitsman. See: J. Mackay Hitsman, *The Incredible War of 1812: A Military History* (Toronto, Ontario: University of Toronto Press, c1965); ibid., *Safeguarding Canada, 1763–1871* (Toronto, Ontario: University of Toronto Press, c1968).

14 For the beginnings of the transition of Canadian history, from avocation to vocation, see: Donald Wright, *The Professionalization of History in English Canada* (Toronto, Ontario: University of Toronto Press, c2005), 28–51.

15 To get a sense of the attitudes among academic historians, see: Carl Berger, *The Writing of Canadian History: Aspects of English-Canadian Historical Writing since 1900*, 2nd ed. (Toronto, Ontario: University of Toronto Press, c1986), 218.

16 Alexander Brian McKillop, *Pierre Berton: A Biography* (Toronto, Ontario: McClelland and Stewart, c2008), 558.

17 Ibid., 560. Regarding the inconsistent treatment of historical evidence, see: Keith Walden, review of *The Invasion of Canada*, by Pierre Berton, in *Canadian Historical Review* LXII, no. 3 (Sept. 1981): 332.

18 McKillop, *Pierre Berton*, 561, 564.

19 The only illustrations Berton used are those which embellish his endpapers. A specially commissioned montage of portraits was designed based on each book's "cast of characters."

Tom McNeely of Toronto was chosen to do the artwork, and he used the profile portrait (pl. 3) for his likeness of Brock.

20 Ludwig Kosche, "Contemporary Portraits of Isaac Brock: An Analysis," *Archivaria* 20 (Summer 1985): 22–66.

CHAPTER I

1 Lieutenant Governor Robinson was the second son of Sir John Beverley Robinson. For the younger Robinson's viceregal appointment, see: Patrick Brode, "Robinson, John Beverley," *Dictionary of Canadian Biography* XII: 908.

2 Lady Edgar [Matilda Ridout], "General Brock's Portrait," *The Canadian Magazine* XXXI, no. 3 (July 1908): 262. In October of 1884, a reporter from the *Toronto World* was invited to tour the nascent art collection at Government House. In the *salle à manger*, or dining room, he found a "Gallery of Governors" consisting of fifteen large-sized oil paintings, being portraits of the "most famous governors-generals and lieut-governors that Canada has possessed." See: *Toronto World* (Toronto, Ontario), 23 Oct., 1884, 1, c. 7.

3 The *Toronto World* reported that "Lieut.-governor Robinson has been most assiduous in his efforts to obtain as good a collection as possible. They are all of them copies of the originals done by the well known artist, M[onsieur] Berthon; some painted directly from the originals, others, when these were unattainable, from photographs. The name of the painter will testify to their excellence." See: *Toronto World*, 23 Oct., 1884, 1, c. 7.

4 Colonel Robinson could not recall precisely when he made his earlier attempt, only that it was some "some 6 or 7 years or more ago." See: Trent University, Thomas J. Bata Library, Trent University Archives (TU), Gilbert and Stewart Bagnani Papers (94–016), General Correspondence (series A), Robinson to Robinson, 19 Apr., 1881.

5 John Charles Dent, *The Canadian Portrait Gallery*, 4 vols (Toronto, Ontario: John B. Magurn, 1880–81), 1: 140; *Globe* (Toronto, Ontario), 13 Apr., 1877, 238, c. 5.

6 A description that accompanies the engraving (fig. 1) credits Dr. Hodgins with having recently procured the "miniature," meaning a photographic copy and not the original profile portrait (fig. 3). See: *Globe*, 13 Apr., 1877, 238, c. 5. In 1906, however, Miss Janet Carnochan claimed that Dr. Egerton Ryerson obtained the photograph, presumably in his capacity as Ontario's chief superintendent of education. Yet, given the contemporaneous nature of the information provided by Dent, it seems more likely that it was Dr. Hodgins who acquired the photograph, and that he did so on behalf of the Normal School, or Teacher's College, specifically for the Educational Museum. See: *Evening Telegram* (Toronto, Ontario), 6 July, 1906, 8, c. 5. For biographical information on Dr. Hodgins, see: Judson D. Purdy, "Hodgins, John George," *Dictionary of Canadian Biography* XIV: 496–9; *Globe*, 24 Dec., 1912, 9, c. 1.

7 *Globe*, 13 Apr., 1877, 238, c. 5; Dent, *Canadian Portrait Gallery*, 1: 140.

8 As Mrs. Huyshe reported to Colonel Robinson early in November of 1881, the portrait in Mrs. Tupper's possession (fig. 3) was "evidently the better of these two." See: TU, Gilbert and Stewart Bagnani Papers (94-016), General Correspondence (series A), Huyshe to Robinson, 2 Nov., 1881.

9 A colour photograph of Mrs. Huyshe's copy of the profile portrait (fig. 4) was located in the Ludwig Kosche Papers at the Canadian War Museum, and appears to show a pastel composition on laid paper. See: Canadian War Museum, Military History Research Centre

(CWM), Ludwig Kosche Papers, Photograph Album (58A3/10.4), Copy of the Profile Portrait of Brigadier General Isaac Brock by Gerrit Schipper, circa 1809–10, photographed by Brian J. Green. An antique photograph of the copy dating to 1881 has also been preserved. See: McCord Museum of Canadian History (MMCH), Notman Photographic Archives, Photograph of a "Miniature of Sir Isaac Brock," by Benjamin Collenette, 1881, cat. MP-0000.2251.2. The copy was eventually bequeathed to the States of Guernsey by a Mrs. Sowels, who died in 1971. This Mrs. Sowels was the former Miss Agnes Bessie Carey, and it was her father's aunt, Mrs. George (Rosa Brock) Huyshe, who inherited the copy from her father, John Savery Brock. After Mrs. Huyshe's death in 1892, the copy went to her nephew, John Savery Carey, who died in 1910. Presumably, the copy then passed to his wife, the former Miss Alice Juliet Hand. She survived until 1929, having outlived her only son, George Savery Carey, who died unmarried in 1917. Eventually, the copy became the joint property of his sisters: Miss Alice Mary Carey (1878–1959), who never married; Miss Florence Ada Carey (1881–1951), who also remained single; and Miss Agnes Bessie Carey (1886–1971), who married Captain Reginald Charles Sowels in 1928. Mrs. Sowels had no children, and it was perhaps for this reason that she decided to bequeath the copy to her cousin, Robert Arthur. However, she later changed her mind in favour of the States of Guernsey. I am grateful to Gillian Lenfestey for providing me with these details, which she discovered in a variety of sources. For information regarding Mrs. Sowels's wills, see: Royal Court House, Greffe, Wills and Intestacies, vol. E/10 (1971–76), will of Realty of Agnes B. (Carey) Sowels, 4 May, 1951; ibid., vol. 71 (new series), will of Personalty of Agnes B. (Carey) Sowels, 6 Sept., 1956. See also: CWM, Ludwig Kosche Papers, Correspondence (58A3/10.25), Rust to Arthur, 10 Nov., 1972.

10 TU, Gilbert and Stewart Bagnani Papers (94-016), General Correspondence (series A), Huyshe to Robinson, 2 Nov., 1881; ibid., Robinson to Robinson, 3 Dec., 1881. Colonel Robinson was of the opinion that much of Mrs. Tupper's anxiety about the original portrait (fig. 3) had to do with the fact that it "rubs easily." See: ibid., 3 Dec., 1881.

11 Ibid., Robinson to Robinson, post 18 Jan., 1882. Unfortunately, Colonel Robinson's letter is missing its first page and consequently the date. However, the colonel mentions having received a letter from Mrs. Tupper's daughter, Mrs. Hubert (Victoria) Le Cocq, which is dated 18 January, 1882. Therefore, Colonel Robinson's letter must have been written after he received Mrs. Le Cocq's reply, or post 18 Jan., 1882. See: ibid., Le Cocq to Robinson, 18 Jan., 1882. The sepia portrait of Brock (fig. 5), although now lost, was used to illustrate Brock's entry in the "Gallery of Local Celebrities"—a series of biographical sketches that appeared in Guernsey's French language newspaper. See: *Bailliage* (St. Peter Port, Guernsey), 24 Sept., 1892, 2, c. 3; ibid., 1 Oct., 1892, 2, c. 1. The portrait was also reproduced as a photogravure print, several of which are preserved in the Priaulx Library, St. Peter Port. A careful examination of one such specimen revealed the monogram of Alice Kerr-Nelson.

12 TU, Gilbert and Stewart Bagnani Papers (94-016), General Correspondence (series A), Robinson to Robinson, 3 Dec., 1881.

13 Ibid. Colonel Robinson also thought the original profile portrait (fig. 3) had "faded with age somewhat, making the face appear flat & whiteish, except in one or two places where the color is bright."

14 Ibid. The photography work was done by Hills and Saunders of London (fig. 7).

15 Colonel Robinson suggested as much when he said: "I think myself that when you see the picture [Miss Kerr-Nelson's portrait of Brock in oils (fig. 6)], it will be bought in Canada,

both as a picture & on account of Sir Isaac's connection with the Country, but, at all events, Berthon would be able from it to make a portrait, of any size." See: ibid.

16 Ibid.

17 Ibid., Robinson to Robinson, post 18 Jan., 1882.

18 Ferdinand Brock Tupper, ed., *The Life and Correspondence of Major-General Sir Isaac Brock, K.B.*, 1st ed. (London, England: Simpkin, Marshall and Company, 1845), 341.

19 While the lieutenant governor's letter does not appear to have survived, his concern regarding Tupper's footnote and the existence of Brock's portrait is addressed in Colonel Robinson's reply. See: TU, Gilbert and Stewart Bagnani Papers (94-016), General Correspondence (series A), Robinson to Robinson, post 18 Jan., 1882.

20 Ibid., Le Cocq to Robinson, 18 Jan., 1882.

21 Ibid., Robinson to Robinson, post 18 Jan., 1882.

22 As Henrietta Tupper herself recognized: "my father was an intense hero-worshipper, & his gallant uncle was his chief hero." See: ibid., Tupper to Robinson, 25 Jan., 1882.

23 Notwithstanding Colonel Robinson's report that there were differences among the various branches of the Brock and Tupper families, it will be seen that Ferdinand Brock Tupper's seeming disapproval of the profile portrait and its copy (figs 3, 4) probably had more to do with aesthetics than animosity.

24 Tupper included an account of Sir Isaac Brock's life in his *Family Records*. A good deal of Brock's correspondence was published in two editions of Tupper's *The Life and Correspondence of Major-General Sir Isaac Brock, K.B.*

25 Morgan's interest probably stemmed from a desire to illustrate his biographical sketch of Brock, which he published the next year. See: Henry J. Morgan, *Sketches of Celebrated Canadians* (Quebec, Canada East: Hunter Rose and Company, 1862), 174–84.

26 Library and Archives Canada (LAC), Henry James Morgan Papers (MG 29, D61), Correspondence, vol. 47, Tupper to Morgan, 13 July, 1861.

27 As Miss Henrietta Tupper later explained, Henry Tupper inherited the portrait (fig. 3) from his uncle, Irving Brock, who died in 1838. See: TU, Gilbert and Stewart Bagnani Papers (94-016), General Correspondence (series A), Tupper to Robinson, 1 Feb., 1882. For Irving Brock's death notice, see: *Gentleman's Magazine* (London, England), Jan.–June 1838, 669, c. 1.

28 TU, Gilbert and Stewart Bagnani Papers (94-016), General Correspondence (series A), Robinson to Robinson, 19 Apr., 1881; ibid., post 18 Jan., 1882. As Captain Arthur S. Cave determined, the officers of the 49th Regiment made their enquiry about Brock's portrait in 1845—the same year Tupper noted the incident in his uncle's biography. Given the timing, it might have been Ferdinand Brock Tupper himself who relayed the disappointing news. See: Tupper, *Life and Correspondence of Major-General Sir Isaac Brock*, 1st ed., 341; Archives of Ontario (AO), Women's Canadian Historical Society of Toronto Papers (F 1180), Correspondence (series 1), file 2 (Jan.–May 1897), Cave to Mickle, 8 May, 1897.

29 Dr. Hodgins acquired his photographic copy of the profile portrait (fig. 3) sometime prior to the publication of Dent's biography of Sir Isaac Brock. This photograph formed the basis of a wood engraving (fig. 2), which appeared in an 1877 issue of the Toronto *Globe*. A note accompanying the illustration claims that it was "engraved from a miniature [no doubt meaning a photograph of the original profile portrait] recently procured from Sir Isaac's relatives in Guernsey." This arrangement must have come about some time after Tupper's

death in December of 1873. See: *Globe*, 13 Apr., 1877, 238, c. 5. For an account of Tupper's death, see: *Star* (St. Peter Port, Guernsey), 23 Dec., 1873, 2, c. 6.

30 TU, Gilbert and Stewart Bagnani Papers (94-016), General Correspondence (series A), Robinson to Robinson, post 18 Jan., 1882.

31 Ibid., Le Cocq to Robinson, 18 Jan., 1882. The niece in question was Miss Caroline Tupper, who later married De Beauvoir de Lisle. Mrs. de Lisle's mother was the former Miss Elizabeth Brock, who became the wife of John Elisha Tupper. For Mrs. de Lisle's obituary, including a brief history of her life, see: *Star*, 27 Feb., 1894, 2, c. 5.

32 TU, Gilbert and Stewart Bagnani Papers (94-016), General Correspondence (series A), Tupper to Robinson, 25 Jan. 1882. Miss Henrietta Tupper's initial letter to Colonel Robinson is largely unrelated to the portraits. However, she does reiterate rather more forcefully Mrs. Le Cocq's explanation about the failure of the officers of the 49th Regiment to obtain a likeness of Sir Isaac Brock. The "reason why the 49th Regt. failed to procure a portrait of Sir Isaac was not that there was no existing likeness, but that there was *no good one*." See: ibid.

33 Ibid., Tupper to Robinson, 1 Feb., 1882.

34 According to Lady Edgar, who wrote an article about Lieutenant Governor Robinson's quest for an authentic portrait of Sir Isaac Brock, the "family in Guernsey seem to have been in ignorance as to when, where, and by whom the profile sketches were made." Still, she speculated that one of them might have been made in Canada between 1806 and 1812, and perhaps by Ensign James Kittermaster of the 49th Regiment, who was an amateur artist. Lady Edgar was influenced in her thinking by Ensign Kittermaster's grand-daughter, who preserved his portfolio of sketches, including several portraits of his fellow junior officers. "What more probable than that the youth [Kittermaster] should have taken a sketch from life of his colonel, which sketch found its way, with the other belongings of Sir Isaac, to his Guernsey home?" It was an interesting proposition, but one that ultimately proved to be incorrect. See: Edgar, "General Brock's Portrait," 265. For Ensign Kittermaster, see: Bernard Burke, *A Genealogical and Heraldic Dictionary of the Landed Gentry of Great Britain and Ireland*, 4th ed., 2 pts (London, England: Harrison, 1863), II: 819.

35 TU, Gilbert and Stewart Bagnani Papers (94-016), General Correspondence (series A), Robinson to Robinson, 31 Mar., 1882.

36 Ibid., Huyshe to Robinson, 3 Apr., 1882.

37 The photograph Miss Tupper sent to Colonel Robinson was a duplicate of the one she gave to David Ross McCord of Montreal in 1889. See: MMCH, Archives and Documentation Centre, McCord Family Papers (P0001), Collecting Correspondence, Tupper to McCord, 26 Apr., 1889. This photograph is now preserved in the McCord Museum of Canadian History. See: MMCH, Notman Photographic Archives, Photograph of a "Miniature of Sir Isaac Brock," by Benjamin Collenette, 1881, cat. MP-0000.2251.2. Miss Tupper described the photograph as having been taken about nine years earlier. Unfortunately, she dated her letter with only the day and month—26 April. It was later guessed to have been written about 1885, which is incorrect. Given that Miss Tupper's letter makes reference to her father, who "has been dead now over 16 years," and as Ferdinand Brock Tupper is known to have died in December of 1873, the letter probably dates to 26 April, 1889. Miss Tupper's calculation that the photograph was taken nine years earlier, which would have been 1880, requires a slight adjustment to 1881—the year she assigned it in her letter

to Colonel Robinson of 15 April, 1882. See: TU, Gilbert and Stewart Bagnani Papers (94-016), General Correspondence (series A), Tupper to Robinson, 15 Apr., 1882. Miss Tupper mentioned this photograph in at least two other letters. See: MMCH, Archives and Documentation Centre, McCord Family Papers (P0001), Collecting Correspondence, Tupper to McCord, 19 Feb., 1897; ibid., 14 Apr., 1897.

38 TU, Gilbert and Stewart Bagnani Papers (94-016), General Correspondence (series A), Tupper to Robinson, 15 Apr., 1882. Although Colonel Robinson dismissed the bronzed silhouette (fig. 8), he thought it might be useful in determining Brock's "true expression," or profile. In fact, this silhouette—which Brock's family considered to be his best likeness—must be of someone other than Brock, as a breast star of the Order of the Garter is prominently displayed on the sitter's chest and Brock never achieved this highest order of British knighthood. It was the late Ludwig Kosche, a former librarian at the Canadian War Museum, who first noticed this discrepancy. See: ibid., Robinson to Robinson, 18 Apr., 1882; Ludwig Kosche, "Contemporary Portraits of Isaac Brock: An Analysis," *Archivaria* 20 (Summer 1985): 58–60.

39 TU, Gilbert and Stewart Bagnani Papers (94-016), General Correspondence (series A), Robinson to Robinson, 18 Apr., 1882.

40 It appears that Miss Augusta Robinson was entrusted with the delivery of this portrait (fig. 6), but a search to determine the date of her arrival in Toronto was unsuccessful. In the process, it was discovered that the lieutenant governor and his wife sailed to England in June of 1882, which suggests the possibility that they might have brought the portrait back themselves. However, the couple did not return until the following September, and in an earlier letter written to the lieutenant governor on 8 August, 1882, Colonel Robinson mentions "Sir I Brock's picture you have in Canada." This "picture" is no doubt a reference to the portrait of Brock by Miss Kerr-Nelson, which seems to have been in Canada for some time. See: AO, John Beverley Robinson Papers (F 44), Calendared Papers, Robinson to Robinson, 8 Aug., 1882; *Globe*, 23 June, 1882, 8, c. 1; ibid., 4 Sept., 1882, 8, c. 4.

41 The Honourable John Beverley Robinson kept the portrait (fig. 6) until his death in 1896. It then passed to his daughter, Mrs. William Forsyth (Minnie Robinson) Grant, who is recorded as having owned the portrait in 1908. Eventually, and presumably after Mrs. Grant's death in 1923, it became the property of her sister, Mrs. Stewart (Augusta Robinson) Houston. In 1924, Mrs. Houston made an unsuccessful attempt to sell the portrait to the Dominion Archives. Later, and sometime prior to 1930, she negotiated a deal with the Canadian financier Ward C. Pitfield. In 1979, Pitfield's son sold the portrait to Brock University, where it remains in the Archives and Special Collections of the James A. Gibson Library. Pitfield's son, it should be noted, is the late Honourable P. Michael Pitfield. See: Edgar, "General Brock's Portrait," 263; *Globe*, 3 Nov., 1923, 3, c. 1; LAC, SNAP File, MB 8320-Brock, Isaac (Sir), Houston to Doughty, 24 June, 1924, 16 July, 1924; ibid., J. Russell Harper Papers (MG 30, D352), [Norman Fee], "List of Paintings, Engravings, and Prints [in the] W.C. Pitfield Collection," 6; Brock University, James A. Gibson Library, Archives and Special Collections, Acquisitions Form, [Kerr-Nelson] Portrait of "General Brock," cat. U2.

42 Although Berthon does not appear to have signed the portrait (fig. 9), it may be that his initials follow an indistinct script in the lower right-hand corner of the canvas—possibly identifying the portrait as being that of Sir Isaac Brock. There is no visible indication of a date. While the attribution to Berthon has never been called into question, the date has been known to range between 1881 and 1883. However, the year 1881 seems too early.

The portrait owned by Mrs. Tupper (fig. 3), which Berthon used as the basis for his own portrait of Brock, was not photographed until late in November of 1881. While Berthon might have received one of the these photographic prints (fig. 7) soon after, it is doubtful that he would have commenced work on his own version until after he had an opportunity of seeing Miss Kerr-Nelson's portrait of Brock (fig. 6), which probably did not arrive in Toronto until rather later—and possibly not until sometime in August of 1882 (see n40). Much credence has been given to a date of 1883, largely because Berthon acknowledged payment for his work on 10 March, 1883. However, Berthon submitted his bill for the portrait to the Government of Ontario before the end of 1882, presumably after he had completed his commission. Based on this fact, and the likelihood that all the necessary reference materials would have been made available to him earlier in that same year, it is reasonable to assume that Berthon's portrait of Brock was both begun and finished in 1882. See: TU, Gilbert and Stewart Bagnani Papers (94-016), General Correspondence (series A), Robinson to Robinson, 3 Dec., 1881; AO, John Beverley Robinson Papers (F 44), Calendared Papers, Robinson to Robinson, 8 Aug., 1882; Art Gallery of Ontario, E.P. Taylor Research Library and Archives, George Theodore Berthon's Sitters' Notebook, 10 Mar., 1883; Ontario, Legislative Assembly, *Sessional Papers*, "Public Accounts of the Province of Ontario," 1882 XV, pt I, no. 1 (1882–83): 32.

43 George Berthon's portrait of Brock (fig. 9) was displayed in Government House at Simcoe and King streets in Toronto until 1912, and then in the new viceregal residence at Chorley Park beginning in 1915. During the intervening years, the portrait may have been on view in the lieutenant governor's temporary lodgings at St. George and College streets, or perhaps put in storage as seems to have been the case with a number of other "pictures." After Chorley Park was closed in 1937, the portrait was transferred to the lieutenant governor's suite in the Legislature, Queen's Park, where it now forms part of the Government of Ontario Art Collection. See: Ontario, Legislative Assembly, *Sessional Papers*, "Report of the Minister of Public Works," 1912 XLV, pt IV, no. 12 (1913): 7, 10; ibid., 1916 XLIX, pt IV, no. 13 (1917): 7, 10; ibid., 1938 LXXI, pt III, no. 8 (1939): 7; ibid., 1939 LXXII, pt III, no. 8 (1940): 7; AO, Government of Ontario Art Collection, "Major-General Sir Isaac Brock, KB," by George Theodore Berthon, 1882, acc. 694,158. See also: Fern Bayer, *The Ontario Collection* (Markham, Ontario: Fitzhenry and Whiteside, 1984), 154.

44 William Kingsford, *The Early Bibliography of the Province of Ontario* (Toronto, Ontario: Rowsell and Hutchison, 1892), 7. As Fern Bayer points out, despite Lieutenant Governor Robinson's diligence, there are significant gaps in the collection. See: Bayer, *Ontario Collection*, 153.

45 William Kingsford, *Canadian Archaeology: An Essay* (Montreal, Quebec: William Drysdale and Company, 1886), 97.

46 Lieutenant Governor Robinson was succeeded by Sir Alexander Campbell in June of 1887. See: *Globe*, 1 June, 1887, 4, c. 2.

47 John W.L. Forster should not be confused with John C.H. Forster, a commercial artist who painted the imaginary portrait of Brock on display at the Fort Malden National Historic Site in Amherstburg, Ontario.

48 According to the inscription on the back of the painting, which is now in the Niagara Falls History Museum (formerly the Lundy's Lane Historical Museum), Forster's portrait of Brock (fig. 10) was "PAINTED FROM AUTHENTIC DATA IN POSSESSION OF HON. JOHN BEVERLEY ROBINSON." See: Niagara Falls History Museum, Oil

Painting of a "Portrait of Maj. General Sir Isaac Brock KB," by John W.L. Forster, 1894, acc. 995.D.067.005. A contemporary newspaper article further reveals that Forster's authentic data consisted of "a copy in oil" of the miniature, or rather the original profile portrait (fig. 3), and also "a photo from it." The "copy in oil" was undoubtedly the painting by Miss Kerr-Nelson (fig. 6), and the "photo from it" was probably one of the several photographs (fig. 7) ordered by Colonel Robinson. See: *Saturday Globe*, 3 Oct., 1896, 1, c. 5.

49 Ben Forster, "Macdonell (Greenfield), John Alexander," *Dictionary of Canadian Biography* XV: 637–9. For John A. Macdonell, see: Henry James Morgan, ed., *The Canadian Men and Women of the Time*, 2nd ed. (Toronto, Ontario: William Briggs, 1912), 686. For Macdonell's obituary, see: *Glengarry News* (Alexandria, Ontario), 18 Apr., 1930, 1, c. 1.

50 *Week* (Toronto, Ontario), 21 Dec., 1894, 91, c. 1. For evidence of Forster's contributions to this newspaper, see: Morgan, *Canadian Men and Women of the Time*, 2nd ed., 412.

51 *Saturday Globe*, 3 Oct., 1896, 1, c. 5.

52 Morgan, *Canadian Men and Women of the Time*, 2nd ed., 412.

53 In 1882, Miss Kerr-Nelson married fellow artist Carl Hirschberg. She and her husband moved to the United States two years later. Mrs. Hirschberg died in 1913. See: Frances E. Willard and Mary A. Livermore, eds., *A Woman of the Century* (Buffalo, New York: Charles Wells Moulton, 1893; reprint ed., Detroit, Michigan: Gale Research Company, 1967), 380–1; *New York Times* (New York, New York), 20 June, 1913, 9, c. 5.

54 This portrait of Brock (fig. 10) remained in John A. Macdonell's possession until his death in 1930, when it was bequeathed to his cousin, Ian M. Macdonell of Toronto. See: AO, Stormont, Dundas and Glengarry Counties Surrogate Court (RG 22), Estate Files, 1800–1967 (series 198), will of John A. Macdonell, 5 Apr., 1930, no. 7,137. Ian Macdonell owned the portrait until his own death in 1992. In 1995, his daughters gave the portrait to the Lundy's Lane Historical Museum (now the Niagara Falls History Museum). I am grateful to the museum's former curator, Kevin Windsor, for information regarding this accession.

CHAPTER 2

1 The Women's Canadian Historical Society of Toronto was incorporated the next year, in 1896. Its objectives were historical, literary, archival, and patriotic in nature. See: "Prefatory Note" and "Preamble of Constitution and By-Laws," Women's Canadian Historical Society of Toronto *Transaction* 1 (1896): 3–6.

2 For biographical information on Miss FitzGibbon, see: "Sketch of Miss FitzGibbon's Life," Women's Canadian Historical Society of Toronto *Transaction* 14 (1914–15): 15–16. Miss FitzGibbon's book about her grandfather, *A Veteran of 1812: The Life of James FitzGibbon*, was published by William Briggs of Toronto in 1894.

3 To learn more about Miss Mickle's life, see: David Kimmel and Janet Miron, "Mickle, Sara," *Dictionary of Canadian Biography* XV: 742–3; *Evening Telegram* (Toronto, Ontario), 3 June, 1930, 2, c. 2.

4 Sara Mickle, comp., *The Cabot Calendar, 1497–1897* (Toronto, Ontario: Toronto Lithographing Company, 1896).

5 Miss FitzGibbon described John Cabot, Samuel de Champlain, the Comte de Frontenac (Louis de Buade), James Wolfe, and Isaac Brock as "the five men whose names are most prominent in the history of Canada." See: *Globe* (Toronto, Ontario), 23 Sept., 1896, 2, c. 5.

6 The portrait used in Dent's biographical sketch of Sir Isaac Brock (fig. 1) was based on the photograph obtained by Dr. J. George Hodgins. The other portrait, which was used by Read as the frontispiece for his book, was painted by Forster for John A. Macdonell (fig. 10). See: John Charles Dent, *The Canadian Portrait Gallery*, 4 vols (Toronto, Ontario: John B. Magurn, 1880–81), 1: 128–9; David B. Read, *Life and Times of Major-General Sir Isaac Brock, K.B.* (Toronto, Ontario: William Briggs, 1894), frontispiece.

7 *Globe*, 23 Sept., 1896, 2, c. 5.

8 Ibid.

9 Ibid.

10 Archives of Ontario (AO), Women's Canadian Historical Society of Toronto Papers (F 1180), Miscellaneous (series 13), file 3, Brock Portrait Notebook, 25. The label on the cover of this notebook is incorrect. The notes are not those of Miss FitzGibbon, but rather Miss Mickle.

11 Ibid., Correspondence (series 1), file 1 (1890–96), Taylor to Mickle, 11 May, 1896.

12 Ibid., Miscellaneous (series 13), file 3, Brock Portrait Notebook, 27.

13 Ibid., 29.

14 Ibid., 27.

15 Regarding the miniature's provenance, see: *Globe*, 23 Sept., 1896, 2, c. 5; Ludwig Kosche, "Contemporary Portraits of Isaac Brock: An Analysis," *Archivaria* 20 (Summer 1985): 43–4. As for Mrs. Dunn's identification of Sir Isaac Brock as the sitter in the miniature (fig. 11), see: AO, Women's Canadian Historical Society of Toronto Papers (F 1180), Correspondence (series 1), file 2 (Jan.–May 1897), Taylor to Mickle, 4 May, 1897. Initially, Miss Mickle and Miss FitzGibbon thought Captain James Brock was a brother to Sir Isaac Brock, but they soon enough corrected their mistake.

16 AO, Women's Canadian Historical Society of Toronto Papers (F 1180), Correspondence (series 1), file 1 (1890–96), Taylor to Mickle, 22 June, 1896.

17 *Globe*, 23 Sept., 1896, 2, c. 5.

18 AO, Women's Canadian Historical Society of Toronto Papers (F 1180), Miscellaneous (series 13), file 3, Brock Portrait Notebook, 31.

19 Ibid. Although Miss Mickle simply identified the person in question as "Elliott the artist," she might have meant Thomas W. Elliott, who was proprietor of the Elliott Illustrating Company. See: *The Toronto City Directory 1897* (Toronto, Ontario: Might Directory Company, 1897), 672.

20 AO, Women's Canadian Historical Society of Toronto Papers (F 1180), Miscellaneous (series 13), file 3, Brock Portrait Notebook, 31.

21 Ibid. In addition to a crack, there were also mildew stains. See: ibid., Correspondence (series 1), file 9 (n.d.), Hayward to Mickle, 14 Aug., 1896.

22 Hayward was born at Port Hope, Canada West (now Ontario), in 1847. He died in 1926. See: Henry James Morgan, ed., *The Canadian Men and Women of the Time*, 2nd ed. (Toronto, Ontario: William Briggs, 1912), 517; *Globe*, 2 Apr., 1926, 18, c. 4; ibid., 1 June, 1926, 9, c. 4.

23 AO, Women's Canadian Historical Society of Toronto Papers (F 1180), Miscellaneous (series 13), file 3, Brock Portrait Notebook, 31, 33, 35, 37, 39, 41. Miss FitzGibbon may have shared in the purchase of Hayward's copy (fig. 13), which she later came to believe

was overpriced. See: ibid., Correspondence (series 1), file 3 (June–Dec. 1897), FitzGibbon to Mickle, 29 June, 1897. This letter is undated, but it describes events that occurred on 29 June, 1897, and appears to have been penned at the close of that same day for Miss Mickle.

24 Although the exact date of Miss Mickle's purchase of the miniature (fig. 11) is unknown, the transaction obviously took place prior to 4 May, 1897, when Mrs. Taylor denied that she ever had any intention of selling it. See: ibid., file 2, (Jan.–May 1897), Taylor to Mickle, 4 May, 1897. Ludwig Kosche, the Canadian War Museum's librarian, was under the mistaken impression that Miss Mickle did not purchase the miniature for herself, but rather on behalf of the Women's Canadian Historical Society of Toronto. In fact, the miniature was owned by Miss Mickle until her death in 1930, and only afterwards was it presented by her family to the society. See: Kosche, "Contemporary Portraits of Isaac Brock," 45; AO, Women's Canadian Historical Society of Toronto Papers (F 1180), Correspondence (series 1), file 3 (1921–39), Mickle to Roberts, 15 Oct., 1930; ibid., Roberts to Mickle and Armour, 20 Oct., 1930.

25 Hayward arrived at this conclusion in association with an unidentified English friend. See: AO, Women's Canadian Historical Society of Toronto Papers (F 1180), Correspondence (series 1), file 9 (n.d.), Hayward to Mickle, 17 Aug., 1896. It later occurred to Miss FitzGibbon that the X might have signified a cross, or plus sign, which was often used to abbreviate the word "and." Thus, 18X6 became 18 and 6, or 1806. See: ibid., Miscellaneous (series 13), file 2, Brock Miniature, "Copies of F. Nowlan's & Alyn Williams's opinions re portraits," 29 June, 1897.

26 Ibid., Correspondence (series 1), file 9 (n.d.), Hayward to Mickle, 17 Aug., 1896. The Dutch refer to Egmont-op-Zee as Egmond aan Zee.

27 The date of delivery appears to have been 21 August, 1896. In an undated note penned on a Wednesday, Hayward advises Miss Mickle that he will go to Toronto the next day and requests her to retrieve the miniatures (figs 11, 13) from him on Friday. In an earlier letter, Hayward mentioned his plans to bring the miniatures to Toronto "this week," by which he meant the week of 16–22 August, 1896, as his letter is dated 17 August, 1896. Since the 17th of August was a Monday, Hayward's undated note was probably written on Wednesday of that same week, or 19 August, 1896. Therefore, Miss Mickle was asked to come for the miniatures the following Friday, meaning 21 August, 1896. See: ibid., 17 Aug., 1896; ibid., 19 Aug., 1896. Miss FitzGibbon subsequently acquired the Hayward copy (fig. 13), which she planned to bequeath to the Women's Canadian Historical Society of Toronto, provided the Society began construction of a memorial hall within ten years of her death. Unfortunately, plans for the hall fell through and eventually the Hayward copy was donated to the Royal Ontario Museum. See: AO, York County Surrogate Court (RG 22), Estate Files, 1800–1968 (series 305), will of Mary Agnes FitzGibbon, 2 Apr., 1915, no. 30,198.

28 For biographical information on Allan Cassels, see: Henry James Morgan, ed., *The Canadian Men and Women of the Time*, 1st ed. (Toronto, Ontario: William Briggs, 1898), 169–70.

29 AO, Women's Canadian Historical Society of Toronto Papers (F 1180), Miscellaneous (series 13), file 3, Brock Portrait Notebook, 45.

30 Ibid., 45, 47.

31 Ibid., Correspondence (series 1), file 1 (1890–96), Cassels to Mickle, 2 Sept., 1896.

32 Hayward was just as pleased that "Mr. Cassels think[s] I am correct about the originality of the miniature, for I never felt more convinced in my life." See: ibid., file 9 (n.d.), Hayward to Mickle, 10 Sept., 1896.

33 *Globe*, 23 Sept., 1896, 2, c. 5. In a letter to the Canadian writer William Kirby, Miss FitzGibbon confessed that both she and Miss Mickle were "almost ecstatic" over the new portrait of Brock (fig. 11). See: AO, William Kirby Papers (F 1076), Miscellaneous Correspondence (series A-23), FitzGibbon to Kirby, 21 Sept., 1896.

34 *Globe*, 23 Sept., 1896, 2, c. 5.

35 Ibid.

36 Ibid., 12 Oct., 1896, 7, c. 2.

37 The former lieutenant governor died during a political rally the previous June. See: ibid., 20 June, 1896, 12, c. 1.

38 In 1896, General Robinson was lieutenant governor and secretary of the Royal Hospital at Chelsea. See: Morgan, *Canadian Men and Women of the Time*, 2nd ed., 956–7. For "Historian's" letter, see: *Globe*, 12 Oct., 1896, 7, c. 2.

39 As an example of "Historian's" careful style of writing, consider the following: "While the full view portrait [fig. 11] will by the supply of detail no doubt enhance the value of the side view [fig. 9], which must give in simpler line the salient features of the original, it will not detract in the least from Miss Mickle's discovery, if the value of the only extant profile portrait of General Brock be spoken of in terms of appreciation." See: *Globe*, 12 Oct., 1896, 7, c. 2.

40 Subtle and not-so-subtle references to Christopher Robinson's retiring nature can be found in his obituaries. See, for example, *Toronto Daily Star* (Toronto, Ontario), 1 Nov., 1905, 5, c. 1; ibid., 6., c. 1; *Evening Telegram*, 1 Nov., 1905, 11, c. 4; ibid., 3 Nov., 1905, 8, c. 1.

41 *Globe*, 27 Oct., 1896, 4, c. 5; AO, Women's Canadian Historical Society of Toronto Papers (F1180), Correspondence (series 1), file 1 (1890–96), Carnochan to Mickle, 8 Oct., 1896. For a biography of Miss Carnochan, see: Cecilia Morgan, "Carnochan, Janet," *Dictionary of Canadian Biography* XV: 183–5.

42 A "Subscriber" to the Toronto *Mail* claimed to have one such variation. It was an oil painting, which was supposedly presented to him by a gentleman who served in the British artillery at the Battle of Queenston Heights. Miss Carnochan soon discovered that the "Subscriber" was Henry A. Garrett of Niagara(-on-the-Lake), and that he acquired the portrait from a Colonel McFarland (actually Major Duncan McFarland). Miss Carnochan was able to view the so-called oil painting, and she immediately recognized it to be a "copy of the picture we all know." She also pronounced it to be "a water color copy, poorly done as a work of art but a good likeness." However, an antique photograph of this supposed "work of art" (fig. 31), which Garrett donated to the Niagara Historical Society Museum, suggests the original was a photograph of Gerrit Schipper's portrait of Brock (fig. 3) that had been overpainted with watercolours. See: *Daily Mail and Empire* (Toronto, Ontario), 25 Sept., 1896, 8, c. 1; AO, Women's Canadian Historical Society of Toronto Papers (F 1180), Correspondence (series 1), file 1 (1890–96), Carnochan to Mickle, 8 Oct., 1896; Niagara Historical Society Museum, Photograph of a Portrait of "General Sir Isaac Brock," by William Quinn, circa 1891, acc. 984.1.127.

43 *Globe*, 27 Oct., 1896, 4, c. 5.

44 Regarding *The Cabot Calendar*'s reception, see, for example: ibid., 28 Nov., 1896, 10, c. 5; ibid., 5 Dec., 1896, 16, c. 2; ibid., 22, c. 3.

45 David Ross McCord probably first learned of Miss Mickle's discovery through Miss FitzGibbon's contributions to the Toronto *Globe*, which were communicated to other Canadian newspapers, including the Montreal *Gazette*. See: *Gazette* (Montreal, Quebec), 25 Sept., 1896, 8, c. 4.

46 McCord Museum of Canadian History, (MMCH) Notman Photographic Archives, Photograph of a "Miniature of Sir Isaac Brock," by Benjamin Collenette, 1881, cat. MP-0000.2251.2. For additional information, see ch. 1, n37.

47 MMCH, Archives and Documentation Centre, McCord Family Papers (P001), Collecting Correspondence, Tupper to McCord, 19 Feb., 1897. By mid-April of 1897, Miss Tupper agreed with McCord "in being very dubious over the Cabot Calendar." See: ibid., 14 Apr., 1897.

48 Specifically, General Robinson questioned the shoulder insignia, which were wings as opposed to epaulettes. See: AO, Women's Canadian Historical Society of Toronto Papers (F 1180), Miscellaneous (series 13), file 3, Brock Portrait Notebook, 79. Brock was appointed a full colonel by brevet on 30 Oct., 1805. See: Library and Archives Canada, British Military and Naval Records, "C" Series (RG 8, I), vol. 17, Gordon to Officer Commanding His Majesty's Forces in Canada, 1 Nov., 1805, 96–8.

49 AO, Women's Canadian Historical Society of Toronto Papers (F 1180), Miscellaneous (series 13), file 3, Brock Portrait Notebook, 79. Regarding the Military General Service Medal, see: Donald Hall and Christopher Wingate, *British Orders, Decorations and Medals* (St. Ives, England: Balfour Publications, 1973), 55.

50 AO, Women's Canadian Historical Society of Toronto Papers (F 1180), Miscellaneous (series 13), file 3, Brock Portrait Notebook, 79.

51 Ibid., 79, 81.

52 Ibid., 79; Canada, Parliament (Commons), *Sessional Papers*, "Report of the Joint Librarians of Parliament, List of Copyrights Deposited in the Library of Parliament," 1896 XXXI, vol. 12, no. 17 (1897): 11. The copyright holder was Mrs. Taylor.

53 AO, Women's Canadian Historical Society of Toronto Papers (F 1180), Miscellaneous (series 13), file 3, Brock Portrait Notebook, 78. As Miss FitzGibbon subsequently observed: "English soldiers understand the 'noblesse oblige,' & do not war with women!" See: ibid., Correspondence (series 1), file 3 (June–Dec. 1897), FitzGibbon to Mickle, 11 June, 1897.

54 Ibid., Miscellaneous (series 13), file 3, Brock Portrait Notebook, 78.

55 Ibid. Miss FitzGibbon was not inclined to blame Mrs. Strachan herself, as "the dear old lady will do what Christopher [Robinson] tells her." It also seemed doubtful that Mrs. Strachan "mentioned the matter to any one out of her own family, but [her niece] Minnie Grant spoke of it before Dr. [George Sterling Ansel] Ryerson—& has probably done so to others." See: ibid., Correspondence (series 1), file 9 (n.d.), FitzGibbon to Mickle, 1 May, 1897. Mrs. William Forsyth (Minnie) Grant was a daughter of Lieutenant Governor John Beverley Robinson. Dr. Ryerson was a nephew of the early Ontario Methodist minister and educator, Rev. Dr. Egerton Ryerson.

56 Forster's client was John A. Macdonell, and the portrait of Brock he commissioned was painted in 1894 (fig. 10). Some of these other materials included a photograph of the original portrait (fig. 7) and the Kerr-Nelson painting (fig. 6). See: *Globe*, 3 Oct., 1896, 1, c. 4.

57 Ibid.

58 *Toronto Saturday Night* (Toronto, Ontario), 27 Mar., 1897, 15, c. 2. Forster appears to have visited Guernsey twice, both before and after his trip to Paris. According to newspaper reports, he was in Paris between approximately 8 June and 22 July, 1897. See: *Star* (St. Peter Port, Guernsey), 8 June, 1897, 2, c. 5; ibid., 22 July, 1897, 2, c. 5.

59 AO, Women's Canadian Historical Society of Toronto Papers (F 1180), Correspondence (series 1), file 2 (Jan.–May 1897), Stuart to Mickle, Easter Tuesday, 20 Apr., 1897.

60 Ibid., file 1, Stuart to Mickle, 29 Oct., 1896. For biographical information on Rev. Stuart, see: Morgan, *Canadian Men and Women of the Time*, 1st ed., 983.

61 Rev. Stuart knew of Carter from his many visits to Trois-Rivières. See: AO, Women's Canadian Historical Society of Toronto Papers (F 1180), Correspondence (series 1), file 2 (Jan.–May 1897), Stuart to Mickle, 12 Apr., 1897.

62 Ibid., Carter to Stuart, 19 Apr., 1897.

63 Ibid.

64 Ibid., Stuart to Mickle, 30 Apr., 1897. Rev. Stuart mistakenly thought that Lieutenant Colonel Short was killed during the attack on Fort Meigs near modern-day Perrysburg, Ohio, in late April of 1813. For additional information on Lieutenant Colonel Short and his death, see: David A.N. Lomax, *A History of the Services of the 41st (the Welch) Regiment* (Devonport, England: Hiorns and Miller, 1899), 75–7, 113. Rev. Stuart gave no reason as to why he doubted the portrait (fig. 15) could be of Brock, or why he thought it might be that of either Captain James Brock or Lieutenant Colonel William C. Short.

65 AO, Women's Canadian Historical Society of Toronto Papers (F 1180), Correspondence (series 1), file 2 (Jan.–May 1897), Taylor to Mickle, 4 May, 1897.

66 Ibid.

67 It was Miss Mickle who noted this living arrangement, which was confirmed by the United States census for 1900. See: ibid., Miscellaneous (series 13), file 3, Brock Portrait Notebook, 74; National Archives and Records Administration, Bureau of the Census (RG 29), Twelfth Census, 1900, Franklin, New Hampshire, sched. 1, dis. 163, sh. 12, nos 80, 83.

68 AO, Women's Canadian Historical Society of Toronto Papers (F 1180), Correspondence (series 1), file 2 (Jan.–May 1897), Short to Mickle, 18 May, 1897.

69 Ibid. By way of an additional argument, Short informed Miss Mickle that his deceased brother, "always said that the Photograph [or rather the miniature (fig. 11)] which you have was that of Sir Isaac." This deceased brother was John Short, the father of Mrs. Taylor and Mrs. de Beaumont.

70 Ibid., Short to Mickle, 26 May, 1897.

71 Ibid.

72 Ibid., Taylor to Mickle, 26 May, 1897.

73 Ibid., 4 May, 1897.

74 Ibid., 26 May, 1897. Lieutenant Dunn suffered from occasional bouts of insanity and had a "tendency to self-destruction." On 23 December, 1850, while acting as paymaster to the 23rd Regiment at Plymouth, he committed suicide by hanging himself. See: *Times* (London, England), 27 Dec., 1850, 7, c. 4.

75 As for the rest of the family, Mrs. Taylor and her uncle agreed that none of them knew anything about the portraits in question. See: AO, Women's Canadian Historical Society of Toronto Papers (F 1180), Correspondence (series 1), file 2 (Jan.–May 1897), Short to Mickle, 26 May 1897; ibid., Taylor to Mickle, 26 May, 1897.

76 George Dunn never held the rank of captain.

77 In the 3 April, 1897 edition of *Toronto Saturday Night*, it was reported that: "Mr. J.W.L. Forster sails to-day for Europe." On 24 April, the same paper reported Miss FitzGibbon's departure: "Miss Fitzgibbon of Jarvis street left for England this week, to be absent all summer." See: *Toronto Saturday Night*, 3 Apr., 1897, 15, c. 2; ibid., 24 Apr., 1897, 4, c. 2.

78 AO, Women's Canadian Historical Society of Toronto Papers (F 1180), Correspondence (series 1), file 9 (n.d.), FitzGibbon to Mickle, 19 Apr., 1897. While this letter was written on board the S.S. *Massachusetts* and appears to have been dated "3rd May," Miss FitzGibbon was already in England when she penned another letter under date of 1 May, 1897. See: ibid., 1 May, 1897. Miss Mickle also questioned the date of 3 May, 1897. See: ibid., Miscellaneous (series 13), file 3, Brock Portrait Notebook, 84–5. Miss FitzGibbon probably meant "3rd day," as in the third day at sea. Since the *Massachusetts* sailed from New York City on 17 April, 1897, Miss FitzGibbon likely wrote her letter on 19 April, 1897. For the sailing of the *Massachusetts*, see: *New York Times* (New York, New York), 17 Apr., 1897, 2, c. 7.

79 AO, Women's Canadian Historical Society of Toronto Papers (F 1180), Correspondence (series 1), file 9 (n.d.), FitzGibbon to Mickle, 1 May, 1897. See also: *Times*, 29 Apr., 1897, 10, c. 5. Later in June, Forster wrote to his mother that "London is crowded, crowded." See: Toronto Reference Library, Marilyn and Charles Baillie Special Collections Centre, Baldwin Collection of Canadiana, John Wycliffe Lowes Forster Papers (S 19), file n.d.–1899, Forster to his mother, 18 June, 1897.

80 The Royal Colonial Institute is now the Royal Commonwealth Society.

81 AO, Women's Canadian Historical Society of Toronto Papers (F 1180), Correspondence (series 1), file 9 (n.d), FitzGibbon to Mickle, 1 May, 1897.

82 Ibid., 4 May, 1897.

83 Ibid. Visitors from Canada could have their mail delivered to the Canadian High Commission while they toured Britain.

84 Ibid.

85 Ibid.

86 As Miss FitzGibbon wrote to Miss Mickle a short time later, "I do not despair especially as I agree with you as do others that the uniform being correct or incorrect does no injury & has no effect upon the authenticity of the portrait [fig. 11]. The medal also is I fear a mere fancy of the artist's own." See: ibid., file 2 (Jan.–May 1897), FitzGibbon to Mickle, 28 May, 1897. Miss FitzGibbon also expressed her opinion of the medal in a letter to Major Holden. After hearing of an extreme case of artistic license, in which a British naval officer was portrayed by a French artist wearing a Napoleonic uniform and decorations, she did "not consider the medal such a stumbling block as it appears to General Robinson." See: ibid., file 3 (June–Dec. 1897), FitzGibbon to Holden, 28 June, 1897.

87 Ibid., file 9, (n.d.) FitzGibbon to Mickle, 4 May, 1897.

88 When Major Holden offered to do anything he could to help Miss FitzGibbon, she took it to mean that he was willing to provide her with a written statement of his opinion regarding the miniature discovered by Miss Mickle (fig. 11). See: ibid. However, it appears that he never complied with her request. A trip to Scotland seems to have been his excuse, but there is also the possibility that Major Holden was restrained by General Robinson's influence. See: ibid., file 3 (June–Dec. 1897), FitzGibbon to Mickle, 29 June, 1897; ibid.,

FitzGibbon to Mickle, 18 July, 1897; ibid., 19 July, 1897; ibid., FitzGibbon to Mickle, 22 July, 1897. For a copy of Miss FitzGibbon's request, see: ibid., FitzGibbon to Holden, 28 June, 1897. Miss FitzGibbon was not particularly bothered by Major Holden's apparent neglect, as she thought she might get a written statement just "as good from some one else." See: ibid., FitzGibbon to Mickle, 18 July, 1897.

89 Ibid., file 9 (n.d.), FitzGibbon to Mickle, 4 May, 1897. As for the legal protection vested in Mrs. Taylor, see: Canada, Parliament (Commons), *Sessional Papers*, "Report of the Joint Librarians of Parliament, List of Copyrights Deposited in the Library of Parliament," 1896 XXXI, vol. 12, no. 17 (1897): 11.

90 AO, Women's Canadian Historical Society of Toronto Papers (F 1180), Correspondence (series 1), file 9, (n.d.) FitzGibbon to Mickle, 4 May, 1897. A short time later, Miss FitzGibbon contradicted herself by raising the possibility of monetary gain through legal action taken in defence of Miss Mickle's discovery. See: ibid., file 3 (June–Dec. 1897), FitzGibbon to Mickle, 29 June, 1897.

91 Ibid., file 9 (n.d.), FitzGibbon to Mickle, 4 May, 1897.

92 Ibid.

93 Ibid. Forster later claimed that he was introduced to the Misses Tupper "through the courtesy of Hon. John Beverley Robinson." Yet, by the time Forster made their acquaintance, the former lieutenant governor had been dead for nearly a year. See: John W.L. Forster, *Under the Studio Light: Leaves from a Portrait Painter's Sketch Book* (Toronto, Ontario: Macmillan Company of Canada, 1928), 140; *Globe*, 20 June, 1896, 12, c. 1.

CHAPTER 3

1 McCord Museum of Canadian History, Archives and Documentation Centre (MMCH), McCord Family Papers (P001), Collecting Correspondence, Tupper to McCord, 19 Feb., 1897. Miss Tupper thought "it would be very interesting to find a solution" as to why the sitter in the miniature (fig. 11), whose likeness was reproduced in *The Cabot Calendar* (fig. 14), differed in appearance from the portrait of Brock at Government House in Toronto (fig. 9)—especially as the latter work was based on the original profile portrait in Guernsey (fig. 3). She also thought Mrs. Taylor, the former owner of the miniature, "might possibly throw some light on the subject." Miss FitzGibbon, however, fulfilled the same function once she arrived in Guernsey.

2 Archives of Ontario (AO), Women's Canadian Historical Society of Toronto Papers (F 1180), Correspondence (series 1), file 2 (Jan.–May 1897), FitzGibbon to Mickle, 17 May, 1897. Forster mistakenly thought that Colonel Groves was curator of the Condé Library. See: John W.L. Forster, *Under the Studio Light: Leaves from a Portrait Painter's Sketch Book* (Toronto, Ontario: Macmillan Company of Canada, 1928), 133. In fact, and as noted in the text, Colonel Groves was librarian of the Candie Library. He was also secretary to the Priaulx Library Council. I am grateful to Gillian Lenfestey for this information.

3 Colonel Groves also considered the Military General Service Medal a possibility, but he quickly changed his mind in favour of the Waterloo Medal. See: AO, Women's Canadian Historical Society of Toronto Papers (F 1180), Correspondence (series 1), file 2 (Jan.–May 1897), FitzGibbon to Mickle, 17 May, 1897. For the report, see: ibid., Miscellaneous (series 13), file 3, Brock Portrait Notebook, 172–6. See also: ibid., Groves to FitzGibbon, 17 May, 1897, 177–8.

4 Miss FitzGibbon initially thought it possible that the medal might have been awarded to Brock for his capture of Detroit in 1812. However, she ruled out this large gold medal once she realized it was meant to be suspended from a ribbon around the neck, and not pinned to the chest as in the miniature (fig. 11). See: ibid., Correspondence (series 1), file 2 (Jan.–May 1897), FitzGibbon to Mickle, 17 May, 1897. Brock's gold medal is preserved in the Greffe, Royal Court House, St. Peter Port, Guernsey.

5 As Miss FitzGibbon put it, "Forster being in Guernsey hampered me much, especially as he got the ear of the Col Groves whom the family thought an authority." See: ibid., file 3 (June–Dec. 1897), FitzGibbon to Mickle, 11 June, 1897.

6 Ibid., file 2 (Jan.–May 1897), FitzGibbon to Mickle, 17 May, 1897.

7 Ibid. Miss Guille recalled the facial features of the men in her family, and she thought the officer in the miniature (fig. 11) "was like *them*." She attested to her belief as follows: "On comparing the photograph of Sir Isaac Brock's miniature (under discussion) with portraits of my maternal Grandfather William Brock Esq. of Brockhurst & his two brothers, first cousins of Sir Isaac Brock's, the resemblance is so very marked & extends also to the next generation, my mother's brothers, there can be no hesitation in recognizing the Brock features of which I have nearly 70 years knowledge." See: ibid., file 3 (June–Dec. 1897), FitzGibbon to Mickle, 15 June, 1897. Miss Guille, however, was mistaken.

8 Ibid., Miscellaneous (series 13), file 3, Brock Portrait Notebook, Tupper to FitzGibbon, 27 May, 1897, 164. The lady in question is simply identified as Mrs. Bubb. However, Gillian Lenfestey determined that she was the former Miss Bertha Tupper, a daughter of Henry Tupper and the wife of Arthur Bubb.

9 The date of the breakfast appears to have been 16 May, 1897. See: ibid., Correspondence (series 1), file 2 (Jan.–May 1897), FitzGibbon to Mickle, 17 May, 1897.

10 Ibid.

11 Ibid.

12 Ibid.

13 Ibid.

14 Ibid. Miss FitzGibbon vowed to write her own letter of protest to General Robinson, but she later decided against it. See: ibid., 28 May, 1897; ibid., file 3 (June–Dec. 1897), FitzGibbon to Mickle, 11 June, 1897.

15 Ibid., file 2 (Jan.–May 1897), FitzGibbon to Mickle, 17 May, 1897.

16 Adolphus Kentish Brock was the son of Rear Admiral Thomas Sausmarez Brock, C.B. After a long career in the Admiralty Office, he retired to Guernsey in 1893 and was elected a douzenier (or parish councillor). He also served as a director and treasurer of Elizabeth College. He died in London on 6 November, 1919. For his obituary, see: *Guernsey Evening Press* (St. Peter Port, Guernsey), 11 Nov., 1919, 3, c. 3.

17 When Miss FitzGibbon wrote to tell Kentish Brock that she had "incontrovertible proof" confirming the authenticity of the miniature (fig. 11), he believed her. See: United Church of Canada Archives (UCCA), John Wycliffe Lowes Forster Papers (3096), Correspondence Re: The Portrait of Sir Isaac Brock, file 10, Brock to Forster, 7 July, 1897.

18 AO, Women's Canadian Historical Society of Toronto Papers (F 1180), Correspondence (series 1), file 3 (June–Dec. 1897), FitzGibbon to Mickle, 20 July, 1897. Included in this letter is the transcript of a note Miss FitzGibbon sent to Kentish Brock on 12 July, 1897. In it, Miss FitzGibbon provided an overview of her research into the miniature discovered by

Miss Mickle (fig. 11). Miss FitzGibbon also wrote out a copy of the reply she received from Kentish Brock, dated 18 July, 1897, in which he acknowledged: "I think the miniature is conclusively shown to be that of Sir Isaac Brock." See: ibid.

19 Kentish Brock was also fully convinced that Miss FitzGibbon might succeed in persuading the States to adorn the Royal Court with an enlarged version of the miniature (fig. 11), as it was a full-faced composition and would therefore be preferable to the profile portrait (fig. 3). See: UCCA, John Wycliffe Lowes Forster Papers (3096), Correspondence Re: The Portrait of Sir Isaac Brock, file 10, Brock to Forster, 7 July, 1897.

20 Miss FitzGibbon returned to London by 25 May, 1897. See: AO, Women's Canadian Historical Society of Toronto Papers (F 1180), Correspondence (series 1), file 3 (June–Dec. 1897), file 2 (Jan.–May 1897), FitzGibbon to Mickle, 25–6 May, 1897.

21 Forster's inscription on the back of the study (fig. 16) reveals that it was painted in May of 1897, which also suggests that it was finished by the end of that same month. For the study, see: Library and Archives Canada, Portrait Gallery of Canada, Oil Painting Study of "Sir Isaac Brock," by John W.L. Forster, 1897, acc. 1991-30-1. The full inscription reads as follows: "This portrait of Sir Isaac Brock, K.B. was painted from the original portrait in the possession of John Savery Carey, Esq., and the coat worn by Genl. Brock in 1812, on the fatal day at Queenston Heights, and now in the possession of the Misses Tupper; by kind permission of the owners. J.W.L. Forster. St. Peter Port May 1897." In fact, the "original portrait" owned by Carey was the copy of Brock's profile portrait (fig. 4). Forster's study was put on display by 8 June, 1897, "though not yet properly framed." See: *Star* (St. Peter Port, Guernsey), 8 June, 1897, 2, c. 5.

22 AO, Women's Canadian Historical Society of Toronto Papers (F 1180), Correspondence (series 1), file 3 (June–Dec. 1897), FitzGibbon to Mickle, 11 June, 1897.

23 Ibid., file 2 (Jan.–May 1897), FitzGibbon to Mickle, 25–6 May, 1897.

24 Ibid., file 3 (June–Dec. 1897), FitzGibbon to Mickle, 11 June, 1897. Although Forster believed that Miss FitzGibbon and Miss Mickle had been deceived with regard to the identity of sitter in the miniature (fig. 11), he let it be known that he would remain silent out of respect for their painstaking work, and also to avoid making himself appear disagreeable. Miss FitzGibbon, however, still did not trust him. See: ibid., FitzGibbon to Mickle, 15 June, 1897.

25 Miss FitzGibbon appears to have entertained the possibility of luring Forster into a confrontation. However, she deferred to Miss Mickle who preferred to avoid unseemly behaviour. See: ibid., FitzGibbon to Mickle, 29 June, 1897.

26 Miss FitzGibbon wrote to Miss Tupper regarding the loan of the portraits (figs 3, 4) on 25 May, 1897. See: ibid., file 2 (Jan.–May 1897), FitzGibbon to Mickle, 25–6 May, 1897.

27 Ibid., Miscellaneous (series 13), file 3, Brock Portrait Notebook, Tupper to FitzGibbon, 27 May, 1897, 161. The copy (fig. 4) was then in the possession of John Savery Carey. He received it as an inheritance from his aunt, Mrs. Rosa (Brock) Huyshe, who died in 1892. While Mrs. Huyshe did not formally bequeath the portrait to John Savery Carey, he was one of her heirs and his ownership is well documented in the local press. See, for example: *Star*, 8 June, 1897, 2, c. 5; ibid., 22 July, 1897, 2, c. 5; ibid., 24 Aug., 1897, 2, c. 7. For Mrs. Huyshe's will, see: Ecclesiastical Court of Guernsey (ECG), Records of the Registrar of Wills and Intestacies, Book of Testaments (Apr. 1889–Aug. 1894), will of Rosa (Brock) Huyshe, 14 Apr., 1892. I am grateful to Gillian Lenfestey for providing me with a copy of this will.

28 This disadvantage became evident when Miss FitzGibbon attended an exhibition of miniatures owned by Dr. John Lumsden Propert. While there, she hoped to learn something about the miniature discovered by Miss Mickle (fig. 11). However, she was told "it would be difficult to do any thing without the original." See: AO, Women's Canadian Historical Society of Toronto Papers (F 1180), Correspondence (series 1), file 3 (June–Dec. 1897), FitzGibbon to Mickle, 11 June, 1897. Regarding the exhibition, see: *Times* (London, England), 16 Apr., 1897, 3, c. 3; ibid., 10 May, 1897, 3, c. 6.

29 As Miss FitzGibbon admitted, "I am worried with all sorts of things." See: AO, Women's Canadian Historical Society of Toronto Papers (F 1180), Correspondence (series 1), file 3 (June–Dec. 1897), FitzGibbon to Mickle, 15 June, 1897.

30 Ibid., 21 June, 1897.

31 Ibid., 15 June, 1897.

32 Ibid.

33 Miss Tupper agreed to bring the portrait (fig. 4) to London on 10 June, 1897, which was anticipated by Miss FitzGibbon in at least two of the letters she wrote to Miss Mickle. See: ibid., FitzGibbon to Mickle, 2 June, 1897; ibid., 7 June, 1897.

34 As Miss FitzGibbon wrote, "I go to Bristol on Wednesday [23 June, 1897] till Friday [25 June, 1897] when, after my return here [to London], there will be a better chance of succeeding in getting an expert to attend to such things as an unknown miniature and to give me an opinion." See: ibid., FitzGibbon to Mickle, 21 June, 1897.

35 Ibid., file 9 (n.d.), FitzGibbon to Mickle, 26 June, 1897.

36 Ibid., file 3 (June–Dec. 1897), FitzGibbon to Mickle, 29 June, 1897.

37 Ibid. Although Miss FitzGibbon did not identify this particular Rowney brother, he was described as being an artist. Apparently, the only one of the three Rowney brothers who was artistically inclined was Walter Rowney. See: ibid. I am grateful to Paul Cox of the National Portrait Gallery, London, England, for information he provided on Walter Rowney.

38 Ibid.

39 For biographical information on Nowlan, see: Daphne Foskett, *A Dictionary of British Miniature Painters*, 2 vols (New York, New York: Praeger Publishers, 1972), 1: 425.

40 AO, Women's Canadian Historical Society of Toronto Papers (F 1180), Correspondence (series 1), file 3 (June–Dec. 1897), FitzGibbon to Mickle, 29 June, 1897. For a biography of Cust, see: Laurence Binyon, revised by Christopher Lloyd, "Cust, Sir Lionel Henry," *Oxford Dictionary of National Biography* 14: 822–3. For biographical information on the solicitor Henry F. Rawstorne (as contained in his obituary), see: *Times*, 25 June, 1924, 16, c. 2.

41 AO, Women's Canadian Historical Society of Toronto Papers (F 1180), Correspondence (series 1), file 3 (June–Dec. 1897), FitzGibbon to Mickle, 29 June, 1897. In letters written to both Miss Mickle and her brother, Henry W. Mickle, Miss FitzGibbon acknowledged receipt of the Jarvis silhouette (fig. 18)—or rather a photographic copy. It is unclear which of these Mickle siblings actually sent the package to Miss FitzGibbon. See: ibid., FitzGibbon to Mickle, 15 June, 1897; ibid., FitzGibbon to Mickle, 15 June, 1897.

42 Ibid., file 1 (1890–96), Jarvis to Mickle, 16 Oct., 1896. Although Ludwig Kosche found a reproduction of this silhouette (fig. 18) in the papers of the Women's Canadian Historical Society of Toronto, a better copy can be found in William Wood's documentary history

of the War of 1812. The fate of the original silhouette, which belonged to Aemilius Jarvis in 1896, is unknown. See: Ludwig Kosche, "Contemporary Portraits of Isaac Brock: An Analysis," *Archivaria* 20 (Summer 1985): 36; William Wood, ed., *Select British Documents of the Canadian War of 1812*, 3 vols (Toronto, Ontario: Champlain Society, 1920–28), I: 32. In his letter to Miss Mickle, cited above, Jarvis stated that his grandmother, Miss Mary Boyles Powell, was engaged to John Macdonell, a claim that was no doubt based on family tradition. However, Macdonell's biographers had good reason to believe otherwise. See: Carol Whitfield and Robert Lochiel Fraser III, "Macdonell (Greenfield), John," *Dictionary of Canadian Biography* V: 522.

43 AO, Women's Canadian Historical Society of Toronto Papers (F 1180), Correspondence (series 1), file 3 (June–Dec. 1897), FitzGibbon to Mickle, 29 June, 1897.

44 Ibid. For a biography of Graves, see: Susanna Avery-Quash, "Graves, Algernon," *Oxford Dictionary of National Biography* 23: 383.

45 AO, Women's Canadian Historical Society of Toronto Papers (F 1180), Correspondence (series 1), file 3 (June–Dec. 1897), FitzGibbon to Mickle, 29 June, 1897. Although this letter is undated, it describes events that are known to have occurred on 29 June, 1897. It also appears to have been penned at the close of that same day, which corresponds with the date of the written opinion given to Miss FitzGibbon by Nowlan. For a transcript of Nowlan's opinion, see: ibid., Miscellaneous (series 13), file 2, Brock Miniature, "Copies of F. Nowlan's & Alyn Williams's opinions re portraits," 29 June, 1897.

46 Ibid., Correspondence (series 1), file 3 (June–Dec. 1897), FitzGibbon to Mickle, 29 June, 1897.

47 For Nowlan's opinion, see: ibid., Miscellaneous (series 13), file 2, Brock Miniature, "Copies of F. Nowlan's & Alyn Williams's opinions re portraits," 29 June, 1897.

48 Ibid., Correspondence (series 1), file 3 (June–Dec. 1897), FitzGibbon to Mickle, 29 June, 1897. The elusive J. Hudson might have been James Hudson, who was listed as a miniature painter in 1823. See: *Kent's Original London Directory: 1823* (London, England: Henry-Kent Causton, 1823), 176.

49 AO, Women's Canadian Historical Society of Toronto Papers (F 1180), Correspondence (series 1), file 3 (June–Dec. 1897), FitzGibbon to Mickle, 29 June, 1897.

50 *Times*, 11 June, 1897, 2, c. 1.

51 AO, Women's Canadian Historical Society of Toronto Papers (F 1180), Correspondence (series 1), file 3 (June–Dec. 1897), FitzGibbon to Mickle, 29 June, 1897.

52 For biographical information on Williams, see: Foskett, *Dictionary of British Miniature Painters*, 1: 579. Williams died in 1941. For his obituary, see: *Times*, 5 Aug., 1941, 6, c. 5.

53 AO, Women's Canadian Historical Society of Toronto Papers (F 1180), Correspondence (series 1), file 3 (June–Dec. 1897), FitzGibbon to Mickle, 29 June, 1897.

54 Miss FitzGibbon had the original profile portrait (fig. 3) photographed a short time earlier. Unfortunately, none of the prints could be located for reproduction here. See: ibid., file 2 (Jan.–May 1897), FitzGibbon to Mickle, 17 May, 1897. After Mrs. Henry Tupper's death in 1882, the profile portrait went to De Vic Tupper. When De Vic Tupper died in 1892, it became the property of his son, Henry Bingham de Vic Tupper. I am grateful to Gillian Lenfestey for this information.

55 Ibid., file 3 (June–Dec. 1897), FitzGibbon to Mickle, 29 June, 1897.

56 Miss FitzGibbon appears to have been especially impressed by Williams's credentials. In a letter to Miss Mickle, she noted that he taught art classes in partnership with the artist who did many of the pictures for the *Illustrated London News*. This partner was probably Edward Linley Sambourne. Miss FitzGibbon considered them to be "quite big enough guns for our purpose." See: ibid., FitzGibbon to Mickle, 18 July, 1897.

57 Ibid., FitzGibbon to Mickle, 29 June, 1897.

58 Ibid., Miscellaneous (series 13), file 3, Brock Portrait Notebook, 134.

59 For Miss FitzGibbon's transcript of Williams's opinion, see: ibid., file 2, Brock Miniature, "Copies of F. Nowlan's & Alyn Williams' opinions re portraits," 29 June, 1897.

60 Ibid., Correspondence (series 1), file 3 (June–Dec. 1897), FitzGibbon to Mickle, 18 July, 1897. According to a letter she addressed to Miss Mickle dated 2 June, 1897, Miss FitzGibbon was already thinking in terms of a duplicate. "I am hoping to get a good copy in pastels if no other way." See: ibid., Mary Agnes FitzGibbon to Mickle, 2 June, 1897. After Miss FitzGibbon's death in 1915, Williams's copy (fig. 19) was bequeathed to the Royal Ontario Museum (acc. 921.42.3). See: AO, York County Surrogate Court (RG 22), Estate Files, 1800–1968 (series 305), will of Mary Agnes FitzGibbon, 2 Apr., 1915, no. 30,198.

61 AO, Women's Canadian Historical Society of Toronto Papers (F 1180), Correspondence (series 1), file 3 (June–Dec. 1897), FitzGibbon to Mickle, 19 July, 1897.

62 John Savery Carey inherited this copy of the profile portrait (fig. 4) from his aunt, Mrs. Huyshe, but not by a provision in her will. See: ECG, Records of the Registrar of Wills and Intestacies, Book of Testaments (Apr. 1889–Aug. 1894), will of Rosa (Brock) Huyshe, 14 Apr., 1892. By 1897, the original profile portrait (fig. 3), formerly owned by Mrs. Henry Tupper, was the property of her grandson, Henry Bingham de Vic Tupper.

63 AO, Women's Canadian Historical Society of Toronto Papers (F 1180), Correspondence (series 1), file 3 (June–Dec. 1897), FitzGibbon to Mickle, 18 July, 1897. From at least early June of 1897, Miss FitzGibbon began to look upon the copy of the profile portrait (fig. 4) as the original. See: ibid., 2 June, 1897. This misconception may have originated with John Wycliffe Lowes Forster, but it was impressed upon Miss FitzGibbon by Alyn Williams.

64 Besides referring to this bronzed silhouette as a bronze profile (fig. 8), Miss Tupper also described it as a "profile in bronze," a "bronze silhouette," and simply a "silhouette." See: MMCH, Archives and Documentation Centre, McCord Family Papers (P001), Collecting Correspondence, Tupper to McCord, 19 Feb., 1897; ibid., 14 Apr., 1897; ibid., 7 July, 1897; Trent University, Thomas J. Bata Library, Trent University Archives, Gilbert and Stewart Bagnani Papers (94-016), General Correspondence (series A), Tupper to Robinson, 15 Apr., 1882. Although several copies of the bronze profile were known to exist at one time, none of them are known to have survived. Fortunately, the image is preserved in a black and white photograph at the McCord Museum of Canadian History, Montreal, Quebec. See: MMCH, Notman Photographic Archives, Photograph of a Bronze Silhouette/Profile of an Unknown Officer (misidentified as "Major General Sir Isaac Brock"), by Robert Dumaresq, 1897, MP-0000.2251.1. There has been some speculation that the sitter in the bronze profile might be Francis Rawdon-Hastings, Earl of Moira, who received the order of the Garter in 1812 and was created Marquess of Hastings in 1817. The style of the bronze profile bears a striking resemblance to those gold-tinted silhouettes produced by the Studio of John Miers in London, England. This particular bronze silhouette appears to have been painted on ivory or plaster circa 1812, and perhaps by John Field (one of Miers's assistants).

Although the sitter in the bronze profile has his hair tied in a queue, which the Duke of York abolished in 1808, some older high-ranking officers—such as Lord Moira was in 1812—ignored the order. See: Herman de Watteville, *The British Soldier: His Daily Life from Tudor to Modern Times* (London, England: J. M. Dent and Sons, 1954), 88.

65 AO, Women's Canadian Historical Society of Toronto Papers (F 1180), Correspondence (series 1), file 3 (June–Dec. 1897), FitzGibbon to Mickle, 7 June, 1897. As Miss FitzGibbon's brother sarcastically remarked, the sitter was a man who "would never see sixty again." Gerald FitzGibbon also told his sister that "no man of forty was ever so developed in head & throat." See: ibid., 19 July, 1897.

66 Ibid., file 2 (Jan.–May 1897), FitzGibbon to Mickle, 17 May, 1897.

67 Ibid., file 3 (June–Dec. 1897), 2 June, 1897. Miss FitzGibbon also wondered if the bronze profile (fig. 8) was an adaptation of the Jarvis silhouette (fig. 18).

68 It appears that this idea first occurred to Miss FitzGibbon towards the end of June 1897. See: ibid., FitzGibbon to Mickle, 29 June, 1897.

69 Ibid., FitzGibbon to Mickle, 19 July, 1897. Miss FitzGibbon's belief that Isaac and Daniel de Lisle Brock resembled one another probably originated with Ferdinand Brock Tupper. See: Ferdinand Brock Tupper, ed., *The Life and Correspondence of Major-General Sir Isaac Brock, K.B.*, 2nd ed. (London, England: Simpkin, Marshall and Company, 1847), 467.

70 AO, Women's Canadian Historical Society of Toronto Papers (F 1180), Correspondence (series 1), file 3 (June–Dec. 1897), FitzGibbon to Mickle, 19 July, 1897.

71 In a letter dated 19 July, 1897, Miss FitzGibbon advised that "it is best to say as little as possible about the Tupper silhouette," meaning the bronze profile (fig. 8). See: ibid.

72 Miss FitzGibbon had arranged to spend a day with Miss Tupper, presumably so that the copy of Brock's profile portrait (fig. 4) could be borrowed and made available for consultation by the art experts. Before the end of June, however, and some two weeks after Miss Tupper's arrival in London, Miss FitzGibbon began to opine: "I will not take her with me to the experts." See: ibid., file 9 (n.d.), FitzGibbon to Mickle, 26 June, 1897.

73 After a voyage of ten days, Miss FitzGibbon arrived back in Canada on 17 August, 1897. See: LAC, Ships Passenger Lists, Quebec City Ships' Manifests (RG 76, C1a), S.S. *Lake Winnipeg*, 17 Aug., 1897, no. 50; *Gazette* (Montreal, Quebec), 17 Aug., 1897, 8, c. 5; *Globe* (Toronto, Ontario), 17 Aug., 1897, 5, c. 1.

74 Forster returned to Guernsey no later than 22 July, 1897, by which time he was engaged in painting a larger portrait of Brock (fig. 21). See: *Star*, 22 July, 1897, 2, c. 5. Although Forster's trip to Guernsey was reported to be for the "express purpose of carrying back to Canada a reliable portrait of Sir Isaac Brock," there was no mention of a client. See: ibid., 8 June, 1897, 2, c. 5. See also: *Globe*, 5 July, 1897, 10, c. 3. Forster seldom overlooked this all-important detail, as name-dropping was quite useful in attracting new customers. Such an omission could only mean one thing: he had no buyer for his portrait of Brock. And sure enough, the study for this intended portrait (fig. 16) remained in Forster's possession until 1913, when he gave it to the Dominion (or Canadian) Archives. Since 2001, the study has formed part of the collections of the Portrait Gallery of Canada, now a program of Library and Archives Canada. While Forster considered it to be a commission for the Government of Ontario, he did not sell a larger version to that province until 1900. See: Forster, *Under the Studio Light*, 140; Ontario, Legislative Assembly, *Sessional Papers*, "Public Accounts of the Province of Ontario," 1900 XXXIII, pt I, no. 1 (1901): 168. I am grateful to Madeleine

Trudeau of Library and Archives Canada for providing me with information regarding Forster's donation.

75 AO, Women's Canadian Historical Society of Toronto Papers (F 1180), Correspondence (series 1), file 2 (Jan.–May 1897), FitzGibbon to Mickle, 25–6 May, 1897. Although an official portrait of Brock was suggested as early as 1885, it did not meet with serious consideration until June of 1897. As the Guernsey *Star* then observed, "A fitting opportunity seems now to have presented itself to secure for Guernsey, if possible, either the picture itself or a *replica* of it before Mr. Forster returns to Canada and we trust that the States may see fit to add General Brock's portrait to their collection in the Royal Court-house, and place it near that of his brother the late Daniel de Lisle Brock, Bailiff of Guernsey." See: *Star*, 7 Mar., 1885, 2, c. 6; ibid., 8 June, 1897, 2, c. 5.

76 Forster, *Under the Studio Light*, 140. Forster recalled that when his study (fig. 16) was finished, "the Bailiff (Governor) of the Island, Sir John Savery Carey, and a deputation including Kentish Brock, Esq., from the 'States' (Parliament) waited upon me." While Forster may have correctly recalled the role of the bailiff in this incident, he was somewhat confused by Guernsey officialdom. The bailiff is not the governor (actually the lieutenant governor), but rather president of the States, or parliament. The lieutenant governor is the monarch's representative in Guernsey. At the time of Forster's visit to Guernsey in 1897, the bailiff was T. Godfrey Carey, not John Savery Carey (who was never knighted). The lieutenant governor was Nathaniel Stevenson.

77 *Star*, 28 Aug., 1897, 3, c. 1. It was at the end of June 1897 that Kentish Brock was officially informed of the preference for a larger painting (fig. 21). See: UCCA, John Wycliffe Lowes Forster Papers (3096), Correspondence Re: The Portrait of Sir Isaac Brock, file 10, Brock to Forster, 29 June, 1897.

78 Forster's return to Toronto was reported on 21 Aug., 1897. See: *Toronto Saturday Night* (Toronto, Ontario) 21 Aug., 1897, 2, c. 4. The proposal had its origin several months earlier. In June of 1897, Kentish Brock wrote to the bailiff asking him to invite the States of Guernsey to deliberate the purchase of either the smaller portrait of Brock (fig. 16), or the larger one (fig. 21). See: Guernsey, States of Deliberation, *Billet d'État* VI (1897): 167–70.

79 *Star*, 2 Sep. 1897, 2, c. 5. It should be noted that deputies in Guernsey are elected members of the States, like members of parliament, while jurats are appointed jury members. Rectors are also unelected.

80 Miss FitzGibbon did not think much of Forster's work. After seeing his study for Brock's portrait (fig. 16) in mid-May of 1897, she expressed her low opinion in the following terms: "It is a better painting than the last," presumably meaning the portrait of Brock painted for John A. Macdonell in 1894 (fig. 10), "but he has lost the likeness still more." See: AO, Women's Canadian Historical Society of Toronto Papers (F 1180), Correspondence (series 1), file 2 (Jan.–May 1897), FitzGibbon to Mickle, 17 May, 1897. Miss FitzGibbon probably viewed Forster's study while it was on display in Thomas Grigg's picture framing shop in St. Peter Port. See: *Star*, 8 June, 1897, 2, c. 5.

81 Mrs. Stevenson was the former Miss Isabella Charlotte Lewin. See: Melville Henry Massue, Marquis of Ruvigny and Raineval, *The Plantagenet Roll of the Blood Royal*, 4 vols (London, England: Melville and Company, 1905–11), Mortimer-Percy, 1: 249.

82 AO, Women's Canadian Historical Society of Toronto Papers (F 1180), Correspondence (series 1), file 3 (June–Dec. 1897), FitzGibbon to Mickle, 11 June, 1897.

83 Both of Forster's portraits of Brock (figs 16, 21) were displayed in Thomas Grigg's picture framing shop in St. Peter Port. Presumably, it was there that the lieutenant governor and members of the Royal Court had an opportunity to view them. See: *Star*, 8 June, 1897, 2, c. 5; ibid., 22 July, 1897, 2, c. 5; ibid., 28 Aug., 1897, 3, c. 1.

84 Guernsey, States of Deliberation, *Billet d'État* VI (1897): 170–1. The letter from Kentish Brock to Bailiff Carey is dated 22 July, 1897. Kentish Brock's letter was no doubt meant to counter Miss FitzGibbon's negative remarks about Forster's work.

85 AO, Women's Canadian Historical Society of Toronto Papers (F 1180), Miscellaneous (series 13), file 3, Brock Portrait Notebook, Tupper to FitzGibbon, postmarked 28 July, 1897, 165, 170.

86 *Star*, 2 Sept., 1897, 2, c. 5. The artist in question was referred to as Mr. Falle, who was actually Rolfe Falls, an Englishman who made his home in Guernsey. See: ibid., 7 Sept., 1897, 2, c. 7; UCCA, John Wycliffe Lowes Forster Papers (3096), Correspondence Re: The Portrait of Sir Isaac Brock, file 10, Hubert to Forster, 5 Oct., 1897.

87 *Star*, 2 Sept., 1897, 2, c. 5.

88 Ibid.

89 As one of Forster's Guernsey friends later explained, Jurat Carey "over-reached himself and exhibited his ignorance of the uniforms in vogue in Gen[eral] Brock's time." See: UCCA, John Wycliffe Lowes Forster Papers (3096), Correspondence Re: The Portrait of Sir Isaac Brock, file 10, Hubert to Forster, 5 Oct., 1897.

90 *Star*, 2 Sept., 1897, 2, c. 5. Deputy Carey further expected that the expert "would be sure to condemn the portrait," as "it was difficult to paint the portrait of a man who is no longer living, especially if there are no good pictures of him in existence."

91 Kentish Brock hastened to tell Forster of the "overwhelming majority." See: UCCA, John Wycliffe Lowes Forster Papers (3096), Correspondence Re: The Portrait of Sir Isaac Brock, file 10, Brock to Forster, 1 Sept., 1897. The vote was twenty-five in favour; six against; and two abstaining. See: *Star*, 2 Sept., 1897, 2, c. 5. Forster was delighted with the news, which he shared with the Toronto *Globe*. He chose, however, to ignore the debate about the quality of his work. See: *Globe*, 15 Sept., 1897, 10, c. 1.

92 This sale was negotiated through the Ontario Ministry of Education, and at a deep discount. Although Forster had already taken $100 off his original asking price of $450, he was forced to deduct a further $100 in order to make the sale. See: AO, Department of Education (RG 2, 42), Select Subject Files, XIV-Pictures, no. 34, "Brock, Sir Isaac—portrait of," Forster to Harcourt, 22 Mar., 1900; Ontario, Legislative Assembly, *Sessional Papers*, "Public Accounts of the Province of Ontario," 1900 XXXIII, pt I, no. 1 (1901): 168. The portrait (fig. 22) is now on display in the foyer of the Ontario Legislative Building, as part of the Government of Ontario Art Collection. In 1957, it was lent for the opening of the General Brock Public School in nearby Scarborough, Ontario. Upon its return, two large tears were discovered in the upper left background, which were thought to have been the work of some vandal. However, given that the tears were only a few inches long, perpendicular, and limited to one side of the background, it now appears that the damage was caused by careless handling. During its subsequent restoration, the painting was also cleaned. See: AO, Government of Ontario Art Collection, Oil Painting of "Major-General Sir Isaac Brock, KB," by John W.L. Forster, 1900, acc. 692,993; *Toronto Daily Star* (Toronto, Ontario), 5 Oct., 1957, 24, c. 1.

93 In 1908, Lady Edgar, who began life in Toronto as Miss Matilda Ridout, published an article in which she recounted the efforts of the Robinson brothers to secure an accurate portrait of Sir Isaac Brock. Although she concluded with the somewhat antagonistic statement that "the portrait by Berthon [fig. 9], in Government House, Toronto, will remain for all time the accredited one of the famous general," there appears to have been no reaction from either Miss Mickle or Miss FitzGibbon. Perhaps they did not view the article as sufficiently threatening, or possibly they were not willing to contest Lady Edgar's authority in the matter—given that she had written a major biography of Brock only a few years earlier. Interestingly, when Forster negotiated the sale of his portrait of Brock (fig. 22) to the Province of Ontario, he informed the minister of education that it "will henceforth be the standard portrait of Sir Isaac Brock, as the uniform is that in which he met his death in defense of Canada." See: Lady Edgar [Matilda Ridout], "General Brock's Portrait," *Canadian Magazine* XXXI, no. 3 (July 1908): 265; AO, Department of Education (RG 2, 42), Select Subject Files, XIV-Pictures, no. 34, "Brock, Sir Isaac—portrait of," Forster to Harcourt, 22 Mar., 1900.

CHAPTER 4

1 Ludwig Kosche was born in Bremen on 5 August, 1929. See: *Ottawa Citizen* (Ottawa, Ontario), 23 May, 2000, F5, c. 8; Ludwig Kosche, "The Turco-German Alliance of August 1914" (Master's thesis, University of Western Ontario, 1969), 277. Kosche received his B.A. and M.A. from the University of Western Ontario, in London, Ontario.

2 Kosche subsequently earned his master's degree in library science from the University of Toronto in 1973. This information was kindly supplied by Kathleen O'Brien, communications and development officer, and Bisa Lovric, assistant to the dean, Faculty of Information Studies, University of Toronto.

3 *Might's Greater Ottawa City Directory, 1974* (Toronto, Ontario: Might Directories, c1974), 390. Kosche was probably hired sometime in 1973.

4 It was not possible to determine the precise date when Kosche began his duties at the Canadian War Museum. His name, however, appears in the first listing for this new position. Given that this information was published in the 1976 edition of the *Canadian Almanac & Directory*, Kosche probably joined the museum sometime in 1975. Although the *Ottawa City Directory* for 1976 continues to list him as an employee of the public library, Kosche likely began his new job after the publishers of the city directory had compiled their data for the upcoming year. See: *Canadian Almanac & Directory, 1976* (Toronto, Ontario: Copp Clark Publishing, 1976), 66; *Might's Greater Ottawa City Directory, 1976* (Toronto, Ontario: Might Directories, c1976), 393.

5 Email, Graves to St-Denis, 11 Jan., 2006. I am grateful to Donald E. Graves for his insights into Kosche's activities at the Canadian War Museum.

6 Ludwig Kosche, "Relics of Brock: An Investigation," *Archivaria* 9 (Winter 1979–80): 55–6.

7 According to Kosche, "Forster's technique of combining his artistry with the use of earlier portraits supplemented by research and artefacts was well-suited to the creation of paintings of historic personages." See: Kosche, "Relics of Brock," 35. Forster's use of the undress or plain coatee is recorded on the back of his study for Brock's portrait (fig. 16). See: ibid., 45. Forster was also assisted by Lieutenant Colonel J. Percy Groves, who advised him regarding the uniform's depiction. See: John W.L. Forster, *Under the Studio Light: Leaves from a Portrait Painter's Sketch Book* (Toronto, Ontario: Macmillan Company

of Canada, 1928), 133. As mentioned elsewhere, Forster used the copy of Brock's profile portrait (fig. 4) as a guide for his own portraits of Brock (figs 16, 21, 22), and probably because he considered the copy to be the original. The copy, incidentally, was then in the possession of John Savery Carey. It should also be noted that the dress or formal coatee is preserved in the McCord Museum of Canadian History in Montreal. Like the undress or plain coatee, it reflects Brock's rank as a brigadier general—a detail first pointed out by Major Nicholas Dawnay in 1953. See: Major Nicholas P. Dawnay, "The Staff Uniform of the British Army, 1767 to 1855," *Journal of the Society for Army Historical Research* XXXI (1953): 78.

8 Canadian War Museum, Military History Research Centre, George Metcalf Archival Collection (CWM), Ludwig Kosche Papers, Correspondence (58A3/10.26), Kosche to Mellish, 9 Apr., 1978.

9 Ibid., 3 June, 1978.

10 Ibid., 29 Oct., 1978.

11 Ibid., Mellish to Kosche, 23 Nov., 1978. It was still nearly mid-April of 1979 before the photographs were delivered. See: ibid., Kosche to Mellish, 10 Apr., 1979.

12 Ibid., Kosche to Mellish, 14 Dec., 1978. This lack of appreciation extended to the research Kosche conducted into other artifacts at the Canadian War Museum. For example, in 1981 Captain Mellish praised Kosche for his research into a watch thought to have belonged to Sir Isaac Brock. Kosche responded by acknowledging the compliment as compensation for the "indifference displayed by the War Museum." See: ibid., 26 Oct., 1981.

13 Ibid., 14 Dec., 1978. Although the coatee (fig. 23) is the same in each of these paintings, Forster's study (fig. 16) has Brock wearing a non-regulation red stock (or neckband of stiff fabric) and a ceinture fléchée (a sash with an arrow design). The portrait sold to the Government of Ontario (fig. 22) provides a more accurate representation of Brock's outfit, as it includes both a regulation black stock and a regulation crimson sash.

14 Kosche, "Relics of Brock," 45; CWM, Ludwig Kosche Papers, Correspondence (58A3/10.26), Kosche to Mellish, 14 Dec., 1978. The original profile portrait (fig. 3) was never the property of John Savery Carey. As mentioned elsewhere, Henry Tupper inherited the portrait from his uncle, Irving Brock, who died in 1838. After Tupper's death in 1875, his widow (Mary Ann Collings Tupper) became the next owner. With Mrs. Tupper's death in 1882, it went to her son, De Vic Tupper, the family's sole male heir. De Vic Tupper died intestate in 1892, and given that his wife (the former Miss Emily Sophia Bingham) had predeceased him in 1890, the portrait passed to their only son, Henry Bingham de Vic Tupper. The portrait then remained in his possession until he died in 1903, after which it became the shared property of his sisters: Miss Beatrice, Miss Constance, and Miss Edith Tupper. At some point, the portrait was lent to their father's cousins, Miss Henrietta and Miss Emilia Tupper, who were allowed to retain it. Miss Henrietta Tupper survived her sister until 1928. While her will makes no mention of the portrait, it was returned to her remaining cousins, Miss Beatrice and Miss Edith Tupper. Their sister, Miss Constance Tupper, who in the meantime had become Mrs. Edward Heathfield Tupper, died in 1914. Upon Miss Beatrice Tupper's death in 1942, Miss Edith Tupper assumed full ownership of the portrait. Miss Edith Tupper died in 1960, and in her will she bequeathed the portrait to Captain Michael H.T. Mellish, a first cousin, once removed. Captain Mellish retained the portrait until 2006, when his son retrieved it for safekeeping. Upon the death of Captain

Mellish in 2007, the portrait became the property of Nicholas T.L. Mellish, who sold it to the Guernsey Museum and Art Gallery early in 2009.

15 There is evidence, however, to suggest that Forster considered using the profile portrait (fig. 3) for his rendering of the uniform. As he wrote in May of 1897, "I have met the misses Tupper, grand [nieces] of General Brock and am going to make a study of the General's coat and face from a portrait they have and the coat itself." See: Toronto Reference Library, Marilyn and Charles Baillie Special Collections Centre, Baldwin Collection of Canadiana, John Wycliffe Lowes Forster Papers (S 19), file n.d.-1899, Forster to his mother, 7 May, 1897.

16 CWM, Ludwig Kosche Papers, Correspondence (58A3/10.26), Kosche to Mellish, 14 Dec., 1978.

17 Ibid., Mellish to Kosche, 23 Feb., 1979.

18 Brock University, James A. Gibson Library, Archives and Special Collections (BU), Guy St-Denis Papers (RG 77), Captain Michael H.T. Mellish Correspondence, Lee to Mellish, 7 June, 1965.

19 Ibid., Mellish to Keeper, Department of Prints and Drawings, British Museum, 20 Aug., 1965.

20 Captain Mellish visited the Niagara Historical Society Museum on 23 June, 1965. He toured Brock University two days later. See: *St. Catharines Standard* (St. Catharines, Ontario), 24 June, 1965, 9, c. 1; ibid., 26 June, 1965, 9, c. 1.

21 BU, Guy St-Denis Papers (RG 77), Captain Michael H.T. Mellish Correspondence, Mellish to Keeper, Department of Prints and Drawings, British Museum, 20 Aug., 1965.

22 Ibid. Presumably, Captain Mellish thought the profile portrait (fig. 3) was a drawing, thus his choice of an expert in the Department of Prints and Drawings at the British Museum.

23 Ibid., Williams to Mellish, 24 Aug., 1965.

24 Captain Mellish instructed Williams by means of a phone call on 27 August, 1965. For Captain Mellish's note about the conversation, see: ibid.

25 Ibid., 21 Oct., 1965

26 Ibid., Mellish to Williams, 13 Dec., 1965.

27 Ibid., Williams to Mellish, 11 Jan., 1966.

28 Williams did not cite the source of this biographical sketch. See: ibid. For the correct information regarding Sharples's travels, see n41. As for the date of the profile portrait (fig. 3), Captain Mellish probably found his information in Tupper's biography of Sir Isaac Brock. During a visit to the Niagara Historical Society Museum in June of 1965, the Captain encountered pictures of Brock that seemed to suggest that the artist might have been either J. Hudson or Alyn Williams. See: Ferdinand Brock Tupper, ed., *The Life and Correspondence of Major-General Sir Isaac Brock, K.B.*, 2nd ed. (London, England: Simpkin, Marshall and Company, 1847), 33, 37–8; BU, Guy St-Denis Papers (RG 77), Captain Michael H.T. Mellish Correspondence, Mellish to Keeper, Department of Prints and Drawings, British Museum, 20 Aug., 1965; *St. Catharines Standard*, 24 June, 1965, 9, c. 1.

29 BU, Guy St-Denis Papers (RG 77), Captain Michael H.T. Mellish Correspondence, Mellish to Williams, 21 Jan., 1966. As Kosche would later determine, neither Sharples nor any of his family of artists "ever ventured as far north as Canada"—meaning Lower

Canada, or the modern-day province of Quebec. See: Ludwig Kosche, "Contemporary Portraits of Isaac Brock: An Analysis," *Archivaria* 20 (Summer 1985): 64.

30 Ibid., Kosche to Mellish, 28 Feb., 1979.

31 Ibid., 27 May, 1979. A search for Andre's letter was unsuccessful. I am, however, grateful to Madeleine Trudeau for her determined effort in trying to locate this elusive document. As for Andre's job description, see: *Might's Metropolitan Toronto City Directory, 1978–79* (Toronto, Ontario: Might Directories, c1979), 34.

32 For a biography of Berczy, see: Ronald J. Stagg, "Berczy, William," *Dictionary of Canadian Biography* V: 70–2.

33 CWM, Ludwig Kosche Papers, Correspondence (58A3/10.26), Mellish to Kosche, 27 May, 1979.

34 For the biography, see: John Andre, *William Berczy: Co-Founder of Toronto* (Toronto, Ontario: Borough of York, 1967).

35 Ibid., opp. 120.

36 Kosche received this photograph of Brock's profile portrait (fig. 3) in August of 1979, which pleased him as it "came out very, very well indeed." See: CWM, Ludwig Kosche Papers, Correspondence (58A3/10.26), Kosche to Mellish, 23 Aug., 1979.

37 Ibid., 28 Jan., 1980; Kosche, "Contemporary Portraits of Isaac Brock," 65. When contacted in 2008, Dr. McNairn could not recall his reason for having agreed with Andre's attribution. "I would think that I relied on my eye rather than any external evidence for concluding that it was indeed a work of Berczy. At the time I was working at the National Gallery of Canada and had some opportunity to look at Berczy's work in some detail. Ludwig Kosche was a close friend of mine and he was meticulous in his research. I am sure that had I made my suggestion in a cavalier fashion he would have prompted me to show him all the visual evidence." See: email, McNairn to St-Denis, 20 Nov., 2008.

38 CWM, Ludwig Kosche Papers, Correspondence (58A3/10.26), Kosche to Mellish, 28 Jan., 1980. In 1984, Kosche once again raised the question of Andre's sources. It appears that the answer he received was no more satisfactory. See: ibid., Kosche to Andre, 19 Mar., 1984.

39 Ibid., Kosche to Mellish, 28 Jan., 1980.

40 Ibid. Although Kosche did not divulge the source of his information regarding Sharples, his article provides a clue. In discussing the attribution of the profile portrait (fig. 3), Kosche makes note of two art histories: Katharine McCook Knox's *The Sharples*, and Basil Long's *British Miniaturists*. A careful examination of these books revealed that Kosche used the one authored by Knox. See: Kosche, "Contemporary Portraits of Isaac Brock," 64; Katharine McCook Knox, *The Sharples: Their Portraits of George Washington and his Contemporaries* (New Haven, Connecticut: Yale University Press, 1930), 24–5; Basil Long, *British Miniaturists* (London, England: Geoffrey Bles, 1929), 395.

41 The possibility of a sitting by Brock was also negated by Sharples's removal from Bath in May of 1806; but it was Brock's whereabouts that effectively undermined the attribution to Sharples. It should be noted that soon after Sharples and his family embarked for America, their ship ran aground off the coast of England. Two of his sons set out on another vessel, but Sharples remained behind with his wife and daughter. They did not return to the United States until 1809. See: Knox, *The Sharples*, 24–32.

42 CWM, Ludwig Kosche Papers, Correspondence (58A3/10.26), Mellish to Kosche, 3 Mar., 1980.

43 Sharples was in England between 1801 and 1809. See: Knox, *The Sharples*, 16, 24–5, 27, 31.

44 Captain Mellish might have known that Brock went on his leave in the autumn of 1805 and that he was back in Canada by September of 1806, as this information was readily available in Tupper's biography of his uncle. See: Tupper, *Life and Correspondence of Major-General Sir Isaac Brock*, 2nd ed., 33, 38.

45 CWM, Ludwig Kosche Papers, Correspondence (58A3/10.25), Andre to Kosche, 9 Feb., 1980. Kosche appears to have shared these observations with Andre, but verbally and by means of a telephone call. Fortunately, they were also put in writing for Captain Mellish. As Kosche observed: "One aspect of Berczy's work which struck me in particular was the similarity of the uniforms in these portraits . . . and that raised the question whether Berczy might have pre-drawn, so to speak, basic components of his portraits, and filled in the details, such as the face, or perhaps the star (as in the Craig portrait) when he did the actual portrait." In other words, Kosche thought that certain parts of Berczy's portraits, including backgrounds and costumes, might have been painted in advance. It was then simply a matter of inserting the face and other details (epaulettes, badges, and other insignia). See: ibid. (58A3/10.26), Kosche to Mellish, 1 Mar., 1980. Kosche, however, failed to consider how Berczy could have worked in the middle of a pre-painted pastel background without smudging it.

46 Ibid. (58A3/10.25), Andre to Kosche, 9 Feb., 1980. Andre's source was not the original letter, but rather a transcript he found in the National Archives of Canada. See: LAC, Collection Baby (MG 24, L3), Papiers Berczy, Correspondance, vol. 27, Viger to Berczy Jr., 28 Sept., 1827, 16640. The portrait of Frontenac may have been intended for a book that the senior Berczy hoped to publish. Unfortunately, the manuscript appears to have gone missing after Berczy's death in New York City in 1813. See: Stagg, "Berczy, William," *Dictionary of Canadian Biography* V: 72; Peter N. Moogk, "William Berczy: Colonization Promoter, 1791–1813," in Mary Macaulay Allodi, et al., *Berczy* (Ottawa, Ontario: National Gallery of Canada, 1991), 106–7. For additional information on Jacques Viger and Sir James H. Craig, see: Jean-Claude Robert, "Viger, Jacques," *Dictionary of Canadian Biography* VIII: 909–13; Jean-Pierre Wallot, "Craig, Sir James Henry," *Dictionary of Canadian Biography* V: 205–14.

47 CWM, Ludwig Kosche Papers, Correspondence (58A3/10.25), Andre to Kosche, 9 Feb., 1980.

48 Ibid. Andre believed that this previous meeting must have taken place in Montreal, simply because there was no indication in any of Berczy's letters that he ever met Brock in Quebec City.

49 Applicants for land grants in Upper Canada made their requests in the form of a written petition, which was submitted to the lieutenant governor presiding over the Executive Council's Land Committee. The members of this committee advised the lieutenant governor in matters relating to the granting of Crown lands. Their decision, usually recommended by the lieutenant governor (or in this case the president), was entered into a minute book commonly called land books. The volumes for 1811 and 1812 were searched, but Berczy's petition was not found. A search among other relevant sources was also unsuccessful.

50 Berczy's letter, or "application," to Brock does not appear to have survived. Nor does the reply he received from Brock, which was written by his aide-de-camp, Captain John B. Glegg. However, a copy of Berczy's letter to Captain Glegg still exists. It both

acknowledges and reiterates Brock's decision to defer the matter of Berczy's land until Lieutenant Governor Gore's return. See: LAC, William von Moll Berczy Papers (MG 23, HII6), Berczy to Glegg, 1 Dec., 1811, 840.

51 Such a realization could only have come about during a search for the petition, which Andre obviously did not undertake. It appears that he simply concluded there was a petition, and furthermore that he based this assumption on a reference Berczy made to his "application." See: ibid.

52 CWM, Ludwig Kosche Papers, Correspondence (58A3/10.25), Andre to Kosche, 9 Feb., 1980. Although Andre could not remember how he was able to date Brock's profile portrait (fig. 3) to 1811, there is the possibility that he was influenced by Walter Nursey's *The Story of Isaac Brock*. For the frontispiece of his book, Nursey reproduced the copy of Brock's portrait painted by Alyn Williams (fig. 19), which was commissioned by Miss FitzGibbon in 1897. In a caption describing this portrait, Nursey made use of information provided by Miss FitzGibbon. In spite of having been led to believe that the copy of Brock's profile portrait (fig. 4) was the original, she seems to have set herself straight by the time of her dealings with Nursey. This she revealed by correctly noting that the original profile portrait (fig. 3) was in the possession of Miss Henrietta Tupper. Miss FitzGibbon also noticed a similarity between the paper on which Brock's portrait was painted and that of his last general orders, which were watermarked with a date of 1811—as if to suggest that his portrait could also date to that year. See: Walter R. Nursey, *The Story of Isaac Brock: Hero, Defender and Saviour of Upper Canada, 1812* (Toronto, Ontario: William Briggs, 1908), 175.

53 CWM, Ludwig Kosche Papers, Correspondence (58A3/10.26), Kosche to Mellish, 1 Mar. 1980.

54 Ibid. Gillian Lenfestey and Helen Conlon confirmed that the stock is solid black, and not green with a plaid design. Kosche came up with a green plaid stock based on his examination of a colour photograph of the profile portrait of Brock (fig. 3), which was provided by Captain Mellish. It would appear that Kosche was thrown off track by some poor colour processing. He might also have been inclined to accept what looked to be a green plaid stock because a red plaid cravat, or rather a scarf, was supposedly included with Brock's uniform when it was donated to Canada. Although a cravat (or long strip of fabric) and a stock (a neckband of stiff fabric) are separate and distinct items of clothing, Kosche appears to have believed that Brock could have worn a cravat over his stock to protect him against the cold, just as he had done with a "stout cotton handkerchief" at the Battle of Egmont-op-Zee (Egmond aan Zee) in 1799. Conceivably, the red plaid cravat might have served the same purpose at the Battle of Queenston Heights, especially as it had what were thought to be gunshot holes corresponding with those in Brock's coatee. As Kosche concluded, a green plain stock was just as plausible as a red cravat. This was not the case, however. When Brock sat for his portrait, he wore a black stock. See: ibid., 23 Aug., 1979; Kosche, "Relics of Brock," 68; W.Y. Carman, "Infantry Clothing Regulations, 1802," *Journal of the Society for Army Historical Research* 19 (1940): 209; email, Lenfestey to St-Denis, 8 May, 2009; ibid., Conlon to St-Denis, 9 Sept., 2009. It should be noted that Brock was portrayed in his plain or undress uniform. Had he worn his fancy or dress uniform to the sitting, and presuming he abided by the dress regulations, then his stock would have been white.

55 Kosche, "Contemporary Portraits of Isaac Brock," 65–6. See also: CWM, Ludwig Kosche Papers, Correspondence (58A3/10.26), Mellish to Kosche, 23 Feb., 1979; ibid., Kosche to Mellish, 1 Mar., 1980.

56 CWM, Ludwig Kosche Papers, Correspondence (58A3/10.26), Kosche to Mellish, 1 Mar., 1980.

57 Ibid.

58 Ibid., Mellish to Kosche, 20 Mar., 1980.

59 Ibid., Kosche to Mellish, 1 Mar., 1980.

60 Ibid., Apr., 1980. The day of the month was left blank. Kosche appears to have subsequently altered the date to 6 May, 1980. See: ibid., Mellish to Kosche, 27 June, 1980.

61 Ibid., Mellish to Kosche, 27 June, 1980. Captain Mellish was away from home, which was his explanation for the delay.

62 Ibid., Kosche to Mellish, 13 Jan., 1981; ibid., 26 Oct., 1981; ibid., 29 May, 1983.

63 Ibid., Mellish to Kosche, 27 June, 1980; ibid, Kosche to Mellish, 15 July, 1980.

64 Ibid., Kosche to Mellish, 13 Jan. 1981. Kosche already had a black and white photograph of the miniature (fig. 11), which he received in 1979 during his research into Brock's uniforms. However, he found it "simply not serviceable." See: ibid., Correspondence (58A3/10.17), Kosche to Procter, 19 Dec., 1979.

65 Kosche sent a copy of this article to Captain Mellish, who expressed his approval by saying "I do certainly like what you are doing." See: ibid., Correspondence (58A3/10.26), Kosche to Mellish, 6 Sept., 1981; ibid., Mellish to Kosche, 26 Sept., 1981. Kosche published his article in the *Organization of Military Museums of Canada Journal*, where he concluded that the pocket watch probably belonged to William Brock, who was a brother to Sir Isaac Brock. See: Kosche, "New Light on an Old Artefact: The Alleged Brock Watch," *OMMC Journal* 8 (1981): 14–24.

66 Kosche was eventually able to determine that Hitler used the car between 1940 and 1943. See: Ludwig Kosche, "The Story of a Car," *After the Battle* 35 (1982): 1–13.

67 CWM, Ludwig Kosche Papers, Correspondence (58A3/10.26), Kosche to Mellish, 6 Sept., 1981. This miniature (fig. 24) was subsequently given to Brock University in 1966, and now forms part of the Brockiana Collection, Archives and Special Collections, James A. Gibson Library. See: *St. Catharines Standard*, 14 Sept., 1966, 9.

68 Kosche mentioned Turner's assistance in a letter to Captain Mellish. See: CWM, Ludwig Kosche Papers, Correspondence (58A3/10.26), Kosche to Mellish, 14 Feb., 1982.

69 Ibid. Kosche had already ruled out the 8th (or King's) Regiment, which Brock had joined as a young ensign, mainly because the miniature (fig. 24) "shows an officer who is no longer young." Brock was only twenty-one years old when he left the 8th Regiment, which departure resulted from his having been appointed the captain of an independent company. Moreover, the facings of the sitter in the miniature were not the right colour for the 8th Regiment. Rather than buff or pale yellow, they should have been blue. See: Kosche, "Contemporary Portraits of Isaac Brock," 24; *London Gazette* (London, England), 29 Jan.–1 Feb., 1791, 63, c. 1.

70 As Kosche admitted to Captain Mellish, "I am beginning to think that I may wish to examine the matter of the various miniatures and portraits further; however, it will probably not be before next year, as I have more than enough to do for the next few

months." See: CWM, Ludwig Kosche Papers, Correspondence (58A3/10.26), Kosche to Mellish, 14 Feb., 1982.

71 Ibid., Mellish to Kosche, 11 June, 1982. This miniature (fig. 25) was one of several inherited by Captain Mellish.

72 Ibid., Kosche to Mellish, 27 June, 1982.

73 Captain Mellish also became somewhat confused, and began to mistake John Brock for his younger brother, John *Savery* Brock. See, for example: ibid., Mellish to Kosch, 7 Sept., 1982.

74 Ibid., Kosche to Mellish, 14 Aug., 1982.

75 The facings comprised the collar, lapels, and cuffs of a uniform. As is the case with most miniatures, the cuffs are not visible. For the colour of the facings of the 49th Regiment, see: Marquess of Cambridge, "De Bosset's Chart of Uniform, 1803," *Journal of the Society for Army Historical Research* XL (1962): 171.

76 *A List of the Officers of the Army* (1799), 278; Cambridge, "De Bosset's Chart of Uniform, 1803," 172.

77 CWM, Ludwig Kosche Papers, Correspondence (58A3/10.26), Kosche to Mellish, 14 Aug., 1982; Kosche, "Contemporary Portraits of Isaac Brock," 39–40.

78 CWM, Ludwig Kosche Papers, Correspondence (58A3/10.26), Kosche to Mellish, 27 June, 1982. See also: Cambridge, "De Bosset's Chart of Uniform, 1803," 170.

79 Ferdinand Brock Tupper, who owned the miniature of Ensign Isaac Brock (fig. 27) in 1861, thought his uncle might have been portrayed somewhat later, when about seventeen years old—which is incorrect. Brock was born in October of 1769, so he was either fifteen or sixteen years old when Jean painted his miniature in 1785 (see n80). Tupper, incidentally, is the earliest recorded owner of this miniature, but how it came into his possession is unknown. The miniature subsequently became the property of Tupper's daughter, Miss Henrietta Tupper. Possibly after Miss Tupper's death in 1928, it passed to her cousin, Miss Edith Tupper. The miniature later came into the possession of Captain Michael H.T. Mellish. In 2004, the captain was asked how he acquired the miniature in question, to which he simply replied that it was an inheritance from a Tupper cousin. It was probably a bequest from the estate of Miss Edith Tupper, who died in 1960. According to the terms of her will, "the portraits of Sir Isaac Brock, and all pictures connected with the Brock family," were to go to Captain Mellish. He retained the miniature until 2006, when his son acquired it—as well as Schipper's profile portrait of Isaac Brock as a brigadier general (fig. 3). Nicholas T.L. Mellish subsequently sold these portraits, as well as that of Lieutenant John Brock (fig. 25) to the Guernsey Museum and Art Gallery in 2009. See: LAC, Henry James Morgan Papers (MG 29, D61), Correspondence, vol. 47, Tupper to Morgan, 13 July, 1861; *Globe* (Toronto, Ontario), 9 July, 1928, 14, c. 4; A. Maude (Cawthra) Brock, *Brock Family Records* (Toronto, Ontario: privately published, 1927), 183; Ecclesiastical Court of Guernsey, Records of the Registrar of Wills and Intestacies, Book of Testaments, vol. 7 (new series), will of Edith Bingham Tupper, 12 Mar., 1949; *St. Catharines Standard*, 20 Feb., 2009, A1. Presumably, the provenance of Lieutenant John Brock's miniature is the same as that of the miniature depicting Ensign Isaac Brock.

80 Kosche, "Contemporary Portraits of Isaac Brock," 24. Helen Conlon of the Guernsey Museum and Art Gallery was able to confirm that the miniatures of Ensign Isaac Brock (fig. 27) and Lieutenant John Brock (fig. 25) were initialled and year-dated by Philip Jean. See: email, Conlon to St-Denis, 19 May, 2010. Unfortunately, some of this vital

information was lost when the miniatures were framed. While enough of the initials survive to identify Jean as the artist, the dates are more problematic. The miniature of Ensign Isaac Brock can be dated to 1785, as the last two digits of the year are still legible. However, the miniature of Lieutenant John Brock must be assigned an approximate date, as only the first two numbers remain. But given that Lieutenant Brock appears to have returned to Guernsey in 1784 and left the 8th Regiment in 1785, his miniature can be fairly safely dated to 1784 or 1785. Curiously, both Kosche and Captain Mellish appear to have been unaware of these dates and initials. See: Kosche, "Contemporary Portraits of Isaac Brock," 24, 40–1.

81 CWM, Ludwig Kosche Papers, Correspondence (58A3/10.26), Kosche to Mellish, 14 Aug., 1982. The relevant portion of this letter is the postscript.

82 Kosche obtained the photograph of the full-length portrait (fig. 28) from the New Brunswick Museum. See: ibid., 1 Mar., 1980.

83 Ibid., 14 Aug., 1982. Mrs. Sowels was the former Miss Agnes Bessie Carey. She married Captain Reginald Charles Sowels in 1928. According to Arthur, she was supposed to leave the full-length portrait (fig. 28) to him, but changed her mind in favour of the States of Guernsey. She must have changed her mind more than once, as the portrait did not go to the States. Or perhaps Arthur was mistaken.

84 Ibid. Captain Mellish was still looking for the full-length portrait (fig. 28) as late as January of 1983. See: ibid., Mellish to Kosche, 7 Jan., 1983.

85 Ibid., Kosche to Mellish, 28 Sept., 1982. This work was carried out in the conservation lab of Canada's National Gallery of Art.

86 This was very likely the portrait painted by Miss Alice Kerr-Nelson (fig. 6), which was commissioned by the Robinsons in 1881. As Kosche related to Captain Mellish, it was formerly owned by Senator P. Michael Pitfield. See: ibid. The painting was subsequently purchased by Brock University in 1979. See: BU, James A. Gibson Library, Archives and Special Collections, Acquisitions Form, [Kerr-Nelson] Portrait of "General Brock," cat. U2.

87 CWM, Ludwig Kosche Papers, Correspondence (58A3/10.26), Kosche to Mellish, 28 Sept., 1982. The earliest known reference to the full-length portrait (fig. 28) is the report of its sale by the auction house of Puttick and Simpson in November of 1927. The winning bidder was a Mr. F. Sabin, who was no doubt the art dealer Frank M. Sabin. By 1930, the portrait had become the property of Ward C. Pitfield, a Montreal financier with an interest in Canadian history. After Pitfield's death in 1939, the portrait passed to his wife and eventually to her son, the Honourable P. Michael Pitfield, who owned it until his death in 2017. See: *Times* (London, England), 12 Nov., 1927, 9, c. 3; LAC, J. Russell Harper Papers (MG 30, D352), [Norman Fee], "List of Paintings, Engravings, and Prints. W.C. Pitfield Collection," 6. For Ward C. Pitfield's obituary, see: *Globe and Mail* (Toronto, Ontario), 12 Jan., 1939, 3, c. 4.

88 CWM, Ludwig Kosche Papers, Correspondence (58A3/10.25), "Report on oil portrait in possession of Senator Michael P. [sic] Pitfield, Ottawa, Ont.," 10 Aug., 1983.

89 Ibid. See also: Kosche, "Contemporary Portraits of Isaac Brock," 54.

90 CWM, Ludwig Kosche Papers, Correspondence (58A3/10.25), Chartrand to Tardif-Côté, 28 Feb., 1984.

91 Ibid.

92 Kosche, "Contemporary Portraits of Isaac Brock," 57. It was the Reverend Percy Sumner who, in 1939, suggested the full-length portrait (fig. 28) was of "General Sir Isaac Brock . . . evidently in the uniform of a captain of the 49th Foot, c. 1792." See: Rev. Percy Sumner, "The Royal Berkshire Regiment," *Journal of the Society for Army Historical Research* XVIII (1939): 122–3.

93 Kosche, "Contemporary Portraits of Isaac Brock," 57.

94 Ferdinand Brock Tupper, ed., *The Life and Correspondence of Major-General Sir Isaac Brock, K.B.*, 1st ed. (London, England: Simpkin, Marshall and Company, 1845), 413; ibid., 2nd ed., 418; Kosche, "Contemporary Portraits of Isaac Brock," 58. In Tupper's *Family Records*, John Brock's death is listed as having occurred in 1802; however, it should have been 1801. According to the regimental history of the 81st Regiment, the duel took place on 5 July, 1801. See: *Historical Record of the Eighty-First Regiment* (Gibraltar: Twenty-Eighth Regimental Press, 1872), 13. Tupper corrected his mistake in both editions of *The Life and Correspondence of Major-General Sir Isaac Brock, K.B.* See: Ferdinand Brock Tupper, *Family Records* (St. Peter Port, Guernsey: Stephen Barbet, 1835), 1.

95 Kosche, "Contemporary Portraits of Isaac Brock," 57–8. For notices regarding John Brock's estate, as well as his death, see: *Cape Town Gazette* (Cape Town, South Africa), 18 July, 1801, 1, c. 1; *Bombay Courier* (Bombay, India), 6 Mar., 1802, 4, c. 2.

96 For the appointment to captain of the Jersey Invalids, see: *London Gazette*, 28 Apr.–2 May, 1801, 463, c. 1.

97 Admittedly, there might be some resemblance between the officer in the full-length portrait (fig. 28) and John Brock (figs 24, 25). The uniform also looks as though it could be that of the Jersey Invalids. Yet, it is difficult to conceive how John Brock could have been portrayed as a captain of the Jersey Invalids, given that he was killed in South Africa only three months after being gazetted to his new company. There is also the possibility that the full-length portrait shows someone other than Captain John Brock. Regardless, the facings are not those of the 49th Regiment, and so the officer displaying them cannot be Captain Isaac Brock, which is all that really matters.

98 CWM, Ludwig Kosche Papers, Correspondence (58A3/10.26), Mellish to Kosche, 7 Jan., 1983. More recent searches in Guernsey have failed to produce the copy of Brock's profile portrait (fig. 4); however, a photograph of this portrait was located in the Ludwig Kosche Papers at the Canadian War Museum. See: ibid., Photograph Album (58A3/10.4), Copy of the Profile Portrait of Brigadier General Isaac Brock by Gerrit Schipper, photographed by Brian J. Green, circa 1980.

99 Ibid., Correspondence (58A3/10.26), Mellish to Kosche, 26 Nov., 1982; ibid., Kosche to Mellish, 31 Jan., 1983.

100 At the time, Miss Procter was seventy-eight years old. See: ibid. (58A3/10.17), Procter to Kosche, 16 Feb., 1983. Kosche began to doubt that the miniature (fig. 11) could portray Brock as early as the spring of 1979. See: ibid., Kosche to Procter, 19 Dec., 1979.

101 Ibid., Procter to Kosche, 16 Feb., 1983. Miss Procter lost faith in Canada Post after an encyclopaedia entrusted to the crown corporation went missing.

102 Ibid., Correspondence (58A3/10.26), Kosche to Mellish, 1 May, 1983. In deciding to deliver the photograph of the miniature (fig. 11) in person, Miss Procter proposed the further loan of a commission signed by Brock and the notebook as well. See: ibid., Correspondence (58A3/10.17), Procter to Kosche, 16 Feb., 1983. Kosche, however, chose to borrow the notebook only.

103 Much of the contents pertain to Miss FitzGibbon's activities, which perhaps explains how the notebook came to be regarded as her property.

104 Kosche was aware of the notebook by December of 1979, and possibly as early as the spring of that same year. See: ibid. (58A3/10.17), Kosche to Procter, 19 Dec., 1979.

105 Ibid. (58A3/10.26), Kosche to Mellish, 1 May, 1983. Kosche appears to have finished the transcription well in advance of the Victoria Day long weekend—the agreed upon date for the notebook's return to Miss Procter. See: ibid. (58A3/10.17), Kosche to Procter, 10 May, 1983.

106 Kosche, "Contemporary Portraits of Isaac Brock," 47. Like General Robinson, Kosche was troubled by certain elements of the uniform worn by the officer, which he first noticed during an examination of a black and white photograph of the miniature (fig. 11) several years earlier. This photograph was supplied to him in the spring of 1979. See: CWM, Ludwig Kosche Papers, Correspondence (58A3/10.17), Kosche to Procter, 19 Dec., 1979.

107 Mrs. Dunn was believed to have inherited the miniature (fig. 11) from her sister, the wife of Captain James Brock, which made sense when it was thought to portray Sir Isaac Brock. But as Kosche was able to determine, the miniature is actually that of Lieutenant George Dunn—Mrs. Dunn's second husband. It would appear, therefore, that Mrs. Dunn inherited the miniature from her husband. The Short sisters, incidentally, had impressive full names. Lucy was *Susannah Lucy Quirk Short*, and Matilda was *Susan Matilda Quirk Short*. See: Archives of Ontario (AO), Women's Canadian Historical Society of Toronto Papers (F 1180), Miscellaneous (series 13), file 3, Brock Portrait Notebook, 51, 53.

108 Mrs. Taylor's paternal grandfather was John Short, who was Mrs. Dunn's brother. This relationship was determined from a provision in Mrs. Dunn's will. See: ibid., 63.

109 Theoretically, the miniature (fig. 11) could also have portrayed Captain James Brock, although Sir Isaac Brock appears to have been a more popular choice.

110 Kosche, "Contemporary Portraits of Isaac Brock," 47–50. Regarding the Waterloo Medal, see: Donald Hall and Christopher Wingate, *British Orders, Decorations and Medals* (St. Ives, England: Balfour Publications, 1973), 56. It should be noted that Kosche made use of a report by Lieutenant Colonel J. Percy Groves, which was submitted to Miss FitzGibbon after he examined the uniform worn by the sitter in Miss Mickle's miniature (fig. 11). Miss Mickle transcribed this report into her notebook, where Kosche eventually found it. See: AO, Women's Canadian Historical Society of Toronto Papers (F 1180), Miscellaneous (series 13), file 3, Brock Portrait Notebook, 172–6.

111 Kosche, "Contemporary Portraits of Isaac Brock," 50, 52. The miniature's apparent date of 1816 coincided with the first year in which the Waterloo Medals were distributed.

112 One of the books was a volume from the official history of the 49th Regiment. See: F. Loraine Petre, *The Royal Berkshire Regiment*, 2 vols (Reading, England: The Barracks, 1925), 1: 86. Lieutenant Dunn's likeness also served as the model for a commemorative bust of Brock, which was sculpted by Miss F. May Simpson in 1912. And when Brock's heroism was used to market the Southam Newspapers chain in 1930, Lieutenant Dunn's miniature (fig. 11) was incorporated into the advertising. See: *Evening Telegram* (Toronto, Ontario), 12 Oct., 1912, 21, cc. 3–4; *Globe*, 9 June, 1930, 15, c. 4. It should be noted that Canada Post redeemed itself somewhat in 2012 with another stamp honouring Brock. Working from the profile portrait painted by Gerrit Schipper (fig. 3), Suzanne Duranceau of Montreal made a good effort in depicting him (even if he looks rather too boyish). Artistic license also accounts for Brock's unrealistically thick hair, and the various shades

of black used for his facings—which should really be dark blue. But at least Duranceau's rendition looks something like Brock, whereas the likeness by Nova Scotia artist Bonnie Ross, which she created for the Royal Canadian Mint's twenty-five cent and four dollar coins, does not.

CHAPTER 5

1 Archives of Ontario (AO), Women's Canadian Historical Society of Toronto Papers (F 1180), Miscellaneous (series 13), file 3, Brock Portrait Notebook, Hayward to Mickle, 17 Aug., 1896, 35, 37, 39.

2 Ibid.

3 Canadian War Museum, Military History Research Centre, George Metcalf Archival Collection (CWM), Ludwig Kosche Papers, Correspondence (58A3/10.17), Kosche to Procter, 10 May, 1983. As Kosche later observed, the facial features suggested a man in his late twenties, and Lieutenant Dunn was twenty-six or twenty-seven years old in 1816. It did not look like the face of a man who was thirty-seven years old, as Brock was in 1806. See: Ludwig Kosche, "Contemporary Portraits of Isaac Brock: An Analysis," *Archivaria* 20 (Summer 1985): 52. This article gives no source for Lieutenant Dunn's age in 1816; however, his obituary confirms that he was twenty-seven years old in 1816. See: *Times* (London, England), 27 Dec., 1850, 7, c. 4.

4 For the authorization, production, and distribution of the Waterloo Medal, see: William S.W. Vaux, "On English and Foreign Waterloo Medals," *Numismatic Chronicle and Journal of the Royal Numismatic Society*, n.s. IX (1869): 109–12.

5 As Kosche explained to Miss Lorna R. Procter in May of 1983, the "key to the authenticity of the miniature rests, in my view, upon the solution of the date." See: CWM, Ludwig Kosche Papers, Correspondence (58A3/10.17), Kosche to Procter, 10 May, 1983.

6 Kosche sought advice from the staff of the Parker Gallery, the National Portrait Gallery, and the Victoria and Albert Museum. See: ibid. (58A3/10.25), Simon to Kosche, 25 May, 1983; ibid., Gold to Kosche, 7 June, 1983; ibid., Murdoch to Kosche, 15 June, 1983. Several years earlier, a representative at Sotheby's in London found the X to be "a curious method of dating." See: ibid., Bainbridge to Kosche, 21 Jan., 1980.

7 Kosche, "Contemporary Portraits of Isaac Brock," 43. Kosche made this discovery in Miss Mickle's notebook. Forster died in 1938. For his obituary, see: *Globe and Mail* (Toronto, Ontario), 26 Apr., 1938, 5, c. 2.

8 Captain Brock's wife was the former Miss Lucy Short, thus the connection. Kosche learned of John Short through H. Douglass Short of Kingston, who made a hobby of studying the genealogy of the Short family. See: CWM, Ludwig Kosche Papers, Correspondence (58A3/10.21), Kosche to Short, 5 Jan., 1983.

9 Kosche, "Contemporary Portraits of Isaac Brock," 50. The portrait (fig. 15) was sent to Kosche in Ottawa, where it was photographed and then returned to John Short by mid-November of 1983. See: CWM, Ludwig Kosche Papers, Correspondence (58A3/10.21), Kosche to Short, 19 Nov., 1983.

10 Kosche, "Contemporary Portraits of Isaac Brock," 51–2.

11 For the transcript, see: AO, Women's Canadian Historical Society of Toronto Papers (F 1180), Miscellaneous (series 13), file 3, Brock Portrait Notebook, Short to Mickle, 26 May,

1897, 139, 141. For the original, see: ibid., Correspondence (series 1), file 2 (Jan.–May 1897), Short to Mickle, 26 May, 1897.

12 Kosche returned to Ottawa on 1 October, 1983. See: CWM, Ludwig Kosche Papers, Correspondence (58A3/10.26), Kosche to Mellish, 2 Oct., 1983.

13 Ibid. (58A3/10.17), Procter to Kosche, 21 Oct., 1983.

14 Kosche began work on his article over the Christmas holidays. See: ibid. (58A3/10.26) Kosche to Mellish, 26 Dec., 1983.

15 Ibid. (58A3/10.25), Helen Durie, "Chronology of the Miniature of Gen. Sir Isaac Brock by J. Hudson, 1806," 1962. See also: Library and Archives Canada, Portrait Files (internal accession records), Brock[, Sir Isaac], no. 207-33. It is not known if Kosche found this document at the archives, or whether he obtained a copy from Miss Procter. Miss Durie's "Chronology" must be treated with care, as it contains a number of errors. One such error is the incorrect statement that it was Miss FitzGibbon who purchased the miniature (fig. 11) from Mrs. Taylor. As detailed elsewhere, Mrs. Taylor sold the miniature to Miss Mickle, who retained it until her death in 1930. According to the terms of Miss Mickle's will, the miniature was bequeathed to the Women's Canadian Historical Society of Toronto. But until such time as the Society's collections could be housed in a fireproof building, the miniature was to be preserved in either the Art Gallery of Toronto (the forerunner of the Art Gallery of Ontario), or the National Gallery of Canada in Ottawa. In accepting the miniature, the ladies of the Society chose to lend it to the Art Gallery of Toronto/Ontario. The miniature remained there until 1962, when it was retrieved and subsequently stored in a safety deposit box at a Toronto, Ontario branch of National Trust. See: AO, Women's Canadian Historical Society of Toronto Papers (F 1180), Correspondence (series 1), file 3 (1921–39), Mickle to Roberts, 15 Oct., 1930; ibid., Roberts to Mickle, 20 Oct., 1930; ibid., Roberts to Mickle, 25 Oct., 1930; *Globe and Mail*, 29 Sept., 1962, 15, c. 4. In 1996, the miniature was donated to the Royal Ontario Museum. See: Royal Ontario Museum, Canadian Collection, Department of World Cultures, Miniature of Lieutenant George Dunn (misidentified as "General Sir Isaac Brock"), by J. Hudson, 1816, acc. 996.58.3.1.

16 Kosche, "Contemporary Portraits of Isaac Brock," 46. Because photocopies were not permitted by the Archives nationales du Québec, Kosche asked a friend to go and examine the file in person. This friend was Henri Serdongs.

17 CWM, Ludwig Kosche Papers, Correspondence (58A3/10.26), Kosche to Mellish, 27 Nov., 1983. See also: Kosche, "Contemporary Portraits of Isaac Brock," 46.

18 CWM, Ludwig Kosche Papers, Correspondence (58A3/10.26), Kosche to Mellish, 27 Nov., 1983.

19 Miss FitzGibbon knew that things such as portraits were considered part of the chattel property and, together with the more mundane contents of a household, were frequently transferred to the rightful heir(s) without the need for legal force. The fact that there was more than one beneficiary of Mrs. Brock's estate was a complication, and so it must have been reassuring to Miss FitzGibbon when she saw that Mrs. Dunn did very well by her sister's will. For a transcript of Mrs. James Brock's will, see: ibid. (58A3/10.25), will of Susannah Lucy Quirk Brock, 24 June, 1857.

20 Ibid. (58A3/10.21), Short to Kosche, 27 Nov., 1983. Douglass Short remembered the portrait (fig. 15) from his youth. His memory was twigged by a photograph, which was provided by Kosche.

21 Ibid. (58A3/10.25), Holme to Kosche, 14 Oct., 1983.

22 Kosche, "Contemporary Portraits of Isaac Brock," 52.

23 CWM, Ludwig Kosche Papers, Correspondence (58A3/10.26), Kosche to Mellish, 4 Feb., 1984. This soft approach ran the risk of further complications, which is exactly what happened when the fifth volume of the *Dictionary of Canadian Biography* was released in 1983. It was in this volume that C.P. (Colonel Charles Perry) Stacey, a highly regarded Canadian military historian, contributed a biographical sketch of Sir Isaac Brock. Colonel Stacey also gave his opinion of the miniature discovered by Miss Mickle (fig. 11), which to him seemed "likely to be a portrait of Sir George Gordon Drummond." See: Charles P. Stacey, "Brock, Sir Isaac," in *Dictionary of Canadian Biography* V: 114. In acknowledging the identification assigned by Colonel Stacey, Kosche questioned why the Short family would have had a miniature of Sir Gordon Drummond. Yet, he made no attempt to argue in favour of Lieutenant George Dunn, even though he knew that Colonel Stacey was wrong. See: Kosche, "Contemporary Portraits of Isaac Brock," 52.

24 CWM, Ludwig Kosche Papers, Correspondence (58A3/10.26), Mellish to Kosche, 21 Feb., 1984.

25 Ibid., Kosche to Mellish, 19 Mar., 1984; ibid., Mellish to Kosche, 30 Mar., 1984. A copy of the article in manuscript form is preserved among Kosche's papers. See: ibid., Miscellaneous Manuscripts (58A3/10.3), Ludwig Kosche, "Isaac Brock in Contemporary Portraiture: An Analysis."

26 AO, Women's Canadian Historical Society of Toronto Papers (F 1180), Correspondence (series 1), file 2 (Jan.–May 1897), FitzGibbon to Mickle, 17 May, 1897.

27 AO, Ferdinand Brock Tupper Papers (F 1081), Glegg to Brock, 30 Dec., 1813.

28 AO, Women's Canadian Historical Society of Toronto Papers (F 1180), Correspondence (series 1), file 2 (Jan.–May 1897), FitzGibbon to Mickle, 17 May, 1897.

29 Ibid., Miscellaneous (series 13), file 3, Brock Portrait Notebook, 98, 100.

30 This observation appears to have been provided by the miniature painter Gerald S. Hayward, and as early as August of 1896. See: ibid., Correspondence (series 1), file 9 (n.d.), Hayward to Mickle, 17 Aug., 1896.

31 Ibid., Miscellaneous (series 13), file 3, Brock Portrait Notebook, 100.

32 Miss Mickle reacted to Glegg's statement as paraphrased by Miss FitzGibbon. See: ibid., 100–1.

33 Ibid., 100. To Miss Mickle's way of thinking, the proof of Major Glegg's ignorance was the watercolour portrait of Brock owned by Henry A. Garrett of Niagara(-on-the-Lake), Ontario (fig. 31), and the silhouette of Brock in the possession of Aemilius Jarvis (fig. 18). Since both of these likenesses were found in Canada, and presumably "taken" there, Major Glegg's knowledge of Brock's portraits was obviously deficient. But despite Miss Mickle's confidence in the portrait owned by Garrett, it was actually nothing more than a photograph of another photograph featuring the profile portrait by Gerrit Schipper (fig. 3), and one that was overpainted with watercolours in a rather clumsy fashion. This copy was eventually given to the Niagara Historical Society and the donor was Garrett himself, who apparently retained the original watercoloured photograph (having obtained it from Major Duncan McFarland sometime earlier). See: Niagara Historical Society Museum, Photograph of a Portrait of "General Sir Isaac Brock," by William Quinn, circa 1891, acc. 984.1.127. As for the Jarvis silhouette, it cannot be authenticated. While the fate of the original silhouette is unknown, a copy was used as an illustration in a documentary history

of the War of 1812 and the image thus preserved. See: William Wood, ed., *Select British Documents of the Canadian War of 1812*, 3 vols (Toronto, Ontario: Champlain Society, 1920–28), I: 32.

34 Miss Mickle doubted Major Glegg's assertion that he was "intimately acquainted with Brock & all his life in Canada," mainly because he "was away from Canada part of the time." See: AO, Women's Canadian Historical Society of Toronto Papers (F 1180), Miscellaneous (series 13), file 3, Brock Portrait Notebook, 100–2. Miss Mickle learned of Major Glegg's absence by conducting a search of *The Quebec Almanac* between 1805 and 1812. This publication lists British army officers posted to the Canadas. Major Glegg, however, never claimed to be "intimately acquainted with Brock & all his life in Canada." As he stated in a letter to William Brock, "I was intimately acquainted my dear Sir with your Brothers sentiments on the most private subjects." See: AO, Ferdinand Brock Tupper Papers (F 1081), Glegg to Brock, 30 Dec., 1813.

35 Major Glegg probably referred to Upper Canada, and specifically the region between Fort York (Toronto) and Fort George (Niagara-on-the-Lake). These were the two posts where Brock spent most of his time in what is now southern Ontario.

36 For Captain Glegg's appointment as co-administrator of Brock's estate, see: AO, Upper Canada Court of Probate (RG 22), Grants of Probate and Administration, Register A, 1796–1816 (series 154), Letters of Administration, estate of Major General Isaac Brock, 10 Nov., 1812.

37 Kosche obtained a copy of the letter for his research into Brock's coatee. See: Ludwig Kosche, "Relics of Brock: An Investigation," *Archivaria* 9 (Winter 1979–80): 79–80. For the original letter, see: AO, Ferdinand Brock Tupper Papers (F 1081), Glegg to Brock, 30 Dec., 1813.

38 Kosche looked for additional correspondence in the Ferdinand Brock Tupper Papers at the Archives of Ontario and also among the descendants of Major Glegg in England, but without success. See: Kosche, "Contemporary Portraits of Isaac Brock," 61.

39 AO, Ferdinand Brock Tupper Papers (F 1081), Glegg to Brock, 30 Dec., 1813; Kosche, "Contemporary Portraits of Isaac Brock," 61. It is not clear if Kosche thought "this Country" was a reference to Upper Canada, or the Canadas as a whole.

40 Kosche, "Contemporary Portraits of Isaac Brock," 61.

41 It should be noted that Miss Mickle did not have access to a complete set of *The Quebec Almanac*, and the entries she found for Major Glegg do not strictly agree with a record of his service. Therefore, the accuracy of her findings is questionable. See: AO, Women's Canadian Historical Society of Toronto Papers (F 1180), Miscellaneous (series 13), file 3, Brock Portrait Notebook, 102; *The Royal Military Calendar*, 3rd ed., 5 vols (London, England: T. Egerton, 1820), V: 205–7.

42 Kosche, "Contemporary Portraits of Isaac Brock," 61. Kosche does not appear to have considered the possibility that Major Glegg might have possessed a sketch of Brock, or perhaps even a silhouette.

43 Savery Brock went to Upper Canada in order to attend to his family's land holdings, which were granted in recognition of Sir Isaac Brock's military service. See: Ferdinand Brock Tupper, ed., *The Life and Correspondence of Major-General Sir Isaac Brock, K.B.*, 2nd ed. (London, England: Simpkin, Marshall and Company, 1847), 398.

44 This letter was eventually donated to the Archives of Ontario. See: AO, Ferdinand Brock Tupper Papers (F 1081), Brock to Tupper, 9 Jan., 1818. Mrs. Charles de Jersey was Savery Brock's sister-in-law. She was the former Miss Mary de Jersey, who married her cousin, Charles de Jersey. I am grateful to Gillian Lenfestey for clarifying the relationship between Savery Brock and Mrs. de Jersey.

45 AO, Women's Canadian Historical Society of Toronto Papers (F 1180), Correspondence (series 1), file 3 (June–Dec. 1897), FitzGibbon to Mickle, 7 June, 1897. Miss FitzGibbon first introduced the subject of this miniature in a letter she wrote to Miss Mickle dated 28 May, 1897. See: ibid., file 2 (Jan.–May 1897), FitzGibbon to Mickle, 28 May, 1897.

46 Ibid., file 3 (June–Dec. 1897), FitzGibbon to Mickle, 7 June, 1897. With regard to the resemblance between the two Brock brothers, Miss FitzGibbon was probably influenced by Ferdinand Brock Tupper. See: Tupper, *Life and Correspondence of Major-General Sir Isaac Brock*, 2nd ed., 467. Initially, Miss FitzGibbon thought the bronze profile (fig. 8) was copied or adapted from the Jarvis silhouette (fig. 18), but she soon opted for Daniel de Lisle Brock having been the model. It then occurred to her that the bronze profile could have been based on Brock's statue in his memorial at St. Paul's Cathedral (fig. 20). Upon closer inspection, however, she discovered that the bronze profile looked nothing like the statue, so she reverted back to her original idea regarding Daniel de Lisle Brock. See: AO, Women's Canadian Historical Society of Toronto Papers (F 1180), Correspondence (series 1), file 3 (June–Dec. 1897), FitzGibbon to Mickle, 2 June, 1897; ibid., 29 June, 1897; ibid., 19 July, 1897.

47 While Miss FitzGibbon was mainly concerned with a more mature likeness of Brock, she appears to have been unaware of the miniature by Philip Jean, which shows a young Ensign Isaac Brock (fig. 27). This ignorance is borne out in her mistaken belief that "until 1818 at the earliest, they [Brock's family] had *no* portrait of Sir Isaac at all!" See: AO, Women's Canadian Historical Society of Toronto Papers (F 1180), Correspondence (series 1), file 3 (June–Dec. 1897), FitzGibbon to Mickle, 7 June, 1897.

48 Ibid., file 3 (June–Dec. 1897), FitzGibbon to Mickle, 7 June, 1897. At the time, Miss FitzGibbon believed that the profile portrait (fig. 3), then owned by Henry Bingham de Vic Tupper, was the original. She subsequently changed her mind when the prominent miniature artist Alyn Williams convinced her that the portrait in John Savery Carey's possession (fig. 4) was done from life, and therefore the original. Williams was mistaken, however, and consequently so too was Miss FitzGibbon. See: ibid., file 2 (Jan.–May 1897), FitzGibbon to Mickle, 28 May, 1897; ibid., file 3 (June–Dec. 1897), FitzGibbon to Mickle, 18 July, 1897. See also: ibid., file 3 (June–Dec. 1897), FitzGibbon to Mickle, 19 July, 1897.

49 Ibid., Miscellaneous (series 13), file 3, Brock Portrait Notebook, 114. Specifically, Miss Mickle referred to the attacks on York (now Toronto) and Fort George (at modern Niagara-on-the-Lake) in April and May of 1813.

50 Ibid., 145.

51 Kosche, "Contemporary Portraits of Isaac Brock," 61–2.

52 Miss FitzGibbon, however, believed that the artist might have been one of Brock's friends. See: AO, Women's Canadian Historical Society of Toronto Papers (F 1180), Correspondence (series 1), file 2, FitzGibbon to Mickle, 28 May, 1897. Perhaps Miss FitzGibbon was influenced by Lady Edgar's article on Brock's portrait, which suggests that Ensign James Kittermaster of the 49th Regiment was responsible for Brock's profile portrait (fig. 3). Lady Edgar thought it was possible, because Ensign Kittermaster was known to

have done portrait sketches while he was posted to Upper Canada in the years leading up to 1812. Unfortunately for Lady Edgar, she was wrong. See: Lady Edgar [Matilda Ridout], "General Brock's Portrait," *Canadian Magazine* XXXI, no. 3 (July 1908): 265.

53 Kosche, "Contemporary Portraits of Isaac Brock," 61.

54 CWM, Ludwig Kosche Papers, Correspondence (58A3/10.26), Mellish to Kosche, 30 Mar., 1984.

55 Ibid., Miscellaneous Manuscripts (58A3/10.3), Kosche, "Isaac Brock in Contemporary Portraiture," 32. Brock's remark about the size of his head is clearly self-deprecating. But even if he had an enormous head, there is no reason to believe it would have been out of proportion with the rest of his body. As for Brock's extraordinary physique, Kosche came up with a waist size of nearly 47 inches (or 119.38 centimetres). This measurement was not taken from the general's trousers (apparently now lost), but rather from his brigadier general's coatee. For this reason, the calculation is highly suspect and it is doubtful that Brock's girth was nearly so extensive as Kosche reckoned. See: Tupper, *Life and Correspondence of Major-General Sir Isaac Brock*, 2nd ed., Isaac Brock to his brother, Irving, 9 July, 1810, 77; Kosche, "Contemporary Portraits of Isaac Brock," 61; ibid., "Relics of Brock," 36. With regard to his belief that Brock was heavyset before he died, Kosche relied on Ferdinand Brock Tupper's impression that his uncle had become "perhaps too portly" in his latter years. How Tupper came up with this idea is unknown, but it might have been reinforced by the bronze profile (fig. 8). This silhouette shows a stout and older man who was thought by the Brock and Tupper families to represent their famous relative. It has since been concluded, however, that this silhouette does not represent Brock. See: Kosche, "Contemporary Portraits of Isaac Brock," 58–61; Tupper, *Life and Correspondence of Major-General Sir Isaac Brock*, 2nd ed., 345.

56 CWM, Ludwig Kosche Papers, Miscellaneous Manuscripts (58A3/10.3), Kosche, "Isaac Brock in Contemporary Portraiture," 36.

57 Ibid., 38, 40.

58 Ibid., 38.

59 Ibid., 31–2.

60 Ibid., Correspondence (58A3/10.26), Mellish to Kosche, 30 Mar., 1984.

61 Ibid. Kosche to Mellish, 19 Mar., 1984.

62 Ibid. (58A3/10.17), Kosche to Procter, 1 Apr., 1984; ibid., 11 Apr., 1984. As the Canadian military historian Donald E. Graves recalled, Kosche was somewhat eccentric, and "not everybody's cup of tea." Still, Graves liked the man and respected his work. See: email, Graves to St-Denis, 11 Jan., 2006.

63 It appears that Miss Procter may have encouraged Kosche to approach the Metropolitan Toronto Historical Board about the possibility of publishing his article. Kosche was thinking in terms of *Archivaria* as early as mid-March of 1984, and possibly even earlier. See: CWM, Ludwig Kosche Papers, Correspondence (58A3/10.26), Kosche to Mellish, 19 Mar., 1984.

64 Ibid., (58A3/10.17), Kosche to Procter, 1 Apr., 1984.

65 The manuscript was submitted by July of 1984. See: ibid. (58A3/10.26), Kosche to Mellish, 2 July, 1984. For the editorial concerns, see: ibid. (58A3/10.25), Nesmith to Kosche, 25 Jan., 1985.

66 Kosche had confirmation that his article would be published in *Archivaria* by the end of September 1984. See: ibid., (58A3/10.26), Kosche to Mellish, 29 Sept., 1984.

67 Ibid. (58A3/10.25), Nesmith to Kosche, 25 Jan., 1985.

68 Ibid., (58A3/10.26), Kosche to Mellish, 28 Feb., 1985.

69 Ibid., Kosche to Mellish, 17 Aug., 1985.

70 Ibid.

71 Captain Mellish thought the article was splendid, and he very much appreciated the acknowledgment Kosche gave him. See: ibid., Mellish to Kosche, 21 Sept., 1985.

72 A notable exception was H. Douglass Short, who expressed his disappointment in finding no reference to a source he thought worthy of inclusion. Kosche replied that the source in question was too erroneous to be used. See: ibid. (58A3/10.21), Short to Kosche, 21 Oct., 1985; ibid., Kosche to Short, 28 Oct., 1985.

73 Ibid. (58A3/10.26), Kosche to Mellish, 17 Aug., 1985.

74 Ibid., 5 Feb., 1986; ibid., 9 July, 1986.

75 Kosche died in Ottawa on 17 May, 2000. For his obituary, see: *Ottawa Citizen* (Ottawa, Ontario), 23 May, 2000, F5, c. 8.

CHAPTER 6

1 For example, Robert Malcomson asserted that "none of the existing portraits of Brock can be said to accurately depict the general." However, Malcomson also admitted that "the best extant images are a miniature that may show a bewigged Brock as a teenaged ensign in the Eighth Regiment of Foot and a pastel side view of the general that may be what Glegg and Brock's family believed was not a good likeness." See: Robert Malcomson, "Picturing Isaac Brock," *The Beaver* 84, no. 5 (Oct.–Nov. 2004): 24. In fact, these are the only authentic portraits of Brock known to exist (figs 3, 27).

2 Canadian War Museum, Military History Research Centre, George Metcalf Archival Collection (CWM), Ludwig Kosche Papers, Correspondence (58A3/10.26), Nesmith to Kosche, 25 Jan., 1985.

3 Kosche was aware of this situation before the end of October 1983, when Miss Lorna R. Procter informed him about it. See: ibid. (58A3/10.17), Procter to Kosche, 21 Oct., 1983.

4 Ibid., Procter to Kosche, 17 Sept., 1985; ibid., 7 Jan., 1986. Regarding the society's decline, see: ibid., 3 Mar., 1985.

5 Ludwig Kosche, "Contemporary Portraits of Isaac Brock: An Analysis," *Archivaria* 20 (Summer 1985): 66.

6 These factors also confirmed the family tradition that identified the sitter as Ensign Isaac Brock of the 8th (or King's) Regiment. Brock became an ensign in March of 1785, when he was fifteen years of age. See: National Archives of the United Kingdom (NAUK), War Office, Returns of Officers' Services (WO 25/744), Brigadier General Isaac Brock, 26 May, 1810. Presumably, this miniature (fig. 27) was painted soon after Brock entered the army. For the facings of the 8th (or King's) Regiment, see: Marquess of Cambridge, "De Bosset's Chart of Uniform, 1803," *Journal of the Society for Army Historical Research* XL (1962): 170.

7 Kosche, "Contemporary Portraits of Isaac Brock," 63.

8 Mary Macaulay Allodi, et al., *Berczy* (Ottawa, Ontario: National Gallery of Canada, 1991). The exhibition ran from 8 November, 1991 until 5 January, 1992.

9 Email, St-Denis to Lenfestey, 13 Dec., 2002.

10 Mary Macaulay Allodi, "Pastel Profiles," in Allodi, et al., *Berczy* (Ottawa, Ontario: National Gallery of Canada, 1991), 304. See also: ibid., 305–7.

11 Ibid., 305.

12 Ibid., 304. Allodi also determined that the mistake dated as far back as the mid-1930s.

13 Ibid., 305.

14 Ibid. John D. Turnbull was an artist, actor, and sometime theatre manager/owner. Jean Riger mistakenly identified him as John Trumbull. See: Jeanne Riger, "New Light on Gerrit Schipper the Painter," *Clarion* 15, no. 1 (Winter 1990): 69.

15 For more information on this incident, see: *Quebec Gazette* (Quebec, Lower Canada), 29 Mar., 1810, 6, c. 2; ibid., 26 Apr., 1810, 2, c. 2; ibid., 31 May, 1810, 3, c. 2; ibid., 4 July, 1811, 3, c.1; *Montreal Gazette* (Montreal, Lower Canada), 26 Mar., 1810, 3, c. 1; ibid., 30 Apr., 1810, 3, c. 1; ibid., 8 Oct., 1810, 3, c. 2; *Canadian Courant* (Montreal, Lower Canada), 23 Apr., 1810, 1, c. 3; ibid., 5 Nov., 1810, 1, c. 4; ibid., 24 Dec., 1810, 2, c. 1.

16 Allodi, "Pastel Profiles," 305. Allodi also made comparisons with other known examples of Schipper's work in the United States. See: ibid., 306.

17 Andre gave no reason for his change of heart. See: *Niagara Arts Journal* (St. Catharines, Ontario), 18 Aug.–26 Sept., 1986, 7–8. He also knew of Schipper at least twenty years earlier, but simply dismissed the Dutch itinerant as one of Berczy's competitors. See: John Andre, *William Berczy: Co-Founder of Toronto* (Toronto, Ontario: Borough of York, 1967), 65–6, 99. Andre died in 2001. See: *Toronto Star* (Toronto, Ontario), 19 Oct., 2001, B6, c. 1.

18 Email, McNairn to St-Denis, 12 Feb., 2009.

19 Ibid., Allodi to St-Denis, 6 Jan., 2003. Allodi, however, questioned whether Brock was actually the sitter, given that the profile portrait (fig. 3) did "not show Brock's reportedly massive head and large, stout, physique." Curiously, her source was Kosche's article "Contemporary Portraits of Isaac Brock," in which he accepts the same portrait as being an authentic likeness of Brock. See: ibid., Allodi to St-Denis, 7 Jan., 2003; Kosche, "Contemporary Portraits of Isaac Brock," 60–1.

20 Riger, "New Light on Gerrit Schipper the Painter," 65–70.

21 Letter, St-Denis to Riger, in care of the Museum of American Folk Art, 31 Oct., 2003.

22 Ibid., Riger to St-Denis, 12 Nov., 2003; ibid., 2 June, 2004.

23 Captain Mellish died on 7 October, 2007, at the age of ninety-two. See: *Guernsey Press* (St. Peter Port, Guernsey), 11 Oct., 2007, 17, c. 1.

24 Letter, Mellish to St-Denis, 8 Feb., 2003.

25 A sister, Miss Beatrice Tupper, was a co-owner of Brock's profile portrait (fig. 3) until her death in 1942. Captain Mellish, however, only mentioned Miss Edith Tupper. She was his first cousin, once removed, and it was according to the terms of her will (proved in December of 1960) that Captain Mellish inherited the portrait. For the will, see: Ecclesiastical Court of Guernsey, Records of the Registrar of Wills and Intestacies, Book of Testaments, vol. 7 (new series), will of Edith Bingham Tupper, 12 Mar., 1949.

26 Conversation with Mellish, 4 May, 2004.

27 Letter, St-Denis to Riger, 30 Mar., 2004; ibid., Riger to St-Denis, 2 June, 2004.

28 Ibid., Riger to St-Denis, 25 June, 2004. Although Riger refers to both of Brock's eyes, the portrait (fig. 3) was painted in profile and so she really only saw one of them.

29 Kosche, "Contemporary Portraits of Isaac Brock," 63.

30 Frick Art Reference Library (FARL), Nicholas L. Schipper, "The Life of Nicholas L. Shipper: Embracing a Period of Sixteen Years, until his Arrival in America in the Year 1826," 1. While the exact date of Gerrit Schipper's death is not known, his burial took place at St. Clement Danes Church, Westminster, England on 27 November, 1825. According to the parish register, Schipper was fifty-five years old and his place of residence was 229 the Strand. His Christian name was also anglicized to George. See: City of Westminster Archives, St. Clement Danes Church, Burial Register, vol. 17 (1819–28), 27 Nov., 1825. This information was provided by Stephen Furniss and Lorraine Saunders, two very determined British genealogical researchers. I am exceedingly grateful to them, and I owe a debt of gratitude to Gillian Lenfestey for having acted as liaison. Schipper, it should be noted, died after a long but unspecified illness, during which he was brought to the "deepest distress" by the prospect of leaving his wife and four children alone and destitute in a foreign land. A public subscription, however, raised the money necessary for his family's return to the United States. See: *Morning Post* (London, England), 23 Feb., 1826, 1, c. 1.

31 Schipper and his family arrived at Portsmouth in late September of 1810. See: NAUK, Foreign Office, Miscellaneous Records (FO 83/21), Lists of Aliens Arriving at English Ports, 1810–11, 27 Sept., 1810. As for Brock's plan to visit Ballston, see: Ferdinand Brock Tupper, ed., *The Life and Correspondence of Major-General Sir Isaac Brock, K.B.*, 2nd ed. (London, England: Simpkin, Marshall and Company, 1847), Isaac Brock to his brothers, 10 Jan., 1811, 88. Ultimately, however, Brock decided against the trip.

32 *Mercantile Advertiser* (New York, New York), 14 May, 1802, 3, c. 3. The last of these advertisements was published on 26 May, 1802, and in them Schipper notes that his "stay in this city will only be to the 12th of June next." Presumably, he went south sometime in mid-June of 1802, but a gap in Schipper's advertising record makes a more precise determination impossible. At the end of March 1803, Schipper announced that he was "lately arrived" in Charleston, South Carolina. See: *City Gazette* (Charleston, South Carolina), 31 Mar., 1803, 3, c. 5. These advertisements were inserted in the *City Gazette* up to and including 16 April, 1803. Schipper appears to have remained in that region until the autumn of 1803, as he established himself at Boston in October of that year, having "lately arrived from the Southern States." See: *Columbian Centinel* (Boston, Massachusetts), 19 Oct., 1803, 3, c. 2; *Independent Chronicle* (Boston, Massachusetts), 28 Nov., 1803, 3, c. 1; *Columbian Centinel*, 14 Jan., 1804, 3, c. 1; ibid., 21 Apr., 1804, 3, c. 1; ibid., 12 May, 1804, 3, c. 2. Although Schipper proposed going to New York City at the beginning of November, 1803, he postponed his departure for a few weeks. However, it was not until January of 1806, after "an absence of four years," that he finally set out. See: *Columbian Centinel*, 19 Oct., 1803, 3, c. 2; *Independent Chronicle*, 28 Nov., 1803, 3, c. 1; *New-York Evening Post* (New York, New York), 11 Jan., 1806, 3, c. 3.

33 *Salem Gazette* (Salem, Massachusetts), 1 June, 1804, 3, c. 2; *New-England Palladium* (Boston, Massachusetts), 17 July, 1804, 1, c. 1; *Massachusetts Spy* (Worcester, Massachusetts), 1 Aug., 1804, 3, c. 5; ibid., 12 Sept., 1804, 3, c. 3. These advertisements continued to be published until 19 June, 1804, 24 July, 1804, 22 August, 1804, and 19 September, 1804, respectively.

34 *Albany Centinel* (Albany, New York), 16 Oct., 1804, 3, c. 4. This advertisement appeared sporadically until 5 March, 1805. A similar advertisement ran from 29 January to 3 May, 1805. See: ibid., 29 Jan. 1805, 1, c. 1. Jeanne Riger, however, mistakenly believed that Schipper went to England for a year beginning in the summer of 1804. Yet, Schipper's advertisements continued to appear in various American newspapers throughout the summer and autumn of 1804. And in the *Albany Centinel*, which is cited above, some of these advertisements carry on well into 1805—leaving no time for a trip abroad. See: Riger, "New Light on Gerrit Schipper the Painter," 66. For a sampling of Schipper's advertisements in the summer of 1804, see: *New-England Palladium*, 17 July, 1804, 1, c. 1; *Massachusetts Spy*, 1 Aug., 1804, 3, c. 5; ibid., 12 Sept., 1804, 3, c. 3. Elsewhere in her article, Riger rejects a claim that Schipper went to England shortly after his marriage to Miss Elizabeth Burt in October of 1806. The source of this claim is Richard Hyer's article on Schipper, which appeared in a 1952 issue of *The New York Genealogical and Biographical Record*. Hyer misjudged the date Schipper and his family set out for London. They actually began their voyage in 1810, some four years later than Hyer calculated. See: Riger, "New Light on Gerrit Schipper the Painter," 69; Richard Hyer, "Gerrit Schipper, Miniaturist and Crayon Portraitist," *New York Genealogical and Biographical Record* LXXXIII, no. 2 (Apr. 1952): 71.

35 Riger, "New Light on Gerrit Schipper the Painter," 66; *Balance* (Hudson, New York), 11 June, 1805, 191, c. 1. On 17 July, 1805, Schipper announced that he had "just arrived" in Hartford, Connecticut. See: *Connecticut Courant* (Hartford, Connecticut), 17 July, 1805, 3, c. 5. See also: *American Mercury* (Hartford, Connecticut), 1 Aug., 1805, 2, c. 5.

36 Schipper arrived in New York City by 11 January, 1806. See: *New-York Evening Post*, 11 Jan., 1806, 3, c. 3. See also: ibid., 24 Jan., 1806, 3, c. 4. Nearly four months later, Schipper announced his plans to leave New York City, which would have been sometime in June of 1806—or perhaps even later. See: ibid., 19 May, 1806, 3, c. 3. Schipper noted his return to Hartford, for a "short stay," in an advertisement dated 14 August, 1806. See: *American Mercury*, 14 Aug., 1806, 3, c. 5. In a subsequent notice, Schipper informed the people of Hartford that he planned to remain among them until 20 September, 1806. See: ibid., 28 Aug., 1806, 3, c. 5. Regarding his drawing academy, see: *Connecticut Courant*, 17 Sept., 1806, 2, c. 4. For additional information, see: ibid., 26 Nov., 1806, 3, c. 5; *American Mercury*, 19 Mar., 1807, 3, c. 5. This last advertisement appears to have been published until 18 June, 1807.

37 Schipper's marriage to Elizabeth Burt took place on 27 October, 1806. See: Hyer, "Gerrit Schipper, Miniaturist and Crayon Portraitist," 71.

38 Riger, "New Light on Gerrit Schipper the Painter," 69.

39 At the end of May 1808, a man named Gerrit Schipper of Albany, New York was declared an insolvent debtor (meaning that he was unable to pay his bills). At the same time, a Gerrit Schipper of Troy, New York met with the same fate. In neither case was the insolvent's occupation disclosed, which would have aided in an identification. Still, the two insolvents were probably one and the same person, and likely Gerrit Schipper the artist. Unfortunately, an attempt to find proof of such a connection among the early insolvency records of New York State proved unsuccessful. For the advertisements declaring Gerrit Schipper an insolvent debtor, see: *Albany Register* (Albany, New York), 10 June, 1808, 3, c. 4; *American Citizen* (New York, New York), 6 July, 1808, 4, c. 3. Schipper's son later claimed that his father was living at Troy when his daughter, Adelia, was born. Since her baptismal record indicates that she was born 28 December, 1807, it would appear

that Gerritt Schipper was residing at Troy by late 1807. The fact that a Gerrit Schipper was declared an insolvent debtor at the same place only five months later hardly seems a coincidence. Under these circumstances, it is not unreasonable to think that Schipper's creditors forced him to head for Lower Canada in October of 1808. For the considerably delayed baptismal record of Adelia Schipper, see: London Metropolitan Archives, St. Marylebone Church, Baptism Register (X023/017), 16 Feb., 1812. See also: FARL, "Life of Nicholas L. Shipper," 1.

40 *Montreal Gazette*, 31 Oct., 1808, 3, c. 2. In this advertisement, Schipper announced that he had "just arrived" in Montreal.

41 Walter W. Jennings, *The American Embargo, 1807–1809*. University of Iowa Studies in the Social Sciences, vol. VIII, no. 1 (Iowa City, Iowa: University of Iowa, 1921), 90–1, 112–22.

42 As John Lambert noted after a visit to Lower Canada in 1808, "The Canadian merchants rejoiced at the embargo, which enriched them while it made their [American] neighbours poor indeed." See: John Lambert, *Travels Through Lower Canada, and the United States in the Years 1806, 1807, and 1808*, 3 vols (London, England: Richard Phillips, 1810), I: 234. In July of 1808, Brock himself observed: "The embargo has proved a famous harvest to some merchants here [at Montreal]." See: Ferdinand Brock Tupper, ed., *The Life and Correspondence of Major-General Sir Isaac Brock, K.B.*, 1st ed. (London, England: Simpkin, Marshall and Company, 1845), Isaac Brock to his brothers, 20 July, 1808, 72. As for the smuggling trade, Lambert reported that the importation of "timber, pot-ash, provisions, and almost every other article brought into the province in 1808, has more than doubled the quantity received from thence [the United States] in 1807." See: Lambert, *Travels Through Lower Canada, and the United States*, I: 253.

43 Regarding Brock's posting to Montreal, see: Library and Archives Canada (LAC), British Military and Naval Records, "C" Series (RG 8, I), vol. 1215, Craig to Gordon, 5 Mar., 1808, 94–5. Brock's transfer to Quebec City was occasioned by Major General Gordon Drummond's having superseded him in the command at Montreal. See: Tupper, *Life and Correspondence of Major-General Sir Isaac Brock*, 2nd ed., Isaac Brock to his brothers, 5 Sept., 1808, 72.

44 There is also evidence to suggest that Schipper was planning his departure from Montreal by late November of 1808. Obviously, he changed his mind. See: *Montreal Gazette*, 28 Nov., 1808, 3, c. 2.

45 In announcing his proposed removal to Quebec City, Schipper also indicated that it would take place sometime after 20 May, 1809. See: *Canadian Courant*, 8 May, 1809, 2, c. 4; *Montreal Gazette*, 8 May, 1809, 3, c. 1.

46 According to a scholarly article, Schipper's most prominent sitter was Isaiah Thomas, the Boston newspaper publisher and founder of the American Antiquarian Society. This might very well have been the case in the United States, but in terms of Lower Canada, no one could have been more important than Sir James H. Craig—who was both a lieutenant general in the British army and the governor-in-chief of British North America. For the above-mentioned article, see: David W. Meschutt and Kevin J. Avery, "Pastels by Gerrit Schipper in the Metropolitan Museum," *Metropolitan Museum Journal* 42 (2007): 134.

47 Jeanne Riger suggests that Governor Sir James H. Craig's portrait was done in Montreal, which is unlikely, as his official residence was at Quebec City. See: Riger, "New Light on Gerrit Schipper the Painter," 69.

48 In 1811, as Governor Craig anticipated his departure from Lower Canada, he gave Brock his favourite horse—Alfred. See: Tupper, *Life and Correspondence of Major-General Sir Isaac Brock*, 2nd ed., Baynes to Brock, 4 Mar., 1811, 99.

49 Brock began his journey to Upper Canada on 17 July, 1810, and was expected to reach Fort George by the end of that same month. See: LAC, British Military and Naval Records, "C" Series (RG 8, I), vol. 1216, Thornton to Gore, 16 July, 1810, 236.

50 In mid-May of 1810, Schipper announced his plans to depart after the fourth of June. See: *Quebec Gazette*, 17 May, 1810, 2, c. 4.

51 LAC, Office of the Governor of Quebec and Lower Canada Governor's Internal Letter Books (RG 7, G15A), vol. 3 (1807–11), Craig to "all to whom these presents may Concern," 8 Aug., 1810, 56. Schipper, it seems, was initially detained by his plans for an engraving of Governor Craig's portrait. At the end of May 1810, he announced that he would accept subscriptions for the engraving until mid-June. See: *Quebec Gazette*, 31 May, 1810, 3, c. 2. Schipper was probably also trying to raise money for his voyage to England.

52 Schipper's arrival at Portsmouth was registered on 27 September, 1810. See: NAUK, Foreign Office, Miscellaneous Records (FO 83/21), Lists of Aliens Arriving at English Ports, 1810–11, 27 Sept., 1810.

53 W.Y. Carman, "Infantry Clothing Regulations, 1802," *Journal of the Society for Army Historical Research* 19 (1940): 200–35.

54 Kosche, "Contemporary Portraits of Isaac Brock," 65.

55 Ibid. Governor Craig appointed Brock to act as brigadier general in Upper Canada, as well as Lower Canada, in early March of 1808. This arrangement was subject to approval, which was received in due course. See: LAC, British Military and Naval Records, "C" Series (RG 8, I), vol. 1215, Craig to Gordon, 5 Mar., 1808, 94–5; ibid., Gordon to Craig, 1 June, 1808, 58; ibid., 6 June, 1808, 60.

56 Major Nicholas P. Dawnay, "The Staff Uniform of the British Army, 1767 to 1855," *Journal of the Society for Army Historical Research* XXXI (1953): 77. Brigadier generals wore the same coat (or coatee) as major generals, with the loops and buttons set in pairs—in other words, two over two. In the case of the brigadier general's coatee, however, a distinction was made on the sleeves and skirts by having two buttons over one. According to Dawnay, the two ranks were indistinguishable prior to this modification. See: ibid., 74, 77–8.

57 Adding to the confusion was a dress regulation dating from 1809, which stipulated that colonels on the staff were to wear the same uniforms as brigadier generals on the staff, with their buttons likewise set in pairs. Apparently, the only difference was the design of the gilt buttons. See: Kosche, "Contemporary Portraits of Isaac Brock," 66; Dawnay, "Staff Uniform of the British Army," 77.

58 Kosche, "Contemporary Portraits of Isaac Brock," 65. Although Kosche was unable to determine when the delivery was made, there is evidence to suggest that Brock had his new uniforms by mid-July of 1810. See: Tupper, *Life and Correspondence of Major-General Sir Isaac Brock*, 2nd ed., Isaac Brock to his brothers, 9 July, 1810, 77.

59 Kosche, "Contemporary Portraits of Isaac Brock," 65. Berczy and Brock were both in Montreal during the spring and part of the summer of 1808, and in Quebec City from August of 1808 to July of 1809. For Brock's postings, see: LAC, British Military and Naval Records, "C" Series (RG 8, I), Craig to Gordon, 5 Mar., 1808, vol. 1215, 94–5; Tupper, *Life and Correspondence of Major-General Sir Isaac Brock*, 2nd ed., Isaac Brock to

his brothers, 5 Sept., 1808, and to his brother Irving, 9 July, 1810, 72, 77–8. For Berczy's whereabouts, see his letters in the following collections: LAC, William von Moll Berczy Papers (MG 23, HII6); Collection Jacques Viger (MG 24, L8). See also: Allodi, "William Berczy: The Canadian Years, 1794–1813," in Allodi, et al., *Berczy* (Ottawa, Ontario: National Gallery of Canada, 1991), 62, 64, 69, 72.

60 CWM, Ludwig Kosche Papers, Correspondence (58A3/10.26), Kosche to Mellish, 1 Mar., 1980; Kosche, "Contemporary Portraits of Isaac Brock," 65–6.

61 The epaulettes were another easy fix. The one shown in Brock's profile portrait (fig. 3) is obviously a replacement, as it is correct for a general officer such as a brigadier general—but not for a colonel who ranked as a regimental officer. Schipper painted the epaulette with a red strap, which is also correct. See: Dawnay, "Staff Uniform of the British Army," 74, 78.

62 After many failed attempts to interpret Brock's uniform within the context of the dress regulations, I consulted Andrew Cormack, a specialist in British army uniforms of the Napoleonic Wars. Cormack noticed oddities, which suggested to him that Brock's uniform was non-regulation. The main oddity, of course, was the placement of the buttons. See: email, Cormack to St-Denis, 13 Feb., 2010. The alterations could have been made by either a regimental or civilian tailor, and there were at least three of the latter description in Quebec City when Brock received his appointment. For their newspaper advertisements, see: *Quebec Gazette*, 30 June, 1808, 1, c. 2.

63 It is also possible that the buttons were left in place to facilitate the coatee's possible reuse, as Brock's appointment to brigadier general was limited to Upper and Lower Canada and therefore potentially temporary.

64 Kosche, "Contemporary Portraits of Isaac Brock," 65. In addition to an informal or undress uniform, Brock would also have received a formal or dress uniform.

65 Brock acknowledged the delivery in a letter to his brother, Irving. "I have a thousand thanks to offer you for the very great attention you have shewn in executing my commissions: the different articles arrived in the very best order, with the exception of the cocked hat, which has not been received." The reference to the cocked hat suggests that the "different articles" were various components of Brock's new military wardrobe. See: Tupper, *Life and Correspondence of Major-General Sir Isaac Brock*, 2nd ed., Isaac Brock to his brothers, 9 July, 1810, 77. This delivery was made in advance of Brock's removal to Upper Canada, and sometime after he sat for Schipper (otherwise he would have worn his new uniform).

66 This approval came earlier, in July of 1808. See: NAUK, War Office, Secretary at War, America, Out-Letters (WO 4/281), Pulteney to Brock, 5 July, 1808, 203/407.

67 As Brock informed his brothers in early September of 1808: "My nominal appointment has been confirmed at home, so that I am really a brigadier." See: Tupper, *Life and Correspondence of Major-General Sir Isaac Brock*, 2nd ed., Isaac Brock to his brothers, 5 Sept., 1808, 72.

68 Kosche was reliably informed that British officers in Brock's day were not strictly bound by the dress regulations. Such was the opinion of the staff at the Prince Consort's Army Library. In "all questions regarding Uniforms of this period, and especially Officers['] Uniforms, one must always bear in mind the considerable latitude allowed to officers at this time in matters of dress." This advice was relayed by Major John J. Price, then curator of the Duke of Edinburgh's Royal Regiment Museum. See: CWM, Ludwig Kosche Papers, Correspondence (58A3/10.25), Price to Kosche, 17 Feb., 1984. For some entertaining

examples of the degree to which adherence to the dress regulations could vary, see: Scott Hughes Myerly, *British Military Spectacle: From the Napoleonic Wars through the Crimea* (Harvard University Press: Cambridge, Massachusetts, 1996), 69–71.

69 Brock acknowledged the local nature of his appointment to brigadier general. In September of 1808, he wrote to his brothers that "were the 49th ordered hence, the rank would not be a sufficient inducement to keep me in this country. In such a case, I would throw it up willingly." See: Tupper, *Life and Correspondence of Major-General Sir Isaac Brock*, 2nd ed., Isaac Brock to his brothers, 5 Sept., 1808, 72.

70 Allodi, "Pastel Profiles," 305.

71 Ibid., 307.

72 *Columbian Centinel*, 14 Jan., 1804, 3, c. 1. With this recommendation, Schipper hoped to entice the discriminating citizens of Boston into having their portraits painted.

73 A sharper image was achieved by focusing two or more colours on the same convergence point.

74 The relatively short sitting time was a strong selling point, and one that Schipper promoted in his various newspaper advertisements. See, for example: *New-York Evening Post*, 11 Jan., 1806, 3, c. 3.

75 Ibid. This guarantee of customer satisfaction can be found in most of Schipper's advertisements, as well as those of other itinerant artists.

76 *Columbian Centinel*, 14 Jan., 1804, 3, c. 1.

77 For an idea of the popularity of the physiognotrace, see: Peter Benes, "Machine-Assisted Portrait and Profile Imaging in New England after 1803," in Peter Benes, ed., *Painting and Portrait Making in the American Northeast*, The Dublin Seminar for New England Folklife Annual Proceedings 19 (Boston, Massachusetts: Boston University, c1995), 139.

78 Ellen G. Miles, "1803—The Year of the Physiognotrace," in ibid., 127–8.

79 Ibid., 131.

80 Allodi, "Pastel Profiles," 306–7. For Schipper's advertisement, see: *Montreal Gazette*, 28 Nov., 1808, 3, c. 2.

81 *Quebec Mercury* (Quebec, Lower Canada), 6 Aug., 1810, 255, c. 2. That Schipper was willing to dispose of his physiognotrace does not indicate a lack of utility, but rather the need to raise money for a passage to England—for which he was also willing to sell his pastels and picture frames. As Mary Allodi noted, the auction took nearly a week after Schipper invoiced the Séminaire de Québec for pastel portraits of bishops Briand and Laval. They were among the last of his commissions in Lower Canada. See: email, Allodi to St-Denis, 28 Oct., 2005; Allodi, "Pastel Profiles," in Allodi, et al., Berczy, 307–8.

82 The sale of Schipper's portrait of Brock (fig. 3) took place in February of 2009. Included in the transaction was the miniature of Brock as a young ensign (fig. 27), and also that of his brother, Lieutenant John Brock (fig. 25), both of which were painted by Philip Jean. See: *St. Catharines Standard* (St. Catharines, Ontario), 14 Feb., 2009, A1; ibid., 18 Feb., 2009, A1; ibid., 20 Feb., 2009, A1.

83 Kosche, "Contemporary Portraits of Isaac Brock," 60.

84 Email, Lenfestey to St-Denis, 23 Apr., 2009. Jane McAusland, an English art on paper conservator, discovered that the mole was actually mould, which she removed during her restoration of the profile portrait (fig. 3) in late 2010.

85 Riger, "New Light on Gerrit Schipper the Painter," 68. For an example of Schipper's signature, see: ibid., 67. A subsequent search for a watermark was also unsuccessful. See: email, St-Denis to Lenfestey, 23 Apr., 2009; ibid., Lenfestey to St-Denis, 24 Apr., 2009.

86 There was also pastel loss consistent with the rubbing caused by an oval mat. This style of mat, however, appears to have been a later replacement. See: ibid., Conlon to St-Denis, 29 May, 2009. The original mat was probably rectangular, like those which still protect several other profile portraits painted by Schipper.

87 During the course of restoration in late 2010, the faint red blur was largely reversed.

88 Email, Lenfestey to St-Denis, 23 Apr., 2009.

89 Ibid., Riger to St-Denis, 2 Dec., 2005.

90 Ibid., Lenfestey to St-Denis, 24 Apr., 2009; ibid., Conlon to St-Denis, 29 May, 2009; ibid., 3 June, 2009. Helen Conlon thought this line was made using a dark coloured or graphite pencil. I later learned that infrared reflectography is more effective in detecting carbon content, such as that used in the lead, or graphite, of pencils. However, the flashlight worked well on this occasion and revealed "a distinctive and clear line following the sitter's profile." See: ibid., Conlon to St-Denis, 13 Nov., 2014.

91 Ibid., Osterman to St-Denis, 26 May, 2009.

92 Conversation with Osterman, 27 May, 2009.

93 For examples of Schipper's full-length portraits, see: Metropolitan Museum of Art, American Paintings and Sculpture, Pastel "Portrait of a Man," by Gerrit Schipper, 1805, acc. 2007.19; Private Collection, "John Knickerbacker and his wife Elisabeth," 1805, reproduced in Riger, "New Light on Gerrit Schipper the Painter," 67.

94 *Columbian Centinel*, 14 Jan., 1804, 3, c. 1.

95 When a Quebec City auctioneer later described Schipper's physiognotrace as being "upon a new construction," he might simply have meant that the fabric or paper covering the glass had been removed. See: *Quebec Mercury*, 6 Aug., 1810, 255, c. 2.

96 Conversation with Osterman, 27 May, 2009. Presumably, Schipper's ability to trace more quickly reduced the amount of time he required to complete a profile portrait, but by how much is unknown.

97 The stages by which Schipper completed his profile portraits were determined by examining his portrait of Sarah (Greene) Jenkins, which is remarkable for having been left unfinished below the neckline—except for a sketch of the upper part of her dress. I am grateful to Helen Conlon, who is Fine Art Curator at the Guernsey Museum and Art Gallery, for her interpretation of this unusual specimen of Schipper's work. See: email, Conlon to St-Denis, 10 Feb., 2014. Schipper's manner of painting with pastels was standard practice by the early nineteenth century. See: Marjorie Shelley, "American Pastels of the Late Nineteenth & Early Twentieth Centuries: Materials & Techniques," in Doreen Bolger, et al., *American Pastels in the Metropolitan Museum of Art* (New York, New York: Metropolitan Museum of Art, 1989), 38. For a description of Schipper's technique, see: Allodi, "Gerritt Schipper," in Mario Béland, *Painting in Quebec, 1820–1850* (Quebec City, Quebec: Musée du Québec, 1992), 186. Sarah Jenkins was the first wife of Elisha Jenkins of Albany, New York, whose own portrait by Schipper was completed in its entirety. Both portraits are in a private collection.

98 During his tours of the United States, Schipper included a frame with the purchase price of his profile portraits. He offered the same incentive at Montreal in 1808, where the $6.00

he asked for a profile portrait included "an elegant gold frame with glass." See: *Montreal Gazette*, 28 Nov., 1808, 3, c. 2. Schipper probably advertised similar terms after his arrival in Quebec City, but a newspaper search failed to produce any evidence of his business practices there. It should be noted that Schipper also made use of rectangular mats, which protected the pastels from being smudged by the glass. In the case of Brock's portrait (fig. 3), it appears that the original mat was replaced with one having an oval cutout. This replacement was discarded at some point, although evidence of its existence (in the form of rubbing) was discovered in 2009 by Helen Conlon, the Fine Art Curator at the Guernsey Museum and Art Gallery. See: email, Conlon to St-Denis, 29 May, 2009.

99 For the quotation, see: Riger, "New Light on Gerrit Schipper the Painter," 69. The blank expression resulted from an obligatory forward gaze, which had to be maintained while Schipper traced the sitter's profile.

100 *Columbian Centinel*, 14 Jan., 1804, 3, c. 1. The only drawback associated with the physiognotrace was its elongated shape, which perhaps made it more cumbersome to transport than the box-type camera obscura. Peter Benes theorizes that Schipper was caught up in the merchandising frenzy that contributed to the popularity of the physiognotrace, and that he responded by promoting the achromatic camera obscura. See: Benes, "Machine-Assisted Portrait and Profile Imaging in New England after 1803," 146–7.

101 These questionable attractions included painted panoramas, acoustical exhibitions, and even electric shock treatments. See: Benes, "Machine-Assisted Portrait and Profile Imaging in New England after 1803," 139–41, 146. It was Shipper's auctioneer who alerted the public to his physiognotrace, and not Schipper himself. See: *Quebec Mercury*, 6 Aug., 1810, 255, c. 2.

CHAPTER 7

1 Ludwig Kosche, "Contemporary Portraits of Isaac Brock: An Analysis," *Archivaria* 20 (Summer 1985): 61.

2 Archives of Ontario (AO), Ferdinand Brock Tupper Papers (F 1081), Glegg to Brock, 30 Dec., 1813.

3 Major Glegg's reply is dated 30 December, 1813, and in it he acknowledges William Brock's letter of 5 September, 1813. While the earlier letter is now lost, it was obviously meant to thank Major Glegg for the delivery of Brock's personal effects. This was William Brock's second attempt to do so, as his initial letter was lost in the *Manchester* packet when it was captured by an American privateer on or about 25 June, 1813. That letter was written circa 5 June, 1813, and probably soon after the trunks containing Brock's personal effects had arrived in England. See: ibid. Regarding the *Manchester*'s capture, see: *Morning Chronicle* (London, England), 13 July, 1813, 3, c. 2; *Liverpool Mercury* (Liverpool, England), 16 July, 1813, 3, c. 4. In a curious twist, the *Manchester* was liberated soon after it was taken—but William Brock's letter was by then at the bottom of the Atlantic Ocean, having been thrown overboard along with the rest of the ship's mail.

4 Kosche, "Contemporary Portraits of Isaac Brock," 62. Kosche found Mrs. de Lisle's recollection in an article published in 1908. See: Lady Edgar [Matilda Ridout], "General Brock's Portrait," *The Canadian Magazine* XXXI, no. 3 (July 1908): 263. Mrs. de Lisle was the daughter of Brock's sister, Elizabeth, who married John Elisha Tupper. It should be noted that Kosche quotes from a letter written to Colonel Charles W. Robinson dated

18 January, 1882, which he claims was written by Miss Henrietta Tupper. The author was in fact Mrs. Hubert Le Cocq (the former Miss Victoria Tupper), who replied to Colonel Robinson on behalf of her mother, Mrs. Henry Tupper. Although the letter lacks Mrs. Le Cocq's signature, there are references to it elsewhere in the Robinson correspondence that serve to confirm the writer's identity.

5 Kosche, "Contemporary Portraits of Isaac Brock," 62.

6 Ibid.

7 Ibid.; Ferdinand Brock Tupper, ed., *The Life and Correspondence of Major-General Sir Isaac Brock, K.B.*, 1st ed. (London, England: Simpkin, Marshall and Company, 1845), 341; ibid., 2nd ed. (London, England: Simpkin, Marshall and Company, 1847), 349. It was Captain Arthur S. Cave who informed Miss Mickle that this attempt was made in 1845. See: AO, Women's Canadian Historical Society of Toronto Papers (F 1180), Correspondence (series 1), file 2 (Jan.–May 1897), Cave to Mickle, 8 May, 1897.

8 Kosche, "Contemporary Portraits of Isaac Brock," 62; Edgar, "General Brock's Portrait," 263. Emphasis added. For the original sources, see: Trent University, Thomas J. Bata Library, Trent University Archives (TU), Gilbert and Stewart Bagnani Papers (94-016), General Correspondence (series A), Le Cocq to Robinson, 18 Jan., 1882. See also: ibid., Tupper to Robinson, 25 Jan., 1882.

9 Kosche, "Contemporary Portraits of Isaac Brock," 62. Major Glegg's admission about not having ever possessed a good likeness of Brock was written in 1813, while Tupper's comment with regard to the disappointed officers of the 49th Regiment was first published in 1845. See: AO, Ferdinand Brock Tupper Papers (F 1081), Glegg to Brock, 30 Dec., 1813; Tupper, *Life and Correspondence of Major-General Sir Isaac Brock*, 1st ed., 341.

10 Kosche, "Contemporary Portraits of Isaac Brock," 60.

11 Ibid, 63.

12 Ibid. No matter how much it might be "straining credulity" to consider the possibility, Tupper was not necessarily all that knowledgeable when it came to the insignia of the Order of the Bath.

13 Mrs. de Lisle was born in 1808, and she always remembered seeing the two portraits of Brock (figs 3, 4) "in the houses of her uncles, brothers of Sir Isaac." See: TU, Gilbert and Stewart Bagnani Papers (94-016), General Correspondence (series A), Le Cocq to Robinson, 18 Jan., 1882.

14 As Kosche noted, "Tupper had Glegg's letter." See: Kosche, "Contemporary Portraits of Isaac Brock," 62.

15 TU, Gilbert and Stewart Bagnani Papers (94-016), General Correspondence (series A), Le Cocq to Robinson, 18 Jan., 1882. The published version of this letter is not verbatim. See: Edgar, "General Brock's Portrait," 263.

16 Kosche, "Contemporary Portraits of Isaac Brock," 61.

17 AO, Women's Canadian Historical Society of Toronto Papers (F 1180), Miscellaneous (series 13), file 3, Brock Portrait Notebook, 145. It will be remembered that Miss Lorna R. Procter allowed Kosche to borrow this notebook for an extended period of time. For the original letter, see: AO, Ferdinand Brock Tupper Papers (F1081), Brock to Tupper, 9 Jan., 1818.

18 AO, Women's Canadian Historical Society of Toronto Papers (F 1180), Correspondence (series 1), file 2 (Jan.–May 1897), FitzGibbon to Mickle, 28 May, 1897.

19 The laid paper on which the profile portrait (fig. 3) is painted measures approximately 8 x 9 inches or, more precisely, 20.3 x 23.4 cm. I am grateful to Gillian Lenfestey for this information.

20 Kosche, "Contemporary Portraits of Isaac Brock," 61.

21 There was also the possibility that Major Glegg was loath to discard the frame, perhaps for fear of damaging the portrait it protected. If so, he exhibited admirable foresight, as the pastels used in the making of Brock's profile portrait (fig. 3) are easily smudged—which is why Gerrit Schipper matted his portraits and framed them under glass. Assuming that Major Glegg did not interfere with the portrait, then the antique gilt frame that still protects it is likely the same one supplied by Schipper.

22 AO, Women's Canadian Historical Society of Toronto Papers (F 1180), Correspondence (series 1), file 2 (Jan.–May 1897), FitzGibbon to Mickle, 28 May, 1897.

23 AO, Ferdinand Brock Tupper Papers (F1081), Glegg to Brock, 30 Dec., 1813. Of course, by "this Country," Major Glegg meant Upper Canada, which is now southern Ontario, as opposed to Lower Canada, or the province of Quebec. Kosche does not appear to have taken these geographical distinctions into consideration.

24 National Archives and Records Administration (NARA), Department of the Navy (RG 45), Captains' Letters, vol. 3 (1 Sept. 1812–31 Dec. 1812), Chauncey to Hamilton, 6 Nov., 1812, no. 167; ibid., 13 Nov., 1812, no. 176; ibid., 17 Nov., 1812, no. 183. See also: University of Michigan, William L. Clements Library, Manuscripts Division (UM), Isaac Chauncey Letter Books, Chauncey to Dearborn, 17 Nov., 1812; ibid., Chauncey to Tompkins, 17 Nov., 1812. Commodore Chauncey also contemplated attacking Kingston "for the purpose of destroying the Guns and publick Stores at that Station." See: NARA, Department of the Navy (RG 45), Captains' Letters, vol. 3 (1 Sept. 1812–31 Dec. 1812), Chauncey to Hamilton, 6 Nov., 1812, no. 167.

25 For additional information on the loss of the *Governor Simcoe*, see: Library and Archives Canada (LAC), Department of Finance, Upper Canada, War of 1812 Losses Claims (RG 19, 5Ea), vol. 3757, file 1, claim of Donald McArthur, no. 1730. In particular, see the letters of Joseph Forsyth to Alexander Wood dated 23 November, 1812 and 8 December, 1812.

26 NARA, Department of the Navy (RG 45), Captains' Letters, vol. 3 (1 Sept. 1812–31 Dec. 1812), Chauncey to Hamilton, 13 Nov., 1812, no. 176. See also: UM, Isaac Chauncey Letter Books, Chauncey to Dearborn, 17 Nov., 1812; ibid., Chauncey to Tompkins, 17 Nov., 1812. Commodore Chauncey mistakenly thought the *Two Brothers* was captured at Armingston, or Armingstown. It was actually Ernestown, which the Canadian historian Lieutenant Colonel Ernest A. Cruikshank noted when he published the commodore's report in 1900. See: NARA, Department of the Navy (RG 45), Captains' Letters, vol. 3 (1 Sept. 1812–31 Dec. 1812), Chauncey to Hamilton, 13 Nov., 1812, no. 176; Ernest A. Cruikshank, ed., *The Documentary History of the Campaign upon the Niagara Frontier*, 9 vols (Niagara Falls, Ontario: Lundy's Lane Historical Society, 1900), IV: II (1812): 208.

27 The date of the *Elizabeth*'s sailing was worked out from Major General Roger Hale Sheaffe's letter to Lieutenant General Sir George Prevost, which mentions that the *Earl of Moira* set sail on the afternoon of 11 November, 1812. According to Commodore Chauncey, the *Elizabeth* was in convoy with the *Earl of Moira*. See: LAC, British Military and Naval Records, "C" Series (RG 8, I), vol. 228, Sheaffe to Prevost, 16 Nov., 1812, 83; NARA, Department of the Navy (RG 45), Captains' Letters, vol. 3 (1 Sept. 1812–31 Dec. 1812),

Chauncey to Hamilton, 17 Nov., 1812, no. 183. See also: UM, Isaac Chauncey Letter Books, Chauncey to Dearborn, 17 Nov., 1812; ibid., Chauncey to Tompkins, 17 Nov., 1812.

28 Although Commodore Chauncey did not mention Captain Brock's wife in his reports, the *Quebec Gazette* certainly noticed her presence on board the *Elizabeth*: "We are happy to state that Capt. Brock and lady, lately captured by the enemy on Lake Ontario, have been released, as also the private property of the late Gen. Brock, has been restored." See: *Quebec Gazette* (Quebec, Lower Canada), 10 Dec., 1812, 2, c. 1. Captain Brock's wife, of course, was the former Miss Susannah *Lucy* Quirk Short.

29 Most of the items purchased by Captain Brock consisted of silverware. See: Toronto Reference Library (TRL), Marilyn and Charles Baillie Special Collections Centre, Baldwin Collection of Canadiana, William Allan Papers (S 123), Miscellaneous Papers (series 6), estate inventory of Major General Sir Isaac Brock, Nov., 1812, 7.

30 Regarding the temporary nature of the grant of administration, see: AO, Upper Canada Court of Probate (RG 22), Grants of Probate and Administration, Register A, 1796–1816 (series 154), Letters of Administration, estate of Major General Isaac Brock, 10 Nov., 1812. In 1817, letters of administration were granted to Brock's brother, John Savery Brock. See: National Archives of the United Kingdom (NAUK), Records of the Prerogative Court of Canterbury, Administration Act Books (PROB 6/193), estate of Sir Isaac Brock, 26 Apr., 1817, 36b.

31 AO, Ferdinand Brock Tupper Papers (F 1081), Glegg to Brock, 25 Oct., 1812. William Brock claimed to have furnished something more than £3,000 for the purchase of his brother Isaac's military commissions. See: LAC, Colonial Office (MG 11-CO 42), vol. 353, Upper Canada, Despatches, Public Offices and Miscellaneous (1812), Brock to Liverpool, 28 Nov., 1812, 218a. See also: Tupper, *Life and Correspondence of Major-General Sir Isaac Brock*, 2nd ed., 110.

32 AO, Upper Canada Court of Probate (RG 22), Estate Files, 1793–1859 (series 155), estate of Major General Isaac Brock, petition of Captain James Brock, 5 Nov., 1812.

33 Cruikshank, *Documentary History* IV: II (1812): 184–5.

34 AO, Upper Canada Court of Probate (RG 22), Estate Files, 1793–1859 (series 155), estate of Major General Isaac Brock, bond of administration, 10 Nov., 1812. As noted elsewhere, the date of Captain Brock's embarkation on board the *Elizabeth* was deduced from a letter written by Major General Roger Hale Sheaffe. In it, he mentioned to Sir George Prevost that the *Earl of Moira*, which escorted the *Elizabeth*, departed York on the afternoon of 11 November. See: LAC, British Military and Naval Records, "C" Series (RG 8, I), vol. 228, Sheaffe to Prevost, 16 Nov., 1812, 83.

35 As Major General Roger Hale Sheaffe informed Colonel Henry Procter, "Murney's sloop [the *Elizabeth*] sailed with her [the *Earl of Moira*]." See: NARA, Papers of the Department of State (RG 59), War of 1812 Papers, Miscellaneous Intercepted Correspondence, British Military Correspondence, Sheaffe to Procter, 20 Nov., 1812. While the *Elizabeth* was a smaller ship, and only lightly armed, the *Earl of Moira* was considered protection enough for both vessels.

36 LAC, British Military and Naval Records, "C" Series (RG 8, I), vol. 228, Sheaffe to Prevost, 16 Nov., 1812, 83.

37 UM, Isaac Chauncey Letter Books, Chauncey to Dearborn, 17 Nov., 1812; ibid., Chauncey to Tompkins, 17 Nov., 1812. Initially, Commodore Chauncey thought his ploy

a failure because the British had discovered his stratagem. But as he later learned, the *Royal George* was put out of commission by having been badly damaged. See: ibid.

38 Commodore Chauncey reported that Master Mix anchored on the southeast side of Long Island, which was another name for modern-day Wolfe Island. See: ibid., Chauncey to Hamilton, 17 Nov., 1812.

39 Ibid., Chauncey to Tompkins, 17 Nov., 1812. The *Elizabeth* was subsequently renamed *Asp*.

40 Ibid. As Commodore Chauncey reported to the secretary of the navy, the wind was "blowing a gale with a severe Snow Storm; the small vessels laboring extremely, and the ice making so fast upon the slides of our carronades that we could not have made use of them." See: ibid., Chauncey to Hamilton, 17 Nov., 1812.

41 The intelligence provided by Captain Brock was relayed to the American secretary of the navy by Commodore Chauncey's private secretary. See: *War* (New York, New York), 28 Nov., 1812, 100, c. 1.

42 Commodore Chauncey had decided to release Captain Brock by 16 November, 1812. UM, Isaac Chauncey Letter Books, Chauncey to Vincent, 16 Nov., 1812.

43 In two official letters, Commodore Chauncey mentions that Captain Brock was captured with part of his cousin's baggage in his charge. See: ibid., Chauncey to Tompkins, 17 Nov., 1812; ibid., Chauncey to Hamilton, 17 Nov., 1812.

44 The generosity of the *Growler*'s crew was hailed in the American press. See, for example: *Buffalo Gazette* (Buffalo, New York), 22 Dec., 1812, 2, c. 1.

45 Commodore Chauncey sent the prisoners to Kingston under a flag of truce on 17 November, 1812. See: UM, Isaac Chauncey Letter Books, Chauncey to Vaughan, 17 Nov., 1812. Captain Thomas Nairne, who was posted with a detachment of the 49th Regiment at Kingston, remarked on the return of Captain Brock and the other British prisoners: "They all unite in praising the good treatment they received from the Yankies." See: LAC, John and Thomas Nairne Papers (MG 23, GIII23), Correspondence, vol. 1, Nairne to Nairne, 15–24 Nov., 1812, 628.

46 Captain Brock confirmed the activity of the Americans "in preparing the most formidable means for establishing a superiority on the lakes." See: LAC, British Military and Naval Records, "C" Series (RG 8, I), vol. 728, Sheaffe to Prevost, 23 Nov., 1812, 115.

47 *Columbian* (New York, New York), 2 Dec., 1812, 3, c. 1.

48 Two crewmen were also detained. See: UM, Isaac Chauncey Letter Books, Chauncey to Vincent, 16 Nov., 1812; ibid., Chauncey to Hamilton, 17 Nov., 1812; *Quebec Mercury* (Quebec, Lower Canada), 8 Dec., 1812, 387, c. 3.

49 *War*, 28 Nov., 1812, 100, c. 1.

50 Ibid.

51 Captain Brock addressed his letter to a Mr. Mower, no doubt Nahum Mower who published the *Canadian Courant* in Montreal. Unfortunately, there are no surviving issues of the *Canadian Courant* for the period in question. However, the captain's letter was widely reprinted in other newspapers, including the *Kingston Gazette*. See: *Kingston Gazette* (Kingston, Upper Canada), 9 Jan., 1813, 3, c. 2. Emphasis added. I am grateful to Chris Raible for clarifying Mower's identity.

52 Ferdinand Brock Tupper described his uncle's personal effects as having been contained in "the trunks belonging to Sir Isaac Brock," by which he appears to have meant that

there were two. Presumably, these trunks were not overly large. See: Tupper, *Life and Correspondence of Major-General Sir Isaac Brock*, 1st ed., v; ibid., 2nd ed., vii.

53 *Quebec Gazette*, 1 July, 1813, 2, c. 3. See also: LAC, British Military and Naval Records, "C" Series (RG 8, I), vol. 689, Chauncey to Prevost, 2 June, 1813, 81. Mrs. Brock was accompanied by the wife of Major James Dennis. I am grateful to the late Stephen Otto for his observations regarding this incident.

54 *Military Monitor* (New York, New York), 23 Nov., 1812, 118, c. 1. It should be noted that the editors of the *Military Monitor* found this account "not probable," as it was related elsewhere that Brock had already been buried. But despite their doubts, the editors went ahead and published the sensational story. Coincidentally, a United States seaman by the name of Ned Myers recited a similar story, which he did for the benefit of James Fenimore Cooper and during a discussion of the American capture of York in 1813. It would appear that Myers, and perhaps the editor of the *Military Monitor*, mistook Brock's body for that of Brigadier General Zebulon Pike, who was killed by the explosion of the powder magazine at Fort York, and whose corpse was preserved in a cask of rum until it could be buried at Sackets Harbor. See: James Fenimore Cooper, *Ned Myers; or, A Life Before the Mast*, 2 vols (London, England: Richard Bentley, 1843), I: 126–7; Robert Malcomson, *Capital in Flames: The American Attack on York, 1813* (Montreal, Quebec: Robin Brass Studio, 2008), 274.

55 According to Asa Grant of Sackets Harbor, Captain Brock "is said to have been the Genl's private secretary & now to have the charge of all his business, that he had his papers & other effects on board the Sloop." See: UM, War of 1812 Collection, Asa Grant to John Grant, 17 Nov., 1812. Brigadier General Jacob Brown of the New York Militia provided a similar report to Nathan Ford of Ogdensburg, which he claimed to have heard from Captain Brock himself. As Ford told his brother, Captain Brock "had on board all the Genl.'s Baggage & property" and "Genl. Brown had a Conversation with Capt. Brock—he gave him the above information." See: AO, Ford Family Papers (F 483), Ford to Ford, Tuesday afternoon. Although this letter is undated, it was probably written sometime in November of 1812.

56 As Murney wrote almost twelve years later: "The Sloop Elizabeth was taken by the enemy in the act of Bringing Capt. Brock and the Baggage of the late General Brock to this place [Kingston]." See: LAC, Department of Finance, Upper Canada, War of 1812 Losses Claims (RG 19, E5a), vol. 3752, file 2, claim of Henry Murney, no. 1176, Murney to Macaulay, 18 Jan., 1824.

57 *Buffalo Gazette*, 22 Dec., 1812, 2, c. 1.

58 Ibid. Ferdinand Brock Tupper, however, thought it was solely through Commodore Chauncey's generosity that Brock's personal effects were saved from the auction block. Many years later, Tupper publicly thanked the commodore for the return of his uncle's property. It was a nice gesture, but about five years too late. The first edition of Tupper's *The Life and Correspondence of Major-General Sir Isaac Brock, K.B.* was published in 1845, but Commodore Chauncey died in 1840. See: Tupper, *Life and Correspondence of Major-General Sir Isaac Brock*, 1st ed., 354; John C. Fredriksen, "Chauncey, Isaac," *American National Biography* 4: 750. Tupper also believed that the box of letters, which he used to compile his uncle's biography, was included with the trunks relinquished by the Americans. See: Tupper, *Life and Correspondence of Major-General Sir Isaac Brock*, 1st ed., v; ibid., 2nd ed., vii.

59 *Columbian*, 2 Dec., 1812, 3, c. 1. According to this newspaper account, Brock's personal effects included his uniform, swords, papers and the equivalent of about $12,000 in specie (or currency). The uniform, swords (although perhaps only one), and the papers all correspond with items Captain Glegg is known to have set aside for William Brock. See: AO, Ferdinand Brock Tupper Papers (F 1081), Glegg to Brock, 30 Dec., 1813; Tupper, *Life and Correspondence of Major-General Sir Isaac Brock*, 1st ed., 354. Tupper, however, refuted the claim about the specie, and Commodore Chauncey made no mention of such a significant prize in his reports. See: Tupper, *Life and Correspondence of Major-General Sir Isaac Brock*, 2nd ed., 362; UM, Isaac Chauncey Letter Books, Chauncey to Dearborn, 17 Nov., 1812; ibid., Chauncey to Tompkins, 17 Nov., 1812; ibid., Chauncey to Hamilton, 17 Nov., 1812. Another equally suspicious contribution to a Quebec City newspaper reported that Brock's furniture was also on the *Elizabeth*, which is completely false. See: *Quebec Mercury*, 8 Dec., 1812, 391, c. 3.

60 Tupper, *Life and Correspondence of Major-General Sir Isaac Brock*, 1st ed., 354; ibid. 2nd ed., 362. For additional references to the plate, see: *Montreal Gazette* (Montreal, Lower Canada), 24 Nov., 1812, 3, c. 1; *Quebec Mercury*, 1 Dec., 1812, 381, c. 2. American sources simply refer to Brock's baggage.

61 TRL, William Allan Papers (S 123), Miscellaneous Papers (series 6), estate inventory of Major General Sir Isaac Brock, Nov. 1812, 7.

62 For a copy of Anderson's letter, see: *War*, 28 Nov., 1812, 100, c. 1.

63 Commodore Chauncey was not above the occasional deception himself. When he sent Captain Henry Murney back to Kingston on 5 December, 1812, he took advantage of the opportunity to spy on the strength of the British defences. Still, and unlike Captain Brock, the American commodore was motivated by public service and not personal gain. See: NARA, Department of the Navy (RG 45), Captains' Letters, vol. 3 (1 Sept. 1812–31 Dec. 1812), Chauncey to Hamilton, 9 Dec., 1812, no. 210.

64 The last ships of the season arrived at Quebec City on or about 11 November, 1812. Presumably, all departures from the port ended at about the same time, which roughly coincided with that of the *Elizabeth* from York. See: *Quebec Gazette*, 12 Nov., 1812, 2, c. 4.

65 AO, Ferdinand Brock Tupper Papers (F 1081), Glegg to Brock, 30 Dec., 1813.

66 According to the *Quebec Gazette*, the first ship of the season arrived on 5 May, 1813. See: *Quebec Gazette*, 6 May, 1813, 2, c. 3.

67 Private Porter was only seventeen years old when he joined the 49th Regiment. See: NAUK, War Office, Records of the Royal Hospital Chelsea, Soldiers Service Documents (WO 97/633), discharge papers of Thomas Porter, 15 Dec., 1813, no. 113. Private Porter, however, did not want for company, as his father and brother were both soldiers in the same regiment. See: Tupper, *Life and Correspondence of Major-General Sir Isaac Brock*, 1st ed., 387; ibid., 2nd ed., 397.

68 Ferdinand Brock Tupper seems to have been under the mistaken belief that Private Dobson died in 1812, and shortly before Brock himself. However, a search of the muster books and pay lists of the 49th Regiment revealed that Private Dobson died on 12 May, 1805. It was also discovered that his death occurred at Quebec City. See: Tupper, *Life and Correspondence of Major-General Sir Isaac Brock*, 1st ed., 5; ibid., 2nd ed., 5; NAUK, War Office, General Muster Books and Pay Lists, 49th Regiment of Foot (WO 12/6041), 25 Apr.–24 May, 1805.

69 Tupper, *Life and Correspondence of Major-General Sir Isaac Brock*, 2nd ed., 5.

70 Ibid., 1st ed., 387; ibid., 2nd ed., 397. It was likely Private Porter himself who suggested his discharge from the army. Also, a letter written by Major Glegg mentions "Porter's arrival" at the residence of William Brock. See: AO, Ferdinand Brock Tupper Papers (F 1081), Glegg to Brock, 30 Dec., 1813.

71 NAUK, War Office, Records of the Royal Hospital Chelsea, Soldiers Service Documents (WO 97/633), discharge papers of Thomas Porter, 15 Dec., 1813, no. 113.

72 Ibid., Commissary General of Musters Office, General Muster Books and Pay Lists, "Pay-List of the Forty Ninth (or Herts) Regiment of Foot," 1811–13 (WO 12/6044), 25 Sept.–24 Dec., 1812, no. 511; ibid., 25 Dec., 1812–24 Mar., 1813, no. 485; ibid., 25 Mar.–24 June, 1813, no. 486. The pay lists for 25 June to 24 December, 1813 indicate that Private Porter was sent home on furlough. See: ibid., 25 June–24 Sept., 1813, no. 464; ibid., 25 Sept.–24 Dec., 1813, no. 463. Moreover, his name is not included in a list of the British prisoners that Commodore Chauncey sent to Lieutenant Colonel John Vincent at Kingston. See: UM, Isaac Chauncey Letter Books, Chauncey to Vincent, 16 Nov., 1812.

73 Even if Captain Brock had received permission to accompany the trunks to England, he would have been prevented from doing so by the terms of his parole. See: UM, Isaac Chauncey Letter Books, Chauncey to Hamilton, 17 Nov., 1812.

74 AO, Ferdinand Brock Tupper Papers (F 1081), Glegg to Brock, 30 Dec., 1813.

75 Ibid. Much private property was confiscated. Included was Major General Sheaffe's own dress coatee, which was auctioned at the American Fort Niagara in the afternoon of 11 May, 1813. See: New-York Historical Society, Patricia D. Klingenstein Library, Manuscript Department, Henry Dearborn Letter Books, Orders of Major General Henry Dearborn, 10 May, 1813, 372; Genevieve Miller, *Wm. Beaumont's Formative Years: Two Early Notebooks, 1811–1821* (New York, New York: Henry Schuman, 1946), 48–9.

CHAPTER 8

1 Early in December of 1812, following a vote of thanks in the House of Lords for Wellington's victory at Salamanca, the Duke of Norfolk enquired whether a similar recognition was intended for the officers who had distinguished themselves in Canada. Lord Liverpool, the prime minister, replied in the negative, but observed that an address would be proposed for a monument to Brock. In July of 1813, the address in question was submitted to the Prince Regent, who approved of the memorial and directed that it be placed in St. Paul's Cathedral. See: *Times* (London, England), 4 Dec., 1812, 2, c. 4; ibid., 14 July, 1813, 2, c. 5; Great Britain, Parliament (Commons), *Journals* vol. 68, 13 July, 1813, 663; ibid., 20 July, 1813, 672; *Ipswich Journal* (Ipswich, England), 17 July, 1813, 2, c. 1.

2 Evidence that William Brock promoted the idea of a monument in honour of his brother was found in a letter he addressed to the British prime minister. In it, Lord Liverpool was reminded of his remark in the House of Lords, namely that an address would be presented to the Prince Regent praying for a monument to Sir Isaac Brock. See: Library and Archives Canada (LAC), Colonial Office (MG 11-CO 42), vol. 354, Upper Canada, Despatches, Public Offices and Miscellaneous (1813), Brock to Liverpool, 11 June, 1813, 198.

3 When Major Glegg's disappointing reply finally came to hand in the late spring of 1814, there was no ambiguity: "I regret to say that I never possessed a good likeness of your Brother, nor did he ever sit for it being taken in this Country." See: Archives of Ontario (AO), Ferdinand Brock Tupper Papers (F 1081), Glegg to Brock, 30 Dec., 1813. This

letter was postmarked at Quebec City on 18 January, 1814, and again on 3 April, 1814. Presumably, it was sent on to London after the opening of navigation on the St. Lawrence River, which did not occur until early in May of 1814 (the first ships of the season arrived there on 4 May). See: *Quebec Gazette* (Quebec, Lower Canada), 12 May, 1814, 2, c. 4; *Quebec Mercury* (Quebec, Lower Canada), 10 May, 1814, 150, c. 3. Another four to six weeks would have passed before the letter was finally delivered to William Brock, sometime in mid-to-late-June of 1814.

4 Richard Westmacott, R.A. entered into the contract on 3 August, 1814. See: Great Britain, Parliament (Commons), *Sessional Papers, Accounts and Papers*, "Erection of Monuments," 1792–1842 XXVI, no. 559 (1842): 505.

5 The cost for this commission was £1,575. See: ibid.

6 The statue on top of Brock's Monument is conjectural, as is the bust by Hamilton MacCarthy dating from 1896. So, too, are all the sculptures of Brock attempted since then. The bust by F. May Simpson, which she created in 1913, might have been the most striking interpretation, had she not based her work on the miniature now known to portray Lieutenant George Dunn. For the busts of Brock by MacCarthy and Simpson, see: AO, Government of Ontario Art Collection, Sculpture of "Major-General Sir Isaac Brock, KB," by Hamilton MacCarthy, 1896, acc. 619,882; ibid., Sculpture of "Major-General Sir Isaac Brock, KB," by F. May Simpson, 1912, acc. 619,885.

7 I found myself in agreement with Ferdinand Brock Tupper, who described his uncle a "very handsome youth." See: LAC, Henry James Morgan Papers (MG 29, D61), Correspondence, vol. 47, Tupper to Morgan, 13 July, 1861.

8 Major John Richardson, *War of 1812* (Brockville, Canada West: John Richardson, 1842), 68. Major Richardson probably saw Brock at Detroit in August of 1812.

9 Tupper had no direct knowledge of Brock's stature, and his description appears to have been based more on family traits than anything else. Thus, his wording: "perhaps too portly." See: Ferdinand Brock Tupper, ed., *The Life and Correspondence of Major-General Sir Isaac Brock, K.B.*, 1st ed. (London, England: Simpkin, Marshall and Company, 1845), 337. Earlier, in 1835, Tupper published the same description, minus the details about his uncle's height. See: Ferdinand Brock Tupper, *Family Records* (St-Peter Port, Guernsey: Stephen Barbet, 1835), 24.

10 AO, Ferdinand Brock Tupper Papers (F 1081), Robinson to Tupper, 19 Jan., 1846, 10.

11 William Stanley Hatch, *A Chapter of the History of the War of 1812 in the Northwest* (Cincinnati, Ohio: Miami Printing and Publishing Company, 1872), 63. For references to Hatch's appointment as acting assistant quarter master general, see: ibid., 19, 30. It should be noted that Hatch was a volunteer in Captain John F. Mansfield's Company of the Cincinnati Light Infantry, which was attached to the Third Regiment of Ohio Militia. See: ibid.; *Roster of Ohio Soldiers in the War of 1812* (Columbus, Ohio: Adjutant General of Ohio, 1916), 72.

12 *Roster of Ohio Soldiers in the War of 1812*, 71.

13 *Cleveland Herald* (Cleveland, Ohio), 18 Nov., 1871, supplement, 5, c. 5. Although Sanderson did not go so far as to mention Brock's ears, I became concerned about the one depicted by Schipper (fig. 3). It looked rather small and perhaps too low, or so I thought. I also began to fear that it was crudely rendered, which caused me to wonder if Schipper might have stylized all of his client's ears for the sake of expediency. However, the expert on Gerrit Schipper disagreed. As Jeanne Riger pointed out, Schipper's portrait

of Bostonian John Dorr (then in her possession) had an ear that was "beautifully done." She also examined photographs of other portraits by Schipper, and in each case the ears were painted with equal care. Given that Schipper completed his profile portraits from life, after the sitter's profile was mechanically reduced and outlined on a piece of paper, his representation of Brock's ear is probably correct. See: letter, St-Denis to Riger, 27 Sept., 2005; email, Riger to St-Denis, 1 Nov., 2005.

14 It was William Stanley Hatch's recollection that Brock had a "very massive and large boned, though not fleshy" physique. This observation was made less than two months before Brock's death, and it seems doubtful that he could have become hefty enough in the interim to justify Tupper's belief that his uncle was "perhaps too portly" in his latter years. See: Hatch, *A Chapter of the History of the War of 1812 in the Northwest*, 63; Tupper, *Life and Correspondence of Major-General Sir Isaac Brock*, 1st ed., 337.

15 With particular reference to Brock's apparent squint, there is no indication that he ever suffered a trauma to either of his eyes. Had there been such an injury, Major Richardson surely would have noted it—just as he did the colour of Brock's eyes. See: Richardson, *War of 1812*, 68.

16 William Kingsford, *Canadian Archaeology: An Essay* (Montreal, Quebec: William Drysdale and Company, 1886), 97.

17 Ludwig Kosche seems to have subscribed to John Andre's belief that "strong men preferably look to the right, ladies and elderly gentlemen to the left." See: Ludwig Kosche, "Contemporary Portraits of Isaac Brock: An Analysis," *Archivaria* 20 (Summer 1985): 64. However, judging from a selection of Schipper's profile portraits, it appears that the direction of a sitter's pose was more often than not a random choice.

18 According to the *Gentleman's Magazine*, William Brock died on 20 December, 1819. See: *Gentleman's Magazine* (London, England), July–Dec., 1819, 639, c. 1.

19 Evidence of Irving Brock's ownership of the profile portrait (fig. 3) is found in a letter from Miss Henrietta Tupper to Colonel Charles W. Robinson. See: Trent University, Thomas J. Bata Library, Trent University Archives (TU), Gilbert and Stewart Bagnani Papers (94-016), General Correspondence (series A), Tupper to Robinson, 1 Feb., 1882. For a published version of this letter, see: Lady Edgar [Matilda Ridout], "General Brock's Portrait," *Canadian Magazine* XXXI, no. 3 (July 1908): 262–4.

20 National Archives of the United Kingdom, Records of the Prerogative Court of Canterbury, Will Registers (PROB 11/1624), will of William Brock, proved 19 Jan., 1820, no. 227.

21 Irving Brock's entire estate was bequeathed to his wife. See: ibid. (PROB 11/1894), will of Irving Brock, proved 28 May, 1838, no. 426.

22 For Irving Brock's obituary, see: *Gentleman's Magazine*, Jan.–June, 1838, 669, c. 1.

23 For Miss Tupper's claim, see: TU, Gilbert and Stewart Bagnani Papers (94-016), General Correspondence (series A), Tupper to Robinson, 1 Feb., 1882.

24 For Henry Tupper's obituary, see: *Star* (St. Peter Port, Guernsey), 6 Apr., 1875, 2. c. 1.

25 Nicholas Mellish also offered the profile portrait (fig. 3) to several other individuals and institutions. These offers preceded his negotiations with the Weir Foundation.

26 Gary Essar and Sandra Lawrence, "Acquisition of the only authenticated portraits of Sir Isaac Brock," Press Release, RiverBrink Art Museum and Weir Foundation, 11 Feb., 2009. See also: *St. Catharines Standard* (St. Catharines, Ontario), 14 Feb., 2009, A1; ibid., 18

Feb., 2009, A1. The profile portrait (fig. 3) might have warranted the extra money because of its larger size.

27 Ibid.

28 *St. Catharines Standard*, 20 Feb., 2009, A1.

29 Guernsey, States of Deliberation, *Billet d'État* IX (2010): 491.

30 The Canadian figures were calculated according to the exchange rates as of 18 February, 2009, the date Nicholas Mellish informed the Weir Foundation that he had accepted the offer of the Guernsey Museum and Art Gallery. See: *St. Catharines Standard*, 20 Feb., 2009, A1.

31 Brock University, James A. Gibson Library, Archives and Special Collections (BU), Guy St-Denis Papers (RG 77), Captain Michael H.T. Mellish Correspondence, Weir to Mellish, 6 Jan., 1964.

32 Ibid.

33 Weir, of course, had his good points, but they were well hidden beneath a very gruff exterior. For examples, see: Mary Willan Mason, *The Consummate Canadian: A Biography of Samuel Edward Weir, Q.C.* (Toronto, Ontario: Natural Heritage, c1999).

34 As Weir's biographer discovered, he "made himself thoroughly familiar with every phase and activity of the Battle of Queenston Heights." See: ibid., 226.

35 Weir was born 12 August, 1898, and so he was sixty-five years old in January of 1964. See: ibid., 9.

36 It is not known how Weir became aware of Captain Mellish and the profile portrait of Brock (fig. 3).

37 BU, Guy St-Denis Papers (RG 77), Captain Michael H.T. Mellish Correspondence, Mellish to Weir, 22 Jan., 1964.

38 Ibid., Weir to Mellish, 11 Feb., 1964.

39 Ibid., Mellish to Weir, 21 Feb., 1964. Captain Mellish had good reason to believe there was a photograph of the profile portrait (fig. 3) in Ottawa, as W. Kaye Lamb (then Dominion Archivist of Canada) reproduced a colour copy of it for the frontispiece of *The Hero of Upper Canada*. Published in 1962, this booklet commemorated the 150th anniversary of the Battle of Queenston Heights.

40 Mason, *Consummate Canadian*, 230, 235.

41 Ibid., 277.

42 It was in anticipation of this gift that the Weir Foundation was established in 1962. See: ibid., 199.

43 Upon completion of high school in 1915, Weir articled with a London, Ontario law office. Beginning in 1917, he attended law school at Osgoode Hall in Toronto. After graduating as a barrister-at-law in 1920, Weir was called to the Ontario bar. Even without a law degree, Weir was qualified to argue cases on behalf of clients. See: ibid., 52, 54, 58–9.

44 Ibid., 112.

45 Conversation with LaBrie, 21 Oct., 2008. This copy of Brock's portrait (fig. 35) was officially presented to Brock University at a dinner party attended by Captain Mellish in October of 1985. See: "Fabulous Forgery," *Surgite* 1, no. 2 (Fall/Winter 1985): 15.

46 Conversation with LaBrie, 21 Oct., 2008. The photography was done in colour.

47 Ibid.

48 RiverBrink Art Museum, Library/Archives (RAM), Weir Foundation Art Collection, Agreement between LaBrie and Abrahams, 13 Aug., 1984. The final measurements were 26 by 22 inches, or 66 by 56 centimetres. See: ibid., Catalogue and location card, Philippa Abrahams painting of "Major-General Sir Isaac Brock," acc. 985.1. I am grateful to James Campbell, former curator of the RiverBrink Art Museum, for providing me with a copy of this and other information regarding the Abrahams commission.

49 RAM, Weir Foundation Art Collection, Agreement between LaBrie and Abrahams, 13 Aug., 1984. The price for the two paintings was £2,400.

50 Canadian War Museum, Military History Research Centre, George Metcalf Archival Collection, Ludwig Kosche Papers, Correspondence (58A3/10.26), Kosche to Mellish, 29 Sept., 1984.

51 Ibid. Kosche communicated with John P.M. Court, Executive Secretary of the Ontario Heritage Foundation (today's Ontario Heritage Trust).

52 Ibid., Mellish to Kosche, 21 Nov., 1984.

53 Ibid.

54 Ibid., Mellish to LaBrie, 13 Apr., 1984.

55 Ibid., Kosche to Mellish, 9 Dec., 1984.

56 This painstaking work was carried out in late 2010 by Jane McAusland, an art on paper conservator based in Suffolk, England. The exhibition was "RiverBrink's War of 1812."

CONCLUSION

1 This mastery was acknowledged in a unique fashion. A few months after Schipper's death in 1825, Sir Thomas Lawrence, Sir William Beechey, and several other notable artists contributed to a fund for the relief of his financially distressed widow. While a sense of charity no doubt influenced their generosity, the quality of Schipper's work presumably warranted some degree of consideration as well. See: *Morning Post* (London, England), 23 Feb., 1826, 1, c. 1.

Bibliography

Manuscripts

CANADA

Archives of Ontario (AO)
Toronto, Ontario

Department of Education (RG 2, 42)
  Select Subject Files, XIV-Pictures
    No. 34, "Brock, Sir Isaac-portrait of," 1900

Ford Family Papers (F 483)

William Kirby Papers (F 1076)
  Miscellaneous Correspondence (series A-23), 1896

John Beverley Robinson Papers (F 44)
  Calendared Papers, 1857–1905

Stormont, Dundas and Glengarry Counties Surrogate Court (RG 22)
  Estate Files, 1800–1967 (series 198), 1930

Ferdinand Brock Tupper Papers (F 1081)

Upper Canada Court of Probate (RG 22)
  Estate Files, 1793–1859 (series 155), 1812
  Grants of Probate and Administration
    Register A, 1796–1816 (series 154), 1812

Women's Canadian Historical Society of Toronto Papers (F 1180)
  Correspondence (series 1), 1890–97, 1921–39, no date.
  Miscellaneous (series 13)
    Brock Miniature
    Brock Portrait Notebook

York County Surrogate Court (RG 22)
Estate Files, 1800–1968 (series 305), 1915

Art Gallery of Ontario
E.P. Taylor Research Library and Archives
Toronto, Ontario

George Theodore Berthon's Sitters' Notebook, 1866–91

Brock University (BU)
James A. Gibson Library, Archives and Special Collections
St. Catharines, Ontario

Acquisitions Form, [Kerr-Nelson] Portrait of "General Brock" (U2)

Guy St-Denis Papers (RG 77)
Captain Michael H.T. Mellish Correspondence, 1964–67

Canadian War Museum (CWM)
Military History Research Centre
Ottawa, Ontario

Ludwig Kosche Papers
Correspondence with:
Lorna Procter and Others (58A3/10.17), 1979, 1983–85
H. Douglass Short (58A3/10.21), 1983, 1985
Various Correspondents (58A3/10.25), 1962, 1972, 1980, 1983–85
Captain Michael H. T. Mellish (58A3/10.26), 1978–86
Miscellaneous Manuscripts (58A3/10.3)
Photograph Album (58A3/10.4)

Library and Archives Canada (LAC)
Ottawa, Ontario

Collection Baby (MG 24, L3)
Papiers Berczy, Correspondance
Volume 27, 1819–34

William von Moll Berczy Papers (MG 23, HII6)

British Military and Naval Records, "C" Series (RG 8, I)
Volume 17, 1805

Volume 228, 1812
Volume 689, 1813
Volume 728, 1812
Volume 1215, 1808
Volume 1216, 1810

Civil Secretary's Correspondence, Upper Canada and Canada West (RG 5, A1)
Upper Canada Sundries
Volume 71, 1815

Colonial Office (MG 11-CO 42)
Upper Canada, Despatches, Public Offices and Miscellaneous
Volume 353, 1812
Volume 354, 1813

Department of Finance, Upper Canada (RG 19, E5a)
War of 1812 Losses Claims
Volume 3752, file 2
Volume 3757, file 1

J. Russell Harper Papers (MG 30, D352)
[Fee, Norman]. "List of Paintings, Engravings, and Prints [in the] W.C. Pitfield Collection"

Henry James Morgan Papers (MG 29, D61)
Correspondence
Volume 47, 1861

John and Thomas Nairne Papers (MG 23, GIII23)
Correspondence
Volume 1, 1762–1865

Office of the Governor of Quebec and Lower Canada, Internal Letter Books (RG 7, G15A)
Volume 3, 1807–11

Portrait Files (internal accession records)
Brock, Sir Isaac, no. 207-33

Ships Passenger Lists, Quebec City Ships' Manifests (RG 76, C1a)
S.S. *Lake Winnipeg*, 1897

SNAP Internal Registry Files
MB 8320-Brock, Isaac (Sir)

Collection Jacques Viger (MG 24, L8)

McCord Museum of Canadian History (MMCH)
Archives and Documentation Centre
Montreal, Quebec

McCord Family Papers (P001)

Collecting Correspondence, 1889, 1897

RiverBrink Art Museum (RAM)
Library/Archives
Queenston, Ontario

Weir Foundation Art Collection

Agreement between LaBrie and Abrahams, 13 Aug., 1984

Catalogue and Location Card, Abrahams Painting of "Major-General Sir Isaac Brock" (985.1)

Toronto Reference Library (TRL)
Marilyn and Charles Baillie Special Collections Centre, Baldwin Collection of Canadiana
Toronto, Ontario

William Allan Papers (S 123)

Miscellaneous Papers (series 6)

Estate Inventory of Major General Sir Isaac Brock, 1812

John Wycliffe Lowes Forster Papers (S 19)

Trent University (TU)
Thomas J. Bata Library, Trent University Archives
Peterborough, Ontario

Gilbert and Stewart Bagnani Papers (94-016)

General Correspondence (series A), 1798-1899

United Church of Canada Archives (UCCA)
Toronto, Ontario

John Wycliffe Lowes Forster Papers (3096)

Correspondence Re: The Portrait of Sir Isaac Brock

GUERNSEY

Ecclesiastical Court of Guernsey (ECG)
St. Peter Port

Records of the Registrar of Wills and Intestacies
 Books of Testaments
  Apr. 1889–Aug. 1894
  Volume 7, 1949

Royal Court House
Greffe
St. Peter Port

Wills and Intestacies
 Volume E/10, 1971–76
 Volume 71, new series

UNITED KINGDOM

College of Arms
London, England

Letters Patent
 Granting Arms to Sir Isaac Brock, 1813
 Granting Supporters to the Arms of Sir Isaac Brock, 1813

London Metropolitan Archives
London, England

St. Marylebone Church
 Baptism Register (X023/017), 1812

National Archives of the United Kingdom (NAUK)
Kew, England

Foreign Office
 Miscellaneous Records, Lists of Aliens Arriving at English Ports
  (FO 83/21), 1810–11

Prerogative Court of Canterbury
 Administration Act Books
  (PROB 6/193), 1817

Will Registers
(PROB 11/1624), 1820
(PROB 11/1894), 1838

War Office
General Muster Books and Pay Lists, 49th Regiment of Foot
(WO 12/6041), 25 Apr.–24 May 1805
(WO 12/6044), 25 Sept.–24 Dec. 1812
Records of the Royal Hospital Chelsea, Soldiers Service Documents
(WO 97/633), 1760–1854
Returns of Officers' Services
(WO 25/744), 1809–10
Secretary at War, Out-Letters. America
(WO 4/281), 1805–09

City of Westminster Archives London, England

St. Clement Danes Church
Burial Register
Volume 17, 1819–28

UNITED STATES

Frick Art Reference Library (FARL) New York, New York

Schipper, Nicholas L. "The Life of Nicholas L. Shipper: Embracing a Period of Sixteen Years, until his Arrival in America in the Year 1826"

National Archives and Records Administration (NARA) Washington, D.C.

Bureau of the Census (RG 29)
Twelfth Census, 1900
Franklin, New Hampshire

Department of the Navy (RG 45)
Captains' Letters
Volume 3, 1 Sept. 1812–31 Dec. 1812

Department of State (RG 59)

War of 1812 Papers

Miscellaneous Intercepted Correspondence, 1789–1814

British Military Correspondence

New-York Historical Society
Patricia D. Klingenstein Library, Manuscript Department
New York, New York

Henry Dearborn Letter Books

Orders of Major General Henry Dearborn, 1813

University of Michigan (UM)
William L. Clements Library, Manuscripts Division
Ann Arbor, Michigan

Isaac Chauncey Letter Books, 1812

War of 1812 Collection

Articles, Books, and Theses

Allodi, Mary Macaulay. "William Berczy: The Canadian Years, 1794–1813." In *Berczy*, Mary Macaulay Allodi, Peter N. Moogk, and Beate Stock, 55–81. Ottawa, Ontario: National Gallery of Canada, 1991.

———. "Pastel Profiles." In *Berczy*, Mary Macaulay Allodi, Peter N. Moogk, and Beate Stock, 304–8. Ottawa, Ontario: National Gallery of Canada, 1991.

———. "Gerritt Schipper." In *Painting in Quebec, 1820–1850*, edited by Mario Béland, 186. Quebec City, Quebec: Musée du Québec, 1992.

Andre, John. *William Berczy: Co-Founder of Toronto*. Toronto, Ontario: Borough of York, 1967.

Auchinleck, Gilbert. "History of the War between Great Britain and the United States of America, during the Years 1812, 1813, and 1814." *Anglo-American Magazine* III, no. 1 (July 1853): 3–17.

———. *A History of the War between Great Britain and the United States of America, during the Years 1812, 1813, and 1814*. Toronto, Canada West: Maclear and Company, 1855.

Avery-Quash, Susanna. "Graves, Algernon." *Oxford Dictionary of National Biography* 23: 383.

Bayer, Fern. *The Ontario Collection*. Markham, Ontario: Fitzhenry and Whiteside, 1984.

Benes, Peter. "Machine-Assisted Portrait and Profile Imaging in New England after 1803." In *Painting and Portrait Making in the American Northeast*, edited by

Peter Benes, 138–50. The Dublin Seminar for New England Folklife Annual Proceedings 19. Boston, Massachusetts: Boston University, c1995.

Berger, Carl. *The Writing of Canadian History: Aspects of English-Canadian Historical Writing since 1900.* 2nd ed. Toronto, Ontario: University of Toronto Press, c1986.

Binyon, Laurence. "Cust, Sir Lionel Henry." *Oxford Dictionary of National Biography* 14: 822–3.

Brock, A. Maude (Cawthra) Brock. *Brock Family Records.* Toronto, Ontario: privately published, 1927.

Brode, Patrick. "Robinson, John Beverley." *Dictionary of Canadian Biography* XII: 906–9.

Burke, Bernard. *A Genealogical and Heraldic Dictionary of the Landed Gentry of Great Britain and Ireland.* 4th ed. 2 pts. London, England: Harrison, 1863.

Cambridge, Marquess of. "De Bosset's Chart of Uniform, 1803." *Journal of the Society for Army Historical Research* XL (1962): 168–73.

Canadian Almanac & Directory, 1976. Toronto, Ontario: Copp Clark Publishing, 1976.

Carman, W.Y. "Infantry Clothing Regulations, 1802." *Journal of the Society for Army Historical Research* 19 (1940): 200–35.

Cooper, James Fenimore. *Ned Myers; or, A Life before the Mast.* 2 vols. London, England: Richard Bentley, 1843.

Cruikshank, Ernest A., ed. *The Documentary History of the Campaign upon the Niagara Frontier.* 9 vols. Niagara Falls, Ontario: Lundy's Lane Historical Society, 1900.

Dawnay, Major Nicholas P. "The Staff Uniform of the British Army, 1767 to 1855." *Journal of the Society for Army Historical Research* XXXI (1953): 64–84.

De Watteville, Herman. *The British Soldier: His Daily Life from Tudor to Modern Times.* London, England: J. M. Dent and Sons, 1954.

Dent, John Charles. *The Canadian Portrait Gallery.* 4 vols. Toronto, Ontario: John B. Magurn, 1880–81.

Edgar, Lady Matilda Ridout. "General Brock's Portrait." *Canadian Magazine* XXXI, no. 3 (July 1908): 262–5.

Essar, Gary, and Sandra Lawrence. "Acquisition of the Only Authenticated Portraits of Sir Isaac Brock." Press Release, RiverBrink Art Museum and Weir Foundation, 11 Feb., 2009.

"Fabulous Forgery." *Surgite* 1, no. 2 (Fall/Winter 1985): 15.

FitzGibbon, Mary Agnes. *A Veteran of 1812: The Life of James FitzGibbon.* Toronto, Ontario: William Briggs, 1894.

Forster, Ben. "Macdonell (Greenfield), John Alexander." *Dictionary of Canadian Biography* XV: 637–9.

Forster, John W.L. *Under the Studio Light: Leaves from a Portrait Painter's Sketch Book.* Toronto, Ontario: Macmillan Company of Canada, 1928.

Foskett, Daphne. *A Dictionary of British Miniature Painters*. 2 vols. New York, New York: Praeger Publishers, 1972.

Fredriksen, John C. "Chauncey, Isaac." *American National Biography* 4: 750–2.

Hall, Donald, and Christopher Wingate. *British Orders, Decorations and Medals*. St. Ives, England: Balfour Publications, 1973.

Harper, John Russell. *Painting in Canada: A History*. Toronto, Ontario: University of Toronto Press, 1966.

Hatch, William Stanley. *A Chapter of the History of the War of 1812 in the Northwest*. Cincinnati, Ohio: Miami Printing and Publishing Company, 1872.

Historical Record of the Eighty-First Regiment. Gibraltar: Twenty-Eighth Regimental Press, 1872.

Hitsman, J. Mackay. *Safeguarding Canada, 1763–1871*. Toronto, Ontario: University of Toronto Press, c1968.

——. *The Incredible War of 1812: A Military History*. Toronto, Ontario: University of Toronto Press, c1965.

Hyer, Richard. "Gerrit Schipper, Miniaturist and Crayon Portraitist." *New York Genealogical and Biographical Record* LXXXIII, no. 2 (Apr. 1952): 70–2.

Jennings, Walter W. *The American Embargo, 1807–1809*. University of Iowa Studies in the Social Sciences VIII, no. 1. Iowa City, Iowa: University of Iowa, 1921.

Kent's Original London Directory: 1823. London, England: Henry-Kent Causton, 1823.

Kimmel, David, and Janet Miron. "Mickle, Sara." *Dictionary of Canadian Biography* XV: 742–3.

Kingsford, William. *Canadian Archaeology: An Essay*. Montreal, Quebec: William Drysdale and Company, 1886.

——. *The Early Bibliography of the Province of Ontario*. Toronto, Ontario: Rowsell and Hutchison, 1892.

Knox, Katharine McCook. *The Sharples: Their Portraits of George Washington and his Contemporaries*. New Haven, Connecticut: Yale University Press, 1930.

Kosche, Ludwig. "Contemporary Portraits of Isaac Brock: An Analysis." *Archivaria* 20 (Summer 1985): 22–66.

——. "New Light on an Old Artefact: The Alleged Brock Watch." *OMMC Journal* 8 (1981): 14–24.

——. "Relics of Brock: An Investigation." *Archivaria* 9 (Winter 1979–80): 33–103.

——. "The Story of a Car." *After the Battle* 35 (1982): 1–13.

——. "The Turco-German Alliance of August 1914." Master's thesis, University of Western Ontario, London, Ontario, 1969.

Lamb, W. Kaye. *The Hero of Upper Canada*. Toronto, Ontario: Rous and Mann Press, 1962.

Lambert, John. *Travels through Lower Canada, and the United States in the Years 1806, 1807, and 1808*. 3 vols. London, England: Richard Phillips, 1810.

A List of the Officers of the Army. London, England: War Office, 1799.

Lomax, David A.N. *A History of the Services of the 41st (the Welch) Regiment*. Devonport, England: Hiorns and Miller, 1899.

Long, Basil. *British Miniaturists*. London, England: Geoffrey Bles, 1929.

Malcomson, Robert. *Capital in Flames: The American Attack on York, 1813*. Montreal, Quebec: Robin Brass Studio, 2008.

——. "Picturing Isaac Brock." *Beaver* 84, no. 5 (Oct.–Nov. 2004): 23–5.

Mason, Mary Willan. *The Consummate Canadian: A Biography of Samuel Edward Weir, Q.C.* Toronto, Ontario: Natural Heritage, c1999.

Massue, Melville Henry, Marquis of Ruvigny and Raineval. *The Plantagenet Roll of the Blood Royal*. 4 vols. London, England: Melville and Company, 1905–11.

McArthur, Glenn, and Annie Szamosi. *William Thomas: Architect, 1799–1860*. Ottawa, Ontario: Archives of Canadian Art/Carleton University Press, c1996.

McKillop, Alexander Brian. *Pierre Berton: A Biography*. Toronto, Ontario: McClelland and Stewart, c2008.

Meschutt, David W., and Kevin J. Avery. "Pastels by Gerrit Schipper in the Metropolitan Museum." *Metropolitan Museum Journal* 42 (2007): 133–7.

Mickle, Sara, comp. *The Cabot Calendar, 1497–1897*. Toronto, Ontario: Toronto Lithographing Company, 1896.

Might's Greater Ottawa City Directory, 1974. Toronto, Ontario: Might Directories, c1974.

Might's Greater Ottawa City Directory, 1976. Toronto, Ontario: Might Directories, c1976.

Might's Metropolitan Toronto City Directory, 1978–79. Toronto, Ontario: Might Directories, c1979.

Miles, Ellen G. "1803—The Year of the Physiognotrace." In *Painting and Portrait Making in the American Northeast*, edited by Peter Benes, 118–37. The Dublin Seminar for New England Folklife Annual Proceedings 19. Boston, Massachusetts: Boston University, c1995.

Miller, Genevieve. *Wm. Beaumont's Formative Years: Two Early Notebooks, 1811–1821*. New York, New York: Henry Schuman, 1946.

Moogk, Peter N. "William Berczy: Colonization Promoter, 1791–1813." In *Berczy*, Mary Macaulay Allodi, Peter N. Moogk, and Beate Stock, 83–111. Ottawa, Ontario: National Gallery of Canada, 1991.

Morgan, Cecilia. "Carnochan, Janet." *Dictionary of Canadian Biography* XV: 183–5.

Morgan, Henry James. *Sketches of Celebrated Canadians*. Quebec, Canada East: Hunter Rose and Company, 1862.

—, ed. *The Canadian Men and Women of the Time.* 1st ed. Toronto, Ontario: William Briggs, 1898.

—, ed. *The Canadian Men and Women of the Time.* 2nd ed. Toronto, Ontario: William Briggs, 1912.

Myerly, Scott Hughes. *British Military Spectacle: From the Napoleonic Wars through the Crimea.* Harvard University Press: Cambridge, Massachusetts, 1996.

Nursey, Walter R. *The Story of Isaac Brock: Hero, Defender and Saviour of Upper Canada, 1812.* Toronto, Ontario: William Briggs, 1908.

Otto, Stephen A. "Brock's Two Monuments." *Cuesta* (1991–92): 15–17.

Petre, F. Loraine. *The Royal Berkshire Regiment.* 2 vols. Reading, England: The Barracks, 1925.

"Prefatory Note." Women's Canadian Historical Society of Toronto *Transaction* 1 (1896): 3–4.

"Preamble of Constitution and By-Laws." Women's Canadian Historical Society of Toronto *Transaction* 1 (1896): 5–6.

Purdy, Judson D. "Hodgins, John George." *Dictionary of Canadian Biography* XIV: 496–9.

The Quebec Almanac. Quebec, Lower Canada: J. Neilson, 1806–12.

Raible, Chris. "Benjamin Lett, Rebel Terrorist." *Beaver* 82, no. 5 (Oct.–Nov. 2002): 10–15.

Read, David B. *Life and Times of Major-General Sir Isaac Brock, K.B.* Toronto, Ontario: William Briggs, 1894.

Reid, Dennis R. *A Concise History of Canadian Painting.* Toronto, Ontario: Oxford University Press, 1973.

Richardson, Major John. *War of 1812.* Brockville, Canada West: John Richardson, 1842.

Riger, Jeanne. "New Light on Gerrit Schipper the Painter." *Clarion* 15, no. 1 (Winter 1990): 65–70.

Robert, Jean-Claude. "Viger, Jacques." *Dictionary of Canadian Biography* VIII: 909–13.

Roster of Ohio Soldiers in the War of 1812. Columbus, Ohio: Adjutant General of Ohio, 1916.

The Royal Military Calendar. 3rd ed. 5 vols. London, England: T. Egerton, 1820.

Shelley, Marjorie. "American Pastels of the Late Nineteenth & Early Twentieth Centuries: Materials & Techniques." In *American Pastels in the Metropolitan Museum of Art,* Doreen Bolger, Mary Wayne Fritzsche, Jacqueline Hazzi, Marjorie Shelley, Mary L. Sullivan, Marc Vincent, and Elizabeth Wylie, 33–45. New York, New York: Metropolitan Museum of Art, 1989.

"Sketch of Miss FitzGibbon's Life." Women's Canadian Historical Society of Toronto *Transaction* 14 (1914–15): 15–16.

Stacey, Charles P. "Brock, Sir Isaac." *Dictionary of Canadian Biography* V: 109–15.

Stagg, Ronald J. "Berczy, William." *Dictionary of Canadian Biography* V: 70–2.

Sumner, Rev. Percy. "The Royal Berkshire Regiment." *Journal of the Society for Army Historical Research* XVIII (1939): 123–4.

The Toronto City Directory 1897. Toronto, Ontario: Might Directory Company, 1897.

Tupper, Ferdinand Brock. *Family Records.* St Peter Port, Guernsey: Stephen Barbet, 1835.

—, ed. *The Life and Correspondence of Major-General Sir Isaac Brock, K.B.* London, England: Simpkin, Marshall and Company, 1845.

—, ed. *The Life and Correspondence of Major-General Sir Isaac Brock, K.B.* 2nd ed. London, England: Simpkin, Marshall and Company, 1847.

Vaux, William S.W. "On English and Foreign Waterloo Medals." *Numismatic Chronicle and Journal of the Royal Numismatic Society* new series IX (1869): 108–17.

Walden, Keith. Review of *The Invasion of Canada*, by Pierre Berton. *Canadian Historical Review* LXII, no. 3 (Sept. 1981): 332–3.

Wallot, Jean-Pierre. "Craig, Sir James Henry." *Dictionary of Canadian Biography* V: 205–14.

Whitfield, Carol, and Robert Lochiel Fraser III. "Macdonell (Greenfield), John." *Dictionary of Canadian Biography* V: 520–3.

Willard, Frances E., and Mary A. Livermore, eds. *A Woman of the Century.* Buffalo, New York: Charles Wells Moulton, 1893; reprint ed., Detroit, Michigan: Gale Research Company, 1967.

Wood, William, ed. *Select British Documents of the Canadian War of 1812.* 3 vols. Toronto, Ontario: Champlain Society, 1920–28.

Wright, Donald. *The Professionalization of History in English Canada.* Toronto, Ontario: University of Toronto Press, c2005.

Newspapers

Albany Centinel (Albany, New York), 1804–05

Albany Register (Albany, New York), 1808

Allen County Democrat (Lima, Ohio), 1859

American Citizen (New York, New York), 1808

American Mercury (Hartford, Connecticut), 1805–07

Bailliage (St. Peter Port, Guernsey), 1892

Balance (Hudson, New York), 1805

Bombay Courier (Bombay, India), 1802

British Colonist (Toronto, Upper Canada), 1840

Buffalo Gazette (Buffalo, New York), 1812

Canadian Courant (Montreal, Lower Canada), 1809–10

Cape Town Gazette (Cape Town, South Africa), 1801

City Gazette (Charleston, South Carolina), 1803

Cleveland Herald (Cleveland, Ohio), 1871

Columbian (New York, New York), 1812

Columbian Centinel (Boston, Massachusetts), 1803–04

Connecticut Courant (Hartford, Connecticut), 1805–06

Daily Mail and Empire (Toronto, Ontario), 1896

Evening Telegram (Toronto, Ontario), 1905–06, 1912, 1930

Gazette (Montreal, Quebec), 1896–97

Gentleman's Magazine (London, England), 1819, 1838

Glengarry News (Alexandria, Ontario), 1930

Globe (Toronto, Ontario), 1859, 1877, 1882, 1887, 1896–97, 1912, 1923, 1926, 1928, 1930

Globe and Mail (Toronto, Ontario), 1938–39, 1962

Guernsey Evening Press (St. Peter Port, Guernsey), 1919

Guernsey Press (St. Peter Port, Guernsey), 2007

Independent Chronicle (Boston, Massachusetts), 1803

Ipswich Journal (Ipswich, England), 1813

Kingston Gazette (Kingston, Upper Canada), 1813

Liverpool Mercury (Liverpool, England), 1813

London Gazette (London, England), 1791, 1801

Massachusetts Spy (Worcester, Massachusetts), 1804

Mercantile Advertiser (New York, New York), 1802

Military Monitor (New York, New York), 1812

Montreal Gazette (Montreal, Lower Canada), 1808–10, 1812

Morning Chronicle (London, England), 1813

Morning Post (London, England), 1826

New-England Palladium (Boston, Massachusetts), 1804

New-York Evening Post (New York, New York), 1806

New York Times (New York, New York), 1897, 1913

Niagara Arts Journal (St. Catharines, Ontario), 1986

Ottawa Citizen (Ottawa, Ontario), 2000

Quebec Gazette (Quebec, Lower Canada), 1808, 1810–14

Quebec Mercury (Quebec, Lower Canada), 1810, 1812, 1814

Salem Gazette (Salem, Massachusetts), 1804

St. Catharines Standard (St. Catharines, Ontario), 1965–66, 2009

Star (St. Peter Port, Guernsey), 1873, 1875, 1885, 1894, 1897

Times (London, England), 1812–13, 1850, 1897, 1924, 1927, 1941

Toronto Daily Star (Toronto, Ontario), 1905, 1957

Toronto Saturday Night (Toronto, Ontario), 1897

Toronto Star (Toronto, Ontario), 2001

Toronto World (Toronto, Ontario), 1884

Upper Canada Gazette (York, Upper Canada), 1824

War (New York, New York), 1812

Week (Toronto, Ontario), 1894

Government Publications

Canada. Parliament (Commons)

Sessional Papers, 1897

"Report of the Joint Librarians of Parliament, List of Copyrights Deposited in the Library of Parliament," 1896

Great Britain. Parliament (Commons)

Journals, 1813

Sessional Papers, Accounts and Papers, 1842

"Erection of Monuments," 1792–1842

Guernsey. States of Deliberation

Billet d'État, 1897, 2010

Ontario. Bureau of Archives

Ninth Report of the Bureau of Archives for the Province of Ontario, 1912

"Journal of the House of Assembly of Upper Canada," 1814

Ontario. Legislative Assembly

Sessional Papers, 1882–83, 1901, 1913, 1917, 1939–40

"Public Accounts of the Province of Ontario," 1882, 1900

"Report of the Minister of Public Works," 1912, 1916, 1938–39

Artworks Cited

Archives of Ontario (AO)
Government of Ontario Art Collection
Toronto, Ontario

Forster, John W.L. Oil painting, "Major-General Sir Isaac Brock, KB," 1900
Accession 692,993

MacCarthy, Hamilton. Sculpture, "Major-General Sir Isaac Brock, KB," 1896
Accession 619,882

Simpson, F. May. Sculpture, "Major-General Sir Isaac Brock, KB," 1912
Accession 619,885

Library and Archives Canada (LAC)
Portrait Gallery of Canada
Ottawa, Ontario

Forster, John W.L. Oil painting, Study of "Sir Isaac Brock," 1897
Accession 1991-30-1

McCord Museum of Canadian History (MMCH)
Notman Photographic Archives
Montreal, Quebec

Collenette, Benjamin. Photograph, "Miniature of Sir Isaac Brock," 1881
Catalogue MP-0000.2251.2

Dumaresq, Robert. Photograph, Bronze Silhouette/Profile of Unknown Officer (misidentified as "Major General Sir Isaac Brock"), 1897
Catalogue MP-0000.2251.1

Metropolitan Museum of Art
American Paintings and Sculpture
New York, New York

Schipper, Gerrit. Pastel painting, "Portrait of a Man," 1805
Accession 2007.19

Niagara Historical Society Museum
Niagara-on-the-Lake, Ontario

Quinn, William. Photograph, Portrait of "General Sir Isaac Brock," circa 1891
Accession 984.1.127

Niagara Falls History Museum
Niagara Falls, Ontario

Forster, John W.L. Oil painting, "Portrait of Maj. General Sir Isaac Brock KB," 1894
Accession 995.D.067.005

Private Collection
Sheffield, Massachusetts

Schipper, Gerrit. Pastel painting, Elisha Jenkins, circa 1805

——. Pastel painting, Sarah (Greene) Jenkins, circa 1805

RiverBrink Art Museum (RAM)
Queenston, Ontario

Abrahams, Philippa. Oil painting, "Major-General Sir Isaac Brock," 1985
Accession 985.1

Royal Ontario Museum
Canadian Collection, Department of World Cultures
Toronto, Ontario

Hudson, J. (James?). Miniature, Lieutenant George Dunn (misidentified as "General Sir Isaac Brock"), 1816
Accession 996.58.3.1

Miscellaneous

Conversations with

F. Eugene LaBrie, 21 Oct., 2008

Captain Michael H.T. Mellish, 4 May, 2004

Mark Osterman, 27 May, 2009

Emails to

Gillian Lenfestey, 13 Dec., 2002; 23 Apr., 2009

Emails from

Mary Allodi, 6 Jan., 2003; 7 Jan., 2003; 28 Oct., 2005

Helen Conlon, 29 May, 2009; 3 June, 2009; 9 Sept., 2009; 19 May, 2010; 10 Feb., 2014; 13 Nov., 2014

Andrew Cormack, 13 Feb., 2010

Donald E. Graves, 11 Jan., 2006

Gillian Lenfestey, 23 Apr., 2009; 24 Apr., 2009; 8 May, 2009

Alan McNairn, 20 Nov., 2008; 12 Feb., 2009

Mark Osterman, 26 May, 2009

Jeanne Riger, 1 Nov., 2005; 2 Dec., 2005

Letters to

Jeanne Riger, 31 Oct., 2003; 30 Mar., 2004; 27 Sept., 2005

Letters from

Michael H.T. Mellish, 8 Feb., 2003

Jeanne Riger, 12 Nov., 2003; 2 June, 2004; 25 June, 2004

Index

www.ingramcontent.com/pod-product-compliance
Lightning Source LLC
LaVergne TN
LVHW052350100826
845147LV00013B/800

* 9 7 8 1 7 7 3 8 5 0 2 0 7 *